PAGE
223
SURVIVAL
GUIDE

VITAL PRACTICAL INFORMATION TO
HELP YOU HAVE A SMOOTH TRIP

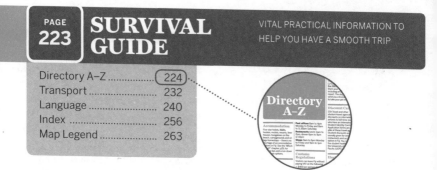

THIS EDITION WRITTEN AND RESEARCHED BY

Dean Starnes,
Celeste Brash, Virginia Jealous

welcome to
Fiji

Throwing Down the (Beach) Towel

Fiji has been in the tourism business for decades, drawing vacationers like pilgrims to a holy land with its promise of white-sand beaches, cloudless skies and the opportunity to fall into a sun-induced coma under a palm tree.

The perennial favourites are the Mamanuca and Yasawa islands, which arc north like a stingray's tail from the body of Fiji's main island, Viti Levu. These are Fiji's movie stars, dangled in front of the world as idyllic South Sea Edens, their reefs and cobalt-blue waters providing cinematic eye candy for films such as Tom Hanks' *Cast Away* and Brooke Shields' vehicle to stardom *The Blue Lagoon*. It is therefore little wonder that, despite a coup in 2006, Fiji's beaches remain flushed with sunburnt tourists.

Wetter is Better

Fiji's underwater scenery is spectacular and some of the finest, and most accessible dives in the Pacific can be found here. Its reputation as the 'soft coral capital of the world' is well justified and its countless reefs, drop-offs, walls and channels will have even experienced divers and snorkellers 'ohhhing' and 'ahhing' into their mouthpieces.

Fiji is also a great surfing destination and now that its surf breaks are open to

Fiji is surely every beach bum's vision of nirvana. Palm-fringed beaches, fish-packed reefs and smiling locals: pack your swimsuit and sunscreen, these sunny isles are so warm they sizzle.

(left) Horse riding on the Coral Coast, Viti Levu
(below) Local life, Yasawa island

all, the legendary waves of Cloudbreak, Swimming Pools and Frigates are free to be enjoyed by anyone experienced and brave enough to take them on.

Beyond the Beach

But the beaches – as lovely as they are – are only part of what Fiji has to offer. To get to grips with the national psyche you have to spend some time on the mainland. Two-thirds of the population live in urban centres and it is on Viti Levu that you'll find the country's two cities: Suva, the capital, and Lautoka, a port town reliant on the sugar-cane farms that surround it. Suva's nightlife and large student population give it a youthful if unexpected vibe.

Those who take their time will discover that there are ample opportunities to stretch the legs and climb a mountain, visit an orchid garden, raft down a river, soak in a hot spring or visit a village. Two islands begging for exploration are Taveuni – known as the Garden Island because of its abundant tropical growth and beautifully weathered mountains – and further south, Kadavu. Life here revolves around the church, the village, the rugby field and the garden. Explorers in these parts are rewarded with meeting some of the warmest and most hospitable people in the Pacific.

›Fiji

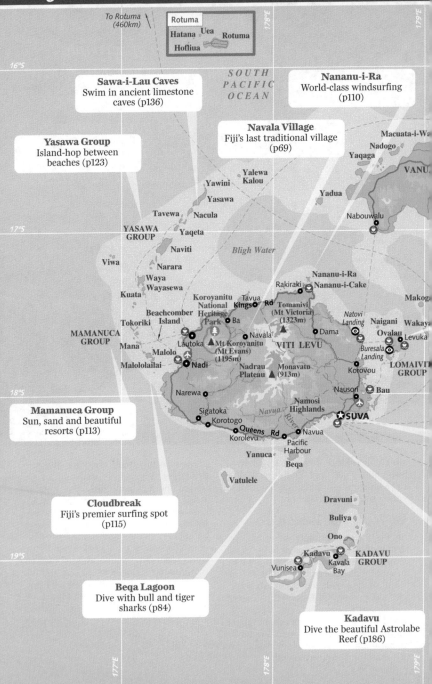

To Rotuma
(460km)

Rotuma
Hatana Uea
Hofliua Rotuma

SOUTH
PACIFIC
OCEAN

Sawa-i-Lau Caves
Swim in ancient limestone
caves (p136)

Nananu-i-Ra
World-class windsurfing
(p110)

Navala Village
Fiji's last traditional village
(p69)

Macuata-i-Wa
Nadogo
Yaqaga

VANU.

Yasawa Group
Island-hop between
beaches (p123)

Yawini

Yalewa
Kalou

Yadua

Nabouwalu

Tavewa Nacula

Yasawa

YASAWA
GROUP Yaqeta

Bligh Water

Viwa

Naviti

Narara

Nananu-i-Ra

Waya Rakiraki Nananu-i-Cake

Makog

Wayasewa

Koroyanitu
National Tavua

Kuata Heritage Kings Rd Tomanivi Natovi

Beachcomber Park Ba (Mt Victoria) Landing Naigani Wakay

Tokoriki Island (1323m) Dama Ovalau Levuka

MAMANUCA Navala VITI LEVU Buresala

GROUP Mana Lautoka ▲ Mt Koroyanitu Landing LOMAIVI

Malolo (Mt Evans) Korovou GROUP

Malololailai Nadi (1195m) Nadrau Monavatu

Plateau (913m) Nausori

Narewa Bau

Namosi SUVA

Sigatoka Highlands

Mamanuca Group Korotogo Navua

Sun, sand and beautiful Queens Rd River

resorts (p113) Korolevu Navua

Yanuca Pacific

Harbour

Vatulele Beqa

Dravuni

Cloudbreak Buliya

Fiji's premier surfing spot
(p115) Ono

Kadavu KADAVU

Vunisea Kavala GROUP

Bay

Beqa Lagoon
Dive with bull and tiger
sharks (p84)

Kadavu
Dive the beautiful Astrolabe
Reef (p186)

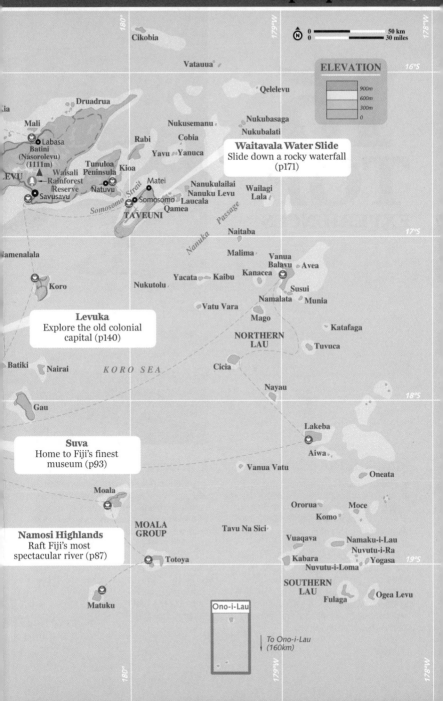

Cikobia

Vatauua

⊕N 0 _____ 50 km
0 _____ 30 miles

ELEVATION

900m
600m
300m
0

16°S

Qelelevu

Druadrua

Mali

Nukusemanu

Nukubasaga

Nukubalati

Waitavala Water Slide
Slide down a rocky waterfall
(p171)

Labasa

Batini
(Nasorolevu)
(1111m)

Rabi

Cobia

Yavu Yanuca

EVU

Wainsali
Rainforest
Reserve
Savusavu

Tunuloa
Peninsula

Natuvu

Kioa

Matei

Somosomo

Qamea

Nanukulailai

Nanuku Levu

Laucala

Wailagi

Lala

TAVEUNI

Somosomo Strait

Nanuka Passage

Naitaba

17°S

Namenalala

Malima

Vanua
Balavu

Avea

Koro

Yacata

Kaibu

Kanacea

Nukutolu

Susui

Namalata

Munia

Vatu Vara

Levuka
Explore the old colonial
capital (p140)

Mago

Katafaga

NORTHERN
LAU

Tuvuca

Batiki

Nairai

KORO SEA

Cicia

Gau

Nayau

18°S

Lakeba

Suva
Home to Fiji's finest
museum (p93)

Aiwa

Vanua Vatu

Oneata

Moala

Ororua

Moce

Komo

Namosi Highlands
Raft Fiji's most
spectacular river (p87)

MOALA
GROUP

Tavu Na Sici

Vuaqava

Namaku-i-Lau

Nuvutu-i-Ra

Totoya

Kabara

Yogasa

Nuvutu-i-Loma

19°S

Matuku

SOUTHERN
LAU

Ogea Levu

Fulaga

Ono-i-Lau

↓ To Ono-i-Lau
(160km)

15 TOP
EXPERIENCES

Mamanucas & Yasawas

1 Hot sun, tepid turquoise sea and cold refreshments are the order of the day in the Mamanuca and Yasawa island groups, off Fiji's west coast. Close to Viti Levu, the Mamanucas (p113) offer water sports of all sorts at island resorts for all budgets and all demographics, along with action-packed day tours from the mainland for the time-poor. Lacing their way northwards, the lower-key Yasawas (p123) beckon with crystal-clear lagoons, ruggedly handsome landscapes, remote villages and heavenly beaches to get stranded on.

Underwater Fiji

2 Even seasoned snorkellers are impressed by the water clarity, which can extend to 30m and beyond, and top facilities ensure that divers keep their logbooks full. From thrilling encounters with massive bull sharks in Beqa Lagoon to sedate drifts over the Great Astrolabe Reef, Fiji has a diverse selection of dives to choose from (see p33). No matter if you are the 'hard-core' or the 'soft-coral' type, Fijian dive-masters will know just the spot to thrill.
Longnose hawkfish

Suva

3 Steamy Suva offers a multicultural mix of colonial and contemporary Fiji (p90). Gracious old buildings and monuments sketch the city's early history along a lively waterfront and harbour. Downtown boasts both air-con shopping malls and crowded handicraft stalls. Open-air eateries and fine dining restaurants get their supplies from the colourful chaos of the don't-miss municipal market. Night owls can sip sunset cocktails at modern bars then dance to the beat of a different drum at loud and lively local nightclubs. Municipal Market, Suva

Navala Village

4 The drive up to Navala, which is nestled in a valley high in the Nausori Highlands (p69), is a treat in itself. Navala is Fiji's most striking village and the country's last bastion of traditional architecture. From the chief's house to the outhouses, all buildings are constructed using age-old techniques that make use of woven bamboo walls, thatched roofs and ropes made of fibre from the surrounding bush. Cooking on an open fire, village women serve up a serious local lunch that's been caught, picked and harvested from the gardens.

PETER SOLNESS / LONELY PLANET IMAGES ©

Sawa-i-Lau Cave

5 A lone limestone island among the volcanic Yasawas, Sawa-i-Lau (p136) hides a secret in its hollow caverns and grottoes: carvings, paintings and inscriptions of unknown age and meaning. They're accessible with a torch and a guide (and a shot of courage) by swimming through a short underwater passage from the cave's main chamber. Those less-submarine-inclined can swim in a more relaxed style, as Brooke Shields did in the 1980 movie *The Blue Lagoon,* in a clear pool beneath the cave's domed ceiling.

Local Life

6 Few travellers escape without downing at least one coconut shell of kava, but culturally Fiji has a lot more to offer than a few kava sessions around a *tanoa* bowl at your hotel. The best place to delve deeper is to visit one of the many villages that dot the countryside. The cornerstones of village life are church, rugby, family values and the observance of traditional etiquette. Fijians are genuinely friendly and if you secure an invitation to a village, expect to be warmly welcomed.

Indo-Fijian Culture

7 Indentured labourers from India first appeared in Fiji in 1879, when they were brought here to toil in British sugarcane and copra plantations. Those days are long gone but the descendants of those people, and the traditions that they brought with them, remain. For a taste of Indo-Fijian culture you need go no further than the local curry house, or visit one of the brightly painted Hindu temples on the mainland. To be transported to India itself, attend a traditional Indian celebration such as Suva's South Indian Fire Walking Festival (p97). Indian sweets for sale

Great Walks

8 Lush. Green. Humid. Fiji is a landlubber's paradise where even the shortest trails lead to rare endemic bird life, gargantuan trees and bizarre rock formations. Many jaunts pass through villages where you may be offered a bowl of kava before heading deeper into the bush. Trails are often muddy but the vibrancy of the foliage and the tranquillity makes this easy to forget – or revel in. Then, just when you think the heat is too much, there's a crystalline waterfall pool or beach to cool you down. Along the Lavena Coastal Walk (p178)

Festivals & Meke

9 Fijians love to sing and many resorts have weekly *meke* nights, including *lovo*-cooked meals, traditional song and dance performances and fire-walking demonstrations. The latter can also be seen during Suva's Hibiscus Festival (p97), which is big on 1970s-style amusement park rides and stalls. For something a little more traditional, the isolated islands of Rotuma (p189) and Lau (p190) have retained some unique and interesting celebrations, and back on the mainland the Indo-Fijian Hindi festivals are those feted with the most flair. *Meke* dance

Namosi Highlands

10 Geology looms large in the humid Namosi Highlands (p87). Sheer canyon walls crowd the Wainikoroiluva River, forming dramatic curtains of rock as the backdrop to Fiji's most scenic river-rafting trip taken aboard a *bilibili* (bamboo raft). The lower, longer, wider reaches of the palm-fringed waterway are usually covered in speedier style, in canoes with outboard motors, alongside villagers making their way up and down the river on slower, local boats laden with pigs, coconuts, taro and leafy green vegetables heading to or from market.

Surfing at Cloudbreak

11 Tubes of up to 250m can form on this colossal left-hand break in the Mamanucas, off Fiji's western edge (p115). Experienced board riders don wetsuits daily in an attempt to catch the perfect wave and competitive professional surfers are regularly drawn to its magnetic blue waters. Although this is no scenic beach-break for picnicking spectators to enjoy, non-surfing mortals who want to get close to the action can join the flotilla of small boats that make the daily pilgrimage offshore.

National Parks

12 Being so small, Fiji doesn't contain any large national parks but you don't have to venture far into those it does have to find colourful parrots, rare and equally beautiful doves and waterfall-fed swimming pools surrounded by lush forests. The most accessible is Colo-i-Suva Forest Park (p95), located just outside the capital city. For something more challenging head to Viti Levu's Koroyanitu National Heritage Park (p63) or Taveuni's Bouma National Heritage Park (p177), the pick of the lot.

Waitavala Water Slide

13 Hang ten or better, just use your bum, to cavort, slip and get a few bruises down this natural cascade of rock slides (p171). Start by watching the local kids to get an idea of what you're in for. They make it look easy, tackling the falls surfer-style, each showing off more than the last in the hope of making it into your top holiday photos. If you try it, believe us, do it sitting first. Your (probably ungraceful) attempt will be rewarded by a cool dip in the pools below.

GRAHAM SIMMONS / PHOTOGRAPHERS DIRECT ©

ROBERT ARMSTRONG / PHOTOLIBRARY / GETTY ©

ROBERT HOLMES / CORBIS ©

Windsurfing & Kitesurfing

14 When the wind blows, windsurfers and kiteboarders come out to play and the wind blows strongest from May through to July on the tiny island of Nananu-i-Ra (p110), off Viti Levu's northern coast. At this time seasonal trade winds pick up and average 10 knots or more most days. The consistent conditions and warm water make this an ideal location to learn and it is possible to hire equipment and take lessons from local experts.

Levuka Colonial Architecture

15 The Wild West meets the South Seas at Levuka, the country's one-time colonial capital turned half-asleep backwater (p140). You can almost imagine scabby sailors rowdily bursting out from the frayed but colourful timber shopfronts. Back then they may have been saloons but nowadays the buildings hold mainly stores of odds and ends. Women from the villages sell *dalo* and produce on the side of the road, a church rises faded and cracked-white against the sky and the only sounds come from the occasional car chugging through town.

need to know

When to Go?

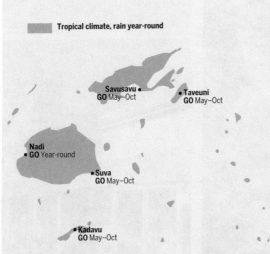

Tropical climate, rain year-round

Savusavu •
GO May–Oct

• Taveuni
GO May–Oct

Nadi
• **GO** Year-round

• Suva
GO May–Oct

• Kadavu
GO May–Oct

High Season
(Jun–Sep)

» Peak season coincides with the school holidays in Australia and New Zealand, including the December–January vacation period.

» Prices are 10% to 20% higher than in the low season; costs peak in June and July.

Shoulder
(May & Oct)

» The shoulder season includes the 'Fijian winter' or 'dry season', from May to October, which brings low rainfall, low humidity, milder temperatures and less risk of extreme weather events such as cyclones.

Low Season
(Nov–Apr)

» Fiji's 'wet season' is from November to April, with the heaviest rains and highest humidity from December to mid-April.

» Fewer tourists mean you're more likely to get discounted rates.

Your Daily Budget

Budget less than
$175

» Dorm including meals: $60-120

» Local transport and markets are good value on the main islands

» A half-day snorkelling excursion: $20-40

Midrange
$175-350

» Double room in a midrange hotel: $150-300

» Local restaurants: $15-25 for a main

» Allow $50 or more for activities

High end over
$350

» Resorts usually include all meals and plenty of activities in their tariffs

» *Bure* range from $300 to $3000 per night

Money

» ATMs and banks are widely available in larger towns on the main islands but scarce or nonexistent on outlying islands. Top-end resorts accept credit cards.

Visas

» Visas are given on arrival to most nationalities and are valid for four months.

Mobile Phones

» Vodafone is the only mobile phone company in Fiji. With an unlocked phone, buy a SIM card and top up with pre-pay units.

Transport

» High-speed catamarans service the Yasawa and Mamanuca Groups. Other islands are best reached by small plane from Nadi.

Websites

» **Fiji Times** (www.fijitimes.com.fj) Fiji's daily newspaper online.

» **Fiji Village** (www.fijivillage.com) Daily news and links to local events.

» **Fiji Visitors Bureau** (www.fijime.com) Fiji's official tourist site – very informative.

» **Lonely Planet** (www.lonelyplanet.com/fiji) Snapshots of the country and the Thorn Tree travel forum.

» **South Pacific Tourism Organisation** (www.spto.org) Useful directory with info on South Pacific countries.

Exchange Rates

Australia	A$1	$1.85
Canada	C$1	$1.79
Europe	€1	$2.38
Japan	¥100	$2.15
New Zealand	NZ$1	$1.46
UK	UK£1	$2.85
US	US$1	$1.78

For current exchange rates see www.xe.com.

Important Numbers

There are no area codes in Fiji, so within the country numbers can be dialled as they are printed in this book.

country code	☏679
international access code	☏00
emergency	☏911
international directory assistance	☏022

Arriving in Fiji

» **Nadi International Airport**

The vast majority of travellers arrive at the country's only international airport in Nadi (see p232).

Hotel shuttle – Most hotels provide free pre-booked transport to and from the airport.

Buses – Local buses from just outside the airport cost $0.90 to downtown Nadi.

Taxi – A taxi fare downtown costs $12 to $15.

» **Ports of Entry**

All yachts must call into an official Port of Entry (Suva, Lautoka, Savusavu, Levuka or Rotuma) before exploring Fijian waters.

Don't Leave Home Without...

» Insect repellent, which is sold in city pharmacies but needed everywhere.

» Plenty to read – bookshops are only found in cities.

» Reef shoes to protect yourself and the reefs that surround most of Fiji's islands.

» Wedding rings if you're here to get hitched.

» Your own snorkel and mask as they'll probably get a daily workout.

» A waterproof camera to capture your marine encounters and make your friends jealous.

» Sunscreen and a raincoat to combat tropical climate conditions.

» Seasickness tablets if you don't have sea legs.

» A Zen-like patience to cope with 'Fiji time', which is more official than GMT.

if you like...

Diving & Snorkelling

The archipelago's warm, clear waters and abundance of reef life make it a magnet for divers and snorkellers. Underwater visibility regularly exceeds 30m and when the current flows, the corals bloom with flower-like beauty.

Beqa Lagoon The only place in the world where it's possible to dive with bull and tiger sharks uncaged (p84)

Snorkelling with manta rays Work your fins to keep up with the giant manta rays that cruise the nearby channel (p130)

E6 (Bligh Water, Lomaiviti Group) A phenomenal seamount that brushes the surface; a magnet for pelagics (p139)

Great White Wall (Taveuni) Possibly the best soft-coral dive in Fiji (p167)

Split Rock (Kadavu) One of the many dives that can be had on the Great Astrolabe Reef, a 100km barrier reef with a vibrant assemblage of hard- and soft-coral formations. This dive is a maze of faults, canyons and tunnels (p36)

Surfing

Fiji has some world-class breaks year-round but from May to October southerly swells form colossal breaks that will have most surfers shivering in their wetsuit.

Cloudbreak Fiji's most famous break and for experienced riders only (p115)

Namotu Left So named after the huge lefties this spot is renowned for (p115)

Frigate Passage Consistently good with waves that seldom drop below head height, this is one of the most underrated spots in the South Pacific (p88)

Restaurants Fast left-hander that will chew you up and spit you out (p115)

Natadola Beach In the right conditions a small break forms that's ideal for beginners (p72)

Sigatoka River Mouth One of the best spots on the main island of Viti Levu (p76)

King Kong Lefts Unlike most Fijian breaks, this is within paddling distance of land and holds great shape when small (p184)

Village Life

A homestay or village visit can be an unexpected highlight and a unique insight into everyday life. Bring a *sevusevu* (gift) of *yaqona* (kava) root and a loud barracking voice for the village rugby-field sidelines. Food generally comes straight from the garden and includes such starchy staples as *tavioka* (cassava) and *dalo* (taro) roots alongside seafood in *lolo* (coconut cream).

Lovoni Join Epi's midland tour and trek to this village built inside the crater of an extinct volcano (p141)

Navala Perched in Viti Levu's highlands, Navala is the only community that insists all homes are built using traditional materials and conform to traditional architectural styles (p69)

Silana Ecolodge A stone's throw from the local village, Seru and his family will soon have you emersed in village life (p147)

Viseisei Village Homestays According to oral tradition, Viseisei is Fiji's oldest village, established by Melanesian explorers hundreds of years ago (p64)

HOLGER LEUE / LONELY PLANET IMAGES ©

» Sailing, Savusavu (p156)

Sailing

A permanent fixture on the Coconut Milk Run, Fiji has long drawn yachts from all over the globe. By law you must call into an official port of entry before fanning out through Fiji's extensive archipelago.

Savusavu With two top marinas and a boatload of facilities, Savusavu is now Fiji's best-resourced port for pleasure cruisers (p156)

Musket Cove Home to Fiji Regatta Week – a weeklong party of fun and sun. Most skippers have this one pencilled in their cruising calendars every September (p122)

Port Denarau Some excellent facilities where yachties can stock up with supplies and arrange repairs (p59)

Royal Suva Yacht Club No longer the institution that it once was but this is the first official port of entry for yachts arriving from Tonga and the east (p96)

Idyllic Beaches

While the main islands have surprisingly few world-class beaches, nearly all of the small offshore islands boast scenery so valued by glossy magazines. With so many to choose between, it seems miserly to single out these few.

Monuriki Ever since Tom Hanks' *Cast Away* was filmed here, tiny Monuriki has become Fiji's biggest star. Its broad lagoon and gorgeous beach have most day trippers wondering why Tom ever left (p119)

Caqalai This tiny island – a mere speck on most maps – has golden beaches backed by swaying palms (p147)

Long Beach The finest beach on Nacula Island and one of the best in the Yasawa chain. It's also only a short boat ride from the original 'Blue Lagoon' (p135)

'Sand bridge' between Waya and Wayasewa Twice the amount of sandy real estate than anywhere else, this strip of sand is lapped by water on both sides (p129)

Birdwatching

A small but dedicated number of travellers come to Fiji in hope of seeing some of its rare and colourful birds. While some, such as the collared lorry, can be seen in hotel gardens, others are more elusive.

Taveuni A great birdspotting site with abundant flora and home to more than 100 species, including the rare orange dove (p169)

Kadavu This island also enjoys a high diversity of bird life, including such endemics as the Kadavu musk parrot. Furthermore, Matava resort has some excellent birding guides (p185)

Vanua Levu Birders should head to Tunuloa Peninsula, home to the rare silktail (p161)

Colo-i-Suva Forest Park Only 11km from downtown Suva, a good network of forest trails offers a good chance to see some of the country's more common native birds (p95)

» Snorkelling in the Blue Lagoon, Sawa-i-Lau (p136)

Romantic Getaways

Beachside dinners, private plunge pools and candlelit massages – these intimate, adult-only resorts leave no pillow unfluffed when it comes to providing honeymooners and those in love with some serious island-style pampering.

Likuliku Lagoon This resort boasts Fiji's only overwater *bure*, each beautifully appointed with traditional touches and oozing style (p121)

Vomo Island Resort With a fantastic coral-fringed beach and some of the smartest *bure* in Fiji, this is South Seas escapism at its finest (p117)

Tokoriki Island Resort The incredibly cute chapel, made of stone and wood, at this resort is the perfect place to tie the knot (p120)

Navini Island Resort A small ecofriendly gem where every *bure* is beachside and every shrub is flowering (p118)

Nanuya Island Resort A short walk from the Blue Lagoon and perched on a hillside with fabulous views. The Nanuya is a long-time favourite with vacationing couples (p134)

Family Fun

If your child is happy with nothing more than a bucket and spade (and possibly a hermit crab or two to harass), then Fiji is one big playground. For other activities suitable for little people try any of the following.

Sabeto Hot Springs For some dirty (but wholesome) fun, kids large and small will love slinging mud at each other in these outdoor pools (p63)

Kula Eco Park This wildlife park on the Coral Coast offers youngsters a chance to get nose-to-beak with rare birds (p78)

Coral Coast Railway Connecting the small Coral Coast town of Yanuca to the beautiful Natadola Beach, this former diesel sugar train is ideal for tiny tots (p73)

Robinson Crusoe Island Children will squeal in delight when 'attacked by cannibals' here (p72)

Sawa-i-Lau Perhaps best suited to slightly older kids, the Sawa-i-Lau caves are a swimming spot with a twist (p136)

Hiking

Although walking for fun might strike most locals as a little odd, there are a few good hikes that will soon have you stretching your legs.

Lavena Coastal Walk Skirting the forest's edge, this 5km walk links beautiful white- and black-sand beaches to isolated villages. Saving the best for last, trekkers can cool off in a brave leap into a pool carved from basalt by twin waterfalls (p178)

Koroyanitu National Heritage Park Options here include treks through *dakua* forests in search of waterfalls, and sweaty scrambles up mountain peaks for breathtaking views (p63)

Colo-i-Suva Forest Park This park offers a network of trails between forest-fringed swimming holes, and gorgeous views (p96)

Des Voeux Peak Nature-lovers are rewarded for the challenging slog to the top with incredible birdwatching opportunities (p172)

month by month

Top Events

1 **Hibiscus Festival**, August

2 **South Indian Fire Walking**, August

3 **Sugar Festival**, September

4 **Fiji Ocean Swim**, October

5 **Fiji Regatta Week**, September

January

Hot and wet. Although temperatures reach above 30°C at this time of year, Fiji's seasonal variations are not pronounced and this is only 5°C above the yearly average. Humidity, however, will make it seem hotter.

✦ New Year's Day New Year's Day is celebrated with much fervour in Fiji, with some parts of the country having festivities the entire month. In Suva, the New Year is seen in with fireworks and street parties.

February

Although only 10 to 15 cyclones strike Fiji each decade (usually between November and April), there is a greater risk of encountering one during February (along with January).

✦ Holi (Festivals of Colour) Holi (also called *phagua* locally) is celebrated by Hindu Indo-Fijians, sometime during February or March, by throwing coloured powder at one another.

March

The wet season continues and this is usually Nadi's wettest month, with an average rainfall of 324mm.

✦ Ram Naumi (Birth of Lord Rama) A Hindu religious festival held in late March or early April, it is mainly celebrated in private homes, although you may see worshippers wade into the water at Suva Bay to throw flowers.

April

Heavier-than-average rains continue until mid-April but, by the end of the month, the wet season will be officially over and humidity levels start to drop.

✦ Fiji International Jazz Festival This three-day jazz festival (www.fijijbfest.org) showcases musicians from around the world and is held in either April or May at Port Denarau.

May

With the start of the dry season, water visibility increases and divers should enjoy excellent clarity from now until October. Fiji's easterly and southeasterly trade winds become more persistent.

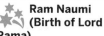 **Surfing** Consistent southerly swells make May a great time to surf. This weather pattern keeps the breaks large until October.

June

Pleasant temperatures, low humidity and fine days kick off Fiji's peak tourist season.

✦ Windsurfing The trade winds that first begin in May continue to provide perfect conditions for windsurfers and kiteboarders around Nananu-i-Ra. Favourable windsurfing conditions persistent here well into next month.

July

July is one of Fiji's coldest and driest months and night temperatures sink to around 18°C. The pleasant days (around 24°C) make this an ideal time to visit.

Bula Festival

One of Fiji's biggest festivals, this is held in Nadi with rides, marching bands, shows and the crowning of 'Miss Bula'.

August

Winter temperatures continue and a light sweater will be needed during the cooler nights. Days remain warm and dry. Ocean temperatures reach their lowest monthly average but are entirely swimmable at 23°C.

Hibiscus Festival

Held in Suva, with floats, food stalls, fair rides and the crowning of 'Miss Hibiscus' (p97).

South Indian Fire Walking

Usually held in August (sometimes July), Hindu devotees at Suva's Mariamma Temple walk across red-hot stones and pierce their bodies with metal skewers (p97).

September

The reliably fine weather continues although Fiji's peak tourist season begins to wind down.

Fiji Regatta Week

Annual regatta luring avid yachties from around the world. Held at Musket Cove (www.musketcovefiji.com).

Sugar Festival

Lautoka comes alive with fun fairs, parades and the crowning of the Sugar Queen.

Friendly North Festival

Similar to Lautoka's Sugar Festival, this is held in Labasa.

October

The cooler dry season ends and temperatures begin to climb as the Southern Hemisphere moves towards its summer.

Ram Leela (Play of Rama)

Primarily a Hindu festival; theatrical performances celebrate the life of the god-king Rama and his return from exile. It's held at the Mariamman Temple (in Vunivau, near Labasa) around the first week of October, and has been celebrated here for more than 100 years.

Diwali (Festival of Lights)

Houses are decorated and candles and lanterns are set on doorsteps to light the way for Lakshmi (the goddess of wealth and prosperity). Held in late October or early to mid-November.

Fiji Ocean Swim

International swim event attracting athletes from around the world who compete in teams or individually in 1km, 2.7km or 19km races (www.fijiswim.com).

November

Fiji's wet season starts in November and continues across summer until April. The mountains of Viti Levu and Vanua Levu create wet climatic zones on their windward (southeastern) sides and dry climatic zones on their leeward (northwestern) sides.

South Pacific World Music Festival

Acclaimed Fijian and international musicians treat Savusavu to five days of global harmony. Held in late November.

December

The rainy season becomes entrenched although travel is still entirely possible. Rain showers are usually heavy but brief and followed by sunny spells.

Fara

Six weeks of dancing and partying kick off on 1 December as Rotumans celebrate Fara (p189)

itineraries

Whether you've got six days or 60, these itineraries provide a starting point for the trip of a lifetime. Want more inspiration? Head online to lonelyplanet. com/thorntree to chat with other travellers.

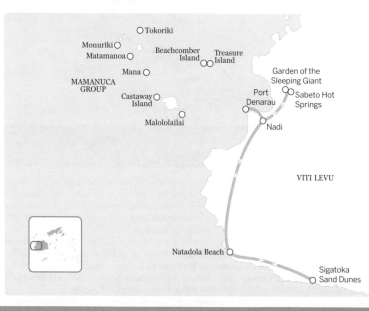

Ten Days
Ten Days in the Sun

> Begin your fling in **Nadi**, by taking a day or two to slow down and reset your internal clock to 'Fiji time'. Some of the best resorts can be found just outside of Nadi at **Port Denarau** and these are also handy to Denarau's golf course, shops and restaurants.
> Spend a morning admiring the orchids at the **Garden of the Sleeping Giant**, and an afternoon immersed in the nearby **Sabeto Hot Springs**. Follow this with a day trip climbing the **Sigatoka Sand Dunes** or horse riding along **Natadola Beach**.

By now you should be suitably relaxed and ready for the beautiful **Mamanuca Group**. It's probably best to base yourself on one island rather than spend your precious vacation packing and unpacking. Which resort you choose will largely depend on the style of vacation you're looking for. **Beachcomber Island** will appeal to party animals while those with families may prefer child-friendly options like **Treasure**, **Mana** and **Malololailai** islands. If you are wanting something more intimate, try romantic **Tokoriki**, the versatile **Matamanoa** or picture-perfect **Castaway**. Before returning to Nadi, be sure to take a day trip to **Monuriki**, made famous in the movie *Cast Away* starring Tom Hanks.

Two to Three Weeks
Once Around the Block

> This itinerary focuses on Fiji's 'mainland', Viti Levu. With roads and regular buses that circumnavigate the island, it's possible to construct your own tour and save a packet in the process. If you wanted you could travel the whole circuit in a day using public transport, although if you allow yourself plenty of time for excursions and beachside relaxation, two or three weeks should be ample.

Assuming you start in **Nadi** – although you could begin anywhere – follow the Coral Coast Hwy to the **Momi Guns**, and **Natadola Beach** for some horse riding. Chug into the verdant interior on the **Coral Coast Scenic Railway** or don your sneakers and trek to the top of the **Sigatoka Sand Dunes**. Kids will love feeding the wildlife at the **Kula Eco Park**, while mum and dad might enjoy a few days poolside at a resort in **Korolevu**.

Make your way towards **Pacific Harbour** to go diving with sharks in **Beqa Lagoon** or take a boat trip out to surf at the underrated **Frigate Passage**. Don't miss the opportunity to raft the canyons of the **Navua River** before heading to **Suva**.

Spend a day or two exploring the nation's capital. Options include taking a crash course on local history at the Fiji Museum or swinging, Tarzan-style, into the refreshing pools at **Colo-i-Suva Forest Park**.

An interesting side trip is to buy a bus/ferry combo ticket to **Ovalau**, a small island off the coast of eastern Viti Levu. During colonial times **Levuka** was the nation's capital and it still retains a good measure of its Wild West vibe.

Back on the mainland complete your Viti Levu loop via the northern Kings Road, windsurfing at **Nananu-i-Ra** or scuba diving at **Rakiraki**. From here, head back to sugar country and visit **Lautoka**, the second-largest city and a great base to explore the **Nausori Highlands**. A good option here is to spend a night or two at the traditional village of **Navala** before heading back to Nadi.

» (above) Sonaisali Island Resort, Naisali (p70)
» (left) Natadola beach, Viti Levu (p72)

The Yasawa Explorer
The Northern Loop

SOUTH PACIFIC OCEAN

Labasa — Cobra Rock
VANUA LEVU
Waisali Rainforest Reserve — Tunuloa Peninsula — Somosomo
Savusavu — Rainbow Reef — TAVEUNI
Waitavala Water Slide — Lavena Coastal Walk

Matacawalevu — Nacula
Nanuya Lailai & Blue Lagoon
Naviti — YASAWA GROUP
Waya
Wayasewa
Beachcomber Island — Treasure Island
VITI LEVU
Port Denarau
Suva (30km)

One to Two Weeks
The Yasawa Explorer

Thanks to a high-speed catamaran, which daily weaves its way from **Port Denarau** through the **Yasawa Group** and back again, this chain is readily explored. Buy yourself a one- or two-week pass for the *Yasawa Flyer* that then allows you to hop on or off the boat at any island you like.

The boat first heads through a few of the Mamanucas before reaching the Yasawa chain, so these islands are a good place to start. With wide sandy beaches and populated by partygoing backpackers, many young people choose **Beachcomber Island** as their first port of call, while families indulge in innumerable water sports on **Treasure Island**.

Spend the next few days on the sliver of sand that connects **Wayasewa** to **Waya** before drifting north to **Naviti** to snorkel with manta rays. Reboard the *Flyer* for a dash up to **Nacula**, or **Nanuya Lailai**, where you can paddle in the **Blue Lagoon**. From here, leapfrog your way back down the chain, stopping at **Matacawalevu** for further bouts of snorkelling and sunbathing on the aptly named and horseshoe-shaped Long Beach.

Ten Days
The Northern Loop

Beginning in **Suva**, spend a morning at the excellent Fiji Museum and then an afternoon stocking up on souvenirs at the craft market. After exhausting Suva's nightlife, hop on a flight to **Vanua Levu** and land yourself in **Labasa**, a sugar town where you can smell the molasses in the air. Visit the **Wasavula Ceremonial Site** and take a side trip to the mystifying **Cobra Rock** inside the Naag Mandir Temple.

Continue your Vanua Levu adventure by jumping on a bus and heading south to **Savusavu**. Spend a day or two taking in the sights, and the evenings talking with visiting skippers over a beer. Take a day trip to the rich and colourful **Waisali Rainforest Reserve**, or rent a 4WD and brave the roads to the lesser-travelled **Tunuloa Peninsula**.

Then it's time to head to gorgeous **Taveuni**. If you've got sea legs, catch a ferry; if not, the flight provides some spectacular views. **Somosomo** is a good base from which to explore the surrounding area. Snorkel or dive at the magnificent **Rainbow Reef**, trek the **Lavena Coastal Walk** and scare yourself silly on the **Waitavala Water Slide** before heading back to Suva.

Which Island?

Top Five Luxury Resorts

Top Five Backpacker Hangouts

Top Five Romantic Getaways

Whatever type of island holiday you're looking for, chances are you'll find it in Fiji. Choose from barebones backpackers and cultural-connection homestays to gorgeously designed, upscale beach bungalows and massive resorts. There's generally a lively scene in the tourist hot spots on Viti Levu and the Mamanuca and Yasawa Groups, while things are quieter but stay pleasantly friendly on less-visited islands like Kadavu and Taveuni.

The Resort Experience

The term 'resort' is bandied around freely in Fiji and can refer to almost anything within a frisbee throw of a beach. Take note of the price and do your homework via the internet to make sure you know what you're getting yourself into. If the tariff is low, chances are you're not booking into a luxury establishment, but it may be a lovely budget choice.

Resort Islands

Viti Levu

» The gateway to the country and the largest of the Fijian islands; boasts a taste of everything the country has to offer.

» Port Denarau, despite having no beach, has a string of big-brand resorts; many packages include a night or two here.

» The Coral Coast and Pacific Harbour have a broad spectrum of resorts including some good midrange options.

FIJIAN HITCH

Many resorts cater to the almost- and newlywed with irresistible honeymoon and wedding packages and can provide you with much of the information and planning you need. The obvious place for romance is the Mamanuca Group, although you'll find a number of adult-only affairs scattered throughout the country.

You'll need to bring the required documentation (including birth certificates and a Statutory Declaration signed by a Justice of the Peace, Notary Public or Solicitor to prove you are not married) to a Registry Office prior to your actual marriage in order to obtain a marriage licence. The **Registrar General's office** (☏331 5280; Ground fl, Suvavou House, Victoria Pde; ☺8.30am-3.30pm Mon-Fri) is in Suva, but there are also **Divisional Registrars** Lautoka (☏666 1708; 1st fl, Rogorogoivuda House, Tavewa Ave; ☺9am-3pm Mon-Fri); Nadi (☏670 0101; Korivolu Ave; ☺8am-1pm & 2-4pm Mon-Fri). There's a $22 fee and you have 28 days to then get hitched.

The following websites can help you plan the perfect Fijian wedding or honeymoon, if not organise it outright:

» www.destination-weddings-abroad.com/fiji/

» www.fijihoneymoon.com

» www.holidaysforcouples.com.au/holidays/special-offers/pacific-islands

» www.weddings-in-fiji.com

Mamanuca Group

» Most Mamanuca islands are around an hour's boat ride away from Nadi.

» Reliably good weather and beautiful beaches mean they remain Fiji's most famous poster child.

» Most cater to vacationing families, honeymooners or romantically inclined couples, although Beachcomber Island has earned its stripes over the years as *the* party destination in Fiji.

Yasawa Group

» Traditionally caters to either backpackers or the well-heeled, but is gradually opening up more for midrange travellers.

» Well connected to the mainland by a high-speed catamaran but is nonetheless remote and has little infrastructure.

Ovalau & the Lomaiviti Group

» Most accommodation on the main island of Ovalau is in the form of small hotels, homestays and lodges.

» Five of the beach-blessed offshore islands have their own isolated resorts: every one of these is fantastic.

» Midrangers will love Koro and Naigani, while you'd be hard-pressed to find more beautiful luxury than at Wakaya.

Vanua Levu

» There are a wide range of resorts (many family-oriented) around pretty Savusavu that are perfect for quiet relaxation and dive holidays.

» There are also a number of offshore island choices: divers and nature lovers should head to Namena, while seekers of luxe will be pampered on Nukubati.

» Other remote getaways can be found on the rugged but spectacular Tunuloa Peninsula and at midrange Palmlea Lodge, northwest from Labasa.

Taveuni

» Great for action seekers of all budgets.

» Most of the posh options are in the north, along with plenty of great-value dive and activity-oriented places.

» Resorts on the offshore islands in this area, including Matagi, Qamea and Laucala, are utterly sublime.

Kadavu

» Nearly all the resorts here are admirably conserving their environment and watching their social impact by growing their own organic vegetables, working in tune with the local villages and much more.

» Only Ono has a very luxurious option, while the rest of the group's choices offer a good level of comfort without too many frills.

What to Expect

If you've organised it in advance, you'll be met at the airport by your resort representative and then soon be transferred to your resort – either by a waiting speedboat, airplane, van or truck. From registration onwards you'll be given the choice to partake in organised activities or just chill and explore the island on your own.

» At the high end expect day spas, landscaped pools and stylish restaurants.

» Midrange resorts will generally have a restaurant and bar and possibly a swimming pool, but not all will have kids clubs or dive operators.

» Resorts for all budgets usually have rates that include nonmotorised (snorkelling, windsurfing and sailing) sports; but diving, parasailing, water-skiing, jet-skiing, fishing and island-hopping excursions generally cost extra.

» Resorts nearly always feature some kind of *bure*-style accommodation, meaning a bungalow, often with a thatched roof and some traditional architecture.

Food & Drink

At luxury resorts you'll find a sumptuous mix of Western, Melanesian, Indian, Asian and fusion specialities, perhaps spread over several restaurants. The bar will be stocked and a good wine selection will be available. Most of the bigger hotels put on a Fijian dance performance, often with buffet meal, a few times a week. Breakfast will often be buffet and at other times meals will be à la carte with more simple options like burgers and sandwiches available at lunch.

Midrange and budget resorts on the bigger islands will almost always have a restaurant with a menu including Western, Fijian and Indian fare. In remote settings these types of places often only serve set meals that are eaten with the other guests, sometimes at individual tables and at other times family style at one big table. You'll be asked when you reserve or check in if you have any special food requirements and they'll do their best to cater to your needs. If you have any serious allergies or dietary restrictions let your hosts know as far in advance as possible so they can get the proper supplies.

The Budget Experience

Many of Fiji's hostels and backpackers are more resort-like than the cheaper hotels, not in terms of luxury, but for their (usually) beachside locations and the activities they offer. To make the choice between a budget hotel or backpacker resort you'll have to decide what's more important to you: a hot-water bathroom, privacy and TV, or socialising, cheap activities and, most often, better beach bumming and snorkelling.

Which Island?

Viti Levu

» Nadi, the country's revolving door, is particularly well represented and backpacker haunts often have their own restaurants, bars, laundries, internet access and tour desks.

» While Nadi rocks out with arriving and leaving tourists you can get your groove on with the locals in Suva.

Mamanuca Group

» Partiers head for Beachcomber Island – the 120-bed *bure* seems less daunting after partaking in the resort's plentiful buffet meals, well-stocked bar and relentless nightly entertainment.

» Quieter nights can be found at South Sea Island, with room for 32 overnighters in the resort's dorm.

Yasawa Group

» Many young partygoers head up the Yasawa chain in search of the perfect beach, but be prepared for the possibility of being the only guest at smaller budget resorts.

» Low-key locally managed Wayalailai Eco Haven Resort offers a wider range of land-based activities than many; while Manta Ray ups the ante with its facilities, food and in-shore reef.

KID SEASON

As Fiji is a popular destination for Australian and New Zealand families, peak season in Fiji coincides with the school holidays in Australia and New Zealand. For the exact dates of antipodean vacation periods search 'school term' at http://australia.gov.au (for Australia) and www.minedu.govt.nz (for New Zealand).

Ovalau & the Lomaiviti Group

» Ovalau has midrange and budget hotels, a B&B and a village stay.

» The resort-cum-backpackers on the outer islands of Caqalai and Leleuvia are the crème de la crème of all-to-yourself budget paradise.

Vanua Levu

» Savusavu has some good, locally run guesthouses/backpackers on the fringes of town – during low season you may feel like the only backpacker in town.

» Very rustic camping and dorms are available on Lesiaceva Point in lush surroundings.

Taveuni

» There are some fabulous, fun and friendly backpacker choices around Matei and on the outer island of Qamea; Beverley Campground in Matei lets you sleep in tents or dorms right on the beach.

» Wonderful, quiet village guesthouses are found in Lavena and Vuna.

What to Expect

» In a well-run establishment you can expect fan-cooled dorms and doubles that are clean and functional with few frills.

» At older establishments rooms can come in a hodgepodge of configurations, many of them hot and airless with poor toilet-to-guest ratios.

NON-RESORT ACCOMMODATION

Camping

There are few campgrounds in Fiji – these usually offer dorms, basic cabins and tents. Some budget resorts do cater for those with a proclivity for canvas, but as campsites are only a few dollars cheaper than dormitories, the hassle of carrying a tent hardly seems worth it.

Nor should you camp without permission. Most of Fiji's land, even in seemingly remote unoccupied areas, is owned by the local *mataqali* (extended family) group or village. Before pitching a tent, present your *sevusevu* (gift) of kava root to the chief and ask his permission. Chances are, you will be invited to stay with a family anyway and to refuse this invitation will likely be misinterpreted as that you find their home beneath you.

Village Homestays

Some villages offer homestays as a way of earning a little extra. Not only is this an affordable way to travel but you will also gain a real insight into Fiji traditions and make a village worth of friends in the process. Viseisei (p64), Navala (p69), Namatakula (p82), Rabi (p163) and Silana (p147) all see a trickle of inquisitive travellers. On remote islands, like those in the Lau, Moala and Rotuma Groups, homestays and village guesthouses are your only option.

CouchSurfing

CouchSurfing is slowly gaining popularity in Fiji and there are around 50 Fiji-based members. CouchSurfers may enjoy free accommodation, but the real reward lies in the chance to meet locals, interact with their families and join in their daily activities. Visit www.couchsurfing.org to join up.

Holiday Rentals

Renting privately owned holiday homes, particularly for those travelling in groups or as a family, can be good value. Rates are by the week – usually around $800 to $3000 – with specified in and out days, and ideal for those looking for a fixed base from which to take day trips. Many are in Pacific Harbour on Viti Levu but there's also plenty on offer in Vanua Levu and Taveuni. We've listed our favourites under the Sleeping headings in this book. To search further, good sites include the following:

» www.harcourts.com.fj

» www.myhome.com.fj

» www.fijilive.com/realestate

» (above) Likuliku Lagoon resort,
   Malolo Island (p121)
» (left) Room interior at Turtle Island
   Resort, Yasawa Group (p135)

» Facilities are generally shared, with cold-water showers.

» Dedicated single rooms are few and far between, so you'll usually have to fork out for a double if you are a solo traveller wanting privacy.

» Few budget resorts include activities in their rates (although they almost always offer them) and most charge for the use of their snorkelling equipment.

Food & Drink

Many hostels, backpackers and cheaper hotels, particularly on the main islands, have their own simple restaurants. Budget lodging in the outer islands, where there are no other eating options, usually offer a plan of two to three meals a day where you'll eat a set meal with the other guests.

Activities

Resorts, upscale boutique places and even hardcore budget lodges will usually have plenty of activities available for their guests or work with independent operators they know and trust.

Action & Adventure

On Viti Levu you can jet boat the Nadi River, take a hot-air balloon ride at sunrise, go on a jet-ski safari around the Mamanucas for the day (from Nadi) and zip line at Pacific Harbour and on the offshore island of Beqa. On other islands you'll have to get your adrenalin the good ol' fashioned way via surfing, diving, hiking or whatever else strikes your fancy.

Birdwatching

There are well over a hundred species of birds in the Fijian islands, with many that are endemic to only one island – so birdwatchers will have their heads spinning with desirable islands to visit. Taveuni and Kadavu have easy access to the interior and you won't have to go far to see some of the species since many have no predators and aren't shy. Guides are available throughout the country – ask at your place of lodging.

On Vanua Levu, the Tunuloa Peninsula is home to the rare silktail. On Viti Levu, Colo-i-Suva Forest Park near Suva is very accessible and Kula Eco Park on the Coral Coast offers birders a chance to get nose-to-beak with the rare, native Pacific black duck. In urban areas you're likely to see the chunky collared lory (a common par-rot) and the brilliant emerald, red-headed parrot finch. Aggressive introduced species, such as Indian mynahs, have forced many native birds into the forest, where you'll hear barking pigeons and giant forest honeyeaters. Some 23 tropical sea birds are also seen in Fiji. Fiji's rarest bird, the *kacau* (petrel), as seen on the back of the $50 note, is only found on Gau in the Lomaiviti Group.

For practical planning tips and inspiration, it is worth reading the field reports posted on the following sites:

» **Fat Birder** (www.fatbirder.com/links_geo/australasia/fiji.html)

» **Travelling Birder** (www.travellingbirder.com)

Diving & Snorkelling

Many resorts have dive centres and those that don't can usually hook you up with diving if it's available on the island. Diving is covered in depth on p33.

Snorkellers are well catered for via boat trips and excursions but it's a good idea to bring your own gear since rental or offered equipment may be in poor shape.

Fishing

Villages have rights over the reefs and fishing in Fiji, so you cannot just drop a line anywhere: seek permission first. Many of the more expensive resorts offer game-fishing tours and boat chartering and tend to favour surface lures and deep and shallow jigging. Budget resorts can organise boats and tackle, although this may be just a simple hand line with baited hooks and sinkers.

SPECIES	SEASON	BEST MONTH
black marlin	Jul-Nov	Aug-Sep
blue marlin	Mar-Aug	Jul-Aug
striped marlin	Jun-Aug	Jul
sailfish	year round	Jun-Sep
wahoo	Jun-Sep	Jul-Aug
dolphinfish	year round	Nov
tanguige	Oct-Mar	Feb
barracuda	Oct-Mar	Feb
giant trevally	Oct-Mar	Feb
yellowfin tuna	May-Jul	Jun
dogtooth tuna	Jun-Oct	Jul
skipjack tuna	May-Aug	Jun

Hiking

Waterfalls, lava-formed coastal trails and lush vistas are plentiful. The best hiking in the country is found on Taveuni, where a huge section of the island has been designated a national park. Viti Levu, Kadavu, Vanua Levu and Ovalau also have fantastic hiking but on these islands it's imperative to hire a guide since most trails pass through village lands and you will need permission (and the proper etiquette; see p221) to go through them.

Horse Riding

The locals around Natadola Beach on Viti Levu make a living out of saddling-up day trippers, while horse riding is also a common resort activity along the Coral Coast. Other opportunities crop up at Vatuwiri Farm in Taveuni and at Bulou's Eco Lodge in the Nausori Highlands.

Kayaking

Many resorts have kayaks for guest use free of charge; others hire them at about $20 and $30 for a half- and full day respectively. The islands of the Mamanucas, Vanua Levu, the Yasawas, Nananu-i-Ra and Kadavu are all great for kayaking. Some keen kayakers paddle Taveuni's rugged Ravilevu Coast, but generally the western sides of the islands are preferred as they're sheltered from the southeast trade winds.

There are also special sea-kayaking tours available during the drier months, between May and November. Some combine paddling with hiking into rainforests, snorkelling, fishing and village visits.

Island Tours & Cruises

Depending on the island, minibuses, tour buses, private cars or 4WDs may be used to take you around the island to see the sites. There are also opportunities for day cruises to smaller offshore islands that can take you to deserted beaches of unimaginable beauty – plus you'll often get a picnic and go snorkelling.

Surfing

Most surf pitches over outer reefs and in passages, and is for intermediate to advanced surfers only. For these reefs you need boats and guides. Marine safety can be lax so ask for oars, life jackets and drinking water

PRICE RANGES

Price ranges are for twin or double rooms during peak season (July to September) and include Fiji's 15% value-added tax (VAT) and the 5% hotel turnover tax. Hotel websites commonly quote prices in various currencies (US$, AU$, NZ$) although we have quoted prices in Fijian dollars throughout this guide for ease of comparison. All room prices in this book include bathrooms unless specified otherwise.

Price ranges are defined as follows:

$ <$150
$$ $150-350
$$$ >$350

as well as a mobile (cell) phone on board. Southerly swells are consistent from May to October, but there is surf year-round. The trade winds are southeast and offshore at the famous breaks. Northerlies, from November to April, are offshore on the Coral Coast.

Cloudbreak, Restaurants and Namotu Left are easily accessed from the Mamanuca islands of Malolo, Malololailai, Namotu or Tavarua. They can be reached just as easily by boat from the resorts near Uciwai Landing on Viti Levu.

Frigates in Beqa Lagoon can be reached from the surf camp on Yanuca island or the more upmarket Waidroka Surf & Dive Resort near Pacific Harbour. To get away from the crowds head to Qamea for its fickle breaks.

The big news in Fijian surfing circles (or should that be pods) is, until very recently, exclusive surfing rights were sold by Fijian villages (who under Fijian law have customary fishing rights) to resorts that would then restrict access to all but their guests. The 2010 Surfing Areas Decree changed all this and now all breaks are open to any brave enough to surf them.

Village Visits

Many tours include a village visit in their activities. Some villages have become affected by bus loads of tourists parading through their backyards every other day and the *sevusevu* (gift) ceremony and *meke* (a dance performance that enacts stories and legends) can seem somewhat contrived. Other

BOOK YOUR STAY ONLINE

For more accommodation reviews by Lonely Planet authors, check out http://hotels.lonelyplanet.com. You'll find independent reviews, as well as recommendations on the best places to stay. Best of all, you can book online.

village tours, especially those run by the villagers, are smaller in scale with perhaps not so much going on; however, the experience can feel more genuine.

Planning & Choosing

Independent Travel

Outside of high season (June through August and mid-December through mid-January) you could arrive just about anywhere in Fiji without any idea of where you're going or what you're doing and have an amazing trip. During the seasonal rush, however, the better places will be booked and flights may be full so it's wise to plan in advance.

Package Tours

A package tour can work out to be a financial godsend but they don't give much leeway to explore at will. Although most tours offer the opportunity to visit more than one island, you will have to prebook one hotel or resort for each destination before departure (meaning you can't swap resorts halfway through if you're not happy).

There's a variety of tour packages available from travel agents and online booking agencies in all Western countries. If you want more than a straightforward combo package, a good travel agent is essential – they can negotiate better prices at the larger hotels and handle the internal flight bookings. In addition to the traditional travel operators, there are agencies that specialise in diving tours. These packages typically include flights, accommodation and diving trips.

Where to Book a Package

Plenty of agents book packages to Fiji but a good place to search and get a feel for pricing is on the websites of the airlines that service the region including Air New Zealand (www.airnewzealand.com), Air Pacific (www.airpacific.com), Jetstar (www.jetstar.com), Qantas (www.qantas.com) and Virgin Australia (www.virginaustralia.com).

Note that most packages quote double occupancy pricing. Solo travellers have to pay a 'single-person supplement'. Extra people can usually share a room, but there's a charge for the extra bed, which varies enormously from resort to resort.

Useful Accommodation Websites

» www.fiji-backpacking.com

» www.fijibudget.com

» www.4hotels.co.uk/fiji

» www.fiji4less.com

» www.fiji.pacific-resorts.com

» www.travelmaxia.com

» www.fijibeaches.com

Diving

Best for Beginner Divers

Fiji is a perfect spot for new divers, as the warm water in the shallow lagoons is a forgiving training environment. Just about anyone in good health, including children aged eight years and over, can learn to dive.
Breath Taker (Nananu-i-Ra, Viti Levu) Great pelagic action on an incoming tide (p109).
Gotham City (Mamanuca Group) Reef species aplenty (p114).
Yellow Wall (Kadavu) An atmospheric site resembling a fairy-tale castle (p183).
Lekima's Ledge (Yasawa Group) A coral-studded underwater cliff (p124).

Best for Experienced Divers

Great White Wall (Taveuni) Possibly the best soft-coral dive in Fiji (p167).
Beqa Lagoon (Viti Levu) Bull sharks galore – a once-in-a-lifetime experience (p84).
Nasonisoni Passage (Vanua Levu) Exhilarating drift dive through a narrow passage (p155).
E6 (Lomaiviti Group) A phenomenal seamount that brushes the ocean's surface (p139).

Some of Fiji's most spectacular scenery is just below the surface and diving in Fiji is truly amazing. The water is warm, clear and teeming with life. You'll see myriad multi-hued fish, canyonlike terrain and vertigo-inducing walls festooned with exquisite soft and hard corals resembling a lush flower garden in full bloom.

Diving Conditions

Although Fiji is diveable year-round, the best season is from April to October. November to March tends to see the most rainfall, which can obscure visibility off the main islands with river run-off.

Keep in mind that many dives are subject to currents, which vary from barely perceptible to powerful. Visibility varies a lot, from a low of 10m at certain sites up to 40m at others. Water temperatures range from 23°C in August to 29°C in January. You won't need anything more than a thin neoprene or a 3mm wetsuit to remain comfortable while diving.

Top Dive Sites

Fiji is often dubbed the 'soft corals capital of the world'. But soft corals are not the only raison d'être of diving in Fiji. You will also find majestic reefs ablaze with techni-coloured critters, spectacular underwater topography, shark dives and drift dives. Fiji's only weak point is the dearth of impressive wrecks.

SHARK FEEDING

A few kilometres off the Viti Levu coast near Pacific Harbour lies Shark Reef. In other parts of the world, shark feeding usually involves grey reef sharks and, if you're lucky, lemon sharks and nurse sharks. Here, up to eight different types of shark turn up: tawny nurse sharks, white-tip, black-tip and grey reef sharks, sicklefin lemon sharks, silvertips, massive bull sharks (except from October to January, when they leave the spot to mate) and even the heavyweight of them all – tiger sharks!

During the dives, divers form a line behind a purpose-built small coral wall. The feeder dips into a huge bin and pulls out hunks of dead fish. For several minutes at a time it may be hard to work out what is happening in the swirl of tails and fins as one shark after another materialises, ripping and tearing at the bait. It's definitely (in)tense, but there's no frenzy to speak of. The sharks approach in surprisingly orderly fashion, even the ponderous-looking bull sharks. If the arena suddenly clears, a 4m tiger shark is about to appear.

While it's certainly thrilling, this is more a show than a dive, and fish feeding is a controversial subject. On the one hand, these artificial encounters undeniably disrupt natural behaviour patterns: sharks grow dependent on 'free lunches' and may unlearn vital survival skills. On the other hand, some experts think that these shows have educational virtue, raising awareness among divers and helping sharks gain some much-needed positive press. We'll let you decide.

Viti Levu

Viti Levu is normally the visiting diver's first glimpse of Fiji. The best diving is found off Nananu-i-Ra island to the north, which has a good balance of scenic seascapes, elaborate reef structures and dense marine life. However, Viti Levu's most noteworthy dive site is undoubtedly Shark Reef in Beqa Lagoon, where you can witness a phenomenal shark-feeding session.

» **Beqa Lagoon (Pacific Harbour)** In addition to going nose-to-nose with massive bull and tiger sharks, other sites include Caesar's Rocks, Side Streets and ET, which features a vast tunnel more than 30m long, densely blanketed with sea fans and soft corals (p84).

» **Rakiraki reefs and Nananu-i-Ra** This area has a good balance of scenic seascapes and elaborate reef structures. Dream Maker and Breath Taker are famous for their dense concentrations of colourful tropicals and the quality of their corals. To the northwest, off Charybdis Reef, Spud Dome is renowned for its dramatic scenery while Heartbreak Ridge offers a chance of spotting pelagics (p109).

Mamanuca Group

Due to their proximity to Nadi and Lautoka on Viti Levu, the Mamanuca islands are very popular with divers and can easily be reached from these two towns by boat. You can also base yourself at any of the island resorts, as diving infrastructure is readily available throughout the Mamanuca Group. Most dive sites are scattered along the Malolo Barrier Reef or off the nearby islets. Diving is probably less spectacular than in other areas of Fiji but it's still rewarding, with diverse marine life, good visibility and a varied topography, as well as a glut of easy sites that will appeal to novice divers; see p114.

» **Plantation Pinnacles** Near Malololailai, this site is notable for its three deep-water rock towers.

» **Sherwood Forest** Near Tokoriki; home to beautiful gorgonian sea fans.

» **Gotham City (Malolo Barrier Reef)** Located inside the barrier-reef lagoon, the site comprises several coral heads surrounded by a smorgasbord of reef fish in less than 20m.

» **Salamanda** The wreck of a 36m vessel that was sunk as an artificial reef near Treasure Island. She rests upright on a rubble seafloor at around 20m and is partly encrusted with soft corals and anemones.

Yasawa Group

The Yasawas are less crowded, with fewer dive boats. This chain of ancient volcanic islands offers excellent corals, pristine reefs and good visibility.

» **Lekima's Ledge** A stunning underwater cliff off Vawa island, suitable for novice divers.

» **Paradise Wall** On the western side of Yasawa island; another recommended wall dive.

» **Passage between Nanuya Balavu and Drawaqa** Frequented by giant manta rays. Although the use of scuba equipment is prohibited, this is an amazing snorkelling experience.

Lomaiviti Group & Bligh Water

Central Fiji roughly covers the area between the country's two main landmasses – it extends from Bligh Water in the west to Namenalala and the Lomaiviti Group in the east. Most sites in this 'golden triangle' can only be accessed by live-aboards and remain largely untouched.

» **E6 (Vatu-i-Ra Channel)** E6 is consistently rated as one of the best sites in Fiji. This seamount rises from 1000m to the surface and acts as a magnet for pelagics. A huge swim-through in the seamount, called the Cathedral, creates a magical atmosphere (p138).

» **Nigali Passage** Also known as Shark Alley, this narrow channel off Gau island is home to an almost ever-present squadron of grey sharks as well as schooling trevally, barracuda, snapper and the occasional ray (p138).

» **Chimneys** At Namenalala Reef, off the southeastern coast of Vanua Levu; has several towering coral pillars, all coated with soft corals, sea fans and crinoids (p162).

» **Blue Ridge (off Wakaya island)** Notable for its abundance of bright-blue ribbon eels.

Vanua Levu

Most dive sites are in or around Savusavu Bay. The underwater scenery is striking, the walls are precipitous and the fish population (which includes pelagics) is diverse.

» **Nasonisoni Passage (Namena Marine Park)** A rip-roaring drift dive in a narrow, current-swept channel. During tidal exchange, divers are sucked into the passage and propelled through the funnel by the forceful current (p155).

» **Dreamhouse (Namena Marine Park)** A small seamount that seems to attract a wealth of pelagics, including grey reef sharks, jacks and tuna (p155).

Taveuni

The Somosomo Strait (p167), a narrow stretch of ocean that is funnelled between Taveuni and Vanua Levu, has achieved Shangri-La status in the diving community, and for good reason. The only downside in Somosomo Strait is the average visibility does not exceed 15m to 20m and when the plankton blooms, during January and February, it is further reduced.

» **Rainbow Reef** Strong tidal currents push the deep water back and forth through the passage, providing nutrients for the soft corals and sea fans that form a vivid tapestry.

» **Purple Wall** An impressive wall suffused with a dense layer of purple soft-coral trees, whip corals and sea fans. Numerous overhangs and arches harbour soldierfish and squirrelfish.

» **Great White Wall** This is one of Fiji's signature drift dives with a phenomenal concentration of white soft coral resembling a snow-covered ski slope when the current is running.

» **Annie's Bommies** An explosion of colour, with several big boulders liberally draped with soft corals and surrounded by swirling basslets.

There are also superb dive sites around neighbouring Matagi, Qamea and Laucala islands and at Motualevu Atoll, some 30km east of Taveuni.

LIVE-ABOARDS

A couple of live-aboards ply the Fiji waters, usually with week-long itineraries. A live-aboard dive trip is recommended for those looking to experience unchartered and uncrowded dive sites beyond the reach of land-based dive operations, especially the sites in Bligh Water and off the Lomaiviti Group. Take a look at the following operators:

Fiji Aggressor (www.aggressor.com)

Nai'a (☑ 345 0382; www.naia.com.fj)

Republic of Diving (☑ 628 2736; www.republicofdiving.com)

Sere-ni-Wai (☑ 336 1171; www.sere.com.fj)

Ɩavu's main claim to fame is the Great ᴀrolabe Reef, a barrier reef that hugs the south and east coasts of the island for about 100km. It's home to a vibrant assemblage of hard- and soft-coral formations and breathtaking walls. Unlike Taveuni, currents are probably easier to handle in this area, but be prepared for rough seas and reduced visibility when it's raining or when the winds blow, especially from November to April.

» **Western side of the Great Astrolabe**
Recommended dive sites include Broken Stone, Split Rock and Vouwa. They more or less share the same characteristics, with scenic underwater seascapes of twisting canyons, tunnels, caverns and arches (p186).

» **Naiqoro Passage** Just off the east coast of Kadavu, this narrow channel is frequently swept by strong tidal currents and offers rewarding drift dives along steep walls (p186).

» **Northwestern side of Kadavu** This area is a bit overshadowed by the Great Astrolabe Reef but novice divers will feel comfortable here. Mellow Reef, Yellow Wall and *Pacific Voyager,* a 63m-long tanker that was intentionally sunk in 30m of water in 1994, are the best dives (p183).

Responsible Diving

The Fiji islands are ecologically vulnerable. By following these guidelines while diving, you can help preserve the ecology and beauty of the reefs:

» Encourage dive operators to establish permanent moorings at appropriate dive sites.

» Practise and maintain proper buoyancy control.

» Avoid touching living marine organisms with your body and equipment.

» Take great care in underwater caves, as your air bubbles can damage fragile organisms.

» Minimise your disturbance of marine animals.

» Never stand on corals, even if they look solid and robust.

DIVING & FLYING

Most divers get to Fiji by plane. While it's fine to dive soon *after* flying, it's important to remember that your last dive should be completed at least 12 hours (some experts advise 24 hours) *before* your flight, to minimise the risk of residual nitrogen in the blood causing decompression. Careful attention to flight times, as compared with diving times, is necessary in Fiji because so much of the interisland transport is by air.

Dive Centres

There are at least 30 professional dive centres in Fiji. All of them are affiliated with one or more internationally recognised certifying agencies, usually PADI or National Association of Underwater Instructors (NAUI). In general you can expect well-maintained equipment, good facilities and knowledgeable staff, but standards may vary from one centre to another. Dive centres are open year-round, most of them every day, and offer a whole range of services, such as introductory dives, night dives, exploratory dives and certification programs. Many are attached to a resort and typically offer two-tank dive trips.

The country has only one recompression chamber, in Suva.

Costs

Diving in Fiji is rather good value, especially if you compare it with other South Pacific destinations. If you plan to do many dives on one island, consider buying a multidive package, which comes out much cheaper. Indicative prices include:

» Introductory dive: about $130

» Two-tank dive: between $200 and $245, including equipment rental

» Open-water certification course: between $700 and $850

Dive centres are detailed in the destination chapters.

Travel with Children

Best Regions for Kids

Nadi, Suva & Viti Levu

On the Coral Coast explore a hill fort, sand dunes, rivers and villages during the day and watch cultural shows at night. Pacific Harbour is perfect for active families, with plenty of adventure sports, highland tours from nearby Navua and off-shore island tours.

The Mamanuca & Yasawa Groups

Take the *Yasawa Flyer* with lots to see on the way then enjoy safe swimming, snorkelling and village visits.

Vanua Levu & Taveuni

Family-oriented resorts let parents dive while the kids get coddled by sitters – or stay longer-term in a fully-equipped holiday rental. On Taveuni, hike to waterfalls and pick fruit in jungle-fringed plantations. Beaches are small and calm and friendly.

Kadavu, Lau & Moala Groups

Snorkel with manta rays, watch the kids catch their first big fish and frolic in waterfall pools with local village kids.

Fiji is a watery playground for all ages but beyond sun and swimming it's also a place of gentle culture and adventures to mangroves, caves, jungles and waterfalls.

Fiji for Kids

Fijians will want to talk with your kids and invite them to join activities or visit homes. Kids will be quickly absorbed into games with local children and fun has no language barrier.

Not all resorts accept children in Fiji but many that do have free kids club for four to 12 year olds and child-friendly pools. Babysitting for toddlers and infants is easily arranged from around $7 per hour or at a fixed rate of $20 for an evening.

Eating Out

Most places in the region have kid-pleaser items such as hamburgers and pasta dishes on their menus, and many children will be happy to try some of the local cuisine such as *dalo*, fish in coconut milk or a mild dhal. Ice cream is frequently available, and it's a real treat in the hot weather. Baby supplies are available in all but the most remote places.

Many restaurants in cities and tourist areas and at well-equipped resorts have high chairs but you're less likely to find these at budget places.

Long-life milk is readily available, as is bottled spring water and fruit juice. While breastfeeding is common among the local population, you'll seldom see it, so follow their example and be discrete.

Water Activities

Babies and toddlers will be happy on a soft beach and with perhaps a hermit crab to hassle. Any place with a shallow sandy bottom is a great place to learn how to swim. Many dive centres offer 'Bubble Maker' courses for kids eight-years and up, where kids take their first breaths under water. Good swimmers over nine can enrol in Junior PADI Open Water courses (see www.padi.com). Sea kayaking is available at most resorts.

Land Lubbers

Over-eights will love tropical interiors choc-a-block with waterfalls with icy swimming pools, ledges to jump from and natural slides. Children of all ages will want to keep an eye out for some spectacular native bird species (including brightly coloured parrots), trees dripping with sleeping fruit bats and native snakes and lizards. Some resorts keep local fauna as pets and fortunately these critters are usually well cared for. Catching a Sunday church service in a small village is often a highlight.

Children's Highlights

Swimming

» **Nacula** Long beach has some of the finest swimming in Fiji.

» **Treasure Island** Lightly sloping beaches, perfect for toddlers.

» **Kadavu** The protected west side holds patches of perfect sandy-bottom lagoon.

» **Leleuvia** Wade into shallow swimming straight from the beach.

Snorkelling

» **Yasawa Group** Plentiful corals, sea turtles and manta rays.

BEST RESORTS FOR KIDS

» Castaway Island (p120)

» Plantation Island Resort (p123)

» Mana Island Resort (p118)

» Jean-Michel Cousteau Fiji Islands Resort (p157)

» Outrigger on the Lagoon (p80)

» Matana Beach Resort Dive Kadavu (p186)

» Leleuvia Island Resort (p148)

» **Mana** Easy snorkelling from the beach with lots of colourful fish.

» **Caqalai** Older kids who can get in the water over some reef will be awestruck by the amount of life here.

» **Kadavu** Take a tour to snorkel with manta rays!

Sandy Stretches

» **Long Beach (Nacula)** A sublime stretch, aptly named for its sandy length.

» **Octopus Resort (Waya)** Wide stretch of wonderful beach with never-want-to-leave charm.

» **Resort islands around Ovalau** All of the resorts on outlying islands of the Lomaiviti Group are encircled with low-key, kid-friendly white beaches.

Cultural Shows & Museums

» **Robinson Crusoe Island** Everything from a 'cannibal attack' on arrival to hermit-crab racing and traditional performances at night.

» **Arts Village (Pacific Harbour)** Disneylike take on a Fijian village with performances including mock battles and dance.

» **Fiji Museum & Thurston Gardens** Lots of big, eye-catching displays and a massive garden to run around.

Village Visits & Homestays

» **Navala village** Be welcomed into the traditional lifestyle of one of Fiji's most scenic villages.

» **Namatakula Village Homestay (Korolevu)** Authentic, hospitable and great for intrepid families.

» **Silana Ecolodge (Ovalau)** You're in with a big family here so the kids will have plenty of company their own age.

Ocean Sports

» **Nananu-i-Ra** Kiteboarding and windsurfing.

» **Natadola Beach** Good for bodysurfing.

» **Natadola Inside Break** The country's best bet for beginner surfers.

Inland Sports

» **Ziplining** Near Pacific Harbour.

» **Jetboating** Through the mangroves at Denarau.

» **Rafting** White water or lower-key *bilibili* (bamboo raft) thrills on the Navua River or around the Namosi Highlands.

» **Trail riding** For all ages, on Viti Levu and at Paradise Taveuni.

PLANNING

Some hotels and resorts have no-children policies (especially under 12s) but then others let kids stay for free – always ask when booking. Some tours and activities are discounted for kids.

Nappies, formula, sterilising solution and baby food are available in pharmacies and supermarkets in the main cities and towns, but if you are travelling to remote areas or islands, take your own supplies.

What to Pack

All ages need the usual suspects: sunscreen, insect repellent, warmer clothes for evenings and rain gear.

BABIES & TODDLERS

☐ A folding stroller is practical for most areas while a baby carrier is a better option if you plan on hiking or staying at a resort with terraced or sandy paths

☐ A portable changing mat, handwash gel etc (baby-changing facilities are a rarity)

☐ Inflatable 'floaties'

SIX TO 12 YEARS

☐ Binoculars for young explorers to zoom in on wildlife, surfers riding reef-breaking waves etc

☐ A camera to inject newfound fun into 'boring' grown-up sights and walks

☐ Field guides to Fijian flora and fauna

Transport & Safety

Large chain car-rental companies can provide baby seats, but local companies and taxis don't. Also bear in mind that local buses have bench seating, no seat belts and can be fairly cramped, so babies and small children will be expected to sit on your lap.

Many small boats don't carry enough life jackets and rarely have child-sized ones; if you're planning to island-hop in small boats, you might want to consider bringing your own.

Critter Encounters

» **Kula Eco Park** Wildlife park with everything from sea turtles to parrots and flying foxes.

» **Treasure Island** Turtle and iguana feeding.

» **Mana** Monthly 'Environment Day' with coral planting.

» **Kadavu** Manta rays.

Jungle Explorers

» **Navua River** Inland villages, hiking and river activities.

» **Colo-i-Suva Forest Park** Walking trails, swimming holes (one with a rope swing), birdlife and pretty vistas.

» **Koroyanitu National Heritage Park** Best for strong walkers; find waterfalls, jungle and traditional villages.

» **Lovoni** Older kids will enjoy this jungle village trek to an extinct crater.

» **Bouma National Heritage Park** Everything from seaside walks to steeper treks to swimmable waterfall pools.

regions at a glance

Most travellers visit the main island, Viti Levu, at least twice – when they arrive and again when they leave. Those that stay find villages to explore and some thrilling activities in the Pacific Harbour region.

The Yasawa and Mamanuca Groups are the stuff tropical postcards are made of. They are easily reached from the 'mainland', and form the backbone of Fiji's tourism industry.

Vanua Levu, Taveuni and Kadavu are famed for their lush forests above the water and beautiful coral gardens beneath. These islands draw yachties, explorers and divers in equal measure.

Only a trickle of trailblazers make it to the Lomaiviti, Lau and Moala Groups. Facilities are scarce and transport erratic, but there are plenty of adventures to be had here.

Nadi, Suva & Viti Levu

Prehistory ✓✓
Culture ✓✓✓
Highlands ✓✓✓

Prehistory & Hill Forts

The Sigatoka area is ripe with historical remnants: there are pot shards and bone fragments in the sand dunes, and hill fortifications with more recent pre-colonial connections between Fiji and Tonga.

Post-Colonial & Multicultural

Colonial buildings of decaying grandeur are dotted around Suva. A more contemporary and multicultural take on life is in the city's streets, the Indo-Fijian sugar-farming communities on the west coast and indigenous Fijian villages along the Kings Road.

Highland Life

The inland landscapes of the Nausori and Namosi Highlands are in sharp contrast to the coastal zone. High mountainous roads, tall forests, clear rivers and remote villages make for a great self-drive adventure.

p44

The Mamanuca & Yasawa Groups

Water Sports ✓✓✓
Beaches ✓✓✓
Wildlife ✓✓

Water Sporting

The Mamanucas are the place to be if you want to get your feet (and the rest) wet. Pretty much everything's on offer here, from high-adrenalin jet-skiing and paragliding to DIY bodyboarding to world-class snorkelling, diving and surfing.

Beach Bumming

If a low-key beach life is what you're after, the Yasawas have it in spades. Choose from stretches of whiter-than-white sand fringing blue lagoons, small sheltered coves and secluded swimming bays.

Wildlife

Underwater, seasonal manta rays and whales add to the all-year attraction of resident sharks and dolphins. On and above ground, the islands are home to iguanas and soaring seabirds. Somewhere in between are turtles, breeding on several islands in the region.

p112

Ovalau & the Lomaiviti Group

Snorkelling ✓✓
Hiking ✓✓
Architecture ✓✓✓

Vanua Levu & Taveuni

Diving ✓✓✓
Hiking ✓✓✓
Surfing ✓

Kadavu, Lau & Moala Groups

Diving ✓✓✓
Snorkelling ✓✓✓
Walking ✓✓

Snorkelling
Snake Island, off Caqalai, isn't for the faint-hearted – in addition to the currents and an entry through a minefield of corals, expect to see the banded sea snakes that give the island its name. The payoff is a wonderland of soft corals, schools of fish and giant Napoleon wrasses.

Hiking
Head to Lovoni crater at the centre of Ovalau to visit the proud village and trek through thick jungle and rivers and take dips in waterfalls.

Architecture
Fabulously rickety-but-still-standing colonial architecture makes Levuka one of the most picturesque towns in the South Pacific. Marvel at shopfronts that look like something out of a John Wayne film and weather-worn cathedral-like churches.

p137

Diving
The Somosomo Strait houses the Rainbow Reef, famed for its soft corals. Dive the Purple Wall, covered in purple coral trees, or the ethereal White Wall, where in the right current, white soft corals open to feed on plentiful plankton.

Hiking
Taveuni is dominated by the excessively lush Bouma National Heritage Park, home to some of Fiji's best hiking. Outside the park are more hikes, such as the strenuous scramble up Des Vouex Peak, where you can look for the rare *tagimaucia*, Fiji's emblem flower.

Surfing
Qamea island, off Taveuni, offers a few fickle, but little known, breaks. When they're working expect clean, fun rides and no crowds.

p150

Diving
The Great Astrolabe Reef is the world's fourth-largest barrier reef; it holds such a long stretch of astounding dive sites many are yet to be discovered. If that wasn't enough, the west side of Kadavu holds other reef networks that are arguably as lovely and also more protected from the trade winds.

Snorkelling
You don't have to dive to see one of the ocean's most spectacular critters: manta rays. Off the Great Astrolabe Reef near Ono island, snorkellers are almost guaranteed the life-altering experience of swimming with these graceful creatures.

Walking
Most resorts have walking trails leading from their doorsteps to villages, waterfalls and plentiful birdwatching.

p181

❯ **Every listing is recommended by our authors, and their favourite places are listed first**

❯ **Look out for these icons:**

 Our author's top recommendation

 A green or sustainable option

FREE No payment required

See the Index for a full list of destinations covered in this book.

On the Road

Nadi, Suva & Viti Levu

Best Places to Eat

» Blue Bure, Nadi (p55)

» Guava, Suva (p101)

» Daikoku, Nadi & Suva
(p56 & p101)

Best Places to Stay

» Five Princes Hotel, Suva
(p98)

» Nanette's Accommoda-
tion, Pacific Harbour (p86)

» Safari Lodge, Nananu-i-Ra
(p111)

» Outrigger on the Lagoon,
Korotogo (p80)

Why Go?

Viti Levu, the largest of the Fijian islands, squats roundly and self-assuredly in the centre of the islands it governs. It wields considerable power and is the pivotal point about which politics, commerce and industry revolve. It is also where roughly three-quarters of the population resides.

From Nadi, Fiji's sunny waterside gateway, the Queens Road hugs the Coral Coast. Opportunities to foray into the interior's dramatic highlands and marvel at the elevated views abound. For the adventurous, it is possible to explore giant sand dunes and dive with truly massive tiger sharks.

Sultry Suva is the largest city in the South Pacific and the merging of island cultures and Indo-Fijian traditions has given the capital a rich heritage and the country's best restaurants and nightlife.

The Kings Road completes Viti Levu's northern loop. Those in the know – usually savvy windsurfers and divers – head for Nananu-i-Ra, home to consistent winds and the beautiful, breathtaking reef.

When to Go

Suva

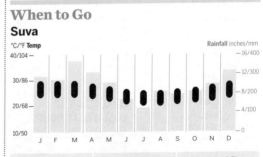

Dec–Mar Trips
upriver to the
Namosi Highlands
can be wetter
than planned.

May–Oct Roads
to the scenic
Nausori High-
lands are most
accessible in the
dry season.

Year-round The
Coral Coast of-
fers activities for
all seasons.

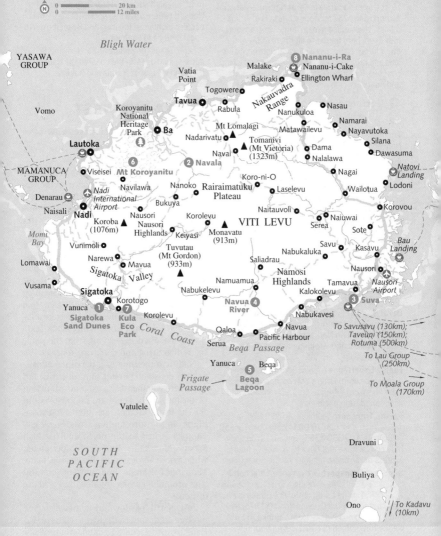

Nadi, Suva & Viti Levu Highlights

1 Slipping and sliding over the **Sigatoka Sand Dunes** (p76) on the lookout for ancient burial relics

2 Catching a local bus into the highlands to **Navala** (p69), Fiji's sole remaining traditional *bure* village

3 Getting to grips with the traditional culture on display at Suva's **Fiji Museum** (p93) and comparing it to today's vibrant urban culture in Suva's **bars** (p102)

4 Kayaking or rafting the mighty **Navua River** (p87) in the rugged Namosi Highlands

5 Diving with the resident tiger sharks in **Beqa Lagoon** (p84)

6 Exploring the lush foothills and high ridges of **Mt Koroyanitu** (p63) with villagers from **Navilawa**

7 Feeding baby turtles and stroking iguanas at the **Kula Eco Park** (p78)

8 Windsurfing and snorkelling on the island's best reefs at **Nananu-i-Ra** (p111)

❶ Getting There & Away

Most travellers arrive in Fiji at Nadi International Airport. See p232 for contact details of airline offices. Nadi is also a main domestic transport hub. From here there are flights to many of the other larger islands as well as reliable boat services and cruises. See p234 and individual island chapters for information on interisland flights and boat services.

❶ Getting Around

AIR

There are regular light-plane flights between Nadi and Suva from around $180.

BUS

Viti Levu has a regular and cheap bus network. Express buses link the main centres of Lautoka, Nadi and Suva, along both the Queens and Kings Roads. Most will pick up or drop off at hotels and resorts along these highways. Slower local buses also operate throughout the island and even remote inland villages have regular (though less frequent) services. Minibuses and carriers (small trucks) also shuttle locals along the Queens Road and taxis are plentiful.

Companies and services available include the following:

Coral Sun Fiji (☑672 3105; www.coralsun fiji.com) Runs comfortable, air-conditioned coaches between Nadi and Suva ($22, four hours, twice daily), stopping only at resorts on the Coral Coast.

Feejee Experience (☑672 5950; www.feejee experience.com) Offers hop-on-hop-off coach transfers from $449, as well as transport and accommodation packages.

Pacific Transport Lautoka (☑666 0499; Yasawa St); Nadi (☑670 0044); Sigatoka (☑650 0088); Suva (☑330 4366) Ten buses run daily between Lautoka and Suva ($14.25, five hours express or six hours regular) via the Coral Coast.

Sunbeam Transport (www.sunbeamfiji.com) Lautoka (☑666 2822; Yasawa St); Suva (☑338 2122/2704) Nine Lautoka–Suva express services go daily via the Queens Road ($17.75, five hours) and nine go daily from Lautoka to Suva via the Kings Road ($20.70, seven hours).

CAR & MOTORCYCLE

Viti Levu is easy to explore by car or motorcycle, but for the unsealed highland roads you'll generally need a 4WD. See p237 for rental details.

Nadi and Suva are linked by the sealed **Queens Road** along the 221km southern perimeter of Viti Levu, which contains a scattering of villages and resorts and is known as the Coral Coast. Many minor roads lead off this road to isolated coastal areas and into the highlands; most of these are unsealed. Between the wetter months of November and April, some roads can become impassable.

Heading north from Suva, the **Kings Road** is mostly sealed and travels for 265km through Nausori (where Suva's airport is located), the eastern highlands, Rakiraki and Ba on the north coast, and on to Lautoka.

Three roads (beginning at Ba, Nadi and Sigatoka) lead up from the coast to the Nausori Highland villages of Navala and Bukuya.

NADI & THE WEST

Nadi

POP 31,400

Most travellers go to Nadi (*nan*-di) twice, whether they like it or not: once on the way in and once on the way out. Its indecently warm air slaps you in the face when you first step from the plane and its airport is the last place to buy sunburn remedies before heading home. For some, two times is twice too often and many people aim to minimise their Nadi exposure to the briefest time possible. Others pause long enough to make the most of the infrastructure before heading out to more picturesque locales. Not that this bothers Nadi. The shops, restaurants, cafes and tour operators strung along Main St can make a decent living from the plane loads of arriving and departing tourists.

Nadi is something of a perennial adolescent in constant pursuit of an identity, not quite sure whether it's a city, tourist junction or business hub. There are no must-sees in the city itself, but there are interesting possibilities in the surrounding areas. Sugar-city Lautoka is just to the north and the lush Sabeto Mountains hug Nadi's perimeter, while gorgeous Natadola Beach, the many Mamanuca islands and ancient cultural sites around Sigatoka are all within striking distance.

Just north of downtown, between the mosque and the Nadi River, Narewa Rd leads west to Denarau island, where you'll find Nadi's top-end resorts. There's also a busy tourist shopping and eating area at Denarau Marina, where boats depart for the Mamanuca and Yasawa Groups.

⊙ Sights & Activities

Sri Siva Subramaniya Swami Temple   TEMPLE

(Map p58; admission $3.50; ☺5.30am-7pm) At the base of Main St, away from Nadi's boisterous main drag, this peaceful Hindu temple is one of the few places outside India where you can see traditional Dravidian architecture. The whole place is painted in colours bright enough to make your eyes ache and looks fantastic against cloudless, blue skies. The wooden carvings of Hindu deities travelled all the way from India, as did the artists who dressed the temple in its colourful coat and impressive ceiling frescos. New murals are still being commissioned and it's quite possible that you'll see resident artist ST Santosh lying, Michelangelo-style, on scaffolding as he paints the temple's ceilings.

If you are having trouble sorting out Lord Shiva's reincarnations and manifestations, ask Mr Prakash Reddy, a temple custodian employed to answer questions and make sense of the Hindu deities.

Nadi's festivals, such as Karthingai Puja (held monthly), Panguni Uthiram Thirunaal (in April) and Thai Pusam (January), attract worshippers from around the world. Devotees circle the temple where they offer banana, smash a coconut, burn some camphor and receive blessing from the priest. Some of these festivals last several days and it's worth attending if they coincide with your plans.

Visitors are welcome as long as they wear neat and modest dress and remove their shoes at the temple entrance. It is fine to take photos in the grounds but not inside the temple. Non-Hindus are asked not to enter the inner sanctum, which is reserved for devotees bringing offerings.

Fiji Surf Company   SURFING
(Map p58; ☑670 5960; www.fijisurfco.com; 2nd fl, cnr Main St & Hospital Rd) Local surf legend Ian Muller is the man to talk to about all things surfing. He passionately promotes surfing within Fiji, along with respect for the water and the people on it. He was instrumental in lobbying for the Surf Decree, which opened Fijian waters to all when it was passed by the government in 2010. Ian and his team of local surf guides run both hardcore and family-friendly surf day tours (one/two or more people per person $230/115) to the monster Mamanuca reef breaks and to the breaks off Natadola and Sigatoka beaches. The surf school (one/two/three people per person $230/$200/$175) is the only one in Fiji endorsed by Surfing Australia. The shop sells, repairs, makes and rents boards ($45 per day) and paddle boards ($80 per day), and can arrange surf packages.

☞ Tours

Nadi is a good base to explore the west side of Viti Levu. From here it is possible to visit the Koroyanitu National Heritage Park, Nausori Highlands, and Namosi Highlands near Pacific Harbour. Many out-of-town tour companies will pick up and drop off in Nadi, so be sure to consult other destination chapters for inspiration.

The Mamanuca and Yasawa island chains, with their necklaces of coral gardens, are the most popular of all the day trips out of the Nadi area. Boats depart from Port Denarau several times daily and offer free hotel pickups and drop-offs. Check out the Yasawa & Mamanuca Groups chapter to read more about your options. Organised trips to Robinson Crusoe Island (p72) just south of Nadi are also an easy and fun day excursion.

✹ Festivals & Events

Nadi's festivals, such as Karthingai Puja (held monthly), Panguni Uthiram Thirunaal (in April) and Thai Pusam (in January), attract worshippers from around the world. Devotees circle Sri Siva Subramaniya Swami Temple. They offer bananas, smash a coconut, burn some camphor and receive the priest's blessing. Some of these festivals last several days and it's worth attending if they coincide with your plans.

⛌ Sleeping

Regardless of what the websites or brochures promise there are no appealing beaches in the Nadi area. That said, the resorts located at the grey-sand New Town and Wailoaloa Beaches are fairly isolated and peaceful. And while Martintar is placed (conveniently and noisily) on the busy main bus route, walk a few metres down its side roads and you're taken to homes, cane fields and a sense of local Fiji.

Expect budget hotels to be clean, sparse and generally air-conditioned. Dorm rooms can be cramped and are generally fan-cooled only, though some hostels offer a range of dorm facilities. Many of Nadi's midrange and top-end hotels are located along the Queens Road between downtown Nadi and the airport. Rooms generally have air-con, a TV, a phone and a fridge. There is usually a swimming pool and space to lounge around it. Most hotels also have tour desks, luggage storage, courtesy airport transfers and restaurants open for breakfast, lunch and dinner. Rates vary widely day to day, depending

Viti Levu

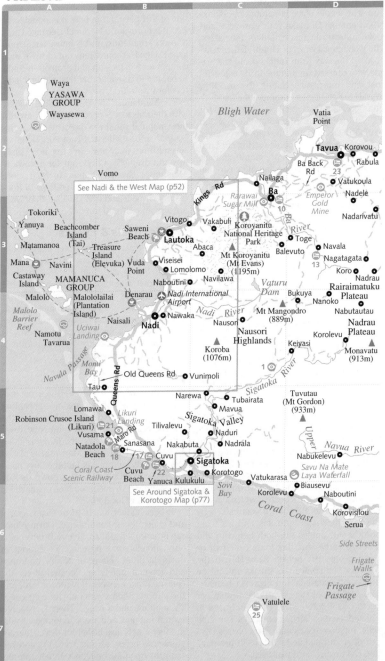

Waya
YASAWA GROUP
Wayasewa

Bligh Water

Vatia Point

Tavua Korovou

Ba Back Rd 23 Rabula

Vomo

See Nadi & the West Map (p52)

Nailaga

Ba Vatukoula

Nadele

Kings Rd

Rarawai Sugar Mill 10

Emperor Gold Mine

Nadarivatu

Tokoriki

Yanuya

Beachcomber Island (Tai)

Saweni Beach

Vitogo Vakabuli

Koroyanitu National Heritage Park

Lautoka Abaca

Ba River

Toge

Navala

Matamanoa

Treasure Island (Elevuka)

Vuda Point

Viseisei

Lomolomo

Mt Koroyanitu (Mt Evans) (1195m)

Balevuto

Nagatagata

Mana

Navini

Naboutini

Navilawa

Vaturu Dam

Koro Nadrau

Castaway Island

MAMANUCA GROUP

Denarau

Nadi International Airport

Bukuya Nanoko

Rairaimatuku Plateau

Malolo

Malololailai (Plantation Island)

Nadi River

Nawaka

Nabutautau

Malolo Barrier Reef

Naisali

Nadi

Nauson

Mt Mangondro (889m)

Korolevu

Nadrau Plateau

Namotu Tavarua

Uciwai Landing

Nausori Highlands

Keiyasi

Monavatu (913m)

Navula Passage

Momi Bay

Old Queens Rd Vunimoli

Koroba (1076m)

Sigatoka River

Tau

Narewa

Tubairata

Tuvutau (Mt Gordon) (933m)

Lomawai

Robinson Crusoe Island (Likuri)

Likuri Landing 21

Mavua

Vusama

Tilivalevu

Sigatoka Valley

Naduri

Upper Navua River

Natadola Beach 18

Sanasana

Nakabuta

Nadrala

Nabukelevu

Coral Coast Scenic Railway

17 Cuvu

22

Cuvu Beach

Sigatoka

Korotogo

Savu Na Mate Laya Waterfall

Yanuca Kulukulu

See Around Sigatoka & Korotogo Map (p77)

Sovi Bay

Vatukarasa

Biausevu

Korolevu

Naboutini

Coral Coast

Korovisilou

Serua

Side Streets

Frigate Walls

Frigate Passage

Vatulele 25

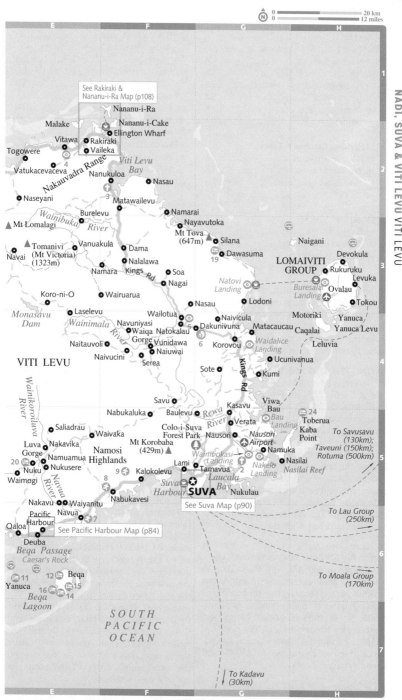

0 ____ 20 km
0 ____ 12 miles

See Rakiraki &
Nananu-i-Ra Map (p108)

Nananu-i-Ra

Malake
Nananu-i-Cake
Ellington Wharf
Vitawa
Rakiraki
Togowere
Vaileka
Viti Levu
Vatukacevaceva
Nakauvadra Range
Bay

Nanukuloa
Nasau
Naseyani

Wainibuka River
Burelevu
Namarai

Mt Lomalagi
Nayavutoka
Vanuakula
Dama
Mt Tova (647m)
Silana

Tomanivi (Mt Victoria) (1323m)
Nalalawa
Kings Rd
Dawasuma
Naigani
LOMAIVITI GROUP
Devokula

Navai
Namara
Soa
19

Rukuruku
Levuka

Koro-ni-O
Wairuarua
Nagai
Natovi Landing
Lodoni
Buresala Landing
Ovalau
Tokou

Monasavu Dam
Laselevu
Wailotua
Nasau
Naivicula
Motoriki

Wainimala River
Navuniyasi
Natokalau
Dakunivuna
Matacaucau
Caqalai
Yanuca
Yanuca Levu

Naitauvoli
Waiqa Gorge
Vunidawa
Korovou
Waidalice Landing
Leluvia

Naivucini
Niauwai
6
Ucunivanua

Serea
Sote
Kumi

Wainikoroiluva River
Savu
Viwa

Nabukaluka
Baulevu
Kasavu
Bau
Toberua
24

Saliadrau
Waivaka
Rewa River
Verata
Bau Landing
Kaba Point
To Savusavu (130km); Taveuni (150km); Rotuma (500km)

Luva Gorge
Nakavika
Colo-i-Suva Forest Park
Nausori
Nausori Airport

Namuamua
Mt Korobaba (429m)
Namuka
Nasilai

20
Nukusere
Namosi Highlands
Kalokolevu
Wainibokasi Landing
Nasilai Reef

Nuku
8
9
Lami
Tamavua
Nakelo Landing

Waimogi
Navua River
Nabukavesi
Suva Harbour
SUVA
Nukulau
Laucala Bay

Nakavu
Waiyanitu
See Suva Map (p90)
To Lau Group (250km)

Qaloa
Pacific Harbour
Navua
7

Deuba
See Pacific Harbour Map (p84)

Beqa Passage
Caesar's Rock
To Moala Group (170km)

11
12
Beqa
Yanuca
16
15
14
Beqa Lagoon

SOUTH PACIFIC OCEAN

To Kadavu (30km)

VITI LEVU

Viti Levu

on season and availability; there are likely to be sizeable discounts on the rates quoted here for walk-ins or phone-a-day-ahead bookings.

See the Denarau section for details on Denarau Island's megaresorts.

ALONG THE QUEENS ROAD

Rosie Serviced Apartments   APARTMENT $
(Map p57; ☑672 2755; fitres@rosie.com.fj; Queens Rd, Martintar; apt $81-139; ❂❈) While this block of apartments is a bit of an ugly duckling from the outside, these studio, one-bedroom and two-bedroom apartments are great value. Ask for a quiet one at the back, overlooking the neighbour's mango tree. There's enough room (even in the studios) to swing several cats and each apartment comes with a furnished balcony, a fully equipped kitchen and use of the laundry and pool in the Mercure Hotel just along the road.

Mercure Hotel Nadi   RESORT $$
(Map p57; ☑672 2255; www.mercure.com; Queens Rd, Martintar; r $135-175; ❂❈@❆) The 85 rooms here are big on creature comforts but smallish in size; those on the third (and top) floor are quietest. Rooms have glossy bathrooms, Sky TV and well-stocked fridges, and most face the pretty pool area. The extensive grounds encompass a mock-beach, sprawling al fresco **restaurant** (mains $30-45) and a tennis court out back.

Tanoa International   RESORT $$
(Map p54; ☑672 0277; ww.tanoahotels.com; Votualevu Rd; r from $178; ❂❈@❆) Another self-contained resort loaded with facilities and distractions (including flood-lit tennis courts, a beauty spa and a gym), making it very popular with package-tour pool addicts, families and regional conferences. The whole place oozes Fijian tropicana, from the lush gardens to the Bula Bar and Mint Café. Kids 12 and below stay free. The fully self-contained Tanoa Apartments on the corner of Queens Road – separate from the hotel but managed by the same company – offer terrific facilities, location and value for self-caterers. Check www.wotif.com for current rates.

Nadi Bay Resort Hotel   RESORT $
(Map p57; ☑672 3599; www.fijinadibayhotel.com; Wailoaloa Rd, Martintar; dm $35-36, s/d without bathroom $75/89, s/d with bathroom & air-con $110/185; ❂❈@❆) One of Nadi's best-equipped budget resorts, this serves up a mixed bag of package-tour guests and backpackers. It's well suited to social animals and the overhead planes leaving the airport are the only interruption to lively banter. The **restaurant** (mains $15-25) is outstanding, the rooms are comfortable and clean, and there's even a free mini movie theatre. The resort's Fijian-food-and-photo book, *Under the Mango Tree,* was shot in and around the hotel grounds with staff and guests – it makes a good souvenir.

Sandalwood Lodge
APARTMENT $

(Map p57; ☑672 2044; www.sandalwoodfiji.com; Ragg St, Martintar; s/d&tr $99/110; ❋@☒) The Lodge offers perky, self-contained rooms with colourful decor, small kitchenettes and TVs. They're clean but tatty, and great value for self-caterers and families, plus the location off the main road promises a good night's sleep. Garden Wing rooms on the ground floor have patio doors leading to the picturesque, free-form pool, while the Orchid Wing rooms upstairs have balconies and more modern and spacious interiors.

Tanoa Skylodge
LODGE $

(Map p54; ☑672 2200; www.tanoahotels.com; Queens Rd, Namaka; 8-bed dm $31, 6-& 4-bed dm $36, r $80-120; ❤❋@☒) This is a good choice, with acres of gardens. The spotlessly clean, somewhat spartan rooms are being progressively renovated. The rooms in the cottages are much larger and lighter than the standard rooms, but both have air-con, private bathrooms, phones, TVs, fridges and towels. There's a pool with plenty of sun loungers, a small restaurant (mains $15-20), pool tables, nightly activities, a travel desk, volleyball courts and a games room. It's a little like a school camp for grown-ups and the current management is slowly aiming for the small-conference market.

Raffles Gateway Hotel
RESORT $$

(Map p54; ☑672 2444; www.rafflesgateway.com; Queens Rd, Namaka; d & tw $103-175; ❤❋@☒⬛) Directly opposite the airport, Raffles is a sound choice behind its mock-colonial entrance. The small water slide gets the kids squealing and those under 16 stay free. The cheaper standard rooms are pinchy but cool and crisp, while the superior rooms are a leap in value with their lounge furniture, TVs and private patios. There's a poolside restaurant (mains $20-35), which also has an air-conditioned section. The grassed central courtyard is flanked by massive bougainvilleas that give an accurate idea of the age of this long-time favourite.

Novotel Nadi
RESORT $$

(Map p54; ☑672 2000; www.novotel.com; Votualevu Rd, Namaka; r from $178; ❋@☒⬛) Formerly the Mocambo, the Novotel got a facelift when the name changed. All the rooms now have internet connections, flat-screen TVs and a very chic brown-on-beige colour scheme. The rooms aren't huge but they are very comfortable. There's also a boutique, business centre, nine-hole golf

---

VITI LEVU FOR KIDS

Fiji's main island has plenty to offer families with little tackers in tow. If you're staying in the Nadi area, try a day cruise to one of the Mamanuca (p115) or Yasawa islands (see the boxed text, p126) or the ever-popular Robinson Crusoe Island (p72).

The Coral Coast is home to a number of attractions that will appeal to kids. A day on the Coral Coast Scenic Railway (p73) is a fun way to gain an appreciation of Fiji's landscape, and the barbecue lunch is a family-oriented affair. Nearby, the Kalevu Cultural Centre (p74) showcases Fijian singing, dancing and ceremonies that will entertain children. A little more kitsch and flashy are the demonstrations, boat tours and mock battles at the Arts Village (p83) in Pacific Harbour. You could also take the kids horse riding at Natadola Beach (p72) or show them Fiji's less-domesticated wildlife at the excellent Kula Eco Park (p78).

The Fiji Museum (p93) is chock-full of exhibits (including cannibal utensils) that will capture inquisitive young minds. Off the northern coast, Nananu-i-Ra (p110) is only a short hop from the mainland and offers calm seas for child-friendly swimming and snorkelling, as well as self-catering accommodation. Kids can also partake in kayaking and windsurfing here.

Many resorts have abundant activities to occupy children. Some kid-friendly resorts include the following:

» Shangri-La's Fijian Resort (p74)

» Hideaway Resort (p82)

» Sonaisali Island Resort (p70)

» Radisson Blu Resort Fiji (p61)

» Outrigger on the Lagoon (p80)

Nadi & the West

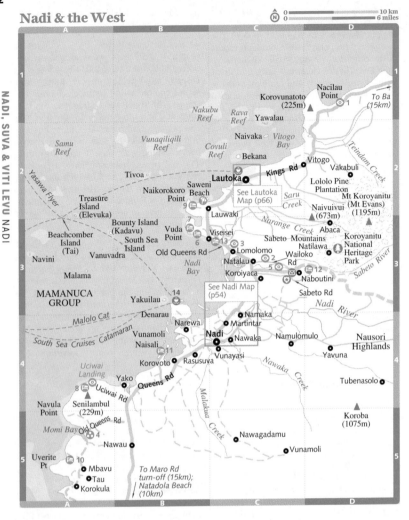

course, day spa and pool. Children under 16 stay for free.

Tokatoka Resort Hotel   RESORT **$$**
(Map p54; ☎672 0222; www.tokatokaresortfiji.com; Queens Rd, Namaka; r $102-300; ❄️✳️@🏊📶👶) This sprawling, low-rise resort is a 'village' of villas connected by a series of covered, mazelike walkways. We got embarrassingly lost – twice. Rooms are well-overdue for refurbishment and redecorating, but those at the back overlook a quiet cane field. The designer pool with its sunshade sail and water slide is also fun. If you can get a rate at the lower end of the price range, it's good value

for the night before an early departure from the airport across the road. Other facilities include a **restaurant** (mains $24-42) and wheelchair-accessible rooms.

Capricorn International   HOTEL **$**
(Map p57; ☎672 0088; www.capricornfiji.com; Queens Rd, Martintar; dm $25, r incl breakfast $105-125, f incl breakfast $175; ❄️✳️@🏊) Everything about the Capricorn is middle-of-the-road. The rooms are dated and faded but essentially still comfortable, and while the pool is small, it's clean and inviting. The pricier deluxe rooms come with a balcony, and if you stay in the 17-bed, all-white dorm, you

Nadi & the West

may well have the place to yourself. Children under 12 stay free; otherwise it's only $20 for an extra guest.

NEW TOWN BEACH & WAILOALOA BEACH

A haul from downtown and the main road, New Town Beach offers budget travellers a cluster of backpacker resorts amid a smattering of wealthy residential properties. It's a peaceful area with great views of the Sabeto Mountains across the water. The New Town places listed here are all within five minutes walk of each other, on the beachfront of Wasawasa Rd or just off it.

Smugglers Cove Beach Resort & Hotel RESORT $
(Map p57; ☎672 6578; www.smugglersbeachfiji.com; Wasawasa Rd; dm incl breakfast $28-38, r incl breakfast $135-195; ✽@☒) Young and brash, with a smart extension opened in 2011, Smugglers Cove upstages some of the older establishments along the beach. There's a bunch of amenities including a tour desk, internet cafe, recommended *restaurant* (mains $20-35), minimart, coin-operated laundry and disabled access. Kayaks and use of the Nadi

Airport Golf Club (Map p54) are free for guests, and all the rooms are modern and comfortable. The cheaper dormitory is dark and cavernous, with 34 bunk beds divided into cubicles of four. The smaller, brighter dorms (including one women-only) are more expensive but better value – quieter and more private – for budget travellers.

Bamboo HOSTEL $
(Map p57; ☎625 0828; www.bamboobackpackers.hostel.com; Wasawasa Rd; dm incl breakfast $12-20, d incl breakfast $50-60; ☏) This is a good addition to the New Town scene: an old-style, low-key, cheap-and-cheerful backpackers' place. Rooms are as small as you'd expect for the price, but it was full of chilled-out travellers relaxing on Fiji time when we visited. As well as breakfast, a variety of beach/sport/cultural activities and an evening kava session are thrown in. There's also a kitchenette for determined self-caterers.

Bluewater Lodge HOSTEL $
(☎672 8858; bluewaterfiji@connect.com.fj; dm incl breakfast $15-40, d incl breakfast $135; ⊝✽@☒) Small and unassuming, this place is the place for travellers beating a retreat from the hollering crowds. The rooms are spotlessly clean, light and airy. There are three- or four-bed dorms and two double rooms, which are often booked well in advance. The wee *restaurant* (mains $16-25) serves breakfast then opens again for dinner only.

Aquarius Fiji RESORT $
(Map p57; ☎672 6000; www.aquarius.com.fj; 17 Wasawasa Rd; dm incl breakfast $31.50-36, d incl breakfast $126-138; ⊝✽@☒) This former luxury home was converted into a professionally run backpackers in 2003 and has never looked back. The whole place swims with warm party vibes. There's a lively restaurant and, for those who overdo it on the nightly cocktail specials, it's only a short stagger around the pool to the hangover-soothing hammocks. All rooms have attached bathrooms, although the larger (and cheaper) 12-bed dorms are slightly airless and cramped when full.

Beachside Resort RESORT $
(Map p54; ☎670 3488; www.beachsideresortfiji.com; Wailoaloa Beach Rd; r incl breakfast $78-155; ⊝✽@☒) The moniker's a tad misleading, but this compact and private resort (away from the beach) provides more comfort than a backpackers and is easier on the wallet than a resort. The rooms are stylish and immaculate and dressed with cheery

Fijian prints. Cheaper rooms are tucked behind the main complex, while others have balconies overlooking the central pool. Windows have screens and wooden shutters – no glass – which makes it dark when the air-con's on. The in-house **Coriander Cafe** (mains $20-25) has a varied blackboard menu.

Club Fiji Resort   RESORT **$$**
(Map p54; 672 0150; www.clubfiji-resort.com; Wailoaloa Beach Rd; bure $118-173, villa $186; ☀✳✉) If you want to stay in Nadi but want quiet beachside atmosphere, this is a good option. The duplex *bure* are comfortable

and clean, and there's a great selection of daily activities, including free windsurfing and kayaking. Game fishing trips (in-house guests only, minimum two people, $30 per person per hour) are popular. The **restaurant** (mains $20-30) boasts Australian steaks, Asian noodles and English roasts.

Tropic of Capricorn   HOSTEL **$**
(Map p57; 672 6607; www.tropicofcapricornfiji.com; Wasawasa Rd; dm $20-25, d $90-120; ☀✳✉) This place gets good reviews from those seeking a home away from home. The older, fan-cooled rooms are still here while a newer three-storey block occupies the prime

Nadi

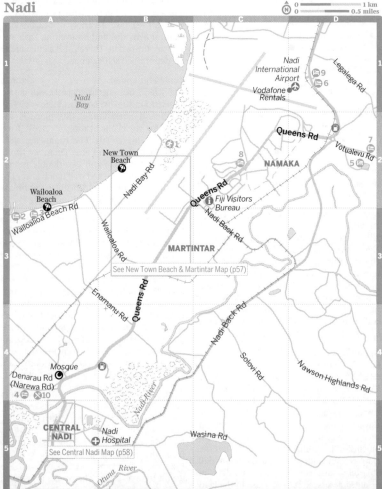

beachfront location. The pool is sandwiched between the two. The meals (mains $10-18) are good value and Mama cooks up a mean mash – reason enough for many to stay.

Horizon Beach Resort
HOSTEL $

(Map p57; ☎672 2832; www.horizonbeachfiji.com; Wasawasa Rd; dm with/without air-con $22/15, d with air-con $80-115, d without air-con $50; ⊛⊛@⊠) Flash it ain't, but this rabbit-warren of a hotel is popular with the backpacker crowd who stay in the cheaper rooms and have access to the upmarket facilities of Smugglers Cove – managed by the same company – next door.

Beach Escape Villas
HOTEL $

(Map p57; ☎672 4442; www.beachescapefiji.com; Wasawasa Rd; dm with/without air-con $25/20, d & tw with/without air-con $50/45; ⊛⊛@⊠) This is a village of clean but very dilapidated villas. Some contain six-bed dorms and others contain two small double rooms, which share a small lounge. Pay $85 and have the whole villa to yourself. For an additional $20, they'll throw in some cooking facilities.

CENTRAL NADI

Blue Bure
HOSTEL $

(Map p54; ☎670 7030; www.fijibluebure.com; cnr Narewa & Queens Rds; dm/s/d incl breakfast $25/40/45; @) A cool, quiet nook five minutes' walk from the hot bustle of Nadi's Main St, these two small, simple rooms and two six-bed dorms – all with shared bathroom – are surrounded by a breezy verandah and tall trees. Outside of serving hours, guests have the run of the spacious and comfortable indoor/outdoor restaurant space.

Nadi

Nadi Sunseekers Hotel
HOSTEL $

(Map p54; ☎670 0400; nadisunseekers@connect. com.fj; Narewa Rd; dm incl breakfast $20, d incl breakfast $50-75; ⊛) This is a decent budget choice, popular with Fijian students and government workers travelling through Nadi. Rooms are clean, simple and air-conditioned. It's quiet towards the back of the building and a wide shady verandah looks down onto a surprisingly large and gleaming pool. The padlocked grille at the open front door can be a bit off-putting. It means staff are working towards the back, so holler and ring the bell.

🍴 Eating

Nadi is a tourist town catering well for a variety of tastes and budgets. Most places serve a mixture of traditional Fijian, Indian, Chinese and Western dishes, and there are lots of cheap lunchtime eateries downtown around the bus station. Some of the resorts have special *lovo* (Fijian feast cooked in a pit oven) nights. The restaurants at most resort hotels welcome nonguests, and most hotels in Denarau have excellent bakeries with eat-in/take-out deli-style sandwiches, salads or sushi on offer at lunchtime.

Self-Catering

Nadi has a large produce market (Map p58; Hospital Rd), which sells lots of fresh fruit and vegetables. Good-quality meat, however, is not so easy to come by. There are several large supermarkets and bakeries downtown and in Martintar, including RB Patel Supermarket Martintar (Map p57); Central Nadi (Map p58) and MH Supermarket (Map p58).

CENTRAL NADI

TOP CHOICE ⟩ Blue Bure
FUSION $$

(Map p54; ☎670 7030; cnr Narewa & Queens Rds; mains $15-25; ☉lunch & dinner Mon-Sat) Tropical green and blue walls and eclectic decor feature in this very low-key funky bar/restaurant. Food is fresh, delicious fusion, reflecting the American/Italian/Tunisian/Fijian mix of the family who runs it. Chicken, coconut and ginger tortellini followed by a shisha pipe and mint tea, perhaps? (Oh, and a visit to the loo is, in the nicest possible way, a must.) Light lunches are around $10.

Saffron & Corner Café
INDIAN $$

(Map p58; ☎670 1233; Jacks Mall, Sagayam Rd; mains $15-25; ☉lunch & dinner Mon-Sat, dinner Sun; ⊛⊛) Two restaurants, one kitchen – a hard choice. The cafe serves light lunches, burgers and noodles while the adjoining, more upmarket Saffron has a tandoori oven and serves up healthy curries, birianis and kormas behind plate-glass windows. It's worth scanning the menu for some interesting Fijian twists on Indian favourites.

Bulaccino
CAFE $$

(Map p58 ☑672 8638; Main St; light meals & snacks $5-20; ☺breakfast & lunch; ☺※@) Bulaccino is arguably the best cafe on Main St although, to be fair, it doesn't have a lot of competition. Lunching alongside the Nadi River on the fan-cooled verandah is bliss, but after a hard day's haggling you might want to bypass the muesli, gourmet sandwiches and crunchy salads in favour of shots of caffeine and one of the scrummy cakes.

Bo Hai Seafood Restaurant
CHINESE $

(Map p58; ☑670 0178; above the Bank of Baroda, Main St; mains $6-25; ☺lunch & dinner; ※) Giving the curry houses a run for their money, Bo Hai has an extensive menu with a heavy emphasis on seafood. Adventurous souls should try the bêche-de-mer combination hotpot. Tasty meals and low prices (many mains go for around $8) mean it's popular with locals.

Mama's Pizza
PIZZERIA $$

(Map p58; ☑670 0221; Main St; pizzas $9-22; ☺lunch & dinner; ☺※) The smell from the wood-fired oven is a great introduction to Mama's downtown, cool, dark interior. Traditionalists may want to stick to the proven crowd-pleasers, but the more adventurous should check out the flip-side of the menu for gourmet treats like garlic-glazed chicken, and eggplant and sun-dried tomato combos. Other branches have opened at Port Denarau and Colonial Plaza – all are good.

Ganga's Veg Restaurant
VEGETARIAN $

(Map p58; Main St; mains $7.50; ☺lunch; ☺※☑) This classic simple Hare Krisna restaurant is a welcome boom for strict vegetarians in any town. The spiced chai and teeth-jarringly sweet sweets will revive flagging energy.

MARTINTAR

Martintar is home to local professionals, expats and several tourist hotels – all things that bode well for its eating and drinking options.

Daikoku
JAPANESE $$

(Map p57; ☑670 3622; cnr Queens Rd & Northern Press Rd; mains $30-52; ☺lunch & dinner Mon-Sat; ☺※) You'll need to brush up on your chopstick skills if you are to match those of the table-side chefs who slice, dice, flip and serve delicious Japanese teppanyaki upstairs at this popular, purpose-built restaurant. If teppanyaki seems too theatrical, you can head downstairs for cosier dining. The lunchtime bento box special ($15) is always great value, and you can try any dishes you missed at the partner restaurant in Suva.

Small Plates
CHINESE $

(Map p57; Queens Rd; dishes from $6; ☺dinner) Think Chinese tapas and you've got the measure of this low-key bar/restaurant set back in a garden off the main road. An odd-seeming mix, perhaps, but it works – and full marks to the crisp and delicious salt-and-pepper squid. The bar opens at 4pm for a happy hour that stretches until 8pm.

Wishbone & Pizzaking
PIZZERIA $

(Map p57; Queens Rd; mains $8-20; ☺lunch & dinner; ※) This is fast food with style – including a bright bar and seating area with TV. It's busy with locals and budget-conscious guests from the nearby hotels. As the name suggests, there's chicken and pizza galore, and the $8 dishes of the day are great value – we ate a much-better-than-average Indian veg thali.

Sitar
INDIAN $$

(Map p57; cnr Queens Rd & Wailoaloa Rd; mains $12-25; ☺lunch & dinner) A pleasant indoor/outdoor restaurant, despite the noisy location. There are comfy sofas in outdoor booths, lots of well-spaced tables and sunset views. Happy hour is from 4pm to 7pm, and if you're lucky (or unlucky, depending on your point of view) you'll get a live band playing oldies but goodies rather than blaringly loud and distorted rap CDs. It does north Indian food well – we enjoyed the rich spinachy, cheesy *palak paneer* ($8.90) with *naan* bread fresh from the tandoor.

Coffee-drinkers can get a decent weekday caffeine hit at Kiss cafe, opposite Rosie Apartments.

🍷 Drinking

Ed's Bar
PUB

(Map p57; ☑672 4650; Lot 51, Queens Rd, Martintar) From the roadside there's little to recommend Ed's Bar, but this is one of Nadi's best watering holes and a big step up from the grog shops in town. Cheap beer, friendly staff, pool tables and the occasional live

New Town Beach & Martintar

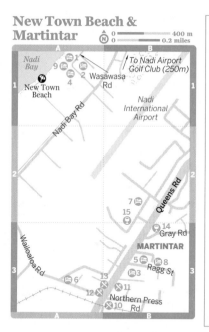

0 — 400 m
0 — 0.2 miles

Nadi Bay
New Town Beach
To Nadi Airport Golf Club (250m)
Wasawasa Rd
Nadi Bay Rd
Nadi International Airport
Queens Rd
Gray Rd
MARTINTAR
Ragg St
Wailoaloa Rd
Northern Press Rd

New Town Beach & Martintar

Sleeping
1 Aquarius Fiji A1
   Bamboo .... (see 1)
2 Beach Escape Villas A1
3 Capricorn International B3
4 Horizon Beach Resort A1
5 Mercure Hotel Nadi B3
6 Nadi Bay Resort Hotel A3
7 Rosie Serviced Apartments B2
8 Sandalwood Lodge B3
   Smugglers Cove Beach Resort &
      Hotel .... (see 1)
9 Tropic of Capricorn A1

Eating
10 Daikoku B3
11 RB Patel Supermarket B3
12 Sitar A3
13 Small Plates B3
   Wishbone & Pizzaking .... (see 11)

Drinking
14 Bounty Bar & Restaurant B3
15 Ed's Bar B2

band draw locals and visiting social animals alike. There's a small dining section inside, but the bar is the main event. Tables outside catch the breeze but they generally fill by early evening, so you'll have to strap on your beer boots early to nab one. Happy hour runs from when it opens at 5pm until 9pm.

Bounty Bar & Restaurant   SPORTS BAR
(Map p57; 672 0840; 79 Queens Rd, Martintar; lunch & dinner;) This convivial restaurant/bar is named in honour of the local rum. The old barrels, large seafaring mural and glass floats provide enough maritime atmosphere to keep most drunken sailors happy. There's a large TV screening important sporting events and a band plays here Friday, Saturday and Sunday, during which times things get loud, beery and fun. Although we wouldn't jump ship for it, the restaurant here serves passable surf-and-turf-style meals (mains $25 to $40).

The bars at the Aquarius Fiji (p53), Smugglers Cove (p53) and Nadi Bay Resort Hotel (p50) are also atmospheric options for a beer. Each of the flashy Denarau resorts (p61) have a six-pack of bars, all tastefully decorated and with attentive staff.

🛍 Shopping

Nadi's Main St is largely devoted to souvenir and duty-free shops, but sadly most items are mass-produced and you're unlikely to find anything truly unique. Much of it isn't even particularly Fijian, just vaguely tribal. The four biggest stores in town (you'll spot them) are all cut from this same cloth and stock more or less identical merchandise aimed unashamedly at the tourist wallet. Your best bet for locally produced souvenirs include printed designs on *masi* (bark cloth), *tanoa* (kava drinking bowls), cannibal forks, war clubs and wood-turned bowls. See p228 for general information.

You may pick up something more authentic at the handicraft market (Map p58; Koroivolu Ave) – and you'll likely enjoy the chat with stallholders.

ℹ️ Information

Emergency
Ambulance (911, 670 1128)
Fire (911, 670 0475)
Police (Map p58; 917, 670 0222; Koroivolu Ave)

NADI, SUVA & VITI LEVU NADI

Internet Access

Internet access is easy to find in downtown Nadi and costs around $3 per hour. Most accommodation offers broadband and, increasingly, wi-fi connections at costs ranging from free to around $10 per hour.

Medical Services

DSM Centre (Map p58; ☑670 0240; www. dsmcentrefiji.com.fj; 2 Lodhia St; ⊗8.30am-4.30pm Mon-Fri, to 12.30pm Sat) Specialises in travel medicine and has radiology and physiotherapy departments. Consultations $50 to $65.

Money

At the airport arrivals concourse there is an ANZ bank (open for all international flights) with an ATM just after you exit customs. There's also an ATM in the domestic terminal. There are ATMs at regular intervals along the Queens Road and Main St, as well as several currency exchange stores and banks including ANZ and Westpac.

Post

Post office Airport (Map p54; ☑672 2045; Nadi International Airport); Downtown (Map p58; ☑670 0001; Sahu Kahn Rd); Port Denerau (Map 60)

Tourist Information

Fiji Visitors Bureau (FVB; Map p54; ☑672 2433; www.fijime.com; Suite 107, Colonial Plaza, Namaka; ⊗8am-4.30pm Mon-Thu, to 4pm Fri) Fiji's official tourism bureau is geared more towards marketing to travel agents than assisting walk-in visitors.

Travel Agencies & Tour Operators

The travel agents at the airport will find you before you've had time to hail a taxi. The major companies have offices and representatives on the ground floor to meet arriving clients, while the agencies upstairs are smaller, local operators. Many of these specialise in budget accommodation and offer good deals, particularly for the islands, but be mindful that you're not receiving independent advice. It may be the commission they earn, not the colour of the coral, that governs their advice.

Domestic plane tickets can be bought directly from the Air Pacific (Fiji Air) office in the international arrivals hall and from the Pacific Sun counter in the departures hall.

These well-regarded agencies are on the ground floor of the arrivals concourse:

ATS Pacific (☑672 2811; www.atspacific. com.fj; Nadi airport concourse) Principally an international inbound operator working with overseas agents but maintains travel desks at many of the Denarau resorts.

Tourist Transport Fiji (☑672 2074; www. touristtransportfiji.com; Nadi airport concourse) This company operates the twice daily **Coral Sun** (p46) Fiji Nadi–Suva scheduled bus services, and **Feejee Experience** (p46) bus transfers and package tours. It also operates **Great Sights Fiji** (☑672 2074; www.tourist transportfiji.com) small-group 4WD tours to destinations including Navilawa in Koroyanitu National Heritage Park ($139 per person) and Navala in the Nausori Highlands ($215 per person).

Rosie Holidays (☑672 2755; www.rosiefiji.com; Nadi airport concourse) The largest and best re-sourced agency in Fiji. Rosie Holidays manages the tour desks at many resorts and organises group multiday treks into the central highlands and Sigatoka Valley, and day treks to the Nausori Highlands. There are also road tours to Sigatoka Valley and Kula Eco Park, Viseisei village and the Garden of the Sleeping Giant, and Pacific Harbour. It is the agent for Thrifty Car Rental.

Popular hotels and backpackers all have tour desks where you can book trips, although like their counterparts at the airport, the advice isn't always impartial.

Websites
Lonely Planet (www.lonelyplanet.com/fiji/viti-levu/nadi)

❶ Getting There & Around
To/From the Airport
Nadi International Airport is 9km north of down-town Nadi and there are frequent local buses stopping just outside the airport that travel along the Queens Road to town ($0.90). A taxi is $12. Most of the hotels have free transfer vehi-cles awaiting international flights.

Boat
Most boat companies, including **Awesome Adventures Fiji** (Map p60; ☑675 0499; www.awesomefiji.com) and **South Sea Cruises** (Map p60; ☑675 0500; www.ssc.com.fj), provide free transfers between Nadi hotels and Port Denarau for clients using their island-bound boats.

Bus
Buses depart regularly from New Town Beach for downtown Nadi ($0.80, 15 minutes, Monday to Saturday).

West Bus Transport runs buses regularly from Monday to Saturday (fewer on Sunday) from Nadi bus station and outside Jack's Handi-crafts to Denarau island. The first is at 8.30am and the last at 5pm ($0.80, 20 minutes).

From Nadi bus station (Map p58), there are buses to Lautoka and Suva and nonexpress buses can be caught at regular bus stops along the Queens Road.

Taxi
Taxis are plentiful and drivers are always on the look out for business. After a much-hyped government-ordered price increase in late 2011, they should be using accurately recalibrated me-ters. A taxi costs $6, $10 or $15 to the Queens Road junction, downtown or the airport.

Around Nadi
DENARAU ISLAND
Proving that money loves company, this small island (2.55 sq km) is laden with fancy resorts manicured to perfection with heavenly pools and designer suites. Although it's only 6km west of Nadi town, the disparity couldn't be starker and staying here offers little insight into everyday Fijian life. But if you're looking to splash some cash, enjoy a dose of pamper-ing and avoid Nadi altogether, then Denarau is the place to go. Be warned though – what the brochures and websites don't advertise is that Denarau is built on reclaimed mangrove mudflats and the beach has dark-grey sand and murky water unsuitable for snorkelling.

Yachties are welcome at the busy Dena-rau Marina (☑675 0600, Marine Channel 14; www.denaraumarina.com), where moorings are $15 per day, and berths cost from $2.50 per 10 metres per day.

✇ Activities
All Denarau resorts have kids clubs and, like most resorts throughout the country, also provide a programme of (mostly free) daily activities that are varied enough to appeal to all. These usually include a combination of Fijian language and cooking courses, *sulu*-tying, palm-frond weaving, coconut pick-ing, husking and jewellery-making lessons, beach volleyball and other sporty things,

HAVE YOUR SAY

Found a fantastic restaurant that you're longing to share with the world? Disa-gree with our recommendations? Or just want to talk about your most recent trip?

Whatever your reason, head to lonelyplanet.com, where you can post a review, ask or answer a question on the Thorntree forum, comment on a blog, or share your photos and tips on Groups. Or you can simply spend time chatting with like-minded travellers. So go on, have your say.

Denarau Island

Yakuilau

Nadi Bay

Golf Course

Narewa Rd

and the strangely ubiquitous (and unexpectedly thrilling) crab-racing.

Adrenalin Fiji   WATER SPORTS
(☑675 0061; www.adrenalinfiji.com) This mob runs the water-sports shops at all of the Denarau resorts and at Port Denarau Retail Centre. It specialises in jet-boat tours ($185 per person), jet-skiing ($120 per 15 minutes) and jetski safaris to Beachcomber, Castaway or Malolo Islands ($500 per person per 2.5 hrs). Adrenalin also offers parasailing ($240), wakeboarding ($110) and diving (PADI Open Water Course/two-tank dive $835/225), hot air ballooning, game fishing, scooter hire...the list goes on.

Nadi Fishing Charters   FISHING
(☑675 0311, 991 6544; www.nadifishingcharters. com) Affable locals John Francis and his son own and work this boat. With 15 years fishing experience – and several fishing trophies – they get a good rap from visitors.

Check out the booths in the passenger terminal at Denarau Marina for other fishing options. Some of the Mamanuca day tour boats also throw a handline out the back of the boat.

Denarau Golf & Racquet Club   GOLF, TENNIS
(☑675 9711; info@denaraugolf.com.fj; ⊙6.30am-6.30pm) This club is open to all and has an immaculately groomed 18-hole golf course with bunkers shaped like sea creatures. Green fees are $145/$95 for 18/nine holes and tennis court hire is $35 per hour. The breezy indoor/outdoor bar and cafe overlooks the course.

☞ Tours

Like those in Nadi, many tour companies based as far away as the Namosi Highlands will organise pick-up and drop-off from Denarau. The helpful staff at **Fiji's Finest Tours** (Port Denarau) will book anything anywhere in Fiji and can offer plenty of suggestions and options.

Denarau Marina (☑675 0600, Marine Channel 14; www.denaraumarina.com) is the port used by catamarans departing to and from the offshore islands. It can be a hive of activity as suitcases are loaded, tired children are soothed and buses drop off guests from their hotel pick-ups. See p115 to read about your Mamanuca Group tour options and p125 to read about boats leaving for the Yasawa Group.

In addition to island transfers, **Island Hoppers** (☑675 0670; www.helicopters.com.fj; Port Denarau) offers scenic helicopter flights over the islands and reefs of the Mamanuca Group and the waterfalls and gorges of Mt Koroyanitu (Mt Evans). Twenty- and 35-minute flights cost $339 and $439 per person respectively; minimum numbers apply. A romantic lunch on a secluded island beach costs $1800 per couple.

🛏 Sleeping

The rates at all of these resorts vary drastically with season and occupancy. They're *very* popular with families during Australia's and New Zealand's school holidays, which may be a plus or minus, depending on the age of your travelling companions. You can be sure that rooms in the following resorts are tastefully decorated and of a high standard, but none offers complimentary snorkelling trips or a beach that compares with those found on the islands.

Fiji Beach Resort & Spa

Managed by Hilton   RESORT $$$

(📞675 6800; www.hilton.com; r from $480; ❄✳@ 🛜✉🏊) A series of seven rectangular, interlocking pools surrounded by artistically simple day beds is a nice architectural change from the other resorts, and the kids club here is free. The long beachfront (the best Denarau has to offer) can be seen from all 273 rooms and the on-site **Nuku** (mains from $40) is arguably Denarau's top restaurant. Its tiny lobby belies the space and light behind.

Sofitel Fiji Resort & Spa   RESORT $$$

(📞675 1111; www.sofitel.com; r from $419; ❄✳@ 🛜✉🏊) The large pavilion-style lobby is flanked by columns of polished, vine-entangled tree trunks on one side and an impressive mezzanine bar overlooking the free-form pool on the other. The Sofitel gets top marks for its restaurant **Salt** (mains $20 to $45), with al fresco dining and a water's-edge location. We liked the kids' height servery at the restaurant buffet, and eyed with longing the baked goods in the resort shopping precinct's cafe. The 296 rooms are in uniform blocks flanking either side of the main building and were being stylishly refurbished at the time of writing.

Radisson Blu Resort Fiji   RESORT $$$

(📞675 6677; www.radisson.com/fiji; r from $442; ❄✳@🛜✉🏊) The 270-room Radisson wins the prize for Fiji's best waterscape. A waterfall spills into a pond from which meanders a series of pools, lagoons, sandy beaches with child-friendly inclines, a white-water tunnel, adult areas and an island containing a day spa. Sun-lounger etiquette is strictly enforced: notices warn that any towel left to bag a spot is removed if the owner disappears for too long! Use of kayaks, windsurfers and catamarans is free.

Sheraton Fiji Resort   RESORT $$$

(📞675 0777; www.starwoodhotels.com; r from $500; ❄✳@🛜✉🏊) The Sheraton is an oldie but a goodie if you like the 264-room family-resort kind of thing. The large entry hall offers views through to pool and ocean. The **Pantry** coffee shop in the lobby offers good take-away wraps and sushi ($15) and, just outside, there's a small shopping area with a deli and cafe.

Westin Denarau Island   RESORT $$$

(📞675 0000; www.starwoodhotels.com; r from $390; ❄✳@🛜✉🏊) The lobby is a synthesis of dark timber and pale sandstone, with a series of alternating high and low ceilings that lead past the resort's many facilities to a designer pool and beachside restaurants. A kids club is available for a one-time $55 fee and there's a small artificial beach, held in place by a bank of stones.

🍴 Eating & Drinking

Each of the Denarau resorts has a handful of restaurants and bars, and it's easy to sample any of them by jumping on the interresort *bula* bus ($7 for unlimited daily travel). Indeed, for many, this is one of the attractions of staying here.

At Port Denarau, there are cafes inside the shopping centre and a swath of cosmopolitan midrange restaurants lining the boardwalk – expect to pay from $25 for a main course. Try **Indigo** for Indian and Asian dishes, **Bonefish** for seafood, the **Hard Rock Cafe Fiji** for classic burgers and **Lulu's** for coffee, juice (or something harder) while waiting to board the interisland boats. More interestingly, **Nadina Authentic Fijian Restaurant** specialises in Fijian cuisine; both the grated cassava in caramel sauce and the pan-fried *walu* in coconut milk make a great introduction to island fare.

The **clubhouse** at the golf course also makes a nice change from the resorts.

🛍 Shopping

Port Denarau Retail Centre   MALL

(www.portdenarau.com.fj) This shopping centre is trying hard to supplant Nadi's Main St as the place to shop. The ever-expanding list of tenants currently includes beachwear, souvenir and video shops, along with banks, a grocery shop, a pharmacy and a post office. Most find it more pleasurable to shop here than contend with the hassles in town. The only thing is that it does tend to feel strangely...what's the word...white?

HINDU SYMBOLIC RITES

Around 35% of Fijians practise Hinduism. The distinctive and sometimes flamboyant temples and shrines in which they worship are dotted liberally around Viti Levu. Sculptured deities and colourful frescos pose photogenically against tropical or mountain backgrounds. Taking a reverent five minutes to pay your respects can be a cathartic experience regardless of your religious persuasion. The most celebrated of Fiji's Hindu temples is the Sri Siva Subramaniya Swami Temple in Nadi, which was constructed and decorated in part by craftsmen flown in from India.

A Hindu temple symbolises the body, the residence of the soul. Union with God can be achieved through prayer and by ridding the body of impurities (meat cannot be eaten on the day of entering the temple).

Water and fire are used for blessings. Water carried in a pot with flowers is symbolic of the Great Mother (the personification of nature), while burning camphor symbolises the light of knowledge and understanding. A trident is used to represent fire, the protector and the three flames of purity, light and knowledge.

Hindus believe that the body should be enslaved to the spirit and denied all comforts. Consequently, fire-walking is practised in order to become one with the Great Mother. Hindus believe life is like walking on fire and that a disciplined approach, like the one required in the ceremony, helps them to achieve balance and self-acceptance, and to see good in everything.

Before entering a Hindu temple, always ask permission and remove your shoes. Photography is generally OK outside the temple but it is considered offensive inside.

❶ Information

Yacht Help (☑675 0911; VHF Marine channel 16; www.yachthelp.com; Shop 5, Port Denarau) This extremely efficient aid to skippers can arrange Lau cruising permits, assemble provision orders and contact tradesmen, and it publishes the comprehensive *Fiji Marine Guide* annually (available online). Poste Restante can also be sent care of Yacht Help at PO Box PD18, Port Denarau.

❶ Getting There & Away

The local **West Bus Transport** operates buses between Nadi and Denarau island ($0.80). Catch it at the main bus station or outside Jack's Handicrafts.

The interresort *bula* bus ($7 for unlimited daily travel) has a thatched roof – who said money can't buy taste? A taxi from Nadi town costs around $12 and from the airport $24.

North of Nadi

FOOTHILLS OF THE SABETO MOUNTAINS

The undulating countryside between Nadi and Lautoka is a lovely area to explore. If the Sabeto (Sa-*mbeto*) Mountain range is cloud-free, look to its far southeast ridge and you'll see the profile of Mt Batilamu or, in local legend, the Sleeping Giant.

◉ Sights

The following sights could all be visited in a morning and are easily accessible from Nadi. A taxi from Nadi will cost around $15 to either the orchid garden or the hot springs. The Wailoko bus ($1.70), which passes both places, leaves Nadi at 9am, 1pm and 4pm and returns at 11am, 2pm and 5pm.

Garden of the Sleeping Giant   GARDENS
(Map p52; ☑672 2701; Wailoko Rd; adult/child $14.50/7.50; ◐9am-5pm Mon-Sat, to noon Sun) This garden was established in 1977 by actor and orchid-enthusiast Raymond Burr of *Perry Mason* and *Ironside* fame (readers born after 1975 may need to look him up). There are now over 1500 varieties of orchid, representing 160 species. Although they won't all be flowering simultaneously (peak flowering season is June to July and November to December), expect a brilliant display year-round. A 50m-long shadecloth-covered walkway leads to a jungle boardwalk that showcases indigenous flora and other tropical beauties. The whole place takes about 45 minutes to walk around unless you bring a picnic and stay longer. Time it right and you can join the 3pm free guided walk – it coincides with any afternoon tour groups, but may not run if there are no bookings.

Sabeto Hot Springs HOT SPRINGS

(Map p52; admission $12; ☉9am-5pm Mon-Sat)
Two kilometres further inland beyond the garden, a series of geothermal hot pools and a mud pool in a field is the place to come clean while getting dirty. The soft, silty, knee-deep mud is covered by a top layer of leaves and the contrasting texture is a little freaky when you first sink into the ooze. The temptation to scoop up a handful of mud to smear over your friends may prove overwhelming.

Lomolomo Guns HISTORIC SITE

(Map p52) There is an abandoned battery of guns at Lomolomo, on a low rise at the foot of the Sabeto Mountains. Built in WWII to protect Nadi Bay, they are hardly a 'must see', but the walk up the hill offers some fine views across sugar-cane fields to the Yasawa Group. To get there, take the second turn-off on the right, 400m after the Lomolomo police post on the main road. Follow the dirt road to the bright pink house and continue the last few hundred metres on foot. The police will happily point you in the right direction – the guns were visible from their post until a palm tree grew too tall.

🛏 Sleeping

Stoney Creek Resort RESORT $

(Map p52; ☎620 3644; www.stoneycreekfiji.net; Sabeto Rd; dm incl breakfast $45, s & d incl breakfast without bathroom $85, bure incl breakfast $150-180; @⛱) When you tire of lying on your beach towel, head here to replace the aqua-blue seascape of the outer islands with the velvet-green landscape of Sabeto Valley. Activities on offer include mountain biking ($25 per person for full-day hire), village visits, guided waterfall treks (October to April or when the water's flowing, $15 per person) and swimming in the river. A mini-golf course was being built when we visited. The 'Love Shack' dorms and rooms are reminiscent of train carriages with shuttered windows, and room number one and the *bure* have sweeping mountain views (although the Seventh Day Adventist campus under construction across the road will undoubtedly alter the landscape). The restaurant (mains $13-25) caters well to both meat-eaters and vegetarians.

The resort repays airport taxi fares for guests staying a minimum of two nights and there are regular 'Sabeto' buses from Nadi bus station ($1.90), every couple of hours between 8am and 5.30pm. A taxi from the airport costs $13 and from downtown Nadi $18.

KOROYANITU NATIONAL HERITAGE PARK

Just half an hour's drive from Nadi airport, Koroyanitu National Heritage Park (Map p52) seems deep within Viti Levu's interior. It's very beautiful, with walks through native *dakua* (a tree of the Kauri family) forests and grasslands, birdwatching, archaeological sites and waterfalls, and gorgeous landscapes of peaks, clouds and sunshine.

There are six small and largely self-sufficient villages within the park that cooperate as part of a conservation project intended to protect Fiji's only unlogged tropical montane forest. Recently, there's been a chequered history of access for travellers. The villages are small and comparatively remote, and, with low numbers of visitors, both track and lodge maintenance has been an issue.

◉ Sights & Activities

Navilawa VILLAGE

As of late 2011, most people access the park from this tiny village, north of Sabeto Rd above Nadi. The rocky 4WD road hugs the Sabeto River, and there are some perfect swimming holes and waterfalls to plunge in. If you're travelling independently, it's polite to ask permission first from any locals you see. The village itself is set in an old volcanic crater with forest and mountains around – a photographer's delight. There's also a short rainforest hike to a cave shelter beside a clear-flowing creek that the villagers use during hurricanes.

Visitors should take a *sevusevu* and make themselves known on arrival for a low-key and very authentic kava welcoming ceremony.

Self-sufficient visitors could spend an interesting couple of days staying here and being part of village life. Villagers will likely be diffident about asking you to join activities but will be delighted if you show interest in, say, spending an hour in someone's garden, cooking with one of the women, rounding up the chooks and goats with the children, or taking a horse ride. A small, simple, self-contained lodge with six beds ($35 per person including shower and flush toilet) is the only accommodation option. Sheets and pillows are provided, but bring your own food.

Abaca VILLAGE

Abaca (Am-*ba*-tha) village, southeast of Lautoka, is another, more logistically challenging, access option to the park. In late 2011, the trails had been unmaintained for months and it wasn't possible to walk without a guide

NADI, SUVA & VITI LEVU NORTH OF NADI

and a machete to clear head-high vegetation. If there's a guide available, it should still be possible to make a day trek to and from Fiji's sleeping giant, Mt Batilamu. This is a strenuous three-hour hike up, and a knee-wobbling couple of hours down. In 2008, a landslide destroyed the section of the trail that joined Abaca with Navilawa. In late 2011, it was still not possible to walk the two-day trek between the villages, though it should be possible to overnight at Abaca's simple Nase Lodge.

❶ Getting There & Away

From Nadi International Airport follow the Queens Road north for a couple of kilometres then turn right onto Sabeto Rd. Follow this to the (unsigned) turn off to Navilawa village – the turn is on the left, 3.9km after Stoney Creek Resort. Pass through Korobebe village and a gold mining exploration camp, and keep veering left whenever the road forks. Navilawa village is 13.2km from Stoney Creek.

You'll need a 4WD with decent clearance; the road is steep and rocky in places, with creek crossings. Public buses make several trips a day from Lautoka and Nadi to Korobebe village, from where it's an hour or so hike up to Navilawa unless you strike it lucky and hitch a ride with a local carrier returning from market.

To get to Abaca, turn right off the Queens Road at Tavakubu Rd – past the first roundabout after entering Lautoka from Nadi. Continue along Tavakubu Rd for about 4.7km, past the police post and the cemetery, then turn right onto the (unsigned) road to Abaca. It's a well-defined road that doubles as the local rubbish dump for the first few hundred metres. At the first causeway, fork right and it's another 10km of gravel road up to the village, suitable for 4WDs only. There is no public transport to Abaca, though you'll be able to charter a carrier from Lautoka.

A good option is to take a half-day guided tour to Navilawa with **Great Sights Fiji** (☑672 2074; www.touristtransport fiji.com). Their affable and knowledgeable guide Kali is a local and has walked the Mt Batilamu trek many times.

VISEISEI & VUDA POINT

About 12km north of Nadi is Viseisei village, which, according to local lore, is the oldest settlement in Fiji. The story goes that the *mataqali* (extended family) here are descendants of the first ocean-going Melanesians who landed 1km north of here around 1500. As if to follow tradition, Fiji's first Methodist missionaries also chose to land here in 1835 and the Centennial Memorial in front of the church is the focal point for 10 October (Fiji Day) celebrations. The ceremonial *bure* opposite the memorial is still used on important occasions and both Queen Elizabeth II and Prince Charles have been received here. To look around you'll need to pay $3 to the ladies who run the tiny craft market (☺8am-6pm Mon-Sat), remove your hat and wear something that covers your shoulders and knees. A bypass on the Queens Road skips Viseisei, so if you're travelling by public transport, be sure to check that the bus you catch actually calls by the village.

Beyond Viseisei, **Vuda Point Marina** (Map p52; ☑666 8214; www.vudamarina.com.fj) is a well-organised and thriving yachties' lure. Facilities include free showers, an excellent noticeboard, a coin-operated laundry, sail makers, a general store, scooter hire (yachties' special offer $59 per day), yacht-repair specialists and a chandlery. Berths cost $0.56 per foot per day and electricity costs $3.88 per day.

Non-yachties can enjoy the ambience, views and good coffee on the boardwalk at **Boatshed Café** (☺breakfast & lunch), and sunset drinks and dinner at the indoor/outdoor **Boatshed Bar & Restaurant** opposite.

🛏 Sleeping & Eating

The beaches around Vuda Point are better than those found near Nadi, but are far from Fiji's best and offer little for the avid snorkeller. Some find staying here a little isolating for anything longer than a few days, though a hire car will widen visitors' horizons.

First Landing Resort   RESORT **$$$**
(Map p52; ☑666 6171; www.firstlandingfiji.com; r incl breakfast $374-469, 2-bed villa incl breakfast $740-840; ⊛✸❋) Perched on the water's edge and dripping in palms and colourful foliage, this resort had a decent facelift in 2011. The *bure* and villas are like cheerful hotel rooms with bright, tiled bathrooms and mosquito-screened verandahs. More expensive villas have private plunge pools and, although the beach isn't great, there's an artificial island in the shape of a footprint and a lagoon-style pool to accommodate sunbathers. The restaurant (mains $25 to $38) serves seafood, pasta, and wood-fired pizza.

Viseisei Village Homestays   HOMESTAY **$**
(Map p52; per person $60) A number of families offer homestays in Viseisei, although they may be hard to contact. Your best bet is to contact **Finau Bavadra** (☑925 5370; dawfin@connect.com.fj): she often welcomes couch surfers or will find a bed elsewhere in the village for you.

Anchorage Beach Resort   RESORT **$$**
(Map p52; ☑666 2099; www.anchoragefiji.com; r incl breakfast $188-388; ☺❋☲) The hilltop wedding *bure* has panoramic views of Nadi Bay and the Mamanuca Group and the grassy lawn can accommodate large numbers. Rather tired mountain-view rooms are set high above the hill. A five-minute walk down the hill leads to beachfront rooms and newer villas (with spa baths built into their private decks), a ho-hum beach, the main **restaurant** (mains $15-40) and a sparkling pool.

At Vuda Point Marina, you can enjoy the ambience, views and good coffee on the boardwalk at **Boatshed Café** (☺breakfast & lunch), and sunset drinks and dinner at the indoor/outdoor **Boatshed Bar & Restaurant** opposite.

Lautoka

POP 52,900

According to legend, Fiji's second-largest city derives its name from a battle cry that means 'spear-hit'. The story goes that when an argument erupted between two local chiefs, one cried out the words *lau toka* as he killed the other by spearing him through the chest, simultaneously stating the obvious and naming the location.

Lautoka's recent history is entwined with the fortunes of sugar, which gives rise to its other name, Sugar City.

Lautoka doesn't have much to detain travellers, but it is a pleasant enough spot with wide streets steeped in foliage, a picturesque esplanade, a couple of decent cafes and the backdrop of Mt Koroyanitu (Mt Evans) to remind everyone that the urban reaches are well and truly finite.

◉ Sights & Activities

Sri Krishna Kaliya Temple   TEMPLE
(Map p66; ☑666 4112; 5 Tavewa Ave; ☺8am-6pm) Fiji has the highest percentage of Hare Krishnas per capita in the world and this temple is the foremost International Society for Krishna Consciousness (ISKCON) temple in the South Pacific. Visitors are welcome anytime, but an interesting time to visit is during the noon *puja* (prayer) on Sunday. Sit according to your gender and expect a whole lot of drum beating, bell ringing, conch blowing and chanting, which is the way Krishnas approach God and achieve transcendental bliss. Keep a donation handy

for the tray that a child circulates at the end of the service. Everyone, whether giving money or not, is invited to the 1pm vegetarian lunch that follows.

Lautoka Sugar Mill   HISTORIC BUILDING
(off Map p66; Nadovu Rd) From Marine Dr, it is possible to walk to this mill, the backbone of the local economy. The mill opened in 1903 and is still by all accounts the largest sugar mill in the southern hemisphere. There are no tours, but you should be able to see the conveyors and pipeline for loading sugar, woodchips and molasses into the waiting cargo boats.

Blue Lagoon Cruises   CRUISE
(Map p66; 183 Vitogo Pde) Blue Lagoon operates its Yasawa Group cruises from Lautoka Port. See p125 for details.

In lieu of beach sports, join the locals who walk, jog, promenade and picnic along Lautoka's **landscaped waterfront** at dawn, dusk and the weekend. The nearest stretch of sand is the unappealing but popular **Saweni Beach**, 8km out of town.

🛏 Sleeping

Northern Club   APARTMENT **$**
(Map p66; ☑666 2469, 992 6469; northernaccom@ yahoo.com.au; apt $120; ❋☲) While you don't have to be a club member to stay here, a member will have to sign you in to the comfortable and relaxed facilities in the main club building. The six self-contained one-bedroom apartments in the landscaped grounds provide everything else you need. They're great value, comfortable and clean as a whistle and just a few minutes walk into town.

Sea Breeze Hotel   HOTEL **$**
(Map p66; ☑666 0717; seabreezefiji@connect. com.fj; Bekana Lane; s $54-70, d $60-76; ☺❋☲) From the outside, the Sea Breeze resembles a jaunty blue-and-white apartment building. Inside, the austere rooms are a clean and tranquil sanctuary to noise-weary travellers. The fan-cooled digs are the cheapest, but the sea-view rooms with air-con are the nicest. The well-maintained pool looks over the water, as does the TV lounge which serves breakfast ($6.60 to $8.80).

Tanoa Waterfront Hotel   HOTEL **$$**
(Map p66; ☑666 4777; www.tanoawaterfront.com; Marine Dr; r $168-188; ☺❋@☲) Lautoka's top-end hotel has a top waterfront location. The cheapest rooms are spotlessly clean and

Lautoka

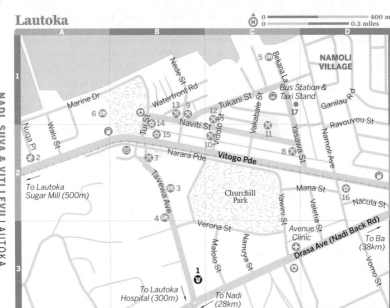

Lautoka

◉ Sights
1 Sri Krishna Kalima Temple B3

◈ Activities, Courses & Tours
2 Blue Lagoon Cruises A2

⊜ Sleeping
3 Cathay Hotel B2
4 Northern Club B2
5 Sea Breeze Hotel C1
6 Tanoa Waterfront Hotel A1

⊗ Eating
7 Blue Ginger Café B2
8 Chilli Bites C2

9 Chilli Tree Café B1
Fins Restaurant .... (see 6)
10 Ganga Vegetarian Restaurant C2
11 Market C2
12 MH Supermarket C1
13 Nang Ying B1

✪ Entertainment
14 Ashiqui Nightclub B1
15 A-SK Pasifika B2
16 Damodar Village Cinema D2

ⓘ Transport
Pacific Transport .... (see 17)
17 Sunbeam Transport C1

have the ambience and trimmings of a mid-range US hotel chain. The more expensive rooms have contemporary interiors, flat-screen TVs and small balconies overlooking two pools. There is a gym, a coin-operated laundry, a small children's playground, a bar and the **Fins Restaurant** on site.

Cathay Hotel HOTEL **$**
(Map p66; ☏666 0205; www.fiji4less.com; Tavewa Ave; dm $24-26, r $61-74; ❊❤) This low-key, budget hotel is the choice of travelling gov-

ernment and NGO workers. Dorms here are good value: they have a maximum of four people to a room and each has its own bath-room. Otherwise, choose between spacious rooms with air-con and simpler but still roomy, fan-cooled rooms with shared bath-rooms. There's a communal TV but no res-taurant or bar so it's quiet – as long as you get a room off the main road – and the pool area is pleasant.

Saweni Beach Apartment Hotel APARTMENT $
(Map p52; ☑666 1777; www.fiji4less.com; dm $23, apt $95-120; ☺❋▩) Situated 8km southwest of town, this hotel offers a series of one-bedroom, self-contained apartments in two long complexes. In addition, there are two dorms that have a total of eight beds and share a communal kitchen and lounge area. It's an inexpensive option for self-caterers and those looking for a base to explore the nearby highlands, but you'll want your own wheels and imagination – there's little to do at the hotel except paddling in the pool.

✖ Eating

Lautoka has fewer restaurants than Nadi or Suva, but there are lots of inexpensive lunch-time eateries frequented by locals.

TOP
CHOICE **Blue Ginger Café** CAFE $
(Map p66; Post Office Roundabout; meals from $6 ☺breakfast & lunch Mon-Sat; ☺❋) Delicious breakfasts (the menu includes homemade yoghurt, fruit and poached eggs) and lunches of wholemeal sandwiches, interesting wraps, fresh salads and buttery cakes and biscuits. Blue Ginger is run by a Swiss–Filipina couple and also serves truly good coffee (and/or a decent glass of wine) to go with the food.

Chilli Bites INDIAN $
(Map p66; Yasawa St; meals from $10-15; ☺break-fast, lunch & dinner Mon-Sat, lunch & dinner Sun; ☺❋) Ignore the scratched formica tables and enjoy this authentic north Indian food made by authentic north Indian Indians. The tandoor breads, rich and flavoursome curries, and sweet or salt yoghurt lassis are cheap and delicious.

Chilli Tree Café CAFE $
(Map p66; ☑665 1824; 3 Tukani St; meals $8-15; ☺breakfast & lunch Mon-Sat, breakfast Sun; ☺❋) This corner cafe is a good place to grab a paper and coffee, build a sandwich and settle into a chair for some serious people watching behind the plate-glass windows.

Nang Ying CHINESE $$
(Map p66; ☑665 2668; Nede St; mains $15-35; ☺lunch & dinner Mon-Sat, dinner Sun; ☺) Twinkly lights, backlit pictures and fake flowers give this place an air of Chinatown authenticity that would do San Francisco proud. Fragrant poultry and noodle dishes, sizzling seafood hotplates and fried-rice specials demonstrate that these cooks know their way around their chopsticks.

Ganga Vegetarian Restaurant VEGETARIAN $
(Map p66; Vidolo St; meals $3-6; ☺breakfast & lunch; ☺❋✍) Popular Hare Krishna restaurant serving good vegetarian meals.

Fins Restaurant INTERNATIONAL $$
(Map p66; ☑666 4777; Marine Dr; mains $25-40; ☺breakfast, lunch & dinner; ☺❋) Themed menus most nights – pizza, barbeque – are the go at this restaurant attached to the Tanoa Waterfront Hotel. It has a scenic outlook onto the waterfront.

Self-catering

Self-caterers can stock up at any one of several supermarkets, including **MH Supermarket** (Map p66; cnr Naviti & Vidolo St) and at the produce market, which is part of the larger, **town market** (Map p66; ☺7am-5pm Mon-Fri, to 3pm Sat).

☕ Drinking & Entertainment

Lautoka lacks the sophistication of Suva and the small number of pubs and clubs are generally on the seedy side.

A-SK Pasifika LIVE MUSIC
(Map p66; ☑666 8989; 151 Vitogo Pde; ☺5pm-1am Mon-Sat) Popular with Fijians who flock here on 'sponsored nights' when the beer is cheaper. A $5 cover charge applies on Friday and Saturday when a band or DJ plays.

Damodar Village Cinema CINEMA
(Map p66; Namoli Ave) Besides the Suva cinema, this is the only other mainstream cinema in Fiji. Tickets are $4.50 for children and $5.50 for adults.

Fighting and drinking are a popular pastime for some and, if you haven't noticed, Fijian men aren't exactly petite; we don't recommend nightclubbing for solo travellers. But, for those with friends, a fun night out dancing can be had at **Ashiqi Nightclub** (Map p66; Lautoka Hotel, Tui St; ☺8pm-1am Fri & Sat), which plays Bollywood hits at alarming decibels.

❶ Information

Emergency
Ambulance (☑911)
Police (Map p66; ☑911, 666 0222; Drasa Ave) There is also a police post on Tui St.

Internet Access
Internet access is cheap and plentiful in Lautoka. Check out the line of shops opposite the mosque and around the market.

Medical Services

Avenue Clinic (Map p66; ☎665 2955; 47 Drasa Ave) Consultation $30.

Lautoka Hospital (off Map p66; ☎666 0399; Thomson Cres) South of the Botanical Gardens.

Money

There are several banks downtown that will change money and travellers cheques. There are ANZ bank ATMs on Vitogo Pde, on Yasawa St and near the cinema on Namoli Ave.

Post

Post office (Map p66; cnr Vitogo Pde & Tavewa Ave) Has public phones.

ℹ Getting There & Around

Local buses depart for Nadi ($2.50, one hour, 33km) via the airport every 15 minutes.

Sunbeam Transport (☎666 2822; Yasawa St) and **Pacific Transport** (☎666 0499; Yasawa St) have offices in Yasawa St opposite the market and both have frequent services to and from Suva ($16, six hours) via the Queens Road. Sunbeam also has seven daily departures to Suva via the Kings Road ($18, seven hours).

Local buses connect Lautoka with Saweni Beach ($1, 45 minutes, six daily). Alternatively any local bus to Nadi will drop you at the turn-off, from where it is an easy walk along 2km of unsealed road. A taxi from Saweni will cost approximately $10 to Lautoka, or $35 to Nadi International Airport.

Arriving yachts wishing to clear customs and immigration at **Lautoka Port** (VHF Marine channel 16; ⊙8am-1pm & 2-4.30pm Mon-Fri) will need to announce their arrival to port authorities and get instructions on where to moor.

Lautoka to Rakiraki

BA

POP 15,800

Although few find reasons to visit Ba, it is Fiji's fifth largest town and characterised by its sizeable Indo-Fijian and Muslim population – most of whom are soccer-mad. Ba boasts Fiji's best racecourse and the town's horse-racing and bougainvillea festivals are in September.

Most who make it to Ba are there to change buses and catch onward transport into the Nausori Highlands. If you're driving yourself, stop off at the roadside headquarters of **Friend** (Map p52; www.friendfiji.com), about 10km from Ba on the way from Lautoka. It's a local non-governmental organisation working with disadvantaged people in Fiji's west. Check out their on-site

small-scale commercial kitchen, the card- and paper-making projects, and the shelves of locally grown and made products for sale at reception. A restaurant is in the pipeline.

Unless for some reason you have to overnight at the **Ba Hotel** (Map p48; 110 Bank St; s & d $80-85; ❄ ⊛ ⊠), head for the more salubrious options on offer in Tavua or Lautoka.

ℹ Getting There & Away

Sunbeam buses travelling between Lautoka ($2, 55 minutes) and Suva ($15, five to six hours) call in at Ba bus station throughout the day.

NADARIVATU, NAVAI & KORO-NI-O

In the dry season, you can head up to the forestry settlement of **Nadarivatu** (30km southeast of Tavua). From here you can **hike** to Fiji's highest peak, **Tomanivi** (1323m, also known as Mt Victoria), or to **Mt Lomalagi** ('sky' or 'heaven' in Fijian). The Mt Lomalagi hike takes about three hours return and has great views. The **District Officer** (☎620 9645) will put you in touch with the Forestry Department in Nadarivatu. Its office is on the side of the road in the village and can arrange camping or a homestay with a local family. Bring provisions and give money or groceries to your hosts to cover costs.

You can also walk from **Navai**, which is 8km southeast of Nadarivatu, to Tomanivi's peak. Allow at least five hours (return) to hike from the village. Guides can be hired for $15. The last half of the climb is practically rock climbing and can be very slippery.

The Wainibuka and Wainimala Rivers (eventually merging to form the Rewa River) originate around here, as does the Sigatoka River. Past Navai, the road deteriorates and a 4WD is needed. **Koro-ni-O** ('village of the clouds' in Fijian) and the **Monasavu Dam** are about 25km to the southeast. The Wailoa/Monasavu Hydroelectric Scheme here provides about 93% of Viti Levu's power needs.

ℹ Getting There & Away

The turn-off to the hills, crossing Fiji's highest mountain range and eventually ending up in Suva, is about 3km east of Tavua. The windy, rough gravel road climbs sharply, affording spectacular vistas of the coast and it takes about 1½ hours by 4WD to Nadarivatu. Nandan local bus service runs between Tavua and Nadarivatu ($3.50) a couple of times a day. Beyond there you may be able to negotiate a lift in a carrier as far as Koro-ni-O. Otherwise you'll need a 4WD to get to Suva.

BRENDON COFFEY, EXECUTIVE CHEF

Brendon Coffey heads up the culinary team at the stylish Sofitel Fiji Resort & Spa (p61).

Top food advice for visitors? I'm a big fan of local produce. So I'd say go to the market and go for what's fresh. Many visitors have never tasted in-season tropical fruit, bought and eaten on the same day it was picked. A hand of truly fresh bananas can be a revelation.

Any particularly interesting dishes to look out for? Anything made with fresh co-conut milk – especially if you're staying somewhere where you can watch local blokes climb a tree to pick a coconut. Have a go at husking it yourself, drink the coconut water (delicious!) and see how the milk is extracted from the flesh.

Any favourite local products? I'm happy to plug any Indian condiments made by Friend, a local organisation that buys from small-scale farmers, employs women in the kitchen and encourages villagers to trial new crops and recipes. Their products are on the shelves of many supermarkets now. I use their tamarind chutney and mango jam in some dishes at the resort – it's great to both expose visitors to authentic Fijian flavours and support local incomes.

Nausori Highlands

In stark contrast to the dense rainforests of the eastern highlands, the Nausori Highlands ascend into the interior in a panorama of grassy moguls. Massive folds of pale green tussle and tumble into the background as the coastline diminishes along the horizon. Patchy areas of forest and small villages are scattered in the hills. The more remote the village, the more traditional the villagers are in their ways. Sunday is a day of rest and worship, so visits to the two main villages of **Navala** and **Bukuya** on this day may be disruptive and unappreciated. The villagers in Navala are Catholic and the villagers in Bukuya are Methodist.

If you have your own transport, the loop from Nadi or Lautoka to Ba, then via Navala to Bukuya, and then back down to Nadi – or down to the Coral Coast via the Sigatoka Valley – is a scenic, fun and usually easy, though long, day trip. You'll need decent weather, a 4WD and a picnic. Check road conditions before heading for the hills.

Tours

Nadi-based tour operators **Great Sights Fiji** (672 2074; www.touristtransportfiji.com) and **Rosie Holidays** (672 2755; www.rosiefiji.com) arrange tours in the Nausori Highlands, including day trips to Navala.

NAVALA
POP 800

Nestled in rugged, grassy mountains, Navala is by far Fiji's most picturesque village. Navala's chief enforces strict town-planning rules: the dozens of traditional thatched *bure* are laid out neatly in avenues, with a central promenade sloping down the banks of the Ba River. All of the houses here are built with local materials; the only concrete block and corrugated iron in sight is for the school, Catholic church and radio shed (which houses the village's emergency radio telephone). The rectangular-plan houses have a timber-pole structure, sloping stone plinths, woven split-bamboo walls and thatched roofs. Kitchens are in separate *bure,* and toilets in *bure lailai* (little houses).

Navala is a photographer's delight, but you need to get permission and pay the $15 entrance fee before wandering around. If arriving independently, ask the first person you meet to take you to the *turaga-ni-koro* (the chief-appointed headman who collects the entrance fee). As the village charges a fee to enter, a traditional *sevusevu* is not required although all other village etiquette rules (p221) apply. If you arrive with Tui from Bulou's Eco Lodge, he will take care of protocol.

Sleeping

Bulou's Eco Lodge   LODGE $

(Map p48; 628 1224; dm/bure per person incl meals $75/180) To experience Fijian hospitality at its finest, a night (or two) spent with Bulou N Talili and her son (and hereditary chief) Tui is highly recommended. Their home and ecolodge is 1km past Navala village, so phone ahead and they can send their tiny truck to meet you at the bus stop. Guests are totally spoilt: expect to be encouraged to 'eat more' of traditional food that is prepared in staggering quantities. Tui is an excellent guide and he accompanies all guests around the village introducing them to his relatives and friends. He will also guide nonguests around for $20 (per group up to four).

There are two very simple traditional *bure* in the garden and a 10-bed dorm attached to the house. There are cold-water showers, flush toilets and a limited electricity supply. It is polite to bring a small *sevu-sevu* (a $5 pack of ground kava is enough) to present to the hosts during the welcoming ceremony (although they will neither ask for nor expect it). Bulou sells her handicrafts (pandanus mats and printed *masi* cloth) for reasonable prices and when you tire of swimming in the backyard river, Tui can arrange horse riding ($25) and trekking ($20) in the surrounding hills.

ⓘ Getting There & Away

BUS The local buses from Ba to Navala ($3) leave Ba bus station at 12.30pm, 4.30pm and 5.15pm Monday to Saturday. Buses return to Ba at 6am, 7.30am and 1.45pm Monday to Friday. Locals pay $45 one way to charter a carrier but it is unlikely that you will be able to get it for this price. The rough gravel road has a few patches of bitumen on the really steep bits. While only 26km away, Navala is about a 1¼-hour drive from Ba, past the Rarawai Sugar Mill, through beautiful rugged scenery.

CAR & MOTORCYCLE If driving from Ba, there are a couple of turns to watch out for. At the police post, take the right turn passing a shop on your right and at the next fork in the road, keep left. The road is rough and rocky, but usually passable as long as the car has high clearance. The Ba River can flood (and does, quite regularly, actually) for a few hours in the evening after heavy afternoon rains. Then the concrete bridge just before the village becomes impassable, so be prepared to sit it out.

BUKUYA
POP 700

Bukuya is a little more commercial than Navala and is not as picturesque, but is still a worthy cultural experience. It is at the intersection of the gravel roads from Sigatoka (66km), Nadi (48km) and Navala (20km). The drive from Sigatoka up the Sigatoka Valley is a stunning two hours or so, as is the journey from Ba via Navala. The journey from Nadi along the Nausori Highlands Rd can take up to three hours.

All roads to Bukuya are rough and unsealed, and no public transport runs this far. It's a bone-crunching ride in the back of a carrier, which will cost around $60 to/from Ba or $18 to/from Navala.

TAVUA
POP 2400

Tavua is a small, quiet agricultural town with lots of temples, churches and mosques. The Emperor Gold Mining Company mined here from the 1930s until 2006 when DRD Gold of South Africa announced it was no longer viable and the mine was closed. Until then, most of the mine's 1800 workers lived in **Vatukoula**, a purpose-built town 9km south of Tavua. The Emperor Gold Mining Company had been Fiji's largest private employer and its subsequent closing has placed considerable hardship on local communities.

South of Nadi

NAISALI

The long, flat island of Naisali (42 hectares) is just 300m off the mainland and about 12km southwest of Nadi. Like Denarau, Naisali is on the edge of mangroves: the beaches aren't ideal for swimming and the dark sand disappoints some.

There's plenty of white sand at the **Sonaisali Island Resort** (Map p52; ☑670 6011; www.sonaisali.com; r incl breakfast $495-682, ste incl breakfast from $891; ❷✳@❋♠), but it's used to create faux beaches and landscape the huge grounds – there's none on the beach. The hub of the resort is a large pool with a swim-up bar and an endless array of activities to keep families happy. These include a free kids club, Fiji's so-far only public paintball ground ($85 per person) and jet skis ($85 per 15 minutes). The nine-course degustation menu ($125) at the **Plantation** signature restaurant looks sensational – book ahead. But the bars are pricey (cocktails $22), so bringing your own booze is a good idea. The hotel-style rooms in the double-storey building are getting tired – at the time of writing, half had been recently renovated, half had not – whereas the semidetached *bure* (especially those set along the beach away from the main action) are far more stylish, with spa baths built into the verandahs.

Naisali is a 25-minute drive followed by a three-minute boat shuttle (free for resort guests) from Nadi airport. A taxi from the airport costs $32 and the resort shuttle $55.

UCIWAI LANDING

Uciwai Landing, used by surfers to access the Mamanuca breaks and island resorts on Namotu and Tavarua, is 25km southwest of Nadi, the last 7km of which is on a slow and

DON'T MISS

TAVUA HOTEL

Tavua's **historic hotel** (Map p48; ☎668 0522; tavuahotel@connect.com.fj; Vatia St; dm/s/d $28/70/105; ⚒☒) is the only place to stay in town, and it's an unexpected gem. Built in the 1930s heydays of the gold boom, it's all polished wood, high breezy rooms and open public spaces. In the original building, the eight bedrooms – all with private bathrooms – have an attractive air of faded elegance. A few newer rooms are laid out in the landscaped grounds. Drop in for a drink or meal at least, and enjoy the old photos on the downstairs walls.

pot-holed road. Surfing is really the only reason to head here.

The lingo and 'tude hang thickly in the air at the **Rendezvous Beach Resort** (Map p52; ☎628 1216; www.surfdivefiji.com; site per person $33, dm $40, r $75-150; ⚒@☒) which caters predominantly to surfers on a budget and Japanese people studying English. It's an interesting combination. Quick access to the Mamanuca surf breaks and dive sites are the attraction and the idea is to spend as much time away from the resort as possible. Accommodation is rudimentary, but the better beach huts have fans. There's a guest kitchen, otherwise three meals per day work out to around $75. The staff here are as languid as the seasoned surfers who visit.

The daily surf boat goes to where the surf's good and costs $100 per person, minimum two people, for three to four hours surfing.

Resort transfers are available from Nadi ($40) and the airport ($60), or there are local buses to Uciwai from Nadi bus station ($2) departing a couple of times a day Monday through Saturday.

MOMI BAY

The first interesting detour off the Queens Road is about 20km south of Nadi, along a sealed road that threads its way between barren hills, pine plantations and sugar-cane fields to Momi Bay and the more impressive WWII Momi Guns. From the bunkers, the site of a more recently raged battle – a legal one – is visible. Construction was well underway on the JW Marriott Fiji Resort and Spa, Fiji's second overwater *bure* resort, until work came to a grinding halt in 2006, at which stage Momi Bay briefly became home to a first-class golf course on which no one has ever played.

◉ Sights & Activities

Momi Guns   HISTORIC SITE

(Map p52; adult/child/family $3/1/6; ☺9am-5pm). Turn off the sealed road at the signpost to the guns, and onto 4km of rattling gravel road. This leads to two 6in guns that were installed here by the New Zealand 30th Battalion in 1941 to defend Fiji against the Japanese. Fiji was, like most other islands, poorly equipped to take on the might of the Imperial Army: an army that had already swept through Papua New Guinea, the Solomon Islands and parts of what is now Vanuatu. A quick scan of the horizon will reveal why this spot was chosen for the battery. The guns (and now tourists) have unobstructed views to Malolo Barrier Reef, the Mamanuca Group and Navula Passage, the only entry into western Fiji for large ships. The war raged on but the guns were only fired once in anger – at a New Zealand Navy ship that failed to signal correctly. An enthusiastic National Trust volunteer rattles off his comprehensive site information as fast as the guns would have fired.

Scuba Bula   DIVING

(☎628 0190; www.scubabula.com) This excellent, independently owned company is based at the Seashell@Momi resort. It is the only company to dive the Outer Navula Barrier Reef, and dive instructor and founder-owner 'Scuba Sam' has over 25 years' experience on local reefs. A two-tank dive including equipment costs $205 and PADI Open Water Course $780. Snorkellers are welcome, and charged $50 for a two-hour outing.

🛏 Sleeping

Seashell@Momi   RESORT **$**

(Map p52; ☎670 6100; www.seashellresort.com; dm/s/d $27/$70/80, bure $128, apt $176; ⊜⚒☒) The Seashell is 13km from the main road and has an undiscovered air about it. While it's far from upmarket, it offers excellent value if you don't mind the dated decor. Accommodation comes in all shapes and configurations, from self-contained *bure* and apartments to sizeable suites, inexpensive lodges and roomy dorms. On-site facilities include a tennis court, a children's playground, two pools, a **restaurant** (mains $10-20) and enough palm trees for a whole island.

People don't come here for the beach (although if you walk around the rocky point, there's a larger bay with better sand). Rather, they come for access to some of Fiji's hottest dive spots and premier surf breaks – or just to kick back away from the crowds for a few days. A 7am surf trip departs daily for a three- to four-hour session ($65 per person, minimum of two people) to the Mamanuca surf breaks.

Transfers to/from Nadi cost $60, and the Nadi–Sigatoka bus ($2.40, three per day) runs via Seashell and drops off at the door.

❶ Getting There & Away

Airport transfers by resort minibus are $30 per person each way (minimum charge $60) and taxis cost about the same. **Dominion Transport** buses leave Nadi Bus Station for Momi Bay at 8am, 12.30pm, 2.30pm and 4pm and cost $2.40. Buses drop off at the door, but do not operate on Sundays.

Robinson Crusoe Island

The **Robinson Crusoe Island Resort** (Map p48; ☑628 1999; www.robinsoncrusoeislandfiji. com; dm $39-45, bure $79-150, lodge $189; ☒) covers all of this small, coral island. Fringed by gorgeous white sand, it's moved away from its former backpacker party-island image, and the upgraded accommodation reflects this shift. Small, simple *bure* and 'lodges' – very smart, light and airy stand-alone rooms with private bathrooms – had a facelift in 2011 and dorms were about to go under the knife when we visited. The bucket-showers in the shared bathrooms remain a source of entertainment and/or frustration.

Popular day tours three times a week are the resort's backbone. The entertainment program is intense and some will undoubtedly find it a little tacky – your boat is 'attacked by cannibals' on your arrival. On the days when day trippers visit (Tuesday, Thursday and Sunday, adult/child $149/75 including Nadi and Coral Coast transfers), the entertainment ramps up to overdrive and before long you'll find yourself singing, dancing, coconut-cracking and *bula*-ing to your heart's content. Kids, old and young, love it. Buffet meals are served in a large horseshoe-shaped shelter surrounding a sandy central area used for performances.

The run-off from the mainland has killed much of the coral and consequently the snorkelling isn't particularly good. If you are keen to see more spectacular marine life, suit up with **Reef Safari** (www.reefsafari.com. fj), who run the dive concession here (one-/two-tank dives $120/225).

Getting stranded on Crusoe outside of day tour days involves a bus/boat return-transfer from Nadi operated by the resort ($99).

Natadola Beach

Gorgeous Natadola Beach is Viti Levu's best. Its vast bank of white sand slides into a cobalt sea, which provides good **swimming** regardless of the tide. Natadola's strong currents often defy the brochures though: instead of glassy, still conditions, you may find sufficient chop for good **body surfing** – just watch the undertows. And there's serious **surfing** here too. Natadola Inside break – which is inside the bay (surprise) – is good for beginners, and Natadola Outside – at the entrance of the channel – is for experienced surfers.

Local villagers tie up their horses under the trees near the car park and pounce on tourists as soon as they arrive. They are fairly persistent and you'll shock them if you don't want a **horse ride** – a gentle 45-minutes or so along the beach costs about $25. Graduating from the same school of high-pressure sales tactics are the coconut and seashell sellers. They're great if you want coconuts or shells but tiring if you don't.

🛏 Sleeping & Eating

Natadola Beach Resort RESORT $$
(Map p48; ☑672 1001; www.natadola.com; ste $195; ☒) This intimate resort has only 11 suites in two blocks and, since there are no children under 16 allowed, it's ideal for travellers wanting some adult time. The resort was built in the faux-Spanish colonial style popular a few years back and has a certain *casa del Fiji* charm about it. Each suite has a spacious bathroom, small private courtyard and tiled interior. The pool meanders through tropical gardens and is long enough to do laps, with plenty of poolside shade for those wishing to snooze. When all that R&R gets too much, grab a boogie board and cross the road to the beach.

The **restaurant/bar** (mains $38-50, lunches $17-20) offers tasty food with small, no-frills servings, is open to nonguests and is a popular stop for day trippers. The resort is bang next door to the InterContinental and is a great overnight option for guests attending (the many) weddings held there, but unable or unwilling to pay the elevated prices. It's perfectly located for strolling over for a sunset cocktail or special dinner.

Yatule Beach Resort APARTMENT **$$**
(Map p48; ☑672 8004; reservation@yatuleresort.com.fj; villas $200-$320, f villa $530; ➌❄@) The thatched roofs of the self-contained *bure* make this small resort look like a Fijian village. Originally built to house the bigwigs involved in the building of the InterContinental, it now offers some excellent beachside accommodation. All the villas have minikitchens, bedrooms and separate lounges. The family villa has four separate bedrooms and is ideal for teenage kids who need privacy. External walls, signs and public areas could do with some TLC but the location is hard to beat.

InterContinental Resort Fiji RESORT **$$$**
(Map p48; www.intercontinental.com; r from $720; ➌❄❀☲) This mammoth resort, a conglomeration of slate-grey buildings somewhat at odds with the tropical land- and seascape, occupies a prime piece of real estate on the beach. The 271 rooms and 91 suites are beautifully appointed and equipped, with spa baths on each balcony. We noticed that block 13 manages to squeeze in an ocean view for garden view rates. The three indoor/outdoor restaurants all offer sunset views along with an occasional howling trade wind, and the attached 18-hole golf course is spruiked as the finest in the southern hemisphere – a sentiment echoed by golfers we met who'd played it.

❶ Getting There & Away

Natadola Beach is fairly isolated and most people visit as part of a day tour from Nadi or the Coral Coast. **The Coral Coast Scenic Railway** is a particularly nice way to arrive. For those with a rental car, turn off the Queens Road onto Maro Rd 36km from Nadi. The road is mostly sealed though the last few kilometres on the old Queens Road are slow, pot-holed going – the beach is signposted. For adventurous drivers, a shortcut involves following the main sealed access-road into the InterContinental and, about 200m before the lobby entrance, turning right onto a well-defined track that cuts over the hill and down to the beach. (It's not a designated road though, so rental cars beware: insurance won't cover any prangs.)

Those with energy could walk here in about 3½ hours by following the track from Yanuca. Catch the train or bus back.

Paradise Transport buses head to Natadola from Sigatoka ($3, one hour, four daily on weekdays). Otherwise catch any bus, ask to be let off at the Maro Rd junction and catch a taxi from there ($7). A taxi costs $75 each way from Nadi.

LOOKING UPWARDS...

...as well as outwards. If you're lucky, you'll see the angular silhouette of a frigatebird, one of the ocean's great airborne wanderers and a resident of this coastline. Its almost two-metre wingspan is unmistakeable as it rides high and cruises the thermals.

And if you're even luckier, you'll see a frigate harassing a gannet in an aerial chase. This results in an exhausted gannet regurgitating its just-caught fish which the frigate then promptly swoops in and swallows. Fast food indeed.

Yanuca & Around

Past the turn-off to Natadola, the Queens Road continues southeast, winding through hills and down to the coast at Cuvu Bay and Yanuca, about 50km from Nadi. Yanuca itself is a blink of a village, but it's home to a couple of good attractions.

◉ Sights & Activities

Coral Coast Scenic Railway SCENIC RAILWAY
(Map p48; ☑652 0434; Queens Rd) The station for the railway is at the causeway entrance to Shangri-La's Fijian Resort. It offers scenic rides along the coast in an old diesel sugar train, past villages, forests and sugar plantations, to beautiful Natadola Beach. The railway was once used for transporting cane and passengers to the Lautoka Mill. The 14km trip takes about 1¼ hours, leaving at 10am on Monday, Wednesday and Friday and returning at 4pm (adult/child $92/46 including barbecue lunch). On Tuesday, Thursday and Saturday, a Sigatoka shopping trip runs east and costs $46/23.

🛏 Sleeping

Namuka Bay Resort RESORT **$$**
(Map p48; ☑670 0243; www.namukabayresort.com; dm incl meals $95, villa $200) These eight, roomy beachfront villas, each comprising two guest rooms with a shared verandah, are tucked 6km down a side-road. It's *very* bumpy, but OK for all vehicles in good weather. The resort fronts a lagoon and 2km of beach, with a historic (deserted) village site on the hill behind and a cave walk just along the coast. It's very secluded and you'd want good weather – or a good supply of

books – to fully enjoy it. There's power for a few hours each evening though there are plans to bring mains electricity the extra mile required. The turn-off is about 5km from the Fijian on the Nadi side.

Gecko's Resort & Kalevu Cultural Centre RESORT $$
(Map p48; ☑652 0200; www.fijiculturalcentre.com; r/f $130/250; ☻✲@✖) Directly opposite the scenic railway station, this resort has 35 new, simple-but-nice-and-roomy hotel rooms. Several have interconnecting doors and convert to family rooms. The **restaurant** (mains $25-50) is recommended and is often busy with dining escapees from the Shangri-La. The complimentary South Pacific dance show on Friday and Sunday evenings is popular. In the landscaped grounds is a purpose-built cultural centre showcasing a collection of traditionally built huts and *bure*, pottery, *masi* and carvings (one-hour guided tour $20 per person between 9.30am and 4pm).

Shangri-La's Fijian Resort RESORT $$$
(The Fijian; Map p48; ☑652 0155; www.shangri-la.com; r incl breakfast from $490; ☻✲@✖) Anchored offshore on its own private island, this resort is one of the Coral Coast's premier (and biggest) hotels. Linked to the mainland by a causeway, the 442 rooms come in a variety of configurations and packages. While mum and dad nip off for a round of golf (nine holes $35) or toddle down to one of the Fijian's swanky day spas or the adults-only pool, they can (lovingly) shunt junior into the child-care centre. If you like big resorts and armies of squealing kids don't daunt you, you'll enjoy the three swimming pools, excellent restaurants, tennis courts and – possibly – even the lovely wedding chapel.

❶ Getting There & Away

The Fijian and surrounds are about a 45-minute drive from Nadi and 11km west of Sigatoka. There are regular express buses, minibuses and carriers travelling along the Queens Road. A taxi to Nadi International Airport is about $75 and the **Coral Sun Fiji** (☑672 3105; www.coralsunfiji.com) coach costs $13.

CORAL COAST

A wide bank of coral offshore gives this stretch of coast between Korotogo and Pacific Harbour its name. Flanked by waves of richly vegetated hills and a fringing reef that drops off dramatically into the deep blue of the South Pacific Ocean, it's the most scenic slice of the Queens Road and resorts of all standards exploit the views. That said, the Coral Coast's beaches are poor cousins to those on Fiji's smaller islands and most swimming is done in hotel pools. Many travellers prefer to focus on inland and other highlights, such as the Sigatoka Sand Dunes, Tavuni Hill Fort, Sigatoka Valley and, near Pacific Harbour, river trips in the Namosi Highlands and diving in the Beqa Lagoon. Lounging in a resort is also a prime pursuit in these parts.

Much of the coast experiences tidal fluctuations that leave a lot of the reef exposed for long lengths of time and (except for some lagoons) it is only possible to swim and snorkel at high tide. Sovi Bay, 2.5km east of Korotogo, is one of the better swimming beaches, but be wary of strong channel currents. The photos you've seen of white, sandy Fijian beaches are unlikely to have been taken along the Coral Coast.

Sigatoka
POP 9500

Sigatoka (sing-a-*to*-ka) is the largest town on the Coral Coast and serves as the commercial hub for the farming communities that grow sugar cane and vegetables upriver in the fertile swathe of the Sigatoka Valley.

Because of its pretty riverside location and accessibility, Sigatoka is a popular day trip from Nadi and the nearby Coral Coast resorts. There is a bustling produce market in the heart of town, a few souvenir shops, a large mosque and a fantasy-style, privately owned mansion overlooking the lot. The Sigatoka River, the second largest in Fiji, flows along the eastern edge of town. If you find your enthusiasm for souvenirs exhausted, stroll across the smaller of the two bridges (the one damaged in a 1994 hurricane) to see if you can spot the shark god, Dakuwaqa, swimming in the murky waters beneath.

Sigatoka's major draws – the sand dunes (p76), surfing (p76) and the Tavuni Hill Fort (p78) – are all a few kilometres out of town, but are easily reached by a short taxi ride.

Sigatoka doesn't offer any outstanding accommodation options, though a few grubby hotel rooms can be found if you go looking.

Sigatoka

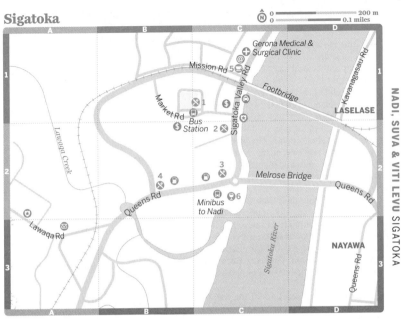

You're better off heading to nearby Korotogo for a bed (p78).

☞ Tours

Adventures in Paradise TOUR
(☑652 0833; www.adventuresinparadisefiji.com; tours per person incl Coral Coast/Nadi hotel transfers $99/119, child 5-12yr half-price) Offers day trips to the Naihehe Cave (p78) on Tuesdays, Thursdays and Saturdays. Lunch and a *bili-bili* (bamboo raft) ride downstream are included – children love it. The Savu Na Mate Laya Waterfall tour leaves Mondays, Wednesdays and Fridays and involves non-strenuous walking to a waterfall-fed swimming hole.

Coastal Inland Tours TOUR
(☑650 1161, 961 8164) A smaller-scale local tour operator, which offers a variety of half-day trips based around the Sigatoka River and nearby villages.

Sigatoka River Safari TOUR
(☑650 1721; www.sigatokariver.com; jet-boat tours per person incl Coral Coast/Nadi hotel transfers $245/265, child 4-15yr $120/130) These popular half-day jet-boating trips include a 45km whirl up the Sigatoka River, a village visit and lunch.

Sigatoka

⊗ Eating
Go Cools Hot Snax	(see 1)
1 Market	C1
2 Morris Hedstrom Supermarket	C2
3 Outback Café	C2
4 Vilisite's Seafood Restaurant	B2

⊖ Drinking
5 Cuppa Bula	C1
6 True Blue Hotel & Restaurant	C2

✖ Eating & Drinking

There's no great foody experience to be had in Sigatoka, but a couple of places are recommended if you find yourself hungry in town.

Vilisite's Seafood Restaurant SEAFOOD **$$**
(Queens Rd; mains $15-20; ⊙lunch & dinner) A long-time local favourite, Vilisite's is still going strong. Picture a tatty tropicana restaurant from the late '70s with faded polyester *lei* and dusty bamboo ceilings and you'll have an idea of what to expect. There are Chinese and curry options on the menu, but everyone recommends seafood (three-course set

menus from $30), followed by an ice-cream cone from the shack outside.

True Blue Hotel & Restaurant and Sigatoka Club
BAR

The draw at this local hangout is its elevated position and lovely views from the cavernous, dancehall-like restaurant and balcony along the mangrove-lined Sigatoka River. The downstairs club has pool-tables and likely a bunch of laconic Sigatokans happy to match you shot for shot. The place is very informal. 'We don't get many visitors from the resorts,' we were told jokingly, 'but when we do, we expect 'em to wear shoes'.

Coffee fiends will find that **Cuppa Bula** makes a decent flat white and vegetarians will find less-than-no-frills but very cheap pure vegetarian food at **Go Cools Hot Snax** (lunch $3.50) at the edge of the market beyond the bus station. **Outback Café** near the main bridge is good for beer and snacks (and cheap internet).

Self-caterers can stock up at the **market** and at **Morris Hedstrom Supermarket** or one of the other many supermarkets in town.

ℹ Information

Westpac and ANZ have banks in town.

Gerona Medical & Surgical Clinic (☑652 0128; Sigatoka Valley Rd; ☺8.30am-1pm, 2-4pm & 7-8pm Mon-Fri, 8.30am-1pm Sat)

T-Wicks Internet Café (☑652 0505; 50 Sigatoka Valley Rd; per hr $2) There's fast connection here. You can burn CDs and DVDs for $2 and $3 respectively.

ℹ Getting There & Around

In addition to a multitude of slower, local buses, **Pacific Transport** (☑650 0088) and **Sunbeam Transport** (www.sunbeamfiji.com) run several express buses a day between Nadi and Sigatoka ($5, 1¼ hours) and between Sigatoka and Suva ($9, three hours) via Pacific Harbour ($6, two hours).

Carriers, minibuses and taxis ply the same Queens Road route. Minibuses will take you to Nadi for $7, Suva for $11 or Pacific Harbour for $7; taxis cost about $70 to Nadi, $120 to Suva or $90 to Pacific Harbour.

Around Sigatoka

SIGATOKA SAND DUNES

One of Fiji's natural highlights, these impressive **dunes** (adult/child/family $10/5/25, child under 6yr free; ☺8am-4.30pm) are a ripple of peppery monoliths skirting the shoreline near the mouth of the Sigatoka River. Windblown and rugged, they stand 5km long, up to 1km wide and on average about 20m high, but rise to about 60m at the western end. Do not expect golden Sahara-like dunes: the fine sand is a grey-brown colour and largely covered with vines and shrubs. The dunes have been forming over millions of years as sediments brought down by the Sigatoka River are washed ashore by the surf and blown into dunes by the prevailing winds. A mahogany forest was planted in the 1960s to halt the dunes' expedition onto the Queens Road and the state-owned part of the area was declared Fiji's first national park in 1989.

Since the coastal margin of the dunes is largely unstable, human bones and early pottery are sometimes exposed and, in many cases, destroyed by slipping slope-faces and eroding winds. Archaeological excavations here have uncovered pottery more than 2600 years old and one of the largest burial sites in the Pacific. The visitor centre houses a few pottery shards and ceramic pots from some of these excavations, along with helpful and enthusiastic staff.

Park access is 4.5km southwest of Sigatoka on the Queens Road. Stick to the designated trails and allow one or two hours for the short or long self-guided walking tours respectively. And if by chance you do come across a thighbone jutting from the sand, know that you'll be cursed forever if you attempt to remove it.

Most buses (excluding express services) travelling between Nadi and Sigatoka can drop you right outside the visitors centre on the main highway. A taxi from Sigatoka town costs $5.

KULUKULU

Viti Levu's premier surfing spot and the country's only beach break can be found in the Kulukulu area between the Sigatoka Sand Dunes National Park and Maunivanua Point at the mouth of the Sigatoka River. Most other areas have fringing reefs but here the fresh water has prevented its formation and the waves break over a large, submerged rock platform covered in sand.

However, surfers should be aware that after heavy rains the murky water flowing from the river mouth can run at about 10 to 15 knots. This creates strong currents and undertows laden with floating logs, coconuts and debris. On top of all that, the place

Around Sigatoka & Korotogo

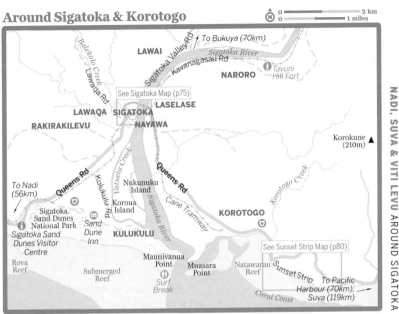

is sharky and a local surfer had his hand badly bitten while surfing here in 2006.

The only place to stay near the beach is **Sand Dune Inn** (☑650 0550; sites per tent $10, dm $29; meals $6-10). It's tatty and basic, sometimes busy with local school camps alongside occasional surfers, and is run by the cheery Mere.

Local buses and minivans run daily between Sigatoka and Kulukulu ($1). A taxi costs about $7.

LOWER SIGATOKA VALLEY

The Sigatoka River's tributaries originate as far away as Tomanivi (Mt Victoria) and the Monasavu Dam. The river has long provided a line of communication between mountain peoples and coast dwellers. Almost 200 archaeological, cultural or historically significant sites have been found in and around the valley, but many are being taken over by farms or housing.

This fertile river valley is known as Fiji's 'salad bowl'. Cereals, vegetables, fruits, peanuts and sugar cane are grown here, mostly on small-scale farms. Much of the produce ends up at the municipal markets, and vegetables such as eggplant, chilli and okra, and root crops such as *dalo* (taro), *tavioka* (cassava) and yams are exported to Canada, Aus-

tralia, New Zealand and the USA. It's overlooked by a wind farm on the horizon, and when we visited in 2011 a major (and much-needed) road upgrade was underway. In the meantime, it's slow-going and pot-holed, but OK for all vehicles in good weather.

Two valley villages are known for their pottery: **Lawai** and **Nakabuta**. Both welcome visitors, who are encouraged to give a community donation of around $5 per person to look around. None of the pots are made using machines or even a potter's wheel. Instead, local sand and clay is mixed together using the heel of the foot and the somewhat uneven pots are then formed by hand. These are sun dried and fired in open fires, along with other small items, such as pottery pigs and *bure*, which are sold by individual families.

ⓘ Getting There & Around

Valley Comfort buses travel up the Sigatoka Valley on the western side of the river to Naduri, and pass Lawai and Nakabuta ($1, one every one to two hours, less frequently at weekends). Lawai is about 2.5km north of Sigatoka. Nakabuta is twice as far ($5 by taxi or a 10-minute drive).

It is possible to catch a 9am bus to Keiyasi village (55km upriver, 2 hrs) and to catch a return bus at 3pm ($6.45 one way, Mon-Sat). An encouragingly honest bus driver told us that the 1230 bus is the most reliable though, since the bus is often out of service. Later afternoon buses overnight in Keiyasi. Take your toothbrush and be prepared for the unexpected.

UPPER SIGATOKA VALLEY

The Naihehe cave (Map p48), about an hour's drive upriver from Sigatoka, was once used as an underground fortress by hill tribes and has the remains of a ritual platform and cannibal oven. The large cathedral-like chamber is quite impressive with its stalactites, flowstones and underground springs. Adventures in Paradise (p78) offers guided tours of the area. Intrepid can drive up Sigatoka Valley Rd to Sautabu village and ask the headman to delegate a villager to take them across the river to the cave.

Closer to town, the remnants of Tavuni Hill Fort (Map p77; adult/child $12/6; ⊘8am-5pm Mon-Sat) provide an excellent insight into the strong precolonial links between Tonga and Fiji. Although there are many forts like it scattered all over Fiji, this is the most accessible for visitors. Built in the 18th century by Tongan chief Maile Latumai, this fort was a defensive site used in times of war and is one of Fiji's most interesting historical sights.

The eldest son of a king, Maile Latumai fled Tonga to escape a dispute during an era of political and social upheaval. He and his entourage of servants sailed all the way in a double-hulled canoe and arrived in the Sigatoka area around 1788. They originally set up in Korotogo (originally Koro-Tonga or 'village/ gathering of Tonga') but were kept on the move by constant tribal warfare. Eventually, the local tribes accepted the newcomers and the chief was given some land and a local wife.

The steep 90m-high limestone ridge at the edge of a bend in the Sigatoka River was an obvious strategic location for a fortification. From this position, the surrounding area could easily be surveyed, both upstream and downstream, and the views are spectacular. Substantial earthworks were carried out to form *yavu* (bases for houses) and terraces for barricade fencing. There are also a number of grave sites, a *rara* (ceremonial ground) and a *vatu ni bokola* (head-chopping stone), as well as some beautiful curtain figs and an *ivi* (Polynesian chestnut tree) on the site.

The information centre here was set up in a combined effort between the Ministry of Tourism and the people of Naroro, and received funding from the EU. After some local management ups and downs, the under-maintained site was once again in the hands of capable and enthusiastic village guides when we visited.

The fort is about 4km northeast of Sigatoka on the eastern side of the river, above Naroro village. Occasional local carriers make the trip past the entrance gate but most visitors drive themselves or hire a taxi to wait while they visit.

Korotogo & Around

The start of the Coral Coast begins in earnest at this condensed group of hotels flanking the water on Sunset Strip. Korotogo is the best area to lodge when exploring the sights around Sigatoka. Korotogo itself is a small village, but travellers will find themselves outside of its confines. At high tide, the lagoon is swimmable and at low tide, you can take a decent-length walk on the beach and poke around in rock pools on the exposed coral shelf.

⊙ Sights & Activities

Kula Eco Park WILDLIFE RESERVE
(Map p80; ✆650 0505; www.fijiwild.com; adult/child $25/12.50; ⊘10am-4pm) This wildlife sanctuary is a must for fans of the furred, feathered and scaled. The park is supported by the National Trust for Fiji and several international parks and conservation bodies, and showcases some magnificent wildlife. This includes hawksbill sea turtles (hand-fed at 11am, 1pm and 3.30pm daily); Fiji's only native land mammal, the Fijian flying fox; and an aviary full of quarrelsome kula parrots, Fiji's national bird and the park's namesake.

The park has come a long way since 1997 and today it runs invaluable breeding programs, with success stories for the Pacific black duck (Fiji's only remaining duck species) and the crested and banded iguana.

Ambling down the wooden walkways, reading the labels on the native plants and poking in and out of the walk-through aviaries is a lot of fun (and less confronting than viewing the owls and raptors in their small individual cages). The park is 100% funded by gate receipts and donations. There's also decent wheelchair access.

🛏 Sleeping

Sandy Point Beach Cottages CABIN $
(Map p80; ✆650 0125; www.sandypointfiji.com; s/d/f $100/120/160; ☀) Five beachside fully self-contained cottages built in the style of roomy Kiwi *baches* (holiday homes) from

CANNIBALISM

Archaeological evidence from food-waste middens shows that cannibalism was practised in Viti Levu from around 500 BC until the mid- to late 19th century, during which time it had become an ordinary, ritualised part of life. In a society founded on ancestor worship and belief in the afterlife, cannibalising an enemy was considered the ultimate revenge. A disrespectful death was a lasting insult to the enemy's family.

Bodies were consumed either on the battlefield or brought back to the village spirit house and offered to the local war god. They were then butchered, baked and eaten on the god's behalf. The triumph was celebrated with music and dance. Men performed the *cibi* (death dance) and women the *dele* or *wate* (an obscene dance in which they sexually humiliated corpses and captives). Torture of captives included being thrown alive into ovens, being bled or dismembered and being forced to watch their own body parts being consumed or eat some themselves.

Mementoes of the kill were kept to prolong the victor's sense of vengeance. Necklaces, hairpins or ear-lobe ornaments were made from human bones, and the skull of a hated enemy was sometimes made into a *tanoa* (kava drinking bowl). Meat was smoked and preserved for snacks, and war clubs were inlaid with teeth or marked with tally notches. To record a triumph in war, the highlanders of Viti Levu placed the bones of victims in branches of trees outside their spirit houses and men's houses as trophies. The coastal dwellers had a practical use for the bones: leg bones were used to make sail needles and thatching knives. Sexual organs and foetuses were suspended in trees. Rows of stones were also used to tally the number of bodies eaten by the chief.

The growing influence of Christianity had a great impact on cannibalism and the practice began to wane in the mid-1800s. By all accounts, it had ended by the turn of the century. Western fascination with the gruesome practice has remained alive and well, however. Original artefacts can be seen in the Fiji Museum in Suva, and souvenir cannibal forks are sold in abundant quantities everywhere. Traditionally, chiefs used these because it was forbidden for human flesh to touch their lips. Considered sacred relics, these forks were kept in the spirit house and were not to be touched by women or children. Today, it would appear, they make interesting wall features.

the '60s. They're quiet, low-key and perfect for independent self-caterers. A rental car is a good idea if you're staying for more than a couple of days. Owner Bob Kennedy is a communications nut and satellite dishes hidden in the grounds provide an interesting array of TV channels.

Bedarra Beach Inn
INN $$

(Map p80; ✆650 0476; www.bedarrafiji.com; Sunset Strip; r $167-180; ✹✵) This modern hotel is a gem. It offers spacious, spotlessly clean rooms with tiled floors and plenty of natural light, most of which have ocean views. There's a good balance between resort-style comfort and do-it-yourself practicality. Everyone who stays here seems to rave about it and most guests are returning Australians. The bar is uniquely designed so that social types can face each other as they sip cocktails, and wi-fi is (erratically) available in most rooms.

New Crow's Nest Resort
RESORT $

(Map p80; ✆650 0230; www.crowsnestfiji.com; Sunset Strip; r $135-145; ✹✵@✵) Nautical

terms abound at these split-level timber bungalows. Each has a lovely balcony and ocean views, and they're in good nick and are good value. The slightly more expensive rooms are self-contained, but all can accommodate a family of four (kids stay free). The **restaurant** (mains $17-25) faces the hillside pool and has a cosmopolitan menu.

Tubakula Beach Bungalows
RESORT $

(Map p80; ✆650 0097; www.fiji4less.com/tuba. html; dm $26, s/tw $58/63, ste $115-164; ✵✵) If it weren't for the palm trees, swimming pool and waterfront setting, this low-key resort would be right at home in the mountains. Simple dorms, singles and twins have shared facilities. The excellent A-frame chalets have strapping timber frames, modern kitchens and verandahs with slouchy wooden seats. It's perfect for self-driving, self-catering, self-sufficient types wishing to escape the crowds. It's right on the beach and free snorkel equipment is available. Though the menu

Sunset Strip

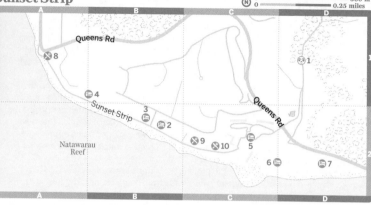

N 0 — 500 m
0 — 0.25 miles

Sunset Strip

is limited, the **restaurant** (mains $10-20; ☺breakfast & dinner) is good value.

TOP CHOICE **Outrigger on the Lagoon** RESORT $$$
(☎650 0044; www.outrigger.com/fiji; r from $567, bure from $990; ☺✳@☀⚐) The 7m outrigger canoe suspended from the ceiling in the main lobby and the stunning balcony views create a powerful first impression at this much-touted resort. From the main building, an artificial stream meanders through lush gardens to a huge, lagoon-style pool. As this is the only pool, it can get noisy with excited kids and the pool loungers are in hot demand. The *bure*, with their high, hand-painted *masi* ceilings, are fabulous, as is the day spa with its superb hilltop location. There's a kids club and children eat for free (depending on which package you have). The Fijian fire-walking show every Tuesday night is fun (per person $18, nonguests welcome). **Dive Away Fiji** runs the dive shop here.

Casablanca Hotel APARTMENT $
(☎652 0600; Casablanca@connect.com.fj; Sunset Strip; s/d $55/65; ☀) This mock-Moroccan mansion offers eight self-contained rooms that are cheap, cheerful and look like they were decorated with furniture picked up at a garage sale. All have fantastic views.

✗ Eating

All restaurants on Sunset Strip are beachfront.

Le Café BISTRO $$
(☎652 0877; Sunset Strip; mains $10-25; ☺breakfast, lunch & dinner) Just west of the shops, pretty Le Café has a Swiss chef who cooks European-style food – tasty pastas and pizzas are the speciality. There's also a daily happy hour from 5pm to 8pm.

**Ocean Terrace Restaurant &
Ebb Tide Cafe** INTERNATIONAL $$$
(☎650 0476; Sunset Strip; mains $25-35; ☺breakfast, lunch & dinner) Slightly pricier than its neighbours and boasting a breezy dining area overlooking the ocean, the food outlets at the Bedarra Inn often lure guests from the Outrigger. It's a great place to try some creative Fijian fusion dishes like *ika vakalolo* (fish poached in coconut milk) served with cassava, but for the less adventurous there's steak, pizza and curries. Light meals and a children's menu are also available.

Mayshaars Cuisine FAST FOOD $
(Johnny's, Beachside Restaurant, Ice Bar; Sunset
Strip; mains $8-18; ⊙lunch & dinner) This place
may have changed its name more times than
its cooking oil, but the food here is still OK.
Diners take their seats on picnic tables in
front of a small supermarket with an outdoor pool table. While the setting is utterly
unsophisticated, you name it, they've got it –
Chinese, Fijian, Italian and Western.

Koko's Café CAFE $$
(Sunset Strip; mains $10-20; ⊙breakfast, lunch & din-
ner) Good coffee and a decent steak sandwich
are among the things on offer at this low-key
cafe, newly opened when we visited. A liquor
licence was pending; in the meantime BYO.

❶ Getting There & Around

Pacific Transport and **Sunbeam Transport**
(www.sunbeamfiji.com) run regular buses along
the Queens Road, stopping at resorts along the
way (about $5 from Nadi, 1½ hours). **Coral Sun
Fiji** (www.coralsunfiji.com) has air-conditioned
coaches that also stop outside resorts ($13 from
Nadi, 1½ hours). The cheapest way from Koro-
togo to Sigatoka is to walk to the roundabout and
catch a local bus for $1. A taxi is $6 to Sigatoka
and around $70 to Nadi.

Korolevu & Around

Further east, the section of the Queens Road
between Korotogo and Korolevu is the most
beautiful. The road winds along the shore,
affording views of scenic bays, beaches, coral
reefs and mountains. Photo opportunities
beg around every bend: it's an especially
spectacular trip at sunrise or sunset. A good
range of accommodation peppers the coast,
each pocketed within its own private cove.

East of Korolevu, the Queens Road turns
away from the shore and climbs over the
southern end of Viti Levu's dividing moun-
tain range. To the east of this range the road
improves and the scenery changes to lush
rainforest as the road winds its way past
wider bays.

🏃 Activities

Besides slumming it at the beach, the most
popular activities are **snorkelling** and **div-
ing**. Resorts ferry guests to and from the
outer reefs daily for close encounters of the
marine kind.

This area is also well served by the tour
companies at Sigatoka (p75) and Pacific Har-
bour (p85), which all pick up from the ho-

tels. **Savu Na Mate Laya Waterfall** is 2.5km
inland from the turn-off to **Biausevu** village,
a 15-minute drive east of Hideaway Resort.
The waterfall is an easy 30-minute walk
from the village. Make sure you read about
village etiquette (p221) before arriving.

Diving
The Korolevu stretch of coast offers some
spectacular diving within close distance of
the shore. Some notable sites include Won-
derwall, with its 'snowdrift' of white soft cor-
als, and, for the experienced, the Gunbarrel,
an adrenalin-laced dive riding a strong cur-
rent through a narrow gorge amid schools
of snapper and surgeon fish. Most dives are
conveniently close to shore.

Dive Away Fiji DIVING
(☑652 0100; www.diveaway-fiji.com) Runs the
dive shops at the Beachhouse, Outrigger (on
the Sunset Strip), Hideaway and Mango Bay
resorts. Most guests are ferried to Hideaway
or Mango Bay from where the dive boats de-
part. A two-tank dive costs $180 plus $30 per
day for gear and the PADI Open Water Course
costs $825 at the upmarket resorts, but guests
at Mango Bay and the Beachhouse get the
same things a little cheaper ($160 and $775).

South Pacific Adventure Divers DIVING
(☑653 0555 ext 609; www.spadfiji.com) Dive op-
erators for the Warwick and Naviti resorts
but, like Dive Away, they'll collect from other
nearby hotels. A two-tank dive costs $190.

Fishing
Sport Fishing Fiji FISHING
(Tropical Fishing; ☑653 0069; www.sportfishingfiji.
com) Based at Mango Bay Resort, this outfit
runs three-quarter-day ($1080) and full-day
($1440) game-fishing charters on an 8.5m
boat. The boat can accommodate five anglers
at a time and drinks, lunch and all equip-
ment are provided. Danny and his crew won
the Fiji 2004 International Game Fishing
Championship and know these waters well.

🛏 Sleeping

Accommodation options here are listed
geographically, from west to east along the
20km or so stretch of coast around Korolevu.

Tambua Sands Beach Resort RESORT $$$
(☑650 0399; www.warwicktabuasands.com; ✉)
Tambua Sands is smeared across a pretty
slice of coast and keeps its guest busy with
village tours, reef-walking excursions and a
tour desk. The manicured lawns are littered

with sun loungers. This friendly resort was taken over by the Warwick Hotel group in 2011 and is going steadily upmarket. By the time you read this, each *bure* should have been rebuilt and will have an individual plunge pool. We saw one completed and it was very stylish – check the website for progress. In the meantime expect good rates to compensate for construction noise; once renovation is complete, anticipate a room rate of several hundred dollars per night.

Hideaway Resort   RESORT $$$
(☑650 0177; www.hideawayfiji.com; r $335-478; ☺✳@✷⊗) Since many of the neighbouring resorts have undergone recent renovations, the Hideaway looks a little tired by comparison and unless a package deal can offer substantial discounts on the rack rate listed here (which is possible – the place was chockers with groups when we visited), you may be better off elsewhere. Nonetheless, the water slide, free kids club and cruise-ship-like entertainment schedule prove popular with families. The manicured grounds include artificial sand alcoves and plenty of grassy sunbaking plots. The tiled restaurant is very noisy at meal times. **Dive Away Fiji** is based here.

Naviti Resort   RESORT $$$
(☑653 0444; www.navitiresort.com.fj; r incl breakfast $285-799; ☺✳@✷⊗) Heavy on the greenery and light on the concrete, the Naviti's 220 rooms have access to all the goodies – four restaurants, five bars, a nine-hole golf course, a swim-up bar, a health spa and a kids club. Unlike most resorts, all-inclusive packages include beer, wine, Sigatoka shopping excursions, a sunset cruise and a choice between à la carte or buffet dining. The two tiny islands offshore are used for weddings and there's an all-tide swimming lagoon to compensate for the poor beach.

Warwick Fiji Resort & Spa   RESORT $$$
(☑653 0555; www.warwickfiji.com; s & d incl breakfast $350-550, ste incl breakfast $740; ☺✳@⊗) Owned by the same crowd that own Naviti (there's a free shuttle between the two and guests can use both resorts' facilities), the Warwick is another feature-laden, activity-rich resort. The somewhat worn public areas feature tile, wooden floors, cane furniture and soft brown furnishings. There are five restaurants, seven bars (one of which has Middle Eastern water pipes) and lagoons with all-tide swimming areas. **South Pa-**

cific Adventure Divers is based here and at Naviti resort.

Beachhouse   HOSTEL $
(☑653 0500; www.fijibeachouse.com; sites per person/dm/d incl breakfast $25/40/119; ☺@⊗) Aimed squarely at backpackers, this long-time favourite combines simple digs with heady social activities in a winning formula. The dorms (including a women-only dorm) are in two-storey houses and the doubles are in colourful duplex bungalows. Buses will stop right outside and there's a pretty pool, a cheap cafe and on-site cooking facilities. Activities include horse riding ($25 per hour) and a recommended 'jungle trek' to the local waterfall ($10).

Namatakula Village Homestay   HOMESTAY $
(www.fijiibure.com/namatakula/index.htm; per adult/child incl meals $130/100) This village homestay is popular with Intrepid Travel groups and with good reason – it's the real deal. Expect basic accommodation, large meals and an excellent opportunity to see a traditional Fijian village firsthand.

Mango Bay Resort   HOSTEL $
(☑653 0069; www.mangobayresortfiji.com; dm incl breakfast $36, d incl breakfast $200, bure incl breakfast $280; ☺@⊗) The dorm, cabins and *bure* are scattered through parklike grounds. Facilities are far better than those found in your average backpackers: the dorms are modern and new, the *bure* have atrium showers and the beach is one of the best on the Coral Coast. Mango targets the 18- to 35-year-old set with plenty of activities of the full-moon-party and sunset-bonfire variety. Snorkelling and diving are with **Dive Away Fiji**, and game fishing can be arranged through **Sport Fishing Fiji**.

Crusoe's Retreat   RESORT $$
(☑650 0185; www.crusoesretreat.com; r incl breakfast from $235; @⊗) Crusoe's may lack the polish of the larger resorts, but its sublime location – hidden down the same dirt track as the Wellesley and boasting a white coral beach – makes up for its slightly tired air. Many of the 28 spacious and fan-cooled *bure* are located on a hillside and the stairs are not ideal for older guests. The pool is small but the **restaurant** (mains $15-25) serves classy fare. **Dive Crusoes** (www.divecrusoes.com) charges $246 for a two-tank dive and $784 for a PADI Open Water Course. Hotel transfers from Nadi International Airport are $130 per person return or about $155 by taxi.

TOP CHOICE / Wellesley Resort
RESORT **$$**

(☑603 0664; www.wellesleyresort.com.fj; Man Friday Rd; d incl breakfast from $179; ❄✳@⛱) Offering top-end style at midrange prices, this adults-only resort oozes comfort, style and tranquillity. The 15 suites saddle a small valley that leads to a pretty cove and even the most ardent adrenalin junkies will soon rediscover their inner sloth. If they don't, they may find this place a little isolated without a rental car (even though tours are available) as it's 4.5km down a dirt road.

TOP CHOICE / Waidroka Surf & Dive Resort
RESORT **$$**

(☑330 4605; www.waidroka.com; r $210, bure $270-330; @⛱) Over a hilly 4.5km of dirt road, Waidroka caters to serious surfers and divers looking for an upmarket alternative to the Yanuca island surf camps. Check out the variety of combined packages on their website. There's a small flotilla of boats on hand to take guests to local breaks ($65, nonguests $75) and Frigate Passage (p88; $90, nonguests $100). The resort crew are skilled at finding the best waves and run the only dive operation to Frigate Walls (p85; two-tank dive $195-235, PADI Open Water Course $775). Non-surfing/diving partners are also well catered for with free snorkelling and kayaking, game fishing (from $250), shopping trips, beachside massages and an excellent restaurant (meal packages $95). Guests stay in either bright orange *bure* or the adjoining terrace rooms – both are very smart. Taxis from Nadi cost $155.

✗ Eating

Vilisite's Restaurant FISH & CHIPS **$$**
(☑650 1030; Queens Rd; mains $15-40; ⊙breakfast, lunch & dinner) If you have a Hawaiian shirt, you'll feel right at home, as this place drips tropical garb. With its sweeping ocean views, it's the nicest restaurant in the area outside of the flashy resorts – it's a couple of kilometres beyond the Naviti. There's Chinese, seafood curries and lobster on offer, but everyone seems to order the fish and chips. Apart from Vilisite's, the resort restaurants are the only eating options.

☆ Entertainment

Evening entertainment is heavily weighted towards the cultural. The Warwick has **fire-walking** on Mondays and Fridays and **Polynesian dancing** on Tuesdays ($45 with beach barbecue). The same fire-walkers also perform at the Naviti on Wednesdays and at the Hideaway on Thursdays (around $15 per person for each performance). Each resort has a **house band** with a repertoire ranging from alternately cheery or soulful Pacific numbers and pop cover versions at sunset to singalong/dance-along numbers later in the evening.

ⓘ Getting There & Around

There are plenty of buses shuttling along the Queens Road (getting to Suva or Nadi costs about $7) and drivers will pick up and drop off at resort gates. The Warwick and the Naviti have a free shuttle bus for guests to Nadi International Airport. A taxi to Sigatoka takes twenty minutes and costs around $10.

Pacific Harbour

Leaving the glorious vegetation and hilly passes of Korolevu in its wake, the Queens Road sweeps across a small bridge into Pacific Harbour, the self-labelled 'Adventure Capital of Fiji'. A range of unique activities, guaranteed to have hearts racing and knees knocking, backs up the claim.

Pacific Harbour began in the 1970s as a canal development. Once the surrounding swamps were drained, roads were laid, waterways were formed and holiday homes were built. The resulting wide culs-de-sac, manicured lawns and orderly river settings are more 'soccer dad and bridge parties' than Fijian. Although the large grassy blocks are brochure-perfect, many are still waiting to be filled by the anticipated boom. It is so at odds with the rest of Fiji that you may feel you've crossed some unseen line and dipped your toes into the twilight zone.

◎ Sights & Activities

Arts Village CULTURAL TOUR
(Map p84;☑345 0065; tours per adult/child from $66/33; ⊙9am-4pm Wed-Sat) This faux village is unashamedly 'Fiji in a theme park' and within its Disneylike confines are a temple, chiefly *bure,* a cooking area with utensils and a weaving hut. Fijian actors dressed in traditional costumes carry out mock battles, preach pagan religion and demonstrate traditional arts. Tours include an island boat tour (for the kids) and an island temple tour. There's also an arts village show and fire-walking. It's good fun for families, but a far cry from authentic village life.

Pacific Harbour

0 —————— 500 m
0 —————— 0.25 miles

River Dr
Qaraniqio River
Fairway Pl
9
4
To Zip Fiji (20km);
Suva (52km)
Hibiscus Dr
Great Harbour Dr
14
15
10
1
12
11
Queens Rd
Belo Circle
7
13
Atoll Pl
6 16
2
5
8
3
To Sigatoka
(79km)
Beqa
Passage
Deuba
Beach
Queens Rd

Pacific Harbour

◎ Sights
1 Arts Village..C2

✪ Activities, Courses & Tours
2 Aqua-Trek Beqa....................................B3
Beqa Adventure Divers.................(see 9)
3 Beqa Island Trips.................................B3
4 Pearl Championship Golf Course..........C1
5 Rivers Fiji...B3

🛏 Sleeping
6 Club Oceanus......................................B3
7 Nanette's Accommodation...................B2
8 Pearl South Pacific..............................C3
9 Studio 6 on the Lake...........................C1
10 Tsulu Backpackers & Apartments.......D2
11 Uprising Beach Resort.........................D2

✴ Eating
12 Baka Blues...C2
Mantarae Restaurant....................(see 8)
Oasis Restaurant............................(see 1)
13 Sakura House.......................................B2
14 Tiki Bar & Melting Pot Restaurant........C2
15 Water's Edge.......................................C2

🛍 Shopping
Arts Village Marketplace...............(see 1)

ℹ Information
16 Batiluva Beach Resort Booking
Office..B3
Rosie's Tours..................................(see 1)

🌿 **Beqa Island Trips**   BOAT TOUR
(📞345 0910; www.beqaislandtrips.com) Run
by the same professional mob as Beqa Adventure Divers, these day tours to Beqa
Lagoon offer a family-friendly beach BBQ/
swimming/snorkelling day at Yanuca island
(Thursday & Sunday, $190 per person) and
a *meke* (dance performance enacting stories
and legends), *lovo* lunch and snorkel in the

locally managed marine protected zone at
Lawaki Beach House on Beqa island (Tuesday & Saturday, $210 per person).

Diving

There are more than 20 dive sites near Pacific Harbour, mostly within **Beqa Lagoon**
and its fantastic soft coral sites. These include ET, which features a vast tunnel more

than 30m long, densely blanketed with sea fans and soft corals. But the main attraction here are the sharks – and we're not talking wimpy white-tips. Beqa Lagoon is one of the few places where it's possible to dive with massive, barrel-chested bull and tiger sharks without being caged or sedated (that's either the sharks or the divers); see the boxed text, p34, for further details about diving with sharks.

Other impressive dives include **Side Streets** (soft corals, coral heads and gorgonian fans), **Frigate Walls** (a 48m wall in Frigate Pass, with large pelagic fish), and **Caesar's Rocks** (coral heads and swim-throughs).

Aqua-Trek Beqa DIVING
(☎345 0324; www.aquatrek.com; Club Oceanus) The first of the shark diving companies. A two-tank dive costs $205, a two-tank shark-feeding dive is $245 and a PADI Open Water Course costs $780. The shark-feeding dives are available Mondays, Wednesdays, Fridays and Saturdays.

Beqa Adventure Divers DIVING
(☎345 0911; www.fiji-sharks.com; Studio 6 on the Lake) Has shark-feeding dives on Monday, Tuesday, Thursday, Friday and Saturday. A two-tank dive costs $210, a two-tank shark-feeding dive $245 and a PADI Open Water Course $720. Keen to be carbon-neutral, the company is offsetting its carbon footprint and that of its clients by supporting a major mangrove restoration programme.

Surfing & Swimming
There is world-class surfing at Frigate Passage but it's easiest accessed from the surf camp on Yanuca island or through Waidroka Surf & Dive Resort (p83) near Korolevu.

Pacific Harbour's main beach, **Deuba Beach**, is reasonable for swimming, but no match for the islands. The snorkelling 500m out from Uprising Beach Resort is surprisingly good.

Fishing & Boating
Pacific Harbour's reefs, shoals, bait schools, current lines and drop-offs are ideal for both trolling and popping. Wahu, mahi mahi, marlin and yellowfin tuna are all regularly caught.

Freedive Fiji FISHING
(☎973 0687; www.freedivefiji.com; half-day $225 per person) If spear- or game-fishing is your thing, this is the outfit for you. Charters too.

Fishing Charters & Pleasure Cruises BOATING
(☎345 0020; www.fcpcfiji.com) Lower-key and lower-priced than Freedive, this mob will take you on options including a gentle lake cruise (two hours from $130), an inland fishing trip (3 hours from $150) and a snorkelling/fishing combination (4 hours from $200).

Golf
Pearl Championship Golf Course GOLF
(☎345 0905; 9 holes with/without club hire $47/24) This golf course has more sand bunkers than some beaches. For those who get hot (and bothered), there's a swimming pool and clubhouse to soothe frayed nerves.

Ziplining
Zip Fiji ADVENTURE SPORTS
(Map p48; ☎930 0545; www.zip-fiji.com; ☺8am-8pm) This outfit lets squealing thrill-seekers whoosh from one platform to another in a series of eight aerial zip lines. The three-hour rainforest canopy tour costs $210 per adult.

Kila Eco Adventure Park ADVENTURE SPORTS
(Map p48; ☎331 7454; www.kilaworld.com; ☺10am-4.30pm) Offers thrills, spills and a few other rope-and-line walks for $199 per person.

🖝 Tours

Rivers Fiji ADVENTURE TOUR
(☎345 0147; www.riversfiji.com; Pearl South Pacific) Rivers offers excellent kayaking and white-water rafting trips into the Namosi Highlands (p87) north of Pacific Harbour. The day trip ($295 per person including lunch) to Wainikoroiluva (Luva Gorge) is highly recommended and the scenery alone is worth the bumpy two-hour carrier trip up to Nakavika village. After the obligatory kava session with the chief, you paddle downstream (four hours) by inflatable kayak over stretches of gentle rapids and past waterfalls to Namuamua village. Here, where the Wainikoroiluva River joins the Upper Navua River, the tour is completed with a motorised longboat ride.

For spectacular gorges and grade-two rapids, try the day trip to the Upper Navua River ($360 per person). It is more physically demanding and involves about five hours on the water. The one-hour road trip to Nabukelevu village is very scenic.

Jetski Tours ADVENTURE TOUR
(☎345 0933; www.jetski-safari.com; 158 Kaka Pl) Jetski Tours takes travellers on a four-hour, full-throttle, 60km jet-ski tour (solo rider $480, twin share $260 per person) around

Beqa Lagoon. Lunch, snorkelling gear, wetsuits and life jackets are included. Book at least a day in advance.

Based just out of town in Navua, but also working the Pacific Harbour hotels, is **Discover Fiji Tours** and **Namuamua Inland Tour** (p88), both of which offer tours into the Navua River area.

🛏 Sleeping

Nanette's Accommodation B&B $
(✐345 2041; www.nanettes.com.fj; 108 River Dr; r incl breakfast $150; ❋❋☎) This four-bedroom villa with swimming pool makes a terrific home-away-from-home. Rooms all have private bathrooms and are big, light and airy. The shared lounge and kitchen are comfortable and vibrantly decorated.

Uprising Beach Resort RESORT $
(✐345 2200; www.uprisingbeachresort.com; dm incl breakfast $38, bure incl breakfast $255-470, villa 375-510; ❋@☎) The Uprising continues to give other resorts a run for their money, recently raising the bar with 12 very swish villas to add to the 12 spacious *bure*. There are nifty outdoor showers (although the novelty of these wears thin if it rains) and bifolding doors to catch the ocean breeze. The 'treehouse' dorm is spotlessly clean and although it isn't in a tree, it does afford beautiful views from the verandah. The restaurant serves global cuisine and there are usually enough barflies buzzing around to give the bar a cheery vibe. There's free internet at reception, jet skis for hire ($95 per 15 minutes) and snorkelling in Beqa Lagoon ($55 per person).

Pearl South Pacific RESORT $$$
(✐345 0022; www.thepearlsouthpacific.com; Queens Rd; r $372-452, ste $698-792; ❧❋@☎) Revamped and reworked with industrial-strength Botox, this is now one of Fiji's finest hotels. No expense is spared in the Fijian-Asian fusion rooms that come themed in six flavours including Red Passion and Moody Blues. Style gurus will overdose on the marble bathrooms, low-slung beds and private decked alcoves with cushioned sun loungers. There's no kids club here (a nanny service is available) but there are plenty of activities to keep adults happy: a day spa, Sunday BBQ with live music, discounted fees at the affiliated golf course and two boats available for fishing ($80 per hour) and surfing (four hours at Frigate Passage for $250) charters.

Tsulu Backpackers & Apartments HOSTEL $
(✐345 0065; dm $35, d $65-88, apt $99-293; ❋@☎) Attached to the Arts Village, the Tsulu has picked up the artistic gauntlet and really, and we mean *really*, run with it. The walls (and in some cases the ceilings) of the dorms, double rooms and self-contained apartments are painted in vibrant murals. One room is bright blue with life-size fish, coral gardens and a snorkeller painted on the ceiling above. It's ridiculously good value.

Club Oceanus MOTEL $
(✐345 0498; www.cluboceanus.com; 1 Atoll Pl; dm/d/f $30/120/130; ❧❋☎) This waterside resort has 10 clean and comfortable rooms in a long, compact block, with kitchen facilities in the dorm. It's good value, located in a convenient spot on the canal within walking distance of the Arts Village complex and with a small cafe on site.

Studio 6 on the Lake RESORT $
(Lagoon Resort; ✐345 2096; studio6onthelake@connect.com.fj; Fairway Pl; r $100-130; ❧❋☎) This grandiose colonial hotel was built in the '80s as a bordello for wealthy Arabs, was painted pink by Korean owners in 1995 and has undergone several changes of ownership and fortune since. It has hosted South Pacific leaders and the cast of the fun-if-instantly-forgettable *Anaconda 2:* the boat from the movie lies in a dilapidated state outside the bar. It was undergoing another metamorphosis when we visited – hence the extremely cheap room rates – so expect prices to have changed by the time you read this.

🍴 Eating

🔝 Baka Blues Cafe FUSION $$
(Arts Village Marketplace; mains $20-30; ⊙lunch & dinner, closed Sun) Bluesy music accompanies the Cajun-influenced menu at this restaurant, which has well and truly lifted the bar for food and wine in the Marketplace. The spicy Cajun-style fish with snappy beans is a great combination.

Mantarae Restaurant FUSION $$$
(✐345 0022; Pearl South Pacific; mains $28-40; ⊙dinner Tue-Sat) This place offers interesting contemporary, fusion-style cuisine that has diners licking their lips from entrée to dessert. The Thai night when we visited was delicious. Sprawled out on a day bed, or sequestered behind the bar with its mirror-backed water feature, it's fine dining all the way – with a wine list to match.

Tiki Bar & Melting Pot Restaurant
INTERNATIONAL **$$**

(Arts Village Marketplace; mains $8-30; ☺lunch & dinner) In keeping with the faux-Fijian theme of the Arts Village, this open-air eatery is on the sand banks of a swimming pool. Overlooked by an 18m-tall, Aztec-like tiki head, this place is great for kids, who can swim in the pool or pickle themselves in the cannibals' 'hot pot' spa. Oh...and the food's not bad either. Day visitors can swim too (adult/child $5/2.50).

Water's Edge
PIZZERIA **$$**

(Arts Village Marketplace; mains $8-28; ☺lunch & dinner) The deckside dining at Water's Edge is surrounded by the water-lily pond and makes a scenic lunch stop. The menu is strong on pizza and Indian (tandoori chicken pizza $20).

Oasis Restaurant
INTERNATIONAL **$$**

(Arts Village Marketplace; mains $16-36; ☺breakfast, lunch & dinner; ☻✳@) Burgers, sandwiches, tortillas, curries and a whole lotta seafood is served at this long-time local favourite. The secondhand books for sale may not be great literature but go really well on a sun lounger.

Sakura House
JAPANESE **$$$**

(☎345 0256; River Dr; mains $25-40; ☺dinner) Although it features other Asian dishes, the Japanese tempura, sashimi, *shabu-shabu* (thinly sliced meat and vegetables cooked tableside in a pot of boiling water) and teriyaki are Sakura's speciality.

🛍 Shopping

Attached to the Arts Village is the **Arts Village Marketplace**, an open-air shopping mall of mock-colonial buildings. It has a supermarket, several cafes (try fresh juices and smoothies at Mai Juice) and several souvenir shops selling Fiji-style resort wear and some good but pricey handicrafts.

ℹ Information

Rosie's Tours (☎345 0655) has a tour desk at Arts Village Marketplace and can book all of the activities within the area. There's also an ATM in the shopping mall and internet can be found at Oasis Restaurant and the Tsulu Backpackers & Apartments arcade.

ℹ Getting There & Around

There are frequent **Pacific Transport** and **Sunbeam Transport** (www.sunbeamfiji.com) buses travelling the Queens Road between Lautoka and Suva, as well as vans and carriers. They all call in at Pacific Harbour.

The first bus from Pacific Harbour to Nadi ($15, 3½ hours) leaves at about 7.50am and the last at around 7pm. The first bus to Suva ($4.15, one hour) leaves at 10.15am and the last at 9.40pm. **Coral Sun Fiji** (www.coralsun express.com) buses stop opposite Rosie's Tours at 8.20am and 4.45pm for Nadi ($18) and at 10.50am and 4.15pm for Suva ($10).

A taxi costs about $40 to Suva and about $145 to Nadi.

Around Pacific Harbour

NAVUA & THE NAMOSI HIGHLANDS

The steamy Namosi Highlands north of Pacific Harbour have some of Fiji's most spectacular mountain scenery, including dense lush rainforests, steep ranges, deep river canyons and tall waterfalls. If you have your own wheels (preferably 4WD and in dry weather), take a detour as far inland as you can from Nabukavesi, east of Navua. Or drive the back road to Suva if you're heading that way. If you intend to visit a village, take along some kava. Sunday is observed as a day of rest. Before visiting a village, see the boxed text on p221.

There would be little to bring a traveller to the township Navua if it were not the base for several interesting tours up the Navua River to the Namosi Highlands. If you are staying on the road, the town's most notable feature is the blindingly purple house that showcases the local proclivity for bright homes.

Early in the 20th century, sugar cane was planted in Navua and a sugar mill was built, but this activity ceased as the drier western region proved more productive. Farmers of the delta region then turned to dairy farming, rice and other crops.

The regular express buses along the Queens Road stop at Navua and there are market boats and local buses to and from Namuamua and Nukusere villages, about 20km up the Navua River. The trip can take up to two hours ($15 each way), depending on the river's water level and general conditions. The boats leave any time between 10am and noon, but do not always return before the next morning (sometime between 6am and 7am).

☞ Tours

Discover Fiji Tours
ADVENTURE TOUR

(Map p48; ☎345 0180; www.discoverfijitours.com) Discover runs several tours to the Navua River area. Tours include waterfall visits, 4WD trips, trekking, kayaking and white-water rafting, and cost between $122 and $159, including transfers from Pacific Harbour or Suva. The popular Jewel of Fiji day tour remains a winner and was raved about by several travellers we met. All day tours last about six hours and include lunch. Some also include *bilibili* rafting, but avoid the Sunday village tours as they don't include the kava ceremony.

Namuamua Inland Tour   CULTURAL TOUR

(✆672 2074; www.touristtransportfiji.com/great-sights-fiji) This tour takes a long boat trip upriver, followed by a visit to Namuamua village, lunch, and a *bilibili* ride and swim on the way home. It's been operating for 18 years, and is one of the oldest locally initiated tours in Fiji supported by **Great Sights Fiji**.

Rivers Fiji (p85), based in Pacific Harbour, also offers longer trips deeper inland to this beautiful wilderness area that travellers otherwise rarely see.

🛏 Sleeping

Navua Upriver Lodge   LODGE $

(Map p48; ✆933 7157; navuaupriverlodge.com; Nuku Village; site per tent/dm/d $30-90) Situated about 25km north of Navua town, this Fijian-run lodge offers travellers a genuine river-village experience. Accommodation and food is simple and the surrounding environment is stunning. Call the lodge from Navua and they'll arrange a *bilibili* transfer. The 1½-hour ride up the Navua passes some 20 waterfalls.

ℹ Getting There & Away

The regular express buses along the Queens Road stop at Navua and there are market boats and local buses to and from Namuamua and Nukusere villages, about 20km up the Navua River. The trip can take up to two hours ($15 each way), depending on the river's water level and general conditions. The boats leave any time between 10am and noon, but do not always return before the next morning (sometime between 6am and 7am).

Offshore Islands

World-class **diving, snorkelling** and **surfing** can be had in the waters that surround the islands off southern Viti Levu and are the principal reason for visiting this area. The easiest way to dive or snorkel on the surrounding coral reefs is with one of the dive-shop operators based in the Pacific Harbour resorts (p84).

For surfers, the left-hand waves at **Frigate Passage**, also known as Kavu Kavu Reef, break on the western edge of Beqa

Barrier Reef, 11km from the nearest land and southwest of Yanuca island. With long rides and reliable barrels, the surf here can reach 6m when the swell is coming from the southeast to southwest. At other times it is far smaller and suitable for intermediate surfers. The break has three sections, which join up under the right conditions: a large take-off zone; a long, walled speed section with the possibility of stand-up tubes; and an inside section breaking over the shallow reef and finishing in deep water. Access is by boat (it's in the middle of nowhere) with Waidroka Surf & Dive Resort (p83) or with Yanuca's Batiluva Beach Resort which specialises in surfing.

Day tours to two of Beqa Lagoon's islands run from Pacific Harbour.

BEQA

The high island of Beqa (be-*n*ga), about 7.5km south of Pacific Harbour and with an area of 36 sq km, is visible from the Queens Road and even from Suva. The island is about 7km in diameter, with a deeply indented coastline and rugged interior that slopes steeply down to the coast. The villagers of Rukua, Naceva and Dakuibeqa are known for their tradition of fire-walking (see the boxed text, but the best place to see it isn't on Beqa. It's now performed chiefly for tourists at the Coral Coast resorts.

🛏 Sleeping

Lawaki Beach House   LODGE $

(Map p48; ✆992 1621, 368 4088; www.lawaki beachhouse.com; sites per tent incl meals $70, dm/d incl meals $130/$280) Aptly named, this small resort sits in front of an isolated beach on the southwestern side of Beqa island. Run by a Fijian–Swiss couple, it's like spending low-key time with family and joining whatever household activities – gardening, fishing – that are happening. The place comprises two double *bure* with en suites and verandahs, and a six-bed dorm. The unobtrusive and cosy set-up blends well with the surrounding environment as do the solar, recycling and water-use practices. Guests mingle together in the communal TV lounge, soaking up the relaxed mood.

There is good snorkelling off the secluded, pristine white-sand beach, as well as visits to the nearby village, diving and surfing ($225 for the boat, plus $25 per hour). The resort offers transfers from Pacific Harbour on a covered aluminium boat (from $220 per one-way transfer). Alternatively, you can

SOME LIKE IT HOT

Of all Fiji's cultural rituals, the extraordinary art of fire-walking is perhaps the most impressive. Watching men display the poise of a lead ballerina while they traverse a pit of blazing embers without combusting is truly baffling. Even more mystifying is the fact that, originally, this ritual was practised in Fiji only on the tiny island of Beqa. Indigenous Fijian fire-walking is known as *vilavilairevo* (literally 'jumping into the oven'). The ability to walk barefoot on white-hot stones without being burned was, according to local legend, granted to a local chief by the leader of the *veli*, a group of little gods. Now the direct descendants of the chief serve as the *bete* (priests) who instruct in the ritual of fire-walking.

Preparations for fire-walking used to occupy a whole village for nearly a month. Firewood and appropriate stones had to be selected, costumes made and various ceremonies performed. Fire-walkers had to abstain from sex and refrain from eating any coconut for up to a month before the ritual. None of the fire-walkers' wives could be pregnant, or it was believed the whole group would receive burns.

Traditionally, *vilavilairevo* was only performed on special occasions in the village of Navakaisese. Today, though, it's performed only for commercial purposes and has little religious meaning. There are regular performances at the Pacific Harbour Arts Village (p83), at the larger resort hotels and at Suva's annual Hibiscus Festival.

catch the small public ferry from the Navua Jetty. The ferry usually leaves between noon and 2.30pm Monday through Saturday, and costs $40 per person one way. It returns to Navua at 7am every day but Sunday.

Beqa Lagoon Resort RESORT $$$
(Map p48; ☎330 4042; www.beqalagoonresort. com; ✳@⊠) The 25 stylish and well-maintained *bure* here come with opulent bathrooms and traditional interiors, and some with plunge pools. The surrounding landscape and calm bay in front lends itself to excellent snorkelling, kayaking, hiking to waterfalls and village visits. There's a large **restaurant-lounge** (meal package $95) serving fabulous food, and a spa and a pool beside a coconut tree-fringed beach. It's a dive resort fair and square, offering all-inclusive seven-day packages for American guests, mostly. Individual travellers should check website for details of costs and packages.

Two other smaller, top-end options on Beqa specialise in diving for couples, who may also choose to get married or honeymoon in them: **Lalati Resort** (www.lalati-fiji.com) and **Kulu Bay Resort** (www.kulubay.com).

YANUCA

Tiny Yanuca island is a hilly speck inside Beqa Lagoon, about 9km west of Beqa. It has comely beaches, good snorkelling and is close to the humbling breaks of Frigate Passage. Unsurprisingly, it lures avid surfers, many of whom come for a week, slip into the lifestyle and stay for a month. If living in your swimmers 24/7 is your idea of bliss, then you've found utopia.

This long-standing camp at **Batiluva Beach Resort** (Map p48; ☎345 1019, 939 1975; www.batliuva.com; dm/d incl meals $200/400) is the stuff of surfers' dreams. The sturdy accommodation houses three spotless and airy dorms, and two double rooms. The per-person price is the same for each, but couples get first dibs on the doubles (there's not much privacy though as the internal dividing wall doesn't reach the ceiling). 'Gourmet jungle meals' (and they are) are included in the tariff, but more importantly, so too is the daily boat out to Frigates for the surf-till-you-drop clientele. The beach here is quite pretty with plenty of fish, but for good snorkelling over coral you need to go on a short boat trip (free of charge). Transfers from Pacific Harbour are $60 return per person. Book at the small office by the bridge at Pacific Harbour (Map p84).

A tiny, locally run surfers' camp, **Yanuca Island Resort**, may also be operating on the island: ask around.

VATULELE
POP 950

The beautiful island of Vatulele (31 sq km) is 32km south of Korolevu, off Viti Levu's southern coast, and west of Beqa Lagoon. It is 13km long and mostly flat. The highest point is just 33m above sea level, and there is scrub and palm vegetation. The western coast is a long escarpment broken by vertical cliffs, formed by fracturing and uplifts. A barrier reef up to 3km offshore forms a lagoon on the eastern and northern ends, with two navigable passages at the northern end.

Vatulele has four villages and one exclusive resort, **Vatulele Island Resort** (Map p48; www.vatulele.com). The villagers live mostly off subsistence farming and fishing and are one of Fiji's two main producers of *masi*. There are also **archaeological sites**, including ancient rock paintings of faces and stencilled hands, and unusual **geological formations**, including limestone caves and pools inhabited by red prawns that are considered sacred.

SUVA

POP 167,975

Suva (*soo*-va), the heart of Fiji, is home to half of the country's urban population and, as the largest city in the South Pacific, it is an important regional centre. Swimming in the urban milieu is the influence of every island and background, a vibrant Indo-Fijian community, university students from around the Pacific, Asian sailors on shore leave, and a growing expat community of Australians and New Zealanders.

Suva is on a peninsula about 3km wide by 5km long, with Laucala Bay to the east and Suva Harbour to the west. Most of the peninsula is hilly, apart from the narrow strip of land on the western edge of the city where you'll find Suva's main drag, Victoria Pde (which holds many of the city's restaurants, shops and clubs), as well as the market and wharf.

The suburb of Toorak tumbles up onto the hill east of Suva Municipal Market. Originally Suva's posh neighbourhood (named after one of Melbourne, Australia's exclusive suburbs), it has fallen from grandeur but leads ultimately to the desirable residences and embassies of ridge-top Tamanvua.

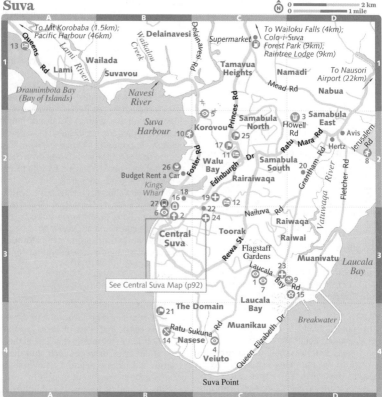

Suva

Downtown is as diverse architecturally as the populace is culturally. A jigsaw of colonial buildings, modern shopping plazas, abundant eateries and a breezy esplanade all form the compact central business district. Small passages transport you to a city somewhere in India with curry houses, sari shops and bric-a-brac traders. Bollywood and Hollywood square off at the local cinema and within the same hour you're likely to see politicians in traditional *sulu* sharing a few shells of kava and denim-clad youth heading to the hottest clubs in the country.

Beyond downtown Suva, there is a string of pretty suburbs dribbled along the hills that crowd the capital's busy port. If Suva is indeed Fiji's heart, there are signs that it may be sick: the ballooning settlement camps of tin sheds on the city outskirts are proof that when 'coup-coup land' misses a beat, the whole country shudders.

On a less serious but equally grey note, clouds tend to hover over Suva, frequently dumping rain on the city (around 300mm each year), which accounts for the lush tropical plants and comparative lack of tourists.

History

Suva's contemporary history has its roots in the fickle mismanagement of Chief Cakobau of Bau, who, with the help of King George of Tonga, proclaimed himself Tui Viti, or King of Fiji, in the 1850s. Cakobau promptly took it upon himself to give away bits and pieces of Fiji to foreign settlers, while concurrently accumulating giant debts with American immigrants. By 1862 his inability to repay the debts became apparent when he attempted to cede Fiji to Britain in exchange for debt clearance.

Up until this time, the only Europeans in the Suva area had come from Melbourne, Australia, seeking new sources of fortune after the decline of the gold rushes and subsequent downturn in the Australian economy. In 1868, the opportunistic Aussies formed the Australian Polynesia Company and agreed to clear Cakobau's debts with the Americans in return for the right to trade in Fiji and a large chunk of land, 90 sq km of which covered the Suva peninsula.

While it was not his land to trade, the powerful Chief Cakobau had the Suva villagers relocated and welcomed new Australian settlers to the area in 1870. The settlers

---

Suva

⊙ Sights

◎ Activities, Courses & Tours

⊜ Sleeping

⊗ Eating

⊙ Entertainment

⊙ Shopping

❶ Information

❶ Transport

Central Suva

Suva Harbour

Scott St

Edward St

Marks St

Thomson St

Cumming St

Waimanu Rd

Stinson Pde

34

17

Suva City Pharmacy

Central St

45

44

11

26

24

Renwick Rd

42

4

Greig St

20

Nabukalou Creek

Ratu Sukuna Park

38

27

Joske St

Murray St

Gordon St

Registrar General's Office

37

16

8

31

Butt St

Macarthur St

Hercules St

5

Holland St

41

29

23

3

Pratt St

Suva City Library

32

Carnarvon St

Kimberley St

St Andrew's Church

Malcolm St

Desvoeux Rd

Berry Rd

Disraeli Rd

Loftus St

36

19

18

Dolphin Arcade

Goodenough St

Thrifty Car Rental

15

Cruickshank Park

25

Loftus St

Thurston St

Gordon St

43

Gorre St

Gladstone Rd

McGregor Rd

Mitchell St

9

Government Buildings

40

35

14

Southern Cross Rd

Kingsford Smith Pavilion

2

Albert Park

Williamson Rd

12

7

Ratu Cakobau Rd

Queen Elizabeth Dr

Victoria Pde

Umaria Park

6

Thurston Gardens

Botanic Gardens Clock Tower

THE DOMAIN

Berkly Cres

1

cleared dense reed from what is now downtown Suva and attempted, unsuccessfully, to grow cotton and sugar cane. In an effort to increase land values, two Melbourne merchants, Thomson and Renwick, encouraged the government to relocate the capital from Levuka to Suva with incentives in the form of land grants. As Levuka had little room for expansion, the government officially moved to Suva in 1882. In the 1880s, Suva was a township of about a dozen buildings, but by the 1920's it was a flourishing colonial centre.

Suva's recent history is inevitably linked to the coups. In May 2000 Suva's parliament buildings became the site of a hostage drama when George Speight and his militia held 36 government officials captive for almost two months (see p203). More recently, in 2006, Suvanites, and indeed the whole country, were once again plunged into political turmoil when Frank Bainimarama seized power (see p204).

◉ Sights

As well as living a cosmopolitan lifestyle, the majority of Suva's residents are very religious, and dash off to temple or church on a regular basis. Chatty and welcoming custodians at most of the city's churches, mosques and temples are happy to talk to visitors.

TOP CHOICE **Fiji Museum** MUSEUM
(Map p92; ☏331 5944; www.fijimuseum.org.fj; Ratu Cakobau Rd; adult/child $7/5; ◷9am-4.30pm Mon-Sat) This museum captivates visitors with a journey into Fiji's archaeological, political, cultural and linguistic evolution. To enjoy the exhibits in chronological order, start with the displays behind the ticket counter and work your way around clockwise. Original examples of musical instruments, cooking apparatus and jewellery – including chiefs' whale-tooth necklaces – and a daunting array of Fijian war clubs and cannibal utensils give a vivid insight into traditional life. Taking centre stage is the massive Ratu Finau (1913), Fiji's last *waqa tabus* (double-hulled canoe), which measures 13.43m long and includes an enclosed deck for inclement weather.

The growing influence of other South Pacific and European cultures is documented in a hall on the other side of the museum shop. It is here that you'll find the well-chewed, but ultimately inedible, shoe of Thomas Baker (see the boxed text, p200), a Christian missionary eaten for his indiscretions in 1867. Upstairs, a small Indo-Fijian

Central Suva

hall chronicles some of the contributions made by the Indian workers and their descendants who were brought to Fiji in the 1870s as indentured labourers. Also on the same floor is a gallery of beautiful *masi* by some of Fiji's finest contemporary artists.

The museum continually undertakes archaeological research and collects and preserves oral traditions. Many of these are published in *Domodomo*, a quarterly journal on history, language, culture, art and natural

history that is available in the museum's gift shop. It also organises craft demonstrations. Contact the museum for times.

After visiting the museum, ponder your new-found knowledge with a wander through the compact but beautiful **Thurston Gardens** (Map p92). The dense conglomeration of native flora and surrounding lawns are less manicured and growing more haphazard with every coup, but it was here that the original village of Suva once stood. It's a lovely spot for a picnic – particularly if you camp yourself under one of the grand and stately fig trees.

Suva Municipal Market

MARKET

(Map p90; Usher St; ⊙6am-6pm Mon-Fri, to 4.30pm Sat) It's the beating heart of Suva and a great place to spend an hour or so poking around with a camera. The boys with barrows own the lanes and they aren't afraid to mow down a few tourists to deliver their cassava on time. Besides the recognisable tomatoes, cabbages and chillies, look out for bitter gourds, *rourou* (boiled *dalo* leaves in *lolo*), kava, jackfruit, *dalo* and sweet potatoes.

Head upstairs to buy your *sevusevu*. *Yaqona* (kava) roots costs anything from $24 to $40 a kilo and a gift of these guarantees 100-watt smiles. Only cheapskates opt for the powdered, less potent, stems.

Colo-i-Suva Forest Park

FOREST

(off Map p90; ☑332 0211; adult/child $5/1; ⊙8am-4pm) Colo-i-Suva (pronounced tholo-ee-*soo*-va) is a 2.5-sq-km oasis of lush rainforest, teeming with tropical plants and vivid and melodic bird life. The 6.5km of walking trails navigate clear natural pools and gorgeous vistas. Sitting at an altitude of 120m to 180m, it's a cool and peaceful respite from Suva's urban hubbub.

Slipping and sliding through the forest over water-worn rocks is the Waisila Creek, which makes its way down to Waimanu River and forms the water catchment for the Nausori and Nasinu areas. The creek gives rise to natural swimming holes. The Lower Pools have a rope swing guaranteed to bring out the Tarzan in anyone.

The mahogany and pines were planted after a period of aggressive logging in the 1940s and '50s to stabilise the topsoil without impinging on the indigenous vegetation. Among the wildlife are 14 different bird species, including scarlet robins, spotted fantails, Fiji goshawks, sulphur-breasted musk parrots, Fiji warblers, golden doves and barking pigeons.

The visitor information centre is on the left of the road as you approach from Suva. Buy your ticket here, check the state of the trails and any current security warnings, then head to the entrance booth on the other side of the road. The recommended route is to follow Kalabu Rd as it skirts the park, turning up Pool Rd to the car park. From here, you take the Nature Trail to the Lower Pools for swimming, the aforementioned rope swinging and, if you remembered to bring it, lunch. It's a sweaty, uphill walk back to the main road via the Falls Trail. Without stopping this loop takes about 1½ hours to complete.

Regarding the security situation: there have been some distressing attacks over the years, but at the time of writing there had been no reported acts of violence for some years. Ask the right questions of the rangers and use your judgement. Rangers will lead guided two-hour walks for $30 if asked. The park receives an annual rainfall of 420cm and the trails can be extremely slippery, so sturdy footwear is essential.

The Sawani bus leaves Suva bus station every half hour ($2, 30 minutes) or a taxi will cost around $8. If driving, follow Princes Rd out of Suva through Tamavua and Tacirua village.

University of the South Pacific

UNIVERSITY

(USP; Map p90; ☑331 3900; www.usp.ac.fj; Laucala Bay Rd) While not necessarily a must-see from a tourist's perspective, this is the foremost provider of tertiary education to the island

---

GRAND DESIGNS

A short stroll along Suva's foreshore towards Albert Park brings you to one of Fiji's most dignified, and yet most neglected, buildings, the **Grand Pacific Hotel** (Map p92). In his book *The World is My Home*, James A Michener describes it as having '...a huge central dining area filled with small tables, each meticulously fitted with fine silver and china...and the barefoot Indians who served the meals [here] had a grace that few hotels in the world could offer and none surpass'.

Built in 1914 by the Union Steamship Company, the splendid white facade still hints at the hotel's former glory, also described by Somerset Maugham when he stayed here in 1916. It closed in 1992 and for a long time remained abandoned and in a continuing state of decay: floorboards upstairs rotted, shutters hung from glassless windows, wallpaper peeled from decaying walls and the army moved in to camp. A string of rescue plans and backers failed to give new life to this grand old dame until finally, in late 2011, restoration and redevelopment of the site began. Watch this space...

nations of the Pacific region. The governments of 12 Pacific countries jointly own the university and mingling among the Fijian students you're likely to see young academics from the Cook Islands, Kiribati, Tonga, Vanuatu and Western Samoa. As this is a fee-paying institution, many of the 11,000 or so students rely on scholarships, and the competition for them is fierce. The USP's main Laucala Campus (built on the site of a New Zealand seaplane base) offers some fascinating people-watching and picturesque strolling through a small **botanical garden**.

On most weekday mornings, the Oceania Dance Theatre and other performance groups can be found rehearsing in the **Oceania Centre for Arts & Culture**, where you can also see temporary exhibits of paintings and carvings. The uni **bookshop** nearby is stocked with many texts of Pacific fact and fiction.

Parliament of Fiji   LANDMARK
(Map p90; ☏330 5811; www.parliament.gov.fj; Battery Rd; admission free) Opened in June 1992, the parliament complex must be one of the world's most striking political hubs. It was designed in the post-1987 atmosphere (see p202 for information on the 1987 coup). The aim of maintaining indigenous Fijian values is apparent through the open-air corridors, traditional arts and structures, and *masi* cloths throughout. The main building, *vale ne bose lawa* (parliament house), takes its form from the traditional *vale* (family house) and has a ceremonial access from Ratu Sukuna Rd. The complex is 5km south of the city centre and, depending on the politics of the day, you may or may not be able to look around – check with the guard at the main entrance or phone ahead.

It's easiest to reach by taxi, but you can hop on a bus along Queen Elizabeth Dr and walk along Ratu Sukuna Rd for 1km.

Shree Laxmi Narayan Temple   TEMPLE
(Map p92; Holland St) Just east of downtown, this bright orange and blue temple generally has a caretaker around to let you in for a look.

Holy Trinity Cathedral   CHURCH
(Map p92; cnr Macarthur & Gordon Sts) This cathedral, with its unique boat-shaped interior, interesting Fijian tapestries and wood-beamed ceiling, is a peaceful retreat. The gigantic tree in front of the church is a showcase of Pacific plants, with cacti and ferns making themselves at home in its branches.

Roman Catholic Cathedral   CHURCH
(Map p92; cnr Murray & Pratt Sts) This 1902 cathedral is built of sandstone imported from Sydney and is one of Suva's most prominent landmarks.

Centenary Methodist Church   CHURCH
(Map p90; Stewart St) For a rousing chorus of song on a Sunday morning, head to the Methodist church. The pitch is more invigorating than dulcet and it often fills the surrounding streets.

If you entered town via the Queens Road, you likely passed **Suva Cemetery** (Map p90). Graves are dug by the inmates from the prison (built in 1913) just down the road, and then decorated with bright cloth.

🏃 Activities

Suva all but closes down on a Sunday, so try to organise activities in advance or attend a Fijian church service to hear some uplifting, boisterous singing.

Trekking
Colo-i-Suva Forest Park is an easy place for bushwalking close to Suva. You can also hike to **Mt Korobaba** (off Map p90), about a two-hour walk from the cement factory near Lami. **Joske's Thumb** is an enticing spectacle for serious climbers. A climb to this peak was featured in the film *Journey to the Dawning of the Day*.

Keen trekkers should contact the **Rucksack Club** for weekly walking adventures either inland or to other islands. There's no website, but your web browser should bring up a link to their current activities and contact details. Membership changes regularly, as many of the members are expats on contract in Fiji.

A gentler but very popular walk (or jog or cycle or skateboard) is the several-kilometre stretch of **Suva waterfront**, on a well-used path that follows the sea wall along the length of Queen Elizabeth drive. It's busy with Suvans exercising at dawn and dusk (but is not a place to exercise after dark).

Sailing
Royal Suva Yacht Club   SAILING
(Map p90; ☏331 2921; www.rsyc.org.fj; ☺office 8am-5pm Mon-Sat, 9am-4pm Sun) The Royal Suva Yacht Club is a popular watering hole for yachties and locals alike. It has great sunset views of the Bay of Islands though the food can be hit and miss. Even without

WINGING IT

Charles Kingsford Smith was the first aviator to cross the Pacific, flying in his little Fokker trimotor, *The Southern Cross*, from California to Australia. The longest leg of the flight was the 34-hour trip from Hawaii to Fiji. Suva's Albert Park, with its hill at one end and the Grand Pacific Hotel at the other, was made into a makeshift landing strip for his arrival. Trees were still being cleared after Kingsford Smith had already left Hawaii. Kingsford Smith and his crew arrived on 6 June 1928 and were welcomed by a crowd of thousands, including colonial dignitaries who had gathered at the Grand Pacific Hotel to witness and celebrate this major event. Because the park was too short to take off with a heavy load of fuel, Kingsford Smith had to unload, fly to Nasilai Beach and reload for take off to Brisbane and Sydney. Kingsford Smith and his crew were presented with a ceremonial *tabua* (whale's tooth) as a token of great respect.

a yacht, overseas visitors are welcome and the atmosphere at the bar can be lively and salty; everyone has a story to tell.

The noticeboard is a good place to find crewing positions and the marina has dockside fuel and water. The **Yacht Shop** handles parts and repairs. Anchorage fees are $5 per day or $50 if you prefer to overnight in one of the marina berths. There are laundry and shower facilities for those who have just arrived, and the office advises on customs and immigration procedures. Yachties use channel 16 to call ahead of arrival.

Sports

Suva has three off-shore breaks for surfers – a left-hand break at Sandbar and two right-handers at Lighthouse and Rat's Tail. You'll need to ask around locally to access them, though. Try the noticeboard at the Yacht Club.

Suva doesn't have a beach. The best places for a swim are listed below.

National Aquatic Centre SWIMMING
(Map p90; ☎331 8185; Laucala Bay Rd; adult/child $5/3; ☼5am-7pm) Built for the 2003 South Pacific Games. Enter by the open side gate before 7am.

Suva Olympic Swimming Pool SWIMMING
(Map p92; 224 Victoria Pde; adult/child $3/1.50; ☼10am-6pm Mon-Fri, 8am-6pm Sat) Absolutely central.

Fiji Golf Club GOLF
(Map p90; ☎338 2872; 15 Rifle Range Rd; ☼7am-last tee-off at 3pm) Nonmembers are welcome except on Saturdays and from noon to 3pm on Tuesdays when the greens are reserved for local competitions. The green fees on this par-72 course are $20 for nine holes and $30 for 18.

Suva Bowls Club BOWLS
(Map p92; ☎331 0596; cnr Graham St & Victoria Pde; green fees $10; ☼9am-5pm Mon-Sat) Lawn bowlers may roll up here, but don't underestimate the breadth of talent in this club. There are only 50 playing members here, but Fiji won silver in the 2008 world championship. The top male player is ranked 6th in the world, the top female player 11th.

☞ Tours

Many of the tour companies based in Pacific Harbour and Navua also pick up from Suva hotels; see those sections for more details.

☆☆ Festivals & Events

Hibiscus Festival BEAUTY PAGEANT
(www.hibiscusfiji.com) Since its inception in 1956, the Hibiscus Festival has grown into a nine-day event, drawing large crowds from around Viti Levu. It is held every August to coincide with the second-term school break. The annual beauty pageant and the crowning of the 'Hibiscus Queen' are the chief draws, but families also flock to Albert Park to ride creaky rides in the amusement park, browse stalls and listen to the free entertainment. Some might find it a little archaic, but if you are in the market for cheap sunglasses and loud shirts, you've struck gold.

South Indian Fire-Walking Festival RELIGIOUS
The extraordinary South Indian fire-walking festival is held at the **Mariamma Temple** (Map p90; ☎337 2773, 338 2357; Howell Rd, Samabula) annually in either July or August. On the day of the ritual, yellow-clad devotees gather at Suva Point, near the National Stadium, to bathe in the sea and make their final preparations for the fire-walking ahead. Temple pundits (Hindu priests) pierce the tongues, cheeks and bodies of the devotees

with three-pronged skewers and smear their faces with yellow turmeric, a symbol of prosperity and a powerful totem over disease. At around 2pm, the participants dance the 3km to the Mariamma Temple (arriving around 4pm) where a large crowd waits. Fire-walking over a bed of hot ash and coals is seen as a sign of devotion and self-sacrifice, the culmination of a 10-day ascetic period during which devotees rely solely on the offerings from the local Hindu community, abstain from sex and eating meat, and meditate to worship the goddess Maha Devi. It is believed that if the fire-walkers are cleansed of physical and spiritual impurities and thus focused on the divine Mother, they will feel no pain.

🛏 Sleeping

Accommodation options in the capital aren't as modish as those found in the more tourist-oriented towns elsewhere on the island. Suva's top hotels are nowhere near the standard set by the resorts in Denarau and cater more to businesspeople than vacationers. Similarly, without the steady stream of backpackers that Nadi enjoys, quality budget accommodation is also rather thin on the ground. Besides the midrange hotels listed here, there are many more to be found along Robertson Rd, particularly the loop it forms between Anand St and Waimanu Rd. A quiet word of warning: some of these are the haunts of prostitutes and their clients. If you notice no other travellers and a lot of traffic, you may prefer to move on.

Five Princes Hotel BOUTIQUE HOTEL $$
(Map p90; ☏338 1575; www.fiveprinceshotel.com; 5 Princes Rd; d $199, bure $230, villa $335; ❈@🛜🏊) The aged 1920s exterior belies the transformation that this one-time colonial villa has undergone on the inside. Solid teak furniture, polished timber floors, power showers, satellite TV and wi-fi connections are all to be had in timelessly appointed rooms. Set in beautifully landscaped gardens, the stand-alone villas are similarly decorated and also include kitchenettes and private verandahs. It's a ten-minute drive from the centre of town.

Quest Serviced Apartments APARTMENT $$
(Map p92; ☏331 9117; www.questsuva.com; Thomson St; studio/one-bed apt $185/237) You'd never know these gems of apartments were here, tucked away on the 6th and 7th floor of the Suva Central building. Central, quiet, well-maintained and secure, they are popular with the long-stay embassy and development agency crowd, but there are always a few units available for overnight and short stays. There's an air-conditioned gym on-site too and breakfast at the coffee shop on the building's 2nd floor is included.

South Seas Private Hotel HOSTEL $
(Map p92; ☏331 2296; www.fiji4less.com; 6 Williamson Rd; s/d without bathroom $39/51, r with bathroom $64; ⊜) The art deco sign out front sets the scene for this grand old dame of the Pacific, set on a quiet street just a step away from the museum and botanic gardens. The sweeping interior verandah, classic white exterior, high ceilings and wide halls speak of the romance of a bygone era. This large colonial house and former girls-only hostel welcomes budget travellers with simple, clean rooms, comfortably ageing lounge furniture and a shared kitchen.

Suva Apartments APARTMENT $
(Map p92; ☏330 4280; www.fijiolympiccommittee.com; 17 Bau St; apt $76-92; ❈) These small, neat and tidy self-contained one-bedroom apartments are great value and well-located just a five-minute bus ride from town and a five-minute walk from shops. They are one of the income-generating ventures of the Fiji Olympic committee, so your stay supports Fiji's athletes.

Nanette's Accommodation B&B $
(Map p90; ☏331 6316; www.nanettes.com.fj; 56 Extension St; r incl breakfast $119, apt incl breakfast $145-195; ⊜❈@) Resort-weary travellers can find solace here in unassuming comfort. This former house is only a 15-minute walk to downtown Suva, but set a world away in tranquil residential surrounds. The four upstairs rooms of varying size share a communal TV lounge and kitchen. All have bathrooms, some with large tubs. Downstairs are three comfortable apartments with their own spacious kitchens and bedrooms.

Novotel Suva Lami Bay HOTEL $$$
(Map p90; ☏336 2450; www.novotelsuva.com.fj; Queens Rd, Lami; r from $300; ⊜@❈🏊) Reopened with a sleek new look and under new management in 2009, these 108 rooms offer business-style accommodation. Popular with the regional conference set, it has a great waterfront location with views across Draunimbota Bay and is a ten-minute drive from central Suva.

Suva Motor Inn HOTEL $$
(Map p92; ☏331 3973; www.hexagonfiji.com; cnr Mitchell & Gorrie Sts; d $119-187; ❈@🏊) Fab for

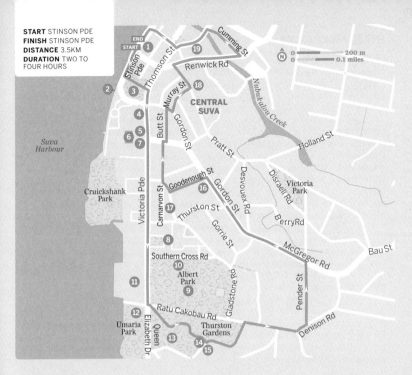

END
START 1
19
Cumming St
Stinson Pde
Thomson St
Renwick Rd
2
3
Murray St
18
CENTRAL
SUVA
Nubukalou Creek
4
Butt St
Gordon St
Pratt St
Holland St
6 5
7
Suva
Harbour
Victoria Pde
Goodenough St
Gordon St
Desvoeux Rd
Disraeli Rd
Victoria
Park
Cruickshank
Park
Carnarvon St
16
Thurston St
BerryRd
17
Gorrie St
McGregor Rd
Bau St
8
Southern Cross Rd
10
Albert
Park
9
Gladstone Rd
Pender St
Denison Rd
11
12
Ratu Cakobau Rd
Umaria
Park
Queen Elizabeth Dr
Thurston
Gardens
13
14
15

0   200 m
N 0   0.1 miles

Walking Tour
Downtown Suva

❯ Downtown Suva has a scattering of colonial buildings and places of interest, making
it a pleasant place to wander around.

Start on Stinson Pde at the ❶ **Suva Curio
& Handicraft Market**. Cross the street and
follow the esplanade south, enjoying the views
of Suva Harbour. Once you reach ❷ **Tiko's
Floating Restaurant**, cross the road and
amble through the tree-lined ❸ **Ratu Sukuna
Park**. Continue south down Victoria Pde, past
the 1926 ❹ **Fintel building** and the 1904
❺ **old town hall**. The ❻ **Suva Olympic
Swimming Pool** is set back between this
building and the 1909 ❼ **Suva City Library**.

Continue down Victoria Pde. On your left
are the stately ❽ **Government buildings**.
Just south is ❾ **Albert Park**, a large sporting field. The ❿ **Kingsford Smith Pavilion**,
named after the famous aviator who landed
here, is on Southern Cross Rd. Opposite the
park is the once-glorious ⓫ **Grand Pacific
Hotel**. Just past Ratu Cakobau Rd is
⓬ **Umaria Park & Suva Bowls Club**, where
you can take a breather with a cold drink.

Cross the road at Queen Elizabeth Dr
and enter ⓭ **Thurston Gardens**. Meander
through this colourful park, stopping at the
⓮ **Botanic Gardens Clock Tower** and the
⓯ **Fiji Museum**.

Continue east, then turn left at Pender St
and left again at McGregor Rd, which turns
into Gordon St. Turn left at ⓰ **St Andrew's
Church**, follow Goodenough St and dog-leg
onto Carnarvon St. If you need a pick-me-up,
drop into the ⓱ **Old Mill Cottage** or **Rave
Bistro** for a traditional Fijian feast and/or a
good coffee.

Stroll north past the bars and clubs to the
⓲ **Roman Catholic Cathedral**, one of Suva's
most prominent landmarks.

Turn left, then right and window-shop your
way to Cumming St, then turn left to immerse
yourself in Suva's little India.

Make your way past the stately
⓳ **Garrick Hotel**, then head back to the
Curio & Handicraft Market. If you've got any
energy left, spend it on a bout of souvenir
shopping.

HOME AWAY FROM HOME

On the outskirts of Suva, away from the flashy shops and colonial homes, tens of thousands of people are living in settlements of tiny, corrugated-iron huts. These dilapidated settlements have little sanitation and often no water or electricity. In 2008, an estimated 35% of Fijians were living below the poverty line and as long as the country's unresolved land issues remain, more and more of the poor are expected to drift towards the urban centres.

Indigenous Fijians have traditional ownership rights to over 80% of the country's land mass, large tracts of which they've leased to Indo-Fijian farmers for the past century. However, with these leases coming to an end and ethnic friction heightened by recent political events, many indigenous landowners are turfing Indo-Fijian farmers off property where their families have lived for generations. Ironically, in many cases the farms that had once been profitably worked by the Indo-Fijian tenants are now lying idle and overgrown. Consequently, the sugar-cane harvest has plummeted from up to 4.3 million tonnes a year at the time of George Speight's coup in 2000 to an estimated 200,000 tonnes in 2011, only fuelling further economic woes.

Meanwhile, the now-landless Indo-Fijians are fleeing to the cities for safety. Unfortunately, with their livelihood gone, many families end up in suburban squatter settlements. However, these impromptu, crowded towns are not strictly Indo-Fijian. The substantial pay cuts and rise in unemployment that have followed the country's coups have left many urban indigenous Fijians unable to pay rent. Their only means of survival is also to head for the squatter settlements.

The government does acknowledge the severe impact this issue has on Fiji's social and economic fabric. Millions of dollars have been spent on squatter resettlement, mostly in the form of estates (primarily around Lautoka) and new housing developments, but for many, this has been too little, too late. With farming leases continuing to expire, it looks certain that the rural-to-urban migration trend will continue. For families who have lost their land, the future continues to look dim.

families, the Suva Motor Inn is a little humble with its title. The four-storey hotel (no lift) is shaped like a 'U' around a small pool into which snakes a water slide. All rooms have balconies (the best with views to Albert Park) and the larger two-bedroom apartments sleep four and have kitchens. It's a solid midrange choice and popular with the visiting NGO crowd.

Holiday Inn HOTEL $$
(Map p92; ☑330 1600; reservations@holidayinn suva.com.fj; Victoria Pde; r $272-497; ❄✳@☎☀) This inn occupies a great location on the harbour shore, across from the Government Buildings and near the museum. Rooms are generically spacious, cool and comfortable and will please picky travellers. The inn patently appeals to business travellers and those on coach tours, and it has the facilities, including wi-fi throughout, to match.

Tanoa Plaza Hotel HOTEL $$
(Map p92; ☑331 2300; www.tanoahotels.com; cnr Gordon & Malcolm Sts; r $248-276, ste $494; ❄✳@☎☀) The rooms here have wi-fi and are comfortable, functional and forgettable.

It's sleek and sophisticated in a minibar and pamper-products-in-the-bathroom kind of way. The views, though, are impressive and the service is one of Suva's best. The Tanoa attracts a stream of visiting politicians and professionals.

Peninsula International Hotel HOTEL $
(Map p92; ☑331 3711; www.peninsula.com.fj; cnr McGregor Rd & Pender St; r $90-130, apt $165; ❄✳☀) Pleasantly situated in a leafy residential area, the Peninsula is a little confused and tired but does its best to provide reasonable value. From the outside, it looks like an apartment block and is recognisable by the overhanging window canopies (which get in the way of what would have been excellent views). There is a small pool, restaurant and bar on site. If you plan to stay here, aim high – the rooms and views get better the higher you go.

Raintree Lodge LODGE $
(Off map p90; ☑332 0113; www.raintreelodge.com; Princes Rd, Colo-i-Suva; dm/d/bure $25/65/165; ❄@☀) It is hard to believe that the tranquil, rainforest-fringed lake that provides such a lush backdrop here was once a rock quarry.

There are rumoured to be two trucks and a bulldozer lying abandoned beneath the lake's glassy surface from when the quarry closed in the 1970s. The three dormitories, communal kitchen, and double and twin rooms with shared bathrooms are clean and comfortable. There are also five *bure* set amongst the trees and these offer excellent value with plump beds, private decks, TVs and DVD players (movies are available). The lakeside bar and restaurant (mains $15-28) is a pretty place to hang out.

The only drawback is the 11km taxi ride ($8) back to town. Alternatively, the Tacirua Transport bus to Sawani passes the Raintree Lodge ($2, 30 minutes) half-hourly Monday through Saturday.

✗ Eating

For a compact city, Suva offers a relatively diverse and multicultural array of eateries. It's the best place in Fiji to try authentic Fijian and Indo-Fijian food, but there are plenty of Western-style options on offer if your tummy and palate are timid.

Guava FUSION $$
TOP CHOICE
(Map p92; ☎362 1051; 22 Marion St; lunch specials $15; ⊗breakfast & lunch; ⊜). Check out this restaurant, housed in a beautifully restored cottage that's a five-minute taxi ride above town. There's great fresh food served in interesting Pacific and Western combinations, with several salads and hot dishes of the day on offer. Run by long-time Suva restaurateur and chef Janey King-Lilo, it's usually full of local identities and expats engaged in various conversations and negotiations.

Old Mill Cottage FIJIAN $
(Map p92; ☎331 2134; 49 Carnarvon St; dishes $5-12; ⊗breakfast & lunch Mon-Sat; ⊜) Officials and government aides from the nearby embassies cram the front verandah of this cheap and cheerful Suva institution to dabble in authentic Fijian fare. Dishes including *palusami* (meat, onion and *lolo* – coconut cream – wrapped in *dalo* leaves) are displayed under the front counter alongside Indian curries and vegetarian dishes.

Rave Bistro BISTRO $$
(Map p92; Carnarvon St; dishes $12-25; ⊗lunch & dinner Mon-Sat; ⊜❀) In an adjoining renovated cottage next to the Old Mill, this bar-bistro gets busy with the after-work crowd in its indoor/outdoor settings. Good laksas are on the eclectic menu and there's decent

coffee. It's cool in all senses – blissfully air-conditioned.

Daikoku JAPANESE $$$
(Map p92; ☎330 8968; Victoria Pde; mains $25-40; ⊗lunch & dinner Mon-Sat) Upstairs past the closet-sized bar, the acrobatic culinary skills of Daikoku's teppanyaki chefs are reason enough to spend an evening here. The seafood, chicken and beef seared on the sizzling teppanyaki plates would hold up in any Tokyo restaurant. Partner restaurant to Daikoku in Nadi, the $15 lunch specials are popular here too. Arrive promptly at midday or be prepared to wait.

Tiko's Floating Restaurant INTERNATIONAL $$$
(Map p92; ☎331 3626; off Stinson Pde; mains $25-40; ⊗lunch & dinner Mon-Fri, dinner Sat; ⊜❀) The only way you could be any more harbourside would be if you were standing in the water. This permanently moored former Blue Lagoon cruise ship is best enjoyed when there's little motion in the ocean. The excellent surf-and-turf fare includes New Zealand steak, fresh local fish (*walu* and *pakapaka*) and an extensive wine list. Everything is served on white linen and in fine china and glassware.

Ashiyana INDIAN $$
(Map p92; ☎331 3000; Old Town Hall Bldg, Victoria Pde; mains $10-20; ⊗lunch & dinner Tue-Sat, dinner Sun) This pint-sized restaurant is a long-standing Indian favourite with some of the best butter chicken in town and curries so spicy even the taxi drivers consider them hot.

Maya Dhaba INDIAN $$
(Map p92; ☎331 0045; 281 Victoria Pde; mains $13-22; ⊗lunch & dinner; ⊜❀) Maya Dhaba looks ready for a refurb, but still screens hip-gyrating Bollywood musicals on flat-screen TVs in Suva's most urbane restaurant. The meals are excellent: wrap your naan around any number of familiar and not so familiar Indian classics, such as goat masala ($20).

Shanghai Seafood House CHINESE $$
(Map p92; ☎331 4865; 6 Thomson St; mains $13-20; ⊗lunch & dinner) In the heart of the shopping district, this 1st-floor restaurant is plush in a kitschy, fake-flower kind of way. The encyclopaedic menu and al fresco seating on the 1914 building's balcony induce long and lazy lunches.

Mango Café SANDWICHES $
(Map p90; Ratu Sukuna Rd, Nasese; mains from $10; ⊗breakfast, lunch & dinner; ⊜❀) This groovy little cafe is the place to stop during a walk

or drive along the Suva waterfront. It serves good coffee and fresh salady wraps, with comfortable cool indoor tables and a garden forecourt.

Esquires Coffee House   CAFE $

(Map p92; ☎330 0828; Renwick Rd; ☺breakfast, lunch & dinner; ☻✳) Popular for informal work meetings, this air-con café serves good coffee ($4 to $5.50) and ordinary cakes and sandwiches ($3 to $9). Regular clientele include government and international workers from the offices opposite.

Barbecue Stands   BARBECUE $

(Map p92; beside the handicraft market; meal boxes $6; ☺5pm-4am Tue-Sat) The teams of cooks here serve Suva's best-value meals into the wee hours of the night. Styrofoam boxes are crammed with enough carbs and cholesterol (taro, sausage, chops, cassava, lamb steak, eggs with a token serve of coleslaw) to arrest the heart of a marathon runner.

Cheap and cheerful curry houses abound. Try **Singh's Curry House** (Map p92; Gordon St) and **Murlidhar's Vegetarian Restaurant** (Map p92; Harbour Centre Food Court).

Suva's **food courts** have large selections of cheap lunchtime eats, especially the ones at **Downtown Boulevard Shopping Centre** (Map p92; Ellery St), **Dolphin Plaza** (Map p92; cnr Loftus St & Victoria Pde), **Harbour Centre** (Map p92; btwn Thomson & Scott St) and **MHCC Department Store** (Map p92; Thomson St; ☺9am-9pm).

Self-Catering

Suva Municipal Market   MARKET

(Map p90; Usher St) The best place for fish, fruit and vegetables.

Victoria Wines & Spirits   SELF-CATERING

(Map p92; Victoria Pde; ☺11am-9pm Mon-Fri, to 2pm Sat) For something to wash it all down with.

Superfresh   SUPERMARKET

(Map p92; Thomson St) The best supermarket in town is in the MHCC Department Store. You can also pick up fresh bread and muffins from the bakery on the ground floor.

🍷 Drinking

Suva has a good mix of drinking and dancing dens. The place to be on Thursday, Friday and Saturday nights is at the bars around Victoria Pde and Macarthur St. Generally, dress standards are very relaxed and although some of the bars may seem rough,

the ones listed here are all fairly safe. If a band is playing or the hour late, expect to pay a small cover charge (usually no more than $5). On the other hand, if you arrive early, entry is free and drinks are discounted between the happy hours of 6pm and 8pm.

Be cautious around other nightclubs. They tend to become dodgier as the night progresses and most locals attend them only with a group of friends – you should do the same. Watch out for pickpockets on the dance floor and always take a taxi after dark, even if you're in a group. The *Fiji Times'* entertainment section lists upcoming events and what's on at the clubs.

O'Reilly's   PUB

(Map p92; ☎331 2322; cnr Macarthur St & Victoria Pde) A combination of **O'Reilly's nightclub**, **Shenanigans bar** (a non-smoking area) and **Bad Dog Café**, O'Reilly's kicks the evening off in relatively subdued fashion: relaxed punters eating, playing pool or watching sport on the numerous TVs. But it brews quite a party as the hours tick by and come 11pm-ish, the place is generally throbbing with a diverse crowd shaking their bits to Europop, soft metal, techno, peppy rock-pop...basically anything that keeps the crowd moving. It is one of the few pubs where a reasonably smart dress code prevails, so dig out your best threads. It's an expat and professional-Fijian haunt more than a welcome-all-comers place.

Traps Bar   LIVE MUSIC

(Map p92; ☎331 2922; Victoria Pde) Something of a subterranean saloon bar with a series of cavelike, dimly lit rooms. Take a seat in the pool room with wide-screen TV (yes, with sports) or join the happy din at the main bar. The crowd is generally young, trendy, relatively affluent and dancing by 11pm. Live music is frequent (usually on Thursdays), as are Bob Marley singalongs.

Bourbon Bluez   BAR

(Map p92; ☎330 0945; cnr Macarthur St & Victoria Pde) Two rooms, two bars and two sets of speakers playing different music at the same time. You'll never quite know what to expect here and if you stand anywhere near the middle of the bar, you'll hear it all. When we arrived, one room was playing ABBA and the other Guns N' Roses. When we left, the band was trying to make itself heard over an enthusiastic karaoke singer. It's a popular hangout for locals.

MOVING TO THE BEAT OF A DIFFERENT DRUM

Dancers pay homage to the steady beat of the drums, seemingly oblivious to the spectators. The poorly lit room is crowded with both tourists and locals yelling 'bula' to one another over the din. As a big, indigenous Fijian man – who better meets the image you may have of a traditional Fijian chief – approaches with a flower behind his ear and a pitcher of beer on his tray, you don't need any reminding that this is no meke (dance performance that enacts stories and legends). This is Saturday night in Suva, when the country's urban youth let down their hair and pole dance to pop music.

Fiji's urban youth face many of the same difficulties as young people around the globe: teenage parenting, crime, drugs and skyrocketing unemployment. However, these youths also find themselves straddling two opposing worlds: the traditional, conservative society of the villages many have left behind, where life was filled with cultural protocols, and the liberal, individualistic lifestyle of the modern and increasingly Westernised city. With 90% of television airtime devoted to Western sitcoms, young people watch a TV screen filled with an irrelevant and often unattainable world. On the positive side, the rising club and cafe culture is bringing together youths from indigenous and Indo-Fijian backgrounds, in the midst of a city filled with ethnic tension. On the negative side, many have difficulty finding a job and returning 'home' to a village sporting dreadlocks and skin-tight jeans isn't much easier. Youth have little room to voice their own opinions and it's not entirely surprising that many look for routes out of the country.

This is not the Fiji of postcards, of grass skirts and beachside lovo (Fijian feast cooked in a pit oven). However, it's well worth grabbing a cappuccino or putting on your dancing shoes to check out Fiji's rising urban youth culture. It's an unexpected eye-opener.

Friends (Map p92; Terry Walk) and **Liquids** (Map p92; upstairs, Harbour Centre) are recommended by locals as having an interesting mix of both music and people, drawn by cheaper drinks than O'Reilly's and Traps.

☆ Entertainment

Fijians are fanatical about their rugby and, even if you aren't that keen on the game, it's worth going to a match. The season lasts from April to September.

National Stadium STADIUM
(Map p90; Laucala Bay Rd) Rugby teams tough it out here and the match atmosphere is huge. You can also catch players training hard at **Albert Park** during the week.

Damodar Village Cinema CINEMA
(Map p92; www.damodarvillage.com.fj; Scott St; adult/child $6/5) Recently released Hollywood and Bollywood films battle it out at Suva's six-screen cinema complex. Check out the Fiji Times' entertainment section for cinema listings.

🛍 Shopping

Your best chance of finding something truly unique is to skip the mass-produced stuff found in the chain tourist stores (which are carbon copies of their Nadi parents) and head straight to the markets.

Suva Curio &
Handicraft Market HANDICRAFTS
(Map p92; Stinson Pde) Strap on your barter boots: this market has endless craft stalls and, if you know your stuff, can offer some fantastic deals. Just be aware that not many of the artefacts are as genuine as the vendor would like you to believe. Only pay what the object is worth to you. A 2.1m by 1.2m ibe (mat) goes for between $45 and $75 (depending on how fine the weaving is) and a completely plain white tapa cloth costs around $45 for a 3.6m by 0.6m length.

Suva Flea Market HANDICRAFTS
(Map p90; Rodwell Rd) Less touristy than the handicraft market previously mentioned, this is another great place to buy masi and traditional crafts, but you might have to sort through the Hawaiian shirts to find them. There's a great secondhand bookshop out the back.

ROC Market CRAFT
(Map p92; Dolphin Plaza, Victoria Pde) The Dolphin Plaza holds a small but eclectic market on the third Sunday of every month. Stalls feature homemade food and arts and crafts at reasonable prices.

Fiji Museum BOOKSHOP

(Map p92; ☑331 5944; www.fijimuseum.org.fj; Thurston Gardens; ☺9.30am-4.30pm Mon-Sat) The gift shop stocks a good selection of Fijian books on history, cooking and birds.

USP Book Centre BOOKSHOP

(Map p90; ☑323 2500; www.uspbookcentre.com; University of the South Pacific) Excellent selection of local and international novels, travel guides and Pacific fiction and nonfiction.

ℹ Information

Dangers & Annoyances

Suva suffers many of the same dangers as most urbanised centres. Walking around during daylight hours is perfectly safe, but as night descends, follow the example of locals and catch a taxi. They are metered, cheap and safe.

Emergency

Ambulance (☑911, 330 2584)
Fire (☑911, 331 2877)
Police (Map p92; ☑911, 331 1222; Pratt St) There is also a police post on Cumming St.

Internet Access

Internet access is cheap and abundant in Suva. Convenient places include the following:
Connect Internet Café (Map p92; Scott St; per hr $3; ☺8.00am-10pm Mon-Fri, 9am-10pm Sat, 9am-8pm Sun)
Suva City Library (Map p92; Victoria Pde; per hr $3; ☺9.30am-5.30pm Mon-Fri, to noon Sat)

Medical Services

Visits to general practitioners are usually between $20 and $30.
Suva Private Hospital (Map p90; ☑330 3404; Amy St)
Colonial War Memorial Hospital (Map p90; ☑331 3444; Waimanu Rd) Fiji's **Recompression Chamber Facility** (☑321 5525; ☺7am-5pm Mon-Fri) is located here. It's on-call 24 hours a day.
Maharaj Medical Centre (Map p90; ☑327 0164; Sports City Centre, Laucala Bay Rd, Laucala Bay; ☺9am-1pm, 2-6pm Mon-Fri, 9am-1pm Sat & Sun) Private medical centre.
Suva City Pharmacy (Map p92; Thomson St) Large and well-stocked pharmacy. There are many in town.

Money

There are plenty of ATMs and Western Union–affiliated currency exchange shops scattered along Victoria Pde. Both the banks listed here have ATMs, foreign-exchange counters and will cash travellers cheques.

ANZ Bank (Map p92; ☑132 411; 25 Victoria Pde)
Westpac Bank (Map p92; ☑132 032; 1 Thomson St)

Post

Post Fiji (Map p92; ☑321 8450; Thomson St)

Tourist Information

There is no longer a visitor centre in Suva, but most hotels have a tours and information desk.
ATS Pacific (Holiday Inn (Map p92; ☑330 1600; Victoria Pde); Novotel Suva Lami Bay (Map p90; ☑336 4086; Queens Rd)) Books local tours and activities, including those at nearby Pacific Harbour.

Travel Agencies

MacQuarie Travel (Map p92; ☑331 5870; Ground fl, Dominion House Arcade, Thomson St) Avoid the queues at Air Pacific and book your domestic and international flights here.

Websites

Lonely Planet (www.lonelyplanet.com/fiji/viti-levu/suva)

ℹ Getting There & Away

Suva is well connected to the rest of the country by air and interisland ferries, and to western Viti Levu by buses and carriers. Most international flights, however, arrive at Nadi International Airport.

Air

Nausori International Airport is around 23km northeast of central Suva. **Nausori Taxi & Bus Service** (☑347 7583) runs regular shuttle buses between the airport and the Holiday Inn hotel in Suva ($10). Otherwise, a taxi from the airport to or from Suva costs around $28.

See p234 for domestic flight routes.

Airline offices in Suva include the following:
Air New Zealand (Map p92; ☑331 3100; www.pacificislands.airnewzealand.com; Queensland Insurance Bldg, Victoria Pde)
Air Pacific & Pacific Sun (Fiji Air; Map p92; ☑330 4388; www.airpacific.com, www.pacificsun.com.fj; Colonial Bldg, Victoria Pde)
Pacific Blue (Map p92; ☑331 5311, www.virginblue.com.au; 81/85 Marks St)
Qantas (Map p92; ☑331 1833; Colonial Bldg, Victoria Pde)

Boat

There are regular ferry services from Suva to Ovalau ($35, four to six hours), Vanua Levu, Taveuni and Kadavu ($50, four to five hours), plus less regular, and far less comfortable, boats to the Lau and Moala Groups. Not many travellers use these boats, and conditions are generally a far cry from anything the words 'a cruise on the South Pacific' might imply. For details about these interisland boats see p235.

Bus & Carrier

There are frequent local buses operating along the Queens Road and Kings Road from Suva's main **bus station** (Map p90; Rodwell Rd). These will stop at resorts along the way upon request. Other buses are operated by the following companies:

Sunbeam Transport (☑338 2122; www.sunbeamfiji.com) Runs several express buses daily to Lautoka via both the southern (Queens Road) and northern (Kings Road) routes.

Pacific Transport (☑330 4366) Runs several daily express buses to Lautoka ($14.20) via the Queens Road, with stops at Pacific Harbour ($3.60), Korolevu ($6.70), Sigatoka ($8.50) and Nadi ($9.35).

Coral Sun Fiji (☑620 3086; www.coralsunexpress.com) Runs a twice-daily service between Suva and Nadi International Airport ($22), stopping at the main resorts on the Queens Road along the way.

Minibuses travelling west along the Queens Road depart from behind the cinema. They are slightly faster than normal buses and depart when full. It costs $5 to Pacific Harbour, $10 to Sigatoka, $15 to Nadi and $17 to Lautoka (per person).

❶ Getting Around

Taxis are cheap for short trips ($3 to $5). The city's one-way looping streets may make you think the taxi driver is taking you for a ride, but along Victoria Pde it's easy to get caught up on a long run around the market and wharf area. Two 24-hr services are listed here:

Matua Taxis (☑5115)
Piccadilly Taxis (☑330 4302)

Local buses are cheap and plentiful, and depart from the main bus station. There are relatively few buses in the evening and barely any on Sundays.

See p237 for a list of car-rental companies in Suva.

KINGS ROAD

Carving a scenic route between Suva and Lautoka, the Kings Road is every bit as spectacular as the faster and more popular Queens Road route. Much fuss is made of the pothole-ridden roads, the ageing buses and the general lack of infrastructure in northern Viti Levu, but for those who don't mind a few bumps – and that's all you'll get – a lush interior and gorgeous views over the

Wainibuka River awaits, with the occasional village meandering its way along the road and river.

The road coils and extends for around 256km, linking the country's two largest cities via the mainland's least developed coast. Promises to upgrade the road have been in the pipeline for many years and work has been carried out at an excruciatingly slow rate. However, by the time of this latest research, only a 20km section of road west of Korovou remained unsealed and earthmovers were in evidence. A Sunbeam Transport (www.sunbeamfiji.com) express bus takes around six hours to trundle between Suva and Lautoka, although most travellers layover at Rakiraki or Nananu-i-Ra.

Nausori & the Rewa Delta

❶ Getting There & Around

The Kings Road from Suva to Nausori is the country's busiest and most congested stretch of highway. Regular buses ($2.50, 30 to 45 minutes) travel this route. The Nausori bus station is in the main street. **Sunbeam Transport** (www.sunbeamfiji.com) has regular buses to Lautoka via the Kings Road ($15.80, 6 hours).

Regular buses run from Nausori to nearby boat landings: Bau Landing, Wainibokasi Landing (for Nasilai village) and Nakelo Landing (for Toberua).

NAUSORI
POP 47,600

The township of Nausori is on the eastern bank of the Rewa River, about 19km northeast of downtown Suva, with the country's second-largest airport on its outskirts. Nausori is a bustling service centre and transport hub for the largely agricultural- and manufacturing-industry workers.

The town developed around the CSR sugar mill that operated here for eight decades between 1881 and 1959, when everyone realised that the canes actually grew better on the drier western side. Recent experiments to grow and mill rice on a large scale proved futile, though in 2011 a new rice mill was opened for local use.

There are many eroded 18th century and earlier ring-ditch fortifications in the Rewa Delta. About 10m wide with steep, battered sides and a strong fence on the inner bank, they were necessary for the survival of a village in times of war, protecting it against a surprise attack.

ⓘ **Getting There & Away**

Nausori International Airport is about 3km southeast of Nausori, 22km from Suva. Despite its name, this is primarily a domestic airport, although at time of research, Air Pacific (Fiji Air) was flying weekly to New Zealand, Tonga and Tuvalu from here. See p234 for details of flying domestically within Fiji.

NASILAI VILLAGE & NAILILILI CATHOLIC MISSION

Nasilai village is home to the well-known potter Taraivini Wati whose work is in the Suva museum. Pottery is a major source of income for the village and when large orders are placed everyone participates in the process – helping to collect and prepare the clay and make the pots. When a baby girl is born in the village, a lump of clay is placed on her forehead. It's believed she will then automatically know how to carry on the pottery-making tradition.

Catholic missionaries from France built the **Naililili Catholic Mission** (Map p48) at the turn of the century. The stained-glass windows were imported from Europe and incorporate Fijian writing and imagery.

There are regular buses to Wainibokasi Landing from Nausori bus station. There you can catch a boat to the Naililili Catholic Mission, which is almost opposite the landing, or take a short trip downriver to Nasilai village. Ask a local for permission to visit the village and take along some kava for a *sevusevu*.

If driving from Nausori, head southeast for 6km on the road that runs parallel to the Rewa River. Pass the airport entrance and turn right at the T-junction. The landing is a further 5km from here, well past the bridge across the Wainibokasi River – follow the sealed road.

BAU

It is bizarre to think that in the 19th century this tiny island was the power base of Cakobau and his father Tanoa (see p198). In the 1780s, there were 30 *bure kalou* (ancient temples) on the small chiefly island, including the famous Na Vata ni Tawake, which stood on a huge *yavu* faced with large panels of flat rock. Also of interest are its **chiefly cemetery**, **old church** and a **sacrificial killing stone** on which enemies were slaughtered prior to being cooked and consumed.

Bau is not an official tourist attraction and to visit you must first be invited by someone who lives there. If you dress conservatively, show polite and genuine interest, take a large *waka* (bunch of kava roots) for presentation to the *turaga-ni-koro* (chief) and ask around at Bau Landing, you'll probably be invited to visit. Failing that, ask for permission from the Tailevu Provincial Council offices at Ratu Cakobau House in Nausori.

There are regular buses from Nausori bus station to Bau Landing, which is northeast of Nausori International Airport. If you are driving from Nausori, turn left onto Bau Rd about 1km before the airport and follow the road to its end. Boats cross to nearby Bau. Boats also leave Bau Landing for the island of **Viwa**, where missionaries lived during Cakobau's time.

TOBERUA

This small island (2 hectares) is just off Kaba Point, the easternmost point of Viti Levu, about 30km from Suva.

All the island's tiny landmass is taken up by low-key **Toberua Island Resort** (Map p48; ☑347 2777; www.toberua.com; bure $612-948; ☒). It's the perfect island hideaway for those seeking some South Pacific solitude. Originally built in 1968 as an American millionaire's hideaway, it's since reinvented itself to cater to unfussy couples and families. Children under 16 stay free. The 15 waterfront *bure* scattered along the beach have gloriously high roofs, minibars, sun decks and stylish bathrooms. The sunset-facing bar and **restaurant** (meal plan adult/child $144/66) serves delicious fresh food, with home-made snacks at cocktail hour and afternoon tea. Toberua only receives about one-third of Suva's annual rainfall so the climate is balmy for most of the year; it's popular with Suva weekenders. At low tide the beach is used for golf and there is snorkelling, paddle boating, and tours to the nearby bird sanctuary and mangroves. A two-tank dive costs $235 and a PADI Open Water Course $868.

Transfers ($192 return per person, up to three children travel free) from Nausori or Suva involve a taxi to Nakelo Landing, followed by a glorious 40-minute boat trip along a stretch of the Rewa River delta and coast.

Korovou to Rakiraki via Kings Road

With any luck, by the time you read this, the Kings Road will be entirely sealed. When we drove it in late 2011, about 20km of road west of Korovou was still under construction, and very slow and pot-holey it was, too. Although locals tackle the unsealed section in two-wheel drive cars, it's best traversed by 4WD and with a prayer to the god of suspension. After a downpour you can throw the complication of mud into the equation. The reward is a green and scenic landscape, devoid of a coastline and commercial infrastructure, which crosses dairy-farming country (land given to returned soldiers after WWII), winds through hills and along the Wainibuka River, and passes many villages. It's one of the prettiest road trips in the country; travelling by bus will afford the views without the hassle.

Korovou is not much more than a transport intersection, about 50km north of Suva. From here, the Kings Road continues to the northwest and over the hills. About 14km from Korovou on the Kings Road, you'll pass the beautiful Uru's Waterfall (Map p48), which descends over a rocky slope on the northern side of the road and ends its journey in a serene pool surrounded by colourful foliage. It's possible to swim here – just ask one of the villagers for permission.

At Wailotua village, 23km west of Korovou, the Snake God Cave (Map p48) is reputedly one of the largest caves in the world. The name is derived from six glittering stalactites in the shape of snakes' heads. During times of tribal war, the village would pack up en masse and seek shelter in the cave's pitch-black labyrinth, which culminates in a huge chamber inhabited by bats. To get here, hop on one of the Suva–Lautoka buses and ask the driver to let you off at the village. Ask the first person you approach if you can visit the cave. They'll organise a couple of lads to guide you through it by lantern. This is the village's main source of income and a $15 donation is well worth the tour and commentary. Wailotua village also entertains Feejee Experience groups, which call in for *bilibili* rafting and visits to local schools on their way to Rakiraki.

Korovou to Rakiraki via the East Coast

A fantastic sealed road (the best we drove on in Viti Levu) follows the coast from Korovou to Natovi Landing. It's a 20-minute drive and there are bus-ferry-bus services to Levuka (Ovalau) from the landing. There is a small general store, and people fishing with handlines from the jetty, but little else. Patterson Brothers runs a Suva–Natovi–Ovalau bus-ferry service ($65, daily except Wednes-

day and Sunday) to Levuka; the boat leaves Natovi around lunchtime.

Transfers to resorts on Leluvia and Caqalai in the Lomaiviti Group of islands are from Waidalice Landing (Map p48), southeast of Korovou; these need to be booked in advance.

Beyond Natovi the road reverts to slow-going gravel.

Sleeping

Natalei Eco-Lodge LODGE $
(Map p48; ☎949 7460; nataleiecolodge@gmail.com; dm/r incl meals $80/120) At Natalei is this low-key, village-based tourism project, about half an hour's drive beyond Natovi, which provides a great opportunity to swerve right off the beaten track and into a cultural adventure. The double and dorm *bure* are frugal (as are the meals – take some snacks), but exploring the surrounding sea and landscape is the real appeal here. Just inland is Mt Tova, where you can hike to waterfalls. Moon Reef, a 20-minute boat ride away, is renowned for snorkelling. Some truly fabulous close encounters with spinner dolphins are (almost always) guaranteed there ($40 per person). It's also a popular destination for Suva weekenders, school groups and NGO workshops. The Suva–Burewai bus ($5.80, three hours) departs three times daily and drops off about 300m from the lodge entrance.

Takalana Bay Retreat BURE $$
(☎991 6338; takalana@gmail.com; d/f incl all meals $220/285) High on a breezy rise above the bay is a two-room *bure*, just along the road from Natalei and run by a family from the same village. While it's more comfortable and private, it's further from the beach.

Beyond Natalei, the gravel road continues north along the coast before curving inland to meet the Kings Road about 30km south of Rakiraki. Locals drive it in all vehicles and in most weather, but we were happy to have the reassuring clearance of a 4WD.

Rakiraki & Around

The scenery continues to be stunning along the Kings Road, winding past Viti Levu Bay and into the beautiful region of Rakiraki, Viti Levu's northernmost tip. The climate on the northern side of the Nakauvadra Range is similar to that of western Viti Levu – drier and suited to growing sugar cane – but far windier. According to local legend, the imposing mountains are the home of the great snake-god Degei, creator of all the islands. The opening and closing of his eyes prompt night and day, and thunder is said to be Degei turning in his sleep.

The turn-off to Ellington Wharf is about 5km east of Rakiraki junction and it is here that resorts collect their guests for the 15-minute boat ride across to Nananu-i-Ra.

West of Rakiraki junction, there is a turn-off that leads past the sugar mill to the small service town of Vaileka. This is where those arriving by bus will be deposited and it's a good place to stock up on provisions before heading offshore. Besides the bus sta-

Rakiraki & Nananu-i-Ra

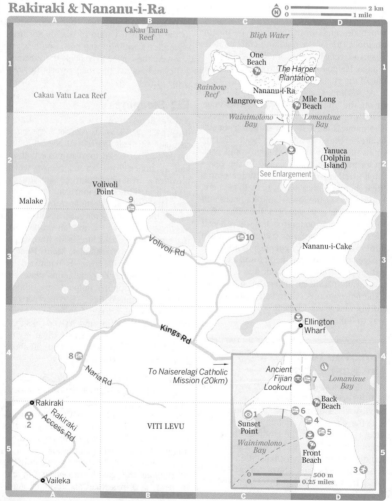

tion itself, town amenities include a New World supermarket, a taxi rank, a produce market, a Westpac bank and a couple of other ATMs, internet places and several fast-food restaurants. We ate a really good, cheap curry – with a staggering array of side dishes – at the **Sunbeam Transport** (www.sunbeamfiji.com) bus ticket office/restaurant.

◉ Sights

Naiserelagi Catholic Mission   CHURCH
(Map p48) About 25km southeast of Rakiraki, overlooking Viti Levu Bay, this 1917 church is famous for its mural depicting a black Christ, painted in 1962 by Jean Charlot. The three panels of biblical scenes depict Christ on the cross in a *masi sulu* (skirt or wrapped cloth worn to below the knees) with a *tanoa* at his feet. Indigenous Fijians are shown offering mats and *tabua* (whale's tooth), and Indo-Fijians presenting flowers and oxen. Visitors are welcome and a small donation is appreciated.

To get there, take the **Flying Prince** local bus ($2, 30 minutes, five to eight daily) from Vaileka or the Kings Road intersection, ideally before 9am when buses are more regular. Otherwise it will cost $36 return by taxi. Naiserelagi is just south of Nanukuloa village, on the right past the school. The mission is on the hill, about 500m up a winding track.

Udreudre's Tomb   HISTORIC SITE
If you have commandeered your own taxi, ask the driver to show you the resting place of Fiji's most notorious cannibal (see the boxed text, p110). The tomb isn't very impressive, just a rectangular block of concrete

---

Rakiraki & Nananu-i-Ra

---

often overgrown with weeds, but it's just by the roadside, on the left about 100m west of the Vaileka/Kings Road intersection.

About 10km west of Rakiraki, near Vitawa, is a large outcrop known as **Navatu Rock** (Map p48). There was once a fortified village on top of the rock and it was believed that from here spirits would depart for the afterlife.

☆ Activities

One of the principal reasons to visit the Rakiraki area is the excellent **scuba diving** to be had on the nearby Cakau Vatu Lacca and Cakau Tanau Reefs, where notable dive sites include **Dream Maker's** large coral heads, **Breath Taker's** concentration of fish, **Spud Dome's** dramatic scenery and the possibility of pelagics at **Heartbreak Ridge**. The mainland resorts and those on Nananu-i-Ra island all use the same dive spots and will happily collect divers from anywhere in the area (usually for around $40, depending on how far they have to come).

Offshore, Nananu-i-Ra is renowned for **windsurfing** and **kiteboarding**.

⌂ Sleeping

Volivoli Beach Resort   RESORT **$**
(☑ 669 4511; www.volivoli.com; dm $31.50, d $126-250, villa $320; ✱⚛) Located on the northernmost point of Viti Levu, Volivoli offers some of the best dorm accommodation in Fiji. Several eight-person dorms, each with two bathrooms, are in a modern and spotlessly clean hillside lodge, sharing a huge deck. Further up the hill is another lodge divided into four doubles that share a communal lounge, two bathrooms and a wide hall that doubles as a kitchen. Far removed from the noisy backpackers and on the opposite side of the **restaurant** (mains $20-35) and bar are self-contained two-bedroom villas with sweeping ocean views and modern, crisp interiors.

If you are disappointed by the mangrove-lined beach, you'll be pleasantly surprised by the picturesque sand spit only a minute's walk around the corner. Here you will find **Ra Divers** (www.radivers.com), which charges $165 for a two-tank dive. Volivoli also offers some dorm-and-dive packages, rents snorkel gear for $10 and shuttles snorkellers to the outer reef for $25.

Wananavu Beach Resort   RESORT **$$$**
(☑ 669 4433; www.wananavu.com; bure incl breakfast from $470; ✱@⚛) Wananavu has an indoor and outdoor **restaurant** (mains $18-$39) with

AN UNEARTHLY APPETITE

In 1849, some time after the death of Ratu Udreudre (p109), the Reverend Richard Lyth asked Udreudre's son, Ratavu, about the significance of a long line of stones. Each stone, he was told, represented one of the chief's victims and amounted to a personal tally of at least 872 corpses. Ratavu went on to explain that his father consumed every piece of his victims of war, sharing none. He ate little else, and had an enormous appetite.

gorgeous views out over the beautiful pool area and across to Nananu-i-Ra island. All the *bure* have timber floors, panelled walls, aircon and their own small decks. They are surrounded by pretty palm- and bougainvillea-filled gardens. Garden *bure* are older and the prices climb dramatically as you head down the hill towards the water. The beach here is entirely artificially created and although the landscapers have done an excellent job, with strategically placed palm trees perfect for slinging a hammock between, most guests end up swimming in the pool. Diving and snorkelling are provided by Reef Safari (www.reefsafari.com), who are based at the resort's small marina.

Tanoa Rakiraki Hotel HOTEL $
(☑669 4101; www.tanoahotels.com; Kings Rd; r 135; ❄☂) Part of the Tanoa chain, this is an ageing midrange hotel, which also offers dorms and cheap singles in a lodge out back (if there are no long-term student groups in residence). It's located 1.8km east of the Vaileka turn-off. Although popular with local business people, it runs a poor second to neighbouring options – there is little, beyond a bowling green, to tempt travellers.

❶ Getting There & Around

If you're not driving yourself, the best way to reach the resorts of Rakiraki and Nananu-i-Ra island is to catch a **Sunbeam Transport** (www.sunbeamfiji.com) express bus along the Kings Road from either Suva ($12.90, 4½ hours) or Nadi ($11.50, 2¼ hours) and get off at Vaileka, Rakiraki's main town. Keep hold of your bus ticket because the conductors on this route are tirelessly dedicated to checking them. From Vaileka, a taxi costs $15 to Volivoli Beach Resort, Wananavu Beach Resort or Ellington Wharf (to catch your prearranged boat to Nananu-i-Ra).

Your other option is to time it for the 7am or 8.30am **Flying Prince** local bus that runs directly to Ellington Wharf from Vaileka or catch any Kings Road local bus and walk the 1.3km from the junction to the wharf.

Nananu-i-Ra

This pocket-sized island is on the itinerary of most travellers to northern Viti Levu. The 3.5-sq-km island is beautifully hilly, and is surrounded by scalloped bays, white-sand beaches and mangroves. There are, however, neither roads nor villages, and accommodation is simple. Former cattle-grazing cleared much of the dense vegetation and today rolling hills of grass inhabit the interior. It's only 3km north of Ellington Wharf, but the atypical landscape and small enclave of wealthy holiday homes exaggerate the distance. Nananu-i-Ra's original inhabitants were wiped out by disease and tribal war, and their land was sold by their surviving heirs, mostly to Fijians of European descent.

Nananu-i-Ra is renowned for its offshore reefs and for windsurfing and kiteboarding. It can get very windy on the east side of the island from May through to July and again from late October to December during the cyclone season. The narrow strip of land that separates the west (Front Beach) from the east (Back Beach) is only 200m wide and no matter which way the wind blows, it's only a short walk to the calmer side. Walking tracks across the inland hills offer a good chance to stretch your legs.

Rumours abound about developing the island, but so far that's all they are...

🏃 Activities

Trekking

The island is good for trekking, with tracks across the top and wonderful views to the mainland. A common sight from the southern side of the island is billowing white clouds swallowing the volcanic Nakauvadra mountain range. The grassy hilltops also provide bird's-eye views of the surrounding turquoise reefs and the aptly named Sunset Point, where Ed Morris, a past president of the International Brotherhood of Magicians, has constructed a (small) labyrinth. If you are lucky, Ed will be around to explain what it all means.

If you time it right with the tides, you can walk around the island in about four to five hours (passing the mangroves at low tide). Part of the island is rocky so shoes are recommended.

Diving & Snorkelling

Snorkelling offshore you can expect to see some coral, abundant fish and, on the north side of the island, many sea snakes. The surrounding reefs and especially the Vatu-i-Ra passage to the north have some amazing dive sites (see p138).

The only PADI dive operation on the island is run by **Safari Lodge** (⌨628 3332, 948 8888; www.safarilodge.com.fj; two-tank dive $185, PADI Open Water Course $690). A local diver (⌨944 4726; papoodivers@gmail.com) with long experience on the island also offers dive trips (two-tank dive $180).

Windsurfing & Kiteboarding

The climate here is relatively dry and the island's exposure to the southeast trade winds make it especially suited for windsurfing. Many windsurfers come here between May to July when winds are generally 10 knots or more on most days. **Safari Lodge** (⌨628 3332, 948 8888; www.safarilodge.com.fj) has both kiteboarding ($220/580 per two/six hours) and windsurfing gear for hire (beginner/advanced equipment $350/500 per week), together with an experienced instructor. Because of the reef, and the possibility of torn sails, a first-time, one-off lesson ($85) is advisable to access your coral-avoiding skills.

🛏 Sleeping & Eating

Most places accept credit cards – check before you go – and are well set up for self-caterers. Safari Lodge, Betham's and McDonald's Beach Cottages have indoor/outdoor cafes with limited menus and small stores selling the basics. Vegetarians might want to bring their own fruit and vegetables from the mainland to ensure supply.

Expect cold-water showers and the generator to be switched off around 10pm at most places.

🏄 **Safari Lodge**   LODGE $
(Map p108; ⌨628 3332, 948 8888; www.safarilodge.com.fj; site per tent/dm/d $10/30/95, r $150, bure $195-320) There's a terrific variety of accommodation here, to suit all styles and budgets. Meal plans ($65) are available, or you can self-cater. Simple, comfortable rooms and balconies peep through foliage to

the ocean, and creep up the hillside towards wide views and breezes. With the great range of outdoor activities available, it's the place to stay for the wind- and water-sports-inclined. The wind and water theme continues throughout. Safari Lodge is heavy on sustainability and light on the environment: a wind turbine provides 24-hour power and solar panels provide hot water.

Betham's Beach Cottages   CABIN $
(Map p108; ⌨669 4132; www.bethams.com.fj; dm/tw/cottage $28/85/145) Betham's has some sound, old-fashioned beach-house accommodation options. The duplex beachfront cottages have large kitchens, tiled floors and can sleep up to five people. The double rooms are good value and there is a large communal kitchen that is shared by those in the spacious eight-bed dorm. The open-air **restaurant** (mains $20-30) here serves hearty meals if you place your order by 1pm.

McDonald's Beach Cottages   CABIN $
(Map p108; ⌨628 3118; www.macsnananu.com; dm/tw $26/90, bure $135-145) McDonald's offers a scattering of supertidy self-contained cabins on a nicely landscaped property right in front of the jetty. The cute blue and yellow cottages are self-contained and it's popular with do-it-yourself types.

Charlie's Beach Cottages   CABIN $
(Map p108; ⌨628 3268; www.charliescottages.com; dm/d $30/115) Charlie's has a large beach cottage made of concrete blocks and is fairly basic. There's a double bed in the bedroom and the lounge can take a further four single beds if required. There is also a seven-bed dorm in a similar but smaller cottage.

ℹ Getting There & Around

Nananu-i-Ra is just a 15-minute boat ride from Ellington Wharf. All the resorts on Nananu-i-Ra have their own boat transfers but you need to arrange your pick-up in advance (there is also a phone at Ellington Wharf for last-minute decisions).

Boat transfers for the budget resorts are around $40 per person return. Coming back, you should spot the taxi that usually waits at the wharf for returning travellers. If there are none, phone ⌨930 9950 and one will come to collect you. A taxi costs $15 to Vaileka, $100 to Lautoka and $130 to Nadi. There is secure parking space at Ellington Wharf in the Safari Lodge compound, free to their guests.

The Mamanuca & Yasawa Groups

Includes »

Best Places to Eat

» Navutu Stars (p131)

» Mantaray Island Resort (p129)

» Nanuya Island Resort (p134)

» Travellers Tea House (p134)

Best Places to Stay

» Navini Island Resort (p118)

» Blue Lagoon Beach Resort (p135)

» Tokoriki Island Resort (p120)

» Castaway Island Resort (p120)

» Wayalailai Eco Haven Resort (p128)

Why Go?

Welcome to Fiji's glittering crown jewels – the Mamanuca and Yasawa Groups.

Like a string of pearls the 20 or so picture-perfect coral atolls and islands of the Mamanucas arc west through the large lagoon formed by the Malolo Barrier Reef and Viti Levu. It's a treasure trove of surf breaks, sea turtles, reef sharks and vast schools of multicoloured tropical fish.

The Yasawas pick up where the Mamanucas left off. They're grander in stature, more isolated in location and mellower in temperament. Today a high-speed catamaran threads its way between these rugged volcanic islands, pulling into one blue lagoon after another to share the riches of abundant sunshine, exquisite beaches, stunning coral gardens and creature comforts enough to ward off any hankerings for an early return to 'civilisation'.

Whatever your style – boutique adults-only, family-friendly, laid-back budget or remote Robinson Crusoe – you'll find it somewhere here.

When to Go
Mamanuca & Yasawa Groups

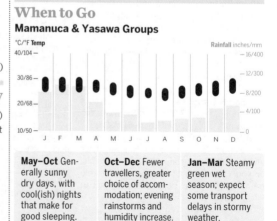

May–Oct Generally sunny dry days, with cool(ish) nights that make for good sleeping.

Oct–Dec Fewer travellers, greater choice of accommodation; evening rainstorms and humidity increase.

Jan–Mar Steamy green wet season; expect some transport delays in stormy weather.

MAMANUCA GROUP

Grab your favourite boardies or bikini, because here they are – the much-trumpeted, widely promoted, photographed and romanticised Mamanuca islands! Wildly popular with visitors, they're valued more for their natural beauty than any contribution they make to the national culture.

Pacific currents sweep nutrients through the passages around the islands and with them come underwater wonders. Above water, with more dive operators, world-class surf, five-star retreats and family-oriented resorts than any other group, the Mamanucas are anything but a well-kept secret.

Each morning a small army of day trippers, fortified with beach towels and factor-15 sunscreen, fan out from the mainland to conquer the white-sand beaches. They meet with no resistance. Most of the habitable islands (and many others that rely on desalination plants or freshwater deliveries) support resorts; this small string of islands forms the backbone of the Fijian tourist industry.

Perhaps because they box so far above their weight when it comes to hauling in the cash, life here bears little resemblance to the harsh realities experienced by most Fijians. Only two resort islands, Mana and Malolo, support Fijian villages but even here tourists outnumber locals. Not that they mind – almost all resorts lease their land from local communities and so, while heavy rain clouds hang over the mainland (both physically and metaphorically), the sun always shines on the magical Mamanucas.

🏃 Activities

The Mamanucas are all about water sports and extreme relaxation. Whether you are staying for a week or visiting for a day, nonmotorised water sports (like snorkelling, windsurfing, kayaking and sailing in catamarans) are nearly always provided free of charge. However, the moment an engine is fired you can expect to be billed. Waterskiing, parasailing and wakeboarding cost about $120 for 15 minutes. Village trips or snorkelling on the outer reef cost between $20 and $40 per person, and reef-fishing trips average around $150 per hour for four people. Island-hopping tours cost anywhere between $80 and $180 per person, depending on how many islands are visited and whether lunch is included. But, whatever you do, don't forget your book – hammocks just aren't the same without one.

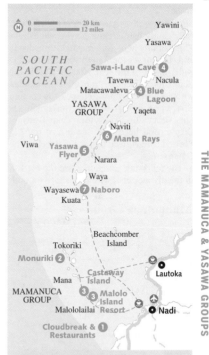

THE MAMANUCA & YASAWA GROUPS

The Mamanuca & Yasawa Groups Highlights

❶ Waxing up your board – the mighty surf breaks of **Cloudbreak** and **Restaurants** (p115) await

❷ Re-enacting your favourite scene from Tom Hanks' *Cast Away* on **Monuriki** (p119), the island where the film was shot

❸ Treating the kids to a holiday they'll never forget at **Malolo Island Resort** (p121) or **Castaway Island** (p120)

❹ Frolicking in the **Blue Lagoon** (p133) waters that helped shoot Brooke Shields to fame and then catching a water taxi to the **Sawa-i-Lau Cave** (p136) where she swam

❺ Island-hopping on the **Yasawa Flyer** (p126) to see if the sand is any whiter at the other end of the island chain

❻ Diving off a boat and doing your best to keep up with the giant **manta rays** (p130)

❼ Hanging out with the locals in Naboro during **Friday afternoon rugby** (p128)

DIVING

Mamanuca dive sites teem with fantastically gaudy fish circling psychedelic corals. The visibility here astounds first-time divers and you can see for 30m to 40m through the water much of the year. Notable sites in the Mamanucas include **Plantation Pinnacles** with its three deep-water rock towers and **Sherwood Forest** with its Gorgonian sea fans. Other sites to look for include **Gotham City's** coral heads, the big fish at the **Big Ws** and the artificial reef at the wreck of the **Salamanda**.

The following companies are the big fish in the diving pond, with dive shops on mul-tiple islands; other long-established resorts have their own equally long-established dive operators, and are detailed in the resort descriptions.

Reef Safari DIVING
(☑675 0566; www.reefsafari.com.fj) Has dive shops at South Sea, Bounty and Amunuca Island Resorts. A two-tank dive costs $205 and a PADI Open Water Course $700.

Subsurface Fiji DIVING
(☑666 6738; www.subsurfacefiji.com) Runs the dive shops at Malolo and Beachcomber, Musket Cove and Treasure Islands. It also offers diving with free pick-ups for guests at

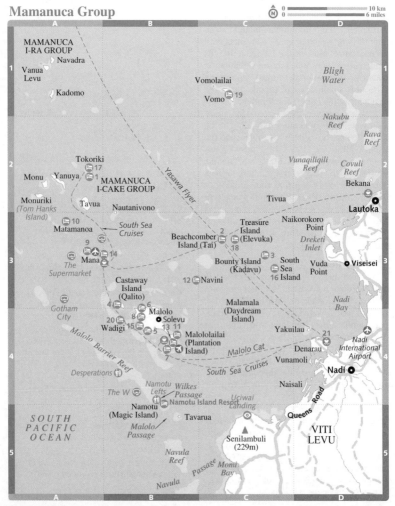

Mamanuca Group

0 — 10 km
0 — 6 miles

MAMANUCA I-RA GROUP
Navadra
Vanua Levu
Kadomo

Bligh Water

Vomolailai
Vomo 19

Nakubu Reef

Rava Reef

Tokoriki 17
Monu Yanuya
MAMANUCA I-CAKE GROUP
Monuriki (Tom Hanks Island)
Tavua
Nautanivono
Matamanoa 10
South Sea Cruises
9
Mana 14
The Supermarket

Vunaqiliqili Reef
Covuli Reef
Bekana

Tivua
Lautoka

Treasure Island (Elevuka) 2
Naikorokoro Point
Beachcomber Island (Tai) 18
Dreketi Inlet

Bounty Island (Kadavu) 3
South Sea Island 16
Vuda Point
Viseisei

Castaway Island (Qalito)
12 Navini
Gotham City
4
20 8 6
Malolo Solevu
Wadigi 15 13 11
5 Malololailai (Plantation Island)
7

Malamala (Daydream Island)
Nadi Bay
Yakuilau 21
Nadi International Airport
Malolo Cat
Denarau
South Sea Cruises
Vunamoli
Nadi

Malolo Barrier Reef
Desperations
The W
Namotu Lefts
Wilkes Passage
Namotu Island Resort
Uciwai Landing
Namotu (Magic Island)
Tavarua
Malolo Passage

Naisali

Queens Road

SOUTH PACIFIC OCEAN

Senilambuli (229m)

VITI LEVU

Navula Reef

Momi Bay

Navula Passage

Namotu, Navini and Tavarua Island Resorts, Wadigi Island Lodge, Resort Walu Beach, Funky Fish Beach Resort and Likuliku Lagoon. A two-tank dive costs $210, and a PADI Open Water Course is $790. Subsurface also offers child-friendly dives.

SURFING

The reefs off the southern Mamanuca islands have some of the world's most formidable breaks including Cloudbreak and Restaurants. And, after years of exclusive resort-held rights, since the Surfing Decree of 2010 they're now open to all.

In brief, the breaks are as follows:

Cloudbreak World famous and for experienced riders only. Hollow left breaking on a reef. Best swell angle is with south-southwest winds, when tubes of up to 250m form.

Restaurants A powerful, superfast left-hander over shallow coral. Up to 200m long for advanced surfers.

Namotu Left A cruising, fun, longboard-type left-hander up to 150m long.

Swimming Pools A fun, easy right. Good for longboarders.

Wilkes Passage Long, fast, down the line right. A swell magnet, it can get as mean as Cloudbreak on some days.

Mini Clouds High-tide break. Best on a south to southwest swell; a quick, short, punchy wave.

Desperations Ideal in southeast swell conditions. Right and left.

🖙 Tours & Cruises

Many, though not all, of the island resorts accept day trippers and every morning a whole armada of launches and yachts leaves Port Denarau with boatloads of people keen to spread their beach towels on some of that glorious white sand.

Captain Cook Cruises   CRUISE
(☑670 1823; www.captaincook.com.au) Offers a day cruise from Denarau island to Tivua, a tiny coral island, on board the sailing ship *Ra Marama* (a 33m former governor's brigantine) for $139 for adults and $69.50 for children. The sunset romance dinner cruise ($99 per adult and $49.50 per child for three hours) includes a three-course meal. Captain Cook Cruises also has popular three-day, two-night cruise/camping trips to the Mamanucas and southern Yasawas.

PJ's Sailing & Snorkelling   CRUISE
(Sailing Adventures Fiji; ☑623 2011; www.sailingadventuresfiji.com) Popular with those who want a small-group fun experience, PJ's takes up to 25 people for a Mamanuca day of cruising, snorkelling and lunch at Plantation Island (adult/child $160/$80).

Seaspray   CRUISE
(☑675 0500; www.ssc.com.fj; cruise per adult/child $165/89) This full-day combination catamaran and sailing cruise aboard the famous

---

Mamanuca Group

◎ Sights
Musket Cove Marina ....(see 11)

✛ Activities, Courses & Tours
Take A Break Cruises...................(see 11)

🛏 Sleeping
1   Amunuca Resort.....................................A2
2   Beachcomber Island Resort................C3
3   Bounty Island Resort............................C3
4   Castaway Island Resort B3
5   Funky Fish Beach Resort B4
6   Likuliku Lagoon....................................B3
7   Lomani Island Resort B4
8   Malolo Island Resort.............................B4
9   Mana Island Resort...............................A3
    Mana Lagoon Backpackers .... (see 14)
10   Matamanoa Island Resort A3
11   Musket Cove Island Resort..................B4

12   Navini Island Resort..............................B3
13   Plantation Island Resort B4
14   Ratu Kini Backpackers...........................B3
15   Resort Walu Beach.................................B4
    Sereana Backpackers...................(see 14)
16   South Sea Island C3
17   Tokoriki Island Resort...........................A2
18   Treasure Island Resort C3
19   Vomo Island Resort C1
20   Wadigi Island Lodge..............................B4

✕ Eating
Coffee Cove .... (see 11)

🛍 Shopping
Musket Cove Trader .... (see 11)

ⓘ Transport
21   Port Denarau D4

Seaspray, a two-masted schooner that featured in the *Adventures of the Seaspray* TV series, is run by South Sea Cruises. You cruise by three uninhabited islands (including Monuriki of *Cast Away* fame) and stop for snorkelling, a barbecue lunch and a village visit. Travel is by catamaran to Mana island where *Seaspray* is docked.

South Sea Cruises   CRUISE

(☎675 0500; www.ssc.com.fj) Apart from the catamaran transfers, these boats are used to ferry day trippers from Port Denarau to various islands and between the islands themselves. The modern catamarans call in to nearly all of the Mamanuca islands on their routes throughout the day, including South Sea Island (adult/child $149/75), Beachcomber ($147/76), Mana Island Resort ($175/96), Castaway Island ($185/139), Treasure Island ($145/80), Bounty ($155/85), Malolo Island Resort ($180/99) and various combinations thereof. Day cruises include lunch, the use of the resort facilities and pick-up and drop-off from Nadi. Half-day options are also available.

ℹ **Information**

Head to **Lonely Planet** (www.lonelyplanet. com/fiji/mamanuca-group) for planning advice, author recommendations, traveller reviews and insider tips.

ℹ **Getting There & Around**

Thanks to their proximity to both Port Denarau and Nadi airport, the Mamanuca islands are easily reached by catamaran, speedboat, seaplane or helicopter. Most people arrive on one of the four high-speed catamarans departing from Port Denarau. All the following boat companies provide free pick-up and drop-off from Nadi hotels.

Awesome Adventures Fiji (☎675 0499; www. awesomefiji.com) Runs the *Yasawa Flyer* (also known as the 'Yellow Boat'), which connects with South Sea Island ($67 one way), Bounty Island ($81 one way), Beachcomber Island ($92 one way) and Vomo ($180 one way in the captain's lounge) on its way north to the Yasawas. See the boxed text, p126, for more information on this boat.

Malolo Cat I & II (☎675 0205) Owned and operated by Plantation Island and Musket Cove Resorts, which use them to bring clients directly to Malololailai. A boat leaves Port Denarau at 10.30am, 2pm and 5pm, and returns at 9am, 12.30pm and 3.30pm. The trip takes 50 minutes ($65 per person).

South Sea Cruises (☎675 0500; www.ssc. com.fj) Operates two fast catamarans that run five or six loops each day from Denarau to most of the Mamanuca islands, including South Sea Island ($67), Bounty Island ($81), Beachcomber Island ($92), Treasure Island ($92), Mana ($109), Matamanoa ($137), Castaway Island ($105), Tokoriki ($137) and Malolo ($105). All fares are one way; children aged five to 15 pay half price, and those aged under five travel free.

A tiny speedboat – *Mana Flyer* – runs between the budget resorts at New Town Beach (approximately $60 one way) to the smaller budget resorts of Bounty and Beachcomber, and to the islands of Malolo and Mana; it's a very wet and bumpy ride in bad weather.

To avoid spending a night on the mainland, you might consider a water taxi. A trip to Mana island with **Mamanuca Express** (☎675 0151, 932 3700; www.mamanucaexpress.com) costs between $408 and $758 for up to four people, depending on the destination.

Alternatively, a light-plane ride over tropical islands with white-sand beaches is more scenic and much quicker (no more than 15 minutes). **Turtle Airways** (☎672 1888; www.turtleair ways.com) and **Pacific Island Air** (☎672 5644; www.pacificislandair.com) offer seaplane charters to the Mamanuca resorts, as does helicopter outfit **Island Hoppers** (☎675 0670; www. helicopters.com.fj).

South Sea Island

South Sea Island is the smallest of the island resorts and little more than a bump of sand with some trees growing on top. You can walk around the whole island in three minutes; if you hurry, you could make it in two. Being so small it can feel a little overrun with the day trippers brought here by South Sea Cruises.

Many backpackers spend a night at South Sea Island (☎675 0500; www.ssc.com .fj/South_Sea_Island.aspx; dm $89; 🐾) on their way to or from the Yasawas. Prices include three meals of varying quality and the use of all nonmotorised water-sport equipment including snorkelling gear, kayaks and a sailing catamaran. The only accommodation is in the 32-bed dorm above the communal lounge, which means night-time crowds are limited and dinner can be a pleasant low-key event on the beach when guest numbers are small. The beach is good for swimming and OK for snorkelling, and there is a small freshwater swimming pool. Reef Safari runs the dive shop here. Transfers are by South Sea Cruises or the *Yasawa Flyer*.

Bounty Island

Bounty Island, also known as Kadavu, is a 20-hectare coral island just 15km offshore from the mainland. It's bigger than its immediate neighbours but it still only takes 20 minutes to walk around or, if you don't stop to tease the clown fish, 1½ hours to snorkel. The white-sand beach attracts both endangered hawksbill turtles and the all-too-common day tripper.

Bounty Island Resort (☑628 3387; www.fiji-bounty.com; dm incl meals $110-120, bure incl meals $334-386; ✳✿) is a notch above South Sea Island in terms of value for budget travellers. Many people come here for a few days' R&R between the mainland and the Yasawas, and it's popular with day trippers. The ageing *bure* with tiled floors and attached bathrooms are basic – and overpriced – by Mamanuca standards, but those returning from the Yasawas will appreciate the hot showers and round-the-clock electricity. The dorms are in a large, partitioned building out the back. Some have air-con and six beds to the room and others are fan-cooled with enough bunks for 20. There's a small pool and the island has a turtle pool and occasionally raises and releases hawksbills. Nonmotorised sports are free and diving can be arranged with Reef Safari. Transfers are with South Sea Cruises or the *Yasawa Flyer*.

Beachcomber Island

Tiny Beachcomber Island (Tai) is 20km offshore from the mainland. It is circled by a beautiful, coconut palm-studded beach.

Beachcomber Island Resort (☑666 1500; www.beachcomberfiji.com; dm incl meals $122, s/d incl meals $282/374, bure incl meals $409-542; ⊜@✿) has the reputation of being *the* party island and tales of drunken debauchery are told far and wide. The truth: over recent years some of the shine has rubbed off Beachcomber's disco ball and, depending on the crowd on the night, the only interesting thing you see might be some weird choreography on the dance floor. Nonetheless, with a huge bar, live music and nightly activities involving the inappropriate use of alcohol, it remains a fun place to spend a night or two. Accommodation options include rooms in the lodge and some clean but pricey private *bure*, although most people opt for a bed in a double-storey screen-sided *bure* that sleeps 120. This may sound like dormitory hell but it gets as many raves as complaints. Snorkelling equipment is free but, unlike other Mamanuca resorts, you'll have to pay for everything else, including beach loungers. Diving is with Subsurface Fiji. Both the *Yasawa Flyer* and South Sea Cruises' catamarans call in here.

Treasure Island

Treasure Island (Elevuka) is another tiny island that takes mere minutes to walk around and is no more than a flyspeck on most maps. The beaches are similar to those found at Bounty, South Sea and Beachcomber Islands.

Treasure Island Resort (☑666 1599; www.fiji-treasure.com; bure/duplex $474/598; ✳@☏✿☝) is one of the oldest resorts (opened in 1972) and caters well for families. The new three-pool complex has plenty of sloping 'beaches' for toddlers and the turtle feeding and minigolf course are ideal for older kids. It has 66 comfortable, recently refurbished, air-conditioned units housed in 34 duplex *bure* with roofs that resemble witches' hats. Many have louvred interconnecting doors, which means – even when they're locked – noise from neighbouring rooms can filter through. It is resolutely midrange despite its top-end prices and relies heavily on repeat guests who return in large numbers – so it must be doing something right. Optional three-meal packages cost $172 per person (half-price for kids under 12), and diving trips are organised with Subsurface Fiji.

The island is serviced by South Sea Cruises' catamarans.

Vomo

This wedge-shaped, 90-hectare island rises to a magnificent high ridge, has two lovely beaches (one or the other will be sheltered if it is windy) and some of the best snorkelling in the Mamanuca islands. It's large enough to be interesting – it takes an hour to walk around – but small enough to be intimate. All in all, Vomo is the very definition of postcard-perfect Fiji.

Vomo Island Resort (☑666 7955; www.vomofiji.com; bure incl meals from $1675; ✳@✿) could make even the most laconic guest wax lyrical. The *bure* are stunningly appointed in dark-brown Pacificana with indigenous wooden floors and separate living areas. The beachside *bure* are so close to the beach you could walk to the water with your flippers on and the hillside *bure* have fantastic views (particularly from Nos 28, 29 and 30). Vomo is the only five-star resort to accept children, but because the grounds are so spacious they have little impact on the tranquillity. The 'honeymoon island', Vomolailai, is just offshore and newlyweds can be dropped here with bubbly, lunch and a two-way radio. Rates include divine meals (all of which are three-course), daily snorkelling trips, access to the nine-hole, pitch 'n' putt golf course and nonmotorised water sports.

Guests arrive by helicopter, seaplane or by the *Yasawa Flyer*.

Navini

From a distance, Navini looks like a round wafer biscuit topped with thick pesto. Up close, this small island is just as delicious. It is surrounded by a white-sand beach and vibrant reef just snorkelling distance offshore. It's owned by the people of Solevu on Malolo, who once held chiefly meetings and fished here. That was until fishing was banned many years ago and a marine sanctuary established. Beware of friendly fish!

TOP CHOICE Navini Island Resort (☑666 2188; www.navinifiji.com.fj; bure $595-790; villa $890; @) is a boutique, ecofriendly resort, which has only 10 *bure*, each spacious, breezy and tastefully decorated. The premier one-bedroom *bure* can sleep three and the two-room *bure* (sleeping up to five) have verandahs at either end; the honeymoon *bure* has a courtyard tiled with pebbles and a private spa; the villa will likely make you want to move in for good. All the *bure* are beachfront, each with its own slice of sand plus a hammock and sun loungers to go with it, and the surrounding hibiscus and bougainvilleas mean that privacy is assured. Guests usually eat at the same long table and meals are a social occasion – if this isn't your thing, more intimate beachside dining can be arranged. The compulsory meal package ($110/98 for three/two meals daily for adults; child rates available) still allows guests to choose from a daily menu and, as there are more staff than guests, the service can't be faulted.

Return transfers from Nadi by resort speedboat ($270/130/780 per adult/child/family) allow you to maximise your time on the island no matter when your plane arrives or leaves.

Mana

The beautiful but literally divided island of Mana is about 30km northwest of Denarau. It's home to the upmarket Mana Island Resort, and a couple of budget backpackers next to the village on the southeastern end. Incredibly, a high chainlink fence, and occasionally even a guard, separates the *bure*-bunnies from the dorm-dwellers, and signs throughout Mana Island Resort warn 'nonguests' that they are not welcome in their restaurants or shops. For their part, the budget resorts welcome everyone (their restaurants can be crowded with mealtime escapees from the big resort) but seem unable to cooperate among themselves.

Fence or no fence, the beaches are (mostly) open to all. Walking around the island isn't really an option because of rocky points on the coast, but there are a couple of 20-minute hikes to Sunset Beach and to a lookout. There's plenty to see underwater in the fish department anywhere off the beach, and decent coral off Sunset. Also check out the south-beach pier for a night snorkel; the fish go into a frenzy under the wharf lights.

🛏 Sleeping & Eating

The backpacker resorts are sewn into a ramshackle Fijian village along the waterfront. If you prebook, beware of paying midrange prices for *very* budget rooms; unless it's peak season you're better off arriving and then booking a bed after shopping around. Savvy travellers go to Malolo or the Yasawas, where standards are far higher for much the same price. Activities on offer at the budget resorts include snorkelling trips (around $25 per person), kayaking ($5 to $10 per hour), hand-line fishing trips ($25) and islandhopping ($60 per person). Nightly activities are as much about beer consumption as they are about entertainment, though sunset on the deck or the beach is a must for all.

Looking landwards from the ferry wharf, the hostels are a few minutes' walk to the right; the resort is to the left. The only eating options are at the accommodation places.

Mana Island Resort   RESORT $$$
(☑665 0423, 666 1455; www.manafiji.com; bure $320-750, honeymoon ste incl breakfast $900; ☢✳@☎☒🚣) One of the oldest and largest (at 300 acres) island resorts in Fiji, the 150 or so rooms and *bure* span the spacious and landscaped low-lying ground between the

north and south beaches. Mana caters for everyone – couples, honeymooners and families – the latter dominating during Australian and New Zealand school-holiday times. Rooms come in a variety of configurations and are constantly getting refurbished, with polished wood and cool stone evident. Stylish split-level suites are winners, each with a bedroom on the mezzanine floor.

Food gets mixed reviews; some guests choose to eat à la carte – or down the beach at Ratu Kini's – rather than go for the meal plans. There are two beautifully situated indoor/outdoor restaurants, a kids club for three- to 12-year-olds (a one-time fee of $25 applies) and a crèche for the littlies while parents unwind in the spa.

Aqua-Trek Mana (www.aquatrekdiving.com) works exclusively for Mana Island Resort. A two-tank dive here costs $240 and a PADI Open Water Course $880, including equipment. Yoshi, the long-term dive instructor, has produced a great resource of photographs of underwater critters along with detailed dive-site descriptions.

Ratu Kini Backpackers   HOSTEL **$**
(☑672 1959; www.ratukini.com; dm incl breakfast/all meals $32/66, d incl breakfast/all meals $120/189; @) A traditional backpacker place, which is slowly expanding along the strip. No-fuss, no-frills, decent-sized dorms share cold-water showers, and quiet, spacious doubles with bathroom extend in a block that melds into the village. The restaurant-cum-bar sits out over the water and is a prime spot for sunset viewing/socialising.

The in-house **Ratu Kini Divers** services Mana's backpacker resorts (and anyone who ducks around the resort fence). It offers two-tank dives for $230 and PADI Open Water Courses for $750.

Sereana Backpackers   HOSTEL **$**
(☑921 9951; dm/d incl meals $55/120, d with bathroom incl meals $150) More village homestay than tourist set-up, the budget travellers we talked here to were enjoying its low-key family feel. The dorm is beachfront, often with a good breeze coming in off the water.

Mana Lagoon Backpackers   HOSTEL **$**
(☑929 2337; tent site/dm/r incl meals $50/72/153) Owned and run by locals, this place seem to have grown organically from sundry concrete walls, panels of plywood and wonky doors; it has a real village feel. There are some nice touches outdoors – like thatched-roof beach shelters, a restaurant-cum-bar with a sand-

covered floor and plenty of beach activities – but, for the price, the rooms leave a lot to be desired: they're hot, small, low and airless.

Tadrai   RESORT **$$$**
(www.tadrai.com; villas from $2400) This new, luxurious five-star resort opened on Mana in late 2011. The super-exclusive resort offers a private stretch of beach and has five villas, each with butler service and a chef-in-room option if the signature restaurant doesn't appeal.

ℹ Getting There & Away

Mana is one of the few resort islands with a wharf. South Sea Cruises' catamarans service the island several times daily, while the budget *Mana Flyer* transfer boat ($60 one way, 55 minutes) makes a daily trip to and from Nadi's New Town Beach.

Matamanoa

Matamanoa is a small, high island just to the north of Mana.

Beautifully refurbished in 2011, **Matamanoa Island Resort** (☑672 3620; www.matamanoa.com; d unit/bure incl breakfast $465/755; ✱@✉) has 20 *bure* overlooking a lovely, white-sand beach. Each has a verandah and beach views (half facing sunrise, half sunset) that, given the size of the island, allows at least an illusion of space and privacy. There are also 13 good-value – but not nearly as nice – air-conditioned, hotel-style units with garden views; the *masi*-decorated ceilings are a knockout. Daily meal plans cost $125, or $81 for dinner only; there's also an à la carte option. As usual, all nonmotorised water sports are free. Other activities include trips to the nearby pottery village on the island of Tavua, and resort diving with **Viti Watersports** (www.vitiwatersports.com); an intro dive is $245 and a two-tank dive $280. The resort doesn't cater for children under 12 and there are no day trippers – there were mostly young professionals and honeymooners in residence when we visited.

Most guests arrive via the South Sea Cruises catamarans, and there is a helipad on the island.

Monuriki

Tiny, uninhabited Monuriki (and ironically not Castaway Island) featured in the 2001 Tom Hanks movie *Cast Away,* and every resort worth its cabanas and cocktails sells day trips to what is increasingly referred to as the Tom Hanks Island. The trips cost around $50 to $80 depending on how far the boat has to travel to get there and what kind of lunch, if any, is included. The island is quite beautiful and the wide lagoon is perfect for snorkelling. An ongoing program with local people to eradicate feral goats and rats has seen native crested iguanas and wedge-tailed shearwaters successfully reintroduced to the island, so keep your eyes open for them.

The two-masted schooner *Seaspray* also sails here as a day trip from Mana.

Tokoriki

The small, hilly island of Tokoriki has a beautiful, fine-white-sand beach facing west to the sunset and is the northernmost island in the Mamanuca group. Guests can walk a track around the point between the two resorts, although an inconvenient (and deliberately placed) rubbish dump inside Amanuca's boundary can make it a bit of an obstacle course.

Sleeping

Tokoriki Island Resort RESORT $$$
(☑672 5926; www.tokoriki.com; d bure from $1092, d villas from $1535; ✳@☀) If you're not married when you arrive here, there's a good chance you will be by the time you leave. This place is the ideal romantic getaway, though singles and families with teenage children are welcome. The whole place drips with orchids, there are queen-sized beds with old-fashioned mosquito-net canopies as well as a gorgeous island-style wedding chapel of stone, wood and stained glass. The 30 beachfront *bure* have indoor and outdoor showers, and it's only a few steps past the hammock to the beach. The five villas have private plunge pools, beautiful interiors and large sandstone terraces. Lunch is served in the pleasant terrace-and-pool area while the gourmet, candlelit dinners (mains from $40; meal plans $198 per person per day) are served on white linen in the restaurant. At eight-seat-only **Oishii Teppanyaki restaurant**, in a garden *bure,* the performance of the dynamic chef is as much of a treat as the food.

Water activities are handled by **Dive Tropex** (www.tokorikidiving.com), whose dive team, Will and Alex, have spent 10 years on the island. Their successful giant-clam reintroduction site is a draw for divers and snorkellers alike, as is Paradise Point, a beautiful coral garden ($40 per person). A two-

tank dive/PADI Open Water Course costs $235/780. Photos of the day trip to Mamanuca-i-Ra, the northernmost Mamanucas known as the Sacred Islands, looked sensational.

Get there a by South Sea Cruises catamaran, a seaplane or helicopter flight, or by water taxi from Nadi or Denarau.

Amunuca Resort RESORT $$$
(☑664 0642; www.amunuca.com; bure $323-794; ✳@☀) Opened in 2007, Amanuca's fortunes have gone up and down like the tide at its beachfront; when we visited it was offering solidly midrange facilities despite the top-end prices. Rooms range wildly in quality from the adults-only, split-level suites to sparsely furnished *bure* with little more than beds and a TV; some attention to maintenance and a new coat of paint in the restaurants and public areas wouldn't go amiss. The beach is good, although the coral shelf is very high here and much of the reef is exposed at low tide. There's a kids club, a 40-seat movie theatre and two pools. Activities and diving are provided by **Let's Get Wet** (letsgetwetwater adventures@gmail.com; intro dive $175, 2-tank dive $250, PADI Open Water Course $800).

Castaway Island

Reef-fringed, 70-hectare Castaway Island, also known as Qalito, is 27km west of Denarau island and just short of paradise. The resort covers about one-eighth of the island – the best bit, on a wide tongue of sand stretching from a bush-clad hill.

Castaway Island Resort (☑666 1233; www.castawayfiji.com; bure $740-985; ✳@☀) is an oldie but a goodie. It's still one of the best family destinations and is also making a splash in the couples market (which avoids school holidays). The 60 spacious *bure* have two sections to accommodate those with children, small verandahs and intricate *masi* (bark-cloth) ceilings. Rooms are well maintained, and bathrooms were renewed throughout the resort in 2011. An adults-only pool was under construction when we visited, and there's a swimming-pool bar, an open-air pizza deck and a great dining terrace overlooking the ocean (all-day casual meals $15 to $25, dinner $30 to $40, or unrestricted meal plan adult/child $118.50/58.80); the lunchtime buffet was truly staggering in its size, variety and quality. The excellent kids club will take three- to 12-year-olds off your hands so you can make use of the well-maintained, and complimentary, nonmotorised water sports. The resort-operated dive centre here charges $155 for a single-tank dive and $920 for a PADI Open Water Course.

Castaway Island is serviced by South Sea Cruises' catamarans.

Wadigi

Pint-sized (1.2 hectares) and privately owned, Wadigi may beckon but it's off limits to all but a few.

Wadigi Island Lodge (☑672 0901; www. wadigi.com; per couple per day incl meals US$1970; ✳@☲) could be your own private island. Guests (a maximum of six) are whisked here by helicopter to unwind in sybaritic seclusion. The luxury three-bedroom suite is perched atop the single hill with gorgeous sea views from the living areas and decks. It has its own infinity-edged pool, two small beaches and seven staff, including two gourmet chefs and a boat captain.

Malolo

Malolo is the largest of the Mamanuca islands and has two villages from which the resorts lease their land. The island's highest point is Uluisolo (218m), which was used by locals as a hill fortification and by US forces in 1942 as an observation point; trekking to the top offers some great panoramic views.

Diving is offered by Subsurface Fiji, which is based at Malolo Island Resort but will happily take guests from neighbouring hotels as well. Malolo is also within striking distance of the great surfing spots mentioned on p115.

🛏 Sleeping & Eating

Malolo Island Resort   RESORT $$$
(☑672 0978; www.maloloisland.com; bure $730-911; ☲✳@☲☑) Small-scale Malolo had a stylish renovation in 2010 and is in great shape. All its 45 rooms can see the sea or are beachfront, and there is no faulting the white-sand beach or lush tropical gardens. There are two pools (one for grown-ups only) and a free kids club. Tariffs include all the usual water activities and are for two adults and up to two children. There are two restaurants (mains around $35, or meal packages), a day spa, an adults-only TV and reading lounge, walking trails and a Subsurface Fiji dive shop.

CLOSE ENCOUNTERS

When American explorer Charles Wilkes sailed through the passage that now bears his name in 1840, Malolo wasn't quite the welcoming place it is today. According to Wilkes' log, when initial trade negotiations turned sour his landing party was forced to take a 'native' hostage and fire two warning shots. This upset the locals and two of Wilkes' crew were killed with throwing clubs. Seeking to set an example, Wilkes' retaliation was swift: both the island villages were razed, their plantations laid waste and their canoes scuttled before the vendetta ceased.

Likuliku Lagoon   LUXURY HOTEL $$$
(☑672 4275; www.likulikulagoon.com; bure $1674-2810; ☲✳@☎☲) The first (and so far only) Fijian resort with overwater *bure* opened on this impossibly azure lagoon in 2007. For couples with the cash to splash, the intimacy and privacy to be had here extend almost scurrilously far beyond a do-not-disturb sign on the door. At the risk of sounding like a promotional advert, even Likuliku's second-tier accommodation boasts private plunge pools, thatched lounging pavilions, his and hers closets, and inside and outside showers. As you would expect in this five star-plus category, a gourmet chef prepares the food and the canapés are tiny and ambrosial.

Funky Fish Beach Resort   RESORT $
(☑651 3180; www.funkyfishresort.com; dm/d $35/108, 1-/2-bedroom bure $170/340; ✳@☲) Funky Fish brings some much-needed professionalism to the budget/midrange spectrum of the Mamanuca market and is run by former Fiji rugby coach and All Black Brad Johnstone. The 12-bed dorm here is modern, spotlessly clean and partitioned into groups of four beds, with a couple of sectioned-off private rooms. The 'rock lobster' *bure* are small, stand-alone constructions with thatched roofs and private outdoor showers, while the larger beachside *bure* can accommodate four. Tasty meals ($60 meal package; mains $18 to $25) are served in an impressive hillside *bure* that enjoys panoramic views over the extremely tidal lagoon in front of the resort. The small beach disappears at high tide and many people who stay here come to surf Cloudbreak and

surrounds ($70 per person, minimum two people), or bring kiteboards and wait for the wind. It's very low-key; big-time party animals might need to look elsewhere for evening entertainment.

Resort Walu Beach   RESORT $$

(☑665 1777; www.walubeach.com; dm incl meals $185, bure from $380; @≋) Pretty Walu Beach was built for the Australian reality TV show *The Resort,* but since that show's cancellation it's been a bit of an orphan. At the time of writing it was being refurbished and heading decidedly upmarket; but while construction's underway there are some good walk-in rates being offered. Beachfront *bure* come in several configurations, and the hillside lodges were being used as (very nice) dorms and let out on a per-person basis. The resort's main restaurant has Sky TV and a bar; the mandatory meal package ($90 per person) features three-course evening meals. Expect all this to change over the coming year or two...

ⓘ Getting There & Away

A South Sea Cruises catamaran does the run from Denarau to Malolo several times daily.

Malololailai

Tranquil Malololailai is approximately 20km west of Denarau island and, at 2.4 sq km, is the second-largest island of the Mamanuca Group. It has long been popular with yachties, who anchor in the protected lagoon and make use of the facilities at the marina. All three resorts are built on the shores of a beautiful, but extremely tidal, lagoon. The beach outside Musket Cove Island Resort is the most affected, and that outside Lomani Island Resort the least affected, by these tides.

◉ Sights & Activities

All the island's diving services are provided by Subsurface Fiji. Dive sites include the **Mamanuca Wall**, **Megabombies** and **Shark Encounter**, as well as a night dive; all are close to the three island resorts.

The excellent surf breaks described on p115 are all accessible from here and from the neighbouring resorts on Malolo, and are about 20 minutes off-shore by boat. A half-day trip runs around $60 per person; ask around at the marina if you'd rather hire a village boat than join a commercial operator.

Musket Cove Marina

(☑666 2215 ext 1279; VHF Marine channel 68; mcyc@musketcovefiji.com) Yachties flock (or should that be school?) to the excellent marina to avail themselves of the services here. There are 27 moorings ($15 per day), 25 marina berths (from $2 per metre, per day), dockside fuel and water (although this can get scarce in the dry season), postal services, a laundry ($6 per load), rubbish disposal, hot showers, book swap, bike hire ($20 per day), a noticeboard and limited repair services. **Musket Cove Trader & Coffee Cove** (General Store; ◷8am-7pm) is probably the best-stocked shop in the Mamanucas – but it doesn't sell alcohol. Yachties can stock up on groceries, meat and vegetables, although not at mainland prices. The attached **coffee shop** (◷10am-6pm) makes a mean coffee and serves light lunches under fans on the verandah, overlooking the marina.

The blackboards outside the activities sheds on the marina and in the resorts list all the fishing and yacht charters available.

In September each year the Musket Cove Yacht Club hosts **Fiji Regatta Week** and the **Musket Cove to Port Vila yacht race**.

Take A Break Cruises   CRUISE, FISHING

(☑925 9469; www.takeabreakcruises.com) Offers a variety of outings, including the popular 'dolphin and snorkel safari' ($90 per person, minimum six people) on Mondays and Thursdays; and 'sunset cruises' ($85 per person including drinks and nibbles, minimum six people) on Tuesdays and Fridays, on a luxury 14m catamaran. Sport-fishing trips ($145 per person, four hours, minimum four people) or private fishing charters are also arranged here.

🛏 Sleeping & Eating

Lomani Island Resort   RESORT $$$

(☑666 8212; www.lomaniisland.com; bure incl breakfast $674-840; ❄🛜≋) This small, adult-only resort has a long and lazy pool, a classy colonial-style bar and a decent outdoor restaurant (full meal plan $224 per person). The 17 gorgeous *bure* have a Mediterranean feel to them – think stucco walls and arched doorways. They're equipped with divan lounges, fridges and DVD players but characterised by the bamboo, four-poster, king-sized bed. Owned by the same family as Plantation Island Resort, the two properties work closely together and guests here piggyback on the other's activities.

Musket Cove Island Resort RESORT **$$**

(☑666 2215; www.musketcovefiji.com; r $276, bure from $590, villa $820; ❄@☎) Musket Cove offers several types of accommodation, from hotel rooms to self-catering thatched *bure*. The Armstrong Island villas – clustered on an artificial island linked to the main one by a bridge – have overwater verandahs and a private pool. The lagoon *bure* have a fridge and breakfast bar and are nicely decorated with traditional weavings. There are free snorkelling trips twice daily to compensate for the low, low tides, along with the usual array of free water sports (but no kids club). Named after the owner, **Dick's Place** bar and restaurant by the pool (mains $35 to $45) often has theme nights, including the popular 'pig-on-a-spit' (although it's not so popular with the pig). The casual **Ratu Nemani Island Bar** is linked to the resort by a walkway and is the place for do-it-yourself barbecues, cold beers and colourful banter with the yachties.

Plantation Island Resort RESORT **$$$**

(☑666 9333; www.plantationisland.com; r $316-650; ❄@☎♠) Plantation is Goliath to David next door. There are kids spilling out everywhere here; they're in the sea, in the pool, painting T-shirts, climbing plaster cows, egg-and-spoon racing, watching TV and eating chips. Most of them are with the free Club Coconut and look to be having a great time. The rooms come in a dizzying array of options and much of the resort was upgraded and/or redecorated in 2011. There are three swimming pools: one for kids (with water slide), one essentially for adults and one for all ages. This place is huge (about 850 people can stay here) and has a slight holiday-camp feel about it. You may have to line up for your buffet or set meal (adult/child full-meal packages $91/51), which is preferable to braving the pretty ordinary snack bar (burgers $8 to $10) down by the dive shop. Your best option is **Ananda's Restaurant** (mains $25 to $35), down by the airstrip.

❶ Getting There & Away

The resorts jointly operate the comfortable *Malolo Cat*, a catamaran that runs four times daily from Port Denarau ($120/60 per adult/child return, 50 minutes).

Namotu Island & Tavarua Island

Namotu and Tavarua are islands at the southern edge of the Malolo Barrier Reef, which encloses the southern Mamanucas. **Namotu Island** (www.namotuislandfiji.com) is a tiny (1.5 hectares) and pretty island; bigger **Tavarua Island** (www.tavarua.com) is 12 hectares, rimmed by beautiful white-sand. Both islands are primarily package surf resorts, geared to the American market. There is no public access.

YASAWA GROUP

POP 5000

The Yasawas are just as beautiful as the Mamanucas, although until relatively recently they have been overshadowed by those bolder upstarts nearby.

But times change. In the 1990s the Yasawa chain was considered prohibitively isolated and, apart from a few hardy souls and an occasional cruise ship, these islands saw few travellers. Today the daily catamaran stops off at almost each one, offloading passengers into a waiting armada of small boats.

The Yasawas have beautiful land- and seascapes – along with enough remoteness and sense of isolation to appeal to the Robinson Crusoe in many a traveller's heart. Which is just as well, as the quality of resorts here varies dramatically: a *bure* could be anything from a hut that you could blow down with a hair dryer to an upmarket villa with an outdoor shower. This new wave of midrange and top-end accommodation options is now enticing families and well-heeled couples into what has traditionally been the stomping ground of backpackers. Before long, they too are nudged surreptitiously into the true meaning of 'Fijian time', where anything more than two snorkels and half an hour on the volleyball court constitutes a busy day at the beach.

The Yasawa chain is composed of 20 or so sparsely populated and surprisingly barren islands. There are no roads, cars, banks or shops and most of the locals live in small, isolated villages, surviving on agriculture and tourism for their livelihoods. Most resorts help make the tourist dollar go further by buying local crops or fish, supporting village schools or sponsoring older kids to get further education on the mainland.

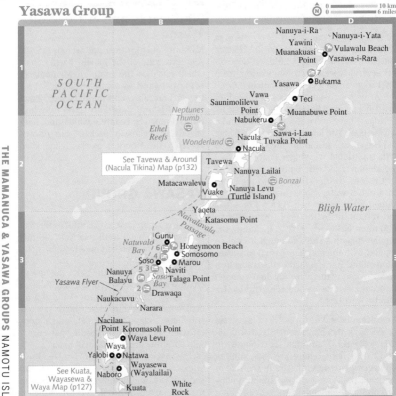

Yasawa Group

The land is mostly hilly; four of the larger islands have summits close to 600m above sea level. While the relatively dry climate is a plus for visitors, the land is prone to drought. During such times the need to conserve water is a priority, and visitors may be asked to take fewer and shorter showers.

History

There is archaeological evidence to suggest that some of the Yasawa islands were occupied thousands of years ago, but with a paucity of fresh water and the threat of tribal war, people have come and gone frequently over that time. The present *mataqali* (extended family or land-owning group) of Waya island, for example, are believed to have arrived only about five generations ago.

At that time most people lived in the mountains, only occasionally venturing down to the foreshore in search of food and fish. Once Christianity was introduced and the wars subsided, the villagers moved down to the sea and have remained there ever since.

Activities
DIVING

The northern Yasawas offer some spectacular diving. Check out **Lekima's Ledge** (good for novice divers) and the popular **Bonsai, Maze** and **Zoo** sites. Saturday's adrenalin-rush shark-encounter dive is offered by most resorts in Nacula, Nanuya Lailai and Tavewa.

CRUISES

The floating hotel/cruise ships are an excellent midrange to top-end option for visiting the Yasawas. With good food and comfortable accommodation laid on, you can take it easy aboard your luxury vessel, pop overboard for excellent snorkelling and diving, drop in on beautiful white-sand beaches and stop to visit local villagers. Children under 15 usually travel at a heavily discounted rate.

Captain Cook Cruises   CRUISE
(☑670 1823; www.captaincook.com.au) Offers an all-inclusive cruise ranging from three to seven nights (from $1295 per person) on board *Reef Endeavour*. The 68m cruise boat has a swimming pool, bars, lounges and air-conditioned accommodation for 135 people spread over three decks. Cruises depart from Denarau Marina, west of Nadi.

Blue Lagoon Cruises   CRUISE
(☑666 1662; www.bluelagooncruises.com; 183 Vitogo Pde, Lautoka) Offers a variety of cruise combinations including three-day (single/double $2068/3136) and seven-day (single/double $3513/6027) trips to the Yasawas aboard motor-cruisers and catamarans. Transfers, on-board activities and food are included, but drinks, snorkelling and

---

ⓘ **ISLAND-HOPPING TIPS FOR BUDGET TRAVELLERS**

» The quality of accommodation rises and falls like the tide. Work the grapevine on the boats and at each island to see which places are currently good value.

» Some accommodation is still little more than simple, thatched *bure* with concrete bathrooms or bunk dorms with shared bathrooms. Mosquito nets should be offered, but may not be – arm yourself with a pack of mozzie coils.

» Double rooms are popular; if you want some time to yourself, consider prebooking these to avoid ending up in a dorm.

» Bed bugs make their way up and down the islands along with whichever traveller is unknowingly carrying them at the time; a dorm that's clear one week can be temporarily infested the next. Most resorts are rigorous about airing mattresses and keeping rooms clean but, if you're worried, having your own bed sheet will offer some protection.

» Some of the budget resorts offer their own, cheaper boat transfers to the Mamanucas; however, be aware that the trip is quite long, that it's across an exposed stretch of water, and that weather conditions can change quickly. Check for life jackets.

» Bring a padlock; security is often relaxed and few resorts have safe-deposit boxes so locking your bags may be your best security option.

» Mobile (cell) phone coverage has improved beyond recognition in the last few years but is still patchy, especially in the Yasawas. Ask the locals for the best spots.

» Meals are included but can be fairly basic – bring snacks if you are a big eater. Be careful where you store these if they'll attract rats and ants.

» Expect intermittent electricity in much of the Yasawas. The generator is usually off for a few hours during the day, on for a few hours after dusk, and then off again when the last bar-fly heads to bed.

» Carrying a tent will save you a little money, but very few places offer camp sites.

» The resorts appreciate it if you make bookings directly with them, as they then don't have to pay commissions.

» In low season it's not unusual to be the only guest at some of the smaller, more isolated Yasawa resorts – be prepared to enjoy the solitude or to move on.

» Snorkelling equipment costs about $10 per day to hire at some resorts. Avid snorkellers may want to bring their own.

» Activities such as village visits, snorkelling trips and hiking all cost around $15 per person.

» Sundays are quiet on the islands but the church services go off.

diving are extra. Cruises depart from Lautoka's Queens Wharf on Viti Levu.

Awesome Adventures Fiji CRUISE
(☑675 0499; www.awesomefiji.com) Offers a selection of budget packages from four nights (single/double per person $881/677) to 11 nights (single/double $1862/1299) travelling aboard the *Yasawa Flyer*. Rates generally include all meals, transfers and nonmotorised activities. It also offers the only scheduled day tour to the Yasawas, to Botaira Beach Resort on Naviti Island (adult/child $103/57). For more information about Awesome Adventures Fiji and *Yasawa Flyer* see the boxed text

SAILING

Captain Cook Cruises SAILING
(☑670 1823; www.captaincook.com.au) Runs sailing trips to the southern Yasawas aboard the tall ship SV *Spirit of the Pacific*. Swimming, snorkelling, fishing, island treks, village visits, campfire barbecues and *lovo* (feasts cooked in a pit oven) are all part of the deal. Accommodation is in simple *bure* ashore at Barefoot Island, or aboard in foldup canvas beds below the deck cabins. Twin share prices, per person, are $599.

Bareboat and crewed yachts can also be chartered to tour the Yasawas; check with the marina offices in Denerau, Musket Cove and Vuda Point or websites such as www.yachtcharterguide.com.

THE YASAWA FLYER

Most people travelling to the Yasawas go by the *Yasawa Flyer* (also called the 'Yellow Boat') operated by **Awesome Adventures Fiji** (☑675 0499; www.awesomefiji.com; Port Denarau). Half the fun of staying in the Yasawas is getting on and off the *Flyer* as it works its way up the chain towards Nacula, and comparing notes with other travellers. The comfortable high-speed catamaran departs at 8.30am daily from Denarau Marina on Viti Levu, calling in at some of the Mamanuca islands (South Sea Island, Bounty Island, Beachcomber Island and Vomo) before reaching the Yasawa Group. It takes about 1¾ hours to Kuata or Wayalailai ($123 per person, one way), two hours to Waya ($130), three hours to Naviti ($136) and 4½ hours to the lagoon shared by Tavewa, Nanuya Lailai and Nacula ($148). Children aged between six and 15 travel half price. In the afternoon it follows the same route back to the mainland, calling in at all of the resorts once more. Coffee and snacks are available, but if you're travelling the length of the chain in one five-hour hit you might want to bring something more substantial to eat.

As the boat pulls up near each island, it is met by a swarm of dinghies that come alongside to take turns collecting and depositing guests, bags and mail. It's worth keeping an eye on your luggage as bags are occasionally offloaded onto the wrong boat.

On board the *Flyer* is a tour desk that can call ahead to book island accommodation. The service is excellent and accepts credit cards, which saves on carrying large amounts of cash. Be warned that your choice of accommodation may be limited to the budget end of the quality scale as some of the more desirable options get booked out well ahead. So, if you've got a firm idea of what you want, you're better off booking your own accommodation separately and in advance.

If you want to linger in the islands without a prebooked itinerary then a **Bula Pass** (7/14/21 days $321/385/482) can be a good deal. The pass enables unlimited island-hopping within the time period, but only one return trip to Denarau. Awesome Adventures Fiji also offers four-/five-/11-night packages. With names such as A Lazy Threesome (six days, five nights, three islands; dorm/twin $771/873 per person), A Great Pair (five days, four nights, two islands; dorm/twin $448/494 per person) and Tropical Awegasm (12 days, 11 nights, five islands; dorm/twin $1215/1482 per person), the packages include accommodation, meals and transport. But as you don't have the choice of where you stay, it's less flexible than a Bula Pass.

The collection boxes on board the boat are for donations to the *Flyer's* Yasawa Trust Foundation. This foundation helps support villagers in the northern Yasawas with infrastructure such as water tanks and school repairs. More information is available at www.vinakafiji.com.fj.

KAYAKING

Southern Sea Ventures

KAYAKING

(www.southernseaventures.com) Australian-operated Southern Sea offers eight-day safaris with six days' kayaking time along the Yasawa chain of islands. The trips (May to October) cost A\$1995 per person for a maximum of 10 people per group. The price includes all meals, two-person fibreglass kayaks, and safety and camping gear. Expect to paddle for three to four hours daily, stopping along the way for snorkelling and village visits. A similar tour is offered by World Expeditions (www.worldexpeditions.com).

ℹ Information

The Yasawas are still remote and isolated, and there are no shops, banks, postal or medical services. Although increased mobile phone range has made communications somewhat easier for locals (and visitors), it can still be a bit erratic when there's a mountain in the way.

Head to **Lonely Planet** (www.lonelyplanet.com/fiji/yasawa-group) for planning advice, author recommendations, traveller reviews and insider tips.

ℹ Getting There & Around

AIR

Pacific Islands Air & Seaplane (☑ 672 5644; www.pacificislandsair.com) provides Yasawa transfers in seven- and 10-seater seaplane and fixed-wheel aircraft, as well as scenic island flights. If you do arrive by seaplane, be sure to inform your resort so they can send their boat into the middle of the lagoon to collect you!

BOAT

Most people access the Yasawas by Awesome Adventures' *Yasawa Flyer* catamaran – it's the only public boat to make the daily trip up and down the island chain.

Once in the islands, water taxis whisk you around locally. While these are usually local motorboats in varying stages of disrepair (and with scant regard for safety equipment), the boatmen know the water and the weather like the back of their hand. Prices are fixed depending on distance and current cost of fuel; in 2011 a one-way transfer from Nacula to Tavewa in the Northern Yasawas, for example, was about \$20.

Kuata & Wayasewa

These two islands mark the first stop in the Yasawa chain. Kuata is separated from Wayasewa by a deep, narrow channel and kayaking between the two islands is a great way to spend a calm-water afternoon.

Kuata, Wayasewa & Waya

Both have unusual volcanic rock formations, with caves and coral cliffs in the waters off the southern end of little Kuata, which is also where you'll find that island's best snorkelling – the island is easily walkable. Kuata's **summit climb** (per person \$15) takes a hot and sticky 30 minutes with a guide – great for sunrise and sunset views.

Wayasewa, also known as Wayalailai (Little Waya), is dominated by a massive volcanic plug (Vatuvula; 349m) that towers dramatically over the beaches below. There's a sunrise and sunset **summit walk** (per person \$10) here, too. The track passes a 'wobbling rock' (pronounced endearingly, by Fijian-speakers, as 'wombling') and is highly recommended; upwards is a good work out for the thighs and the downhill slopes are not for the fainthearted or weak-kneed; you'll likely find your legs, too, wombling on return. The views towards Kuata, Vomo and Viti Levu are phenomenal.

THE MAMANUCA & YASAWA GROUPS KUATA & WAYASEWA

The Fijian government declared Wayasewa's Namara village unsafe and moved it north to two present locations, **Naboro** and Yamata, in 1985 after a rock slide damaged some of the buildings, though some die-hard locals refused to move and still live in Namara. Naboro's **rugby** sessions are the stuff of local legend, and kick off every Friday afternoon at the village school. The rugby field is in poor condition, the teams unruly and the atmosphere great – we highly recommend attending. Staff from local resorts attend and, if you are willing to cheer for their team, will happily keep you company.

Yamata, on the northwestern side of the island, also receives tourists on village visits. It is far more low-key and visitors should expect a stroll through the village, a look at the small church and occasional stalls selling shells and jewellery.

A 15-minute boat ride away from the resorts, at a local reef, is a spot renowned for **shark snorkelling**. The sharks, which are mostly white-tip reef sharks, are totally harmless but their sleek looks and stealth-like appearance make for a thrilling outing. The local divers are able to grab hold of their tails by distracting the sharks with food hidden in rock crevices. For more on the issue of shark feeding, see the boxed text, p34. Snorkelling with the sharks with/without gear costs $40/25 and, along with other activities described here, can be arranged through any of the resorts.

Dive Trek Wayasewa is based at the Wayalailai Eco Haven Resort, services all the resorts on both islands, and offers intro/two-tank dives/PADI Open Water Courses for $115/180/650.

🛏 Sleeping & Eating

None of the resorts yet had 24-hour power when we visited.

Wayalailai Eco Haven Resort   HOSTEL **$**
(☎603 0215; www.wayalailairesort.com; incl meals sites per person $60, dm $80, d $180-200) Owned and operated by the Wayasewa villagers, whose cheery voices ring out loud around the grounds from dawn, this rustic budget resort was one of the first backpackers to open in the Yasawas. Over the years it has grown, and accommodation now ranges from a couple of eight- and 10-bed dorms, to singles and doubles with private bathrooms (and very thin walls) in the renovated former schoolhouse, to spacious traditional *bure* with private balconies above the beach. Sitting squarely

at the base of Vatuvula's granite facade, the property has a dramatic setting and is tiered over two levels above the beach. Buffet meals are served in a bar-restaurant with a lovely raised deck overlooking the beach and shaded by sails. This place lacks the homely welcome of the smaller establishments, but it's an excellent introduction to things to come further up the line and is very popular with the sociable backpacking crowd.

Naqalia Lodge   LODGE **$$**
(☎977 4696; www.naqalialodge-yasawa.com; dm/d incl meals $117/234) A few minutes' boat ride further along the beach from Wayalailai is this simple lodge, covered in wildly colourful artwork. It has four big, light, airy and well-maintained traditionally built *bure* with private bathrooms, and a simple 12-bed dorm. It's also run by Wayasewa villagers and, unlike Wayalailai, targets travellers looking for something small-scale and low-key – it's lovely, but it's not the place for party animals. The same daily activities – guided walks, snorkelling trips, village visits – are offered, but evenings are quiet.

Kuata Natural Resort   HOSTEL **$**
(☎862 8262; sites per person/dm/d incl meals $50/72/172) Sitting behind a coarse sandy beach with Wayasewa hovering in the near distance, Kuata appeals to that unfussy backpacker with a taste for beer and the simple life. The resort has one four-bed and one 28-bed dorm, and many basic traditional-style double *bure* with private bathrooms and fans; all beds have mosquito nets. The standards are pretty modest, as is the food, though major renovations of the kitchen were underway when we visited.

Waya

Waya is exquisite on the eyes, with picture-postcard scenery. It has rugged hills, beautiful beaches and lagoons, and a coastline that alternates between long, sandy beaches and rocky headlands. Waya is also unusually blessed with natural springs that percolate up through the volcanic rock, so it is unlikely you will face water restrictions here. There are four villages (Nalauwaki, Natawa, Yalobi and Waya Levu), a nursing station and a boarding school on the island.

Hiking unguided across the island is not recommended. The land is privately owned, the terrain unforgiving and the hiking trails largely overgrown as many islanders now rely on motorised boats to get around. The best opportunity to work the pins is the **summit trek to Ului Nakauka** (three hours return). The track from Nalawauki village circles around the back of a huge rock outcrop before ascending to its summit. The views south across Waya and north towards Naviti are spectacular, and you may find yourself in the company of feral goats.

A thick rim of coral follows Waya's shoreline and provides good **snorkelling** just off the beach in front of Octopus Resort. Yachties often anchor on one side or the other (depending on the wind) of the **natural sand bridge** that has formed between Waya and Wayasewa.

🛏 Sleeping & Eating

Octopus Resort RESORT **$$**
(🏠666 6337; www.octopusresort.com; dm $45-55, d $255-479; 🌐❄@♨🛜) Every day feels like a lazy Sunday at Octopus, with its breezy bar-restaurant, swaying hammocks and a wide sandy beach peppered with thatched sun huts and padded sun loungers. It's a mostly midrange option of stand-alone thatched and fan-cooled *bure*; there's also a small air-con dorm and several decidedly top-end villas and lodge rooms – the range of guests and families checking in is as varied as the rooms. The compulsory meal package ($77) includes excellent à la carte lunches and set dinners in a sand-floored restaurant, though the communal dining tables might not suit all. A multitude of activities include Fijian cookery classes, quiz nights and movies by the pool; diving costs $185/595 for a two-tank dive/PADI Open Water Course. Octopus also offers direct boat transfers from Vuda Point marina (adult/child $150/110 one way, 1¼ hours) for guests who don't wish to island-hop the *Flyer*'s route.

Naviti & Around

One of the largest (33 sq km) and highest (up to 380m high) islands of the group, Naviti has a rugged volcanic profile. Along with the two smaller islands of Nanuya Balavu and Drawaqa at the southern end, three very different and equally inviting resorts welcome travellers.

The islands' main attraction is an amazing snorkelling site where you can swim with **mantarays**. The best time to see the giant rays is between June and August, although they may be spotted as early as May and as late as September, cruising the channel near

FAST FOOD

On 29 April 1789 mutineers set Captain William Bligh and 18 loyal crew members adrift of the HMS *Bounty* in an open boat just 7m long and 3m wide. The epic journey that followed passed through treacherous waters littered with shallow reefs and islands inhabited by cannibals; two Yasawa war canoes put to sea from Waya in pursuit of them. Fortunately a squall swept in some much-needed wind to raise the mainsail and blow them to the safety of the open sea. This body of water is today referred to as Bligh Water and while the Yasawas remain relatively undeveloped, the locals are considerably friendlier.

Mantaray Resort. All the resorts in the area offer snorkelling trips to the rays for around $35 per person plus snorkel hire, with spotters heading out in the mornings ahead of the tours to check where the animals are. Once the rays are spotted, everyone dives overboard and it will be up to you to keep up with the rays. If they are swimming against the current you'll have to kick like an Energizer bunny to stay anywhere near them. It can be a bit of a free-for-all – watch for the flipper in the face. Those able to free dive the seven-or-so metres down to the rays may have a really close encounter, with 'look, don't touch' as the guiding principle.

Awesome Adventures Fiji offers day trips to Naviti that include return transport, lunch and three hours at Botaira Beach Resort (adult/child $103/57).

🛏 Sleeping & Eating

Mantaray Island Resort RESORT **$**
(🏠603 0202; www.mantarayisland.com; dm $41, d $139-250; @) Mantaray occupies its own wee island of Nanuya Balavu, spreading over a small hill between two pretty beaches. Excellent snorkelling is a few strokes offshore and its proximity to the manta rays' favoured stomping grounds is a huge plus. The modern dorm is divided into cubicles of four bunk beds, each with its own fan and light. The cheaper 'treehouse' *bure* share the self-composting toilets and showers with the dorm and offer greater privacy (though they're still *very* close to each other), while the stylish 'jungle' *bure* have private bathrooms. The $77 meal plan is compulsory and

SWIMMING WITH THE DEVIL

It's hard not to feel a little nervous at the sight of a large dark object approaching from the depths towards you, but the graceful flying carpet that emerges is something to admire, not fear. Also known as devil rays (because of their hornlike pectoral fin extensions), manta rays are the largest of the rays and typically measure 4m to 5.5m across at maturity. The largest recorded specimen was a massive 7.6m (2300kg) and, due to their size, only four aquariums in the world have ever kept them successfully. Despite their bulk, manta rays are capable of great speed and are known to leap out of the water, landing with a resounding slap – but mostly they glide effortlessly in seemingly synchronised swimming manoeuvres.

the food is fresh and inventive. A yacht or two is often moored in the bay, with yachties coming over for wood-fired pizza on the beach ($5 per big slice) during cocktail hour. Mantaray is professionally run and deservedly popular so it's worth booking ahead. Depending on the night's crowd, it can be a party destination – and with the music, and the proximity of the gen shed, the dorm can be pretty noisy – but the jungle *bure* along the beach are the very essence of peace and quiet.

Barefoot Lodge
LODGE $

(☏777 5250; www.captaincook.com.au; bure per person incl meals $99) This is a mellow, very low-key resort on tiny Drawaqa island. Small, clean and simple *bure* made with lattice walls and thatched roofs are owned and operated by Captain Cook Cruises. Most who stay here arrive on the sailing ship *Spirit of the Pacific* and spend their days on prearranged 'sailing safaris', returning only in the afternoon to make use of Drawaqa's three beaches; other resort guests are welcome to join ship for the day ($100 per person). If you are looking for a quiet, simple alternative to the party islands, and want to be close to the mantas, this is an excellent choice. The *bure* have fans (there's 24-hour power), accommodate two, and all facilities are shared. **Reef Safari** (www.reefsafari.com.fj) is based here, and charges $225 for a two-tank dive.

Botaira Beach Resort
RESORT $$$

(☏670 7002; www.botaira.com; dm/d incl meals $125/470) Botaira makes a great day-tour destination – there's a beautiful open-air restaurant with elevated decks, and landscaped grounds with orchards and vegetable gardens. The beach extends over a long cove, thick with palm trees, and the snorkelling along the reef edge is very good; it's a treat to see the reintroduced giant clams. Its accommodation targets the more discerning traveller who is after space and privacy, but while the 11 *bure* are certainly stylish, the jump in price is not commensurate with the facilities offered by other resorts in the same price range. Other amenities – like a pool and the option to deviate from set menus – are conspicuous by their absence, though at the time of writing 24-hour power was expected to be available in 2012.

White Sandy Beach
HOSTEL $

(☏666 4066, 912 5254; whitesandybeach_diveresort @yahoo.com; dm/d incl meals $72/162) A slow, mellow budget resort with a clean, 10-bed dorm, several simple *bure* and hammocks under the palms on the water's edge. The resort was upgrading as we visited; the construction of a 30-bed dorm split into five-bed cubicles, below a 1st-floor reading-room-cum-restaurant, was well underway. A small dive centre here offers two-tank dives for $210.

White Sandy Beach shares a protected, long stretch of white sand about halfway up the west coast of Naviti with Korovou Eco-Tour Resort – it's a great sunset location. Swimming is only possible at high tide here – low tide exposes a wide bank of dead reef and mosslike seaweed. Fortunately a steep short track next to White Sandy Beach crosses over a hill (about a 10-minute walk) to the pretty and secluded Honeymoon Beach; a lovely swath of white sand. Visitors make a $2 donation to the village to visit this little cove, but the pay-off is calm and tranquil waters and decent snorkelling.

The hostel has a generator that shuts down for a few hours during the day and from about 11pm, but is aiming for 24-hour power and at the time of writing had plans to be solar by 2012.

Korovou Eco-Tour Resort
HOSTEL $$

(☏603 0050; www.korovoufiji.com; dm/d/villas incl meals $120/286/330; @☒) Korovou can accommodate about 70 travellers and can be packed with young and sociable troops. Two 20-bed dorms have wooden bunks and fans.

The newly built stone-and-wood villas each have a separate lounge, a fridge and a stone bathroom. The cheaper wooden lodges have their own verandahs and bathrooms, and are spotlessly clean. Work off the filling meals with a snorkel on the reef shelf in front of the restaurant; the coral's not great, but there are lots of fish.

Korovou's generator is shut down at similar times to White Sandy Beach, but is also aiming for 24-hour power.

Matacawalevu & Yaqeta

Matacawalevu is a 4km-long hilly volcanic island protected by the large Nasomo Bay on its eastern side. Nanuya Levu (Turtle Island) is to the east, and to the south, across a protected lagoon used for seaweed farming, is Yaqeta. The island has two villages: Matacawalevu on its northeast end and Vuake in Nasomo Bay.

🛏 Sleeping

TOP CHOICE Navutu Stars   BOUTIQUE HOTEL **$$$**
(☏664 0553; www.navutustarsfiji.com; Yaqeta; d $525-892; ☏✳@⊠) Yaqeta's beautiful boutique hotel specialises in opulent decadence, Pacific-style – with petal-sprinkled baths, intimate sunset dining if you choose and complimentary massages on arrival. The nine whitewashed villas have king-sized beds, exquisitely detailed 7m-high roofs, and fantastic views north from their private decks. Food is fabulous – think Italian, with good use of local produce (meal packages are available from $120 per person per day, or à la carte). And full marks for the small-scale, successful and ongoing coral regeneration

gardens just offshore; snorkel out with enthusiastic Seruvi and plant a patch yourself.

Long Beach Backpackers   HOSTEL **$**
(☏603 1020; longbeach_vuaki@yahoo.com; Matacawelevu; sites/dm incl meals $60/70, d incl meals $250) Low-key and mellow, this welcoming family-run hostel has several double *bure* with private bathrooms, and a clean eight-bed dorm with a tired bathroom. The big draw here is the long, horseshoe-shaped beach and a breezy deck overlooking tiny Deviulau island – you can wade over at low tide and scramble to the top for great views.

Bay of Plenty Lodge   HOSTEL **$**
(☏995 1341; bayofplentylodge@yahoo.com; Matacawalevu; dm/d incl meals $72/165) Five small hillside villas opened here in 2008. They have tiled floors, attached bathrooms, excellent views and are soundly constructed. It's not the place to stay if you want to walk out and snorkel – the mangrove-fringed beach has brownish sand and, being extremely tidal, resembles an estuary for much of the day, but a likely bonus is helping the cook and staff wade out with nets and slap the water to catch fish for dinner. A walking track along the ridge offers good island views. Guests are picked up ($10 return transfer) from the *Yasawa Flyer*'s Blue Lagoon drop-off point.

Tavewa, Nanuya Lailai & Nacula

These islands are right in the middle of the Yasawa Group, but house some of the group's northernmost resorts. Nacula marks the end of the *Yasawa Flyer* route, and there's a

---

BEACH BUSINESS

All the resorts in the Yasawas are on the waterfront, but not all can claim idyllic beaches. If white sand, turquoise depths and simmering in a sun-coma are what you came for, the following resorts should be just the ticket.

Blue Lagoon Beach Resort (Nacula) (p135) It's on the best of the Yasawas' resort-based beaches. Protected from the trade winds, the water is still, clear and deep. A large bank of coral provides excellent snorkelling.

Nanuya Island Resort (Nanuya Lailai) (p134) The resort occupies an enviable and isolated position on a quiet beach in front of the renowned Blue Lagoon.

Octopus Resort (Waya) (p129) The beach in this protected cove is beautiful for swimming at high tide and great for sunbaking and wandering at low tide.

Botaira Beach Resort (Naviti) (p130) Botaira's beach is a length of soft white sand with ample room to park a towel. The calm water has a good stretch of shallows before it drops into the deep.

Tavewa & Around (Nacula Tikina)

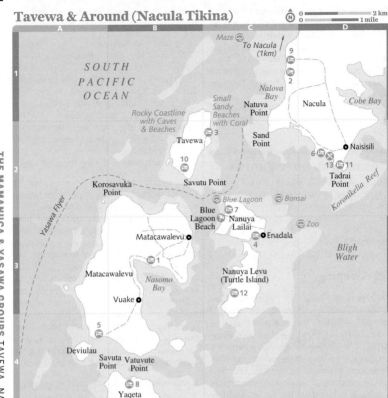

Tavewa & Around (Nacula Tikina)

Activities, Courses & Tours

Dive Yasawa Lagoon	(see 3)
Vertical Blue Diving	(see 2)
Westside Watersports	(see 7)

Sleeping

1 Bay of Plenty Lodge	B3
2 Blue Lagoon Beach Resort	C1
3 Coral View Resort	C2
4 Gold Coast Inn	C3
5 Long Beach Backpackers	A4
6 Nabua Lodge	D2
7 Nanuya Island Resort	C2
8 Navuta Stars	B4
9 Oarsman's Bay Lodge	C1
10 Otto & Fanny's	B2
11 Safe Landing Resort	D2
12 Turtle Island Resort	C3

Eating

Lo's Tea Shop	(see 4)
13 Travellers Tea House	D2

Shopping

Grandma's Shell Market	(see 4)

busy hour or so of loading and unloading at the turn-around point mid-lagoon. Budget resorts on Nacula may charge around $10 for their transfers to and from the *Yasawa Flyer*, but then again may not. Travelling be-tween the resorts by water taxi costs around $25 per trip.

All the resorts offer boat trips to the Blue Lagoon (around $20 per person) and trips to Sawa-i-Lau caves (around $45 per person).

Each island has a dive shop, which also picks up from other resorts nearby. Recommended dive spots include the big wall dives at the **Zoo** and **Bonsai** and the swim-throughs and tunnels at the **Maze**. Every Saturday and Wednesday there's a **shark dive**, where you are likely to see two resident 4m lemon sharks and, occasionally, 2m grey reef sharks. A two-tank dive/PADI Open Water Course costs around $180/750, including equipment.

TAVEWA

A pleasant beach unfurls itself on the southeastern coast of this small island (3 sq km) but it's often plagued by buffeting trade winds (which are great, however, for kiteboarders). You need to head west to the beach around the bend of Savutu Point to find relief from the gales and you're best off doing so at low tide. The snorkelling just offshore here is excellent. An ambling ascent of the central crest affords photogenic views of the Yasawa chain, which is particularly spectacular at sunset; the track crosses several stretches of private land, so ask your accommodation to get the OK from the owners before you head up.

Diving is provided by **Dive Yasawa Lagoon** (666 2648; VHF Marine channel 72; www.diveyasawalagoon.com) at Coral View Resort.

🛏 Sleeping & Eating

Coral View Resort HOSTEL **$**
(922 2575; www.coralviewfiji.com; dm/s/d incl meals $76/140/185; ❄ @) This well-run budget resort is popular with young Brits returning from their antipodean adventures. Having failed to drink New Zealand and Australia dry, they make a good attempt at polishing off this island, and the nightly entertainment often features beach parties and bonfires. The three 20-bed dorms are simple, clean and air-conditioned. The small, stone cottages, with their high-pitched roofs and *masi*-and-bamboo-lined interiors, are excellent value; there's even 24-hour electricity. There are jetskis available to zip across the bay and interesting snorkelling to be had right offshore but, as the virtually nonexistent beach loses the afternoon sun (thanks to the low hills behind the resort), you'll need to cover the distance to the southeast beach for serious sunbaking.

Otto & Fanny's HOMESTAY **$**
(996 3108; ottofanny@connect.com.fj; dm/d incl meals $100/210; @) On a sprawling property amid a former copra plantation, this quiet, homely place has several *bure* with private bathrooms and a spacious 12-bed dorm. The flat, grassy grounds are inundated with coconut trees but offer plenty of wide open spaces. Travellers talk up the meals here and the afternoon tea of banana cake or scones is legendary. This place has a real family feel to it – it's more of a quiet homestay than hostel, and sees returning guests of all ages – and is closest to Tavewa's best patch of beach.

NANUYA LAILAI

This is it, folks – home to that celebrity of all the Yasawas' beaches, the **Blue Lagoon**. Crystalline and glossy, it doesn't disappoint the bevy of swimmers, snorkellers, divers, and people on cruise boats or yachts who dabble in its gorgeous, lucent depths. Actually, it's not dissimilar to many of the lagoons scattered around the Yasawas. The snorkelling here is rich in fish but the coral has taken a hammering over recent years. Travellers are advised by signs, and enforced at times by security staff, to stay clear of Nanuya Levu as well as the section of Blue Lagoon beach used by Blue Lagoon Cruises.

The settlement of **Enadala** is on the eastern side of Nanuya Lailai, and the beach

---

CREATING AN OCTOPUS'S GARDEN

As activities' coordinator at Navutu Stars Resort in the Yasawas – and as a local villager – Seruvi Iosefo is a passionate advocate of coral gardening. After all, as he says, it may be slow going but it's not rocket science. 'It's just like planting cassava. You break a bit off, find a good place to put it, make sure the new conditions are right. If the bottom's attached after a couple of weeks, you know it'll survive!' It's a great way to explain the simplicity of the process to visitors.

Armed with snorkel, mask and flippers Seruvi swims off. Pointing out the bright blue tips of a healthy staghorn coral he snaps a piece off, fins away to a bleached, barren patch of tired reef and pokes the just-picked stem into a crevice. He indicates small, single-stemmed corals next to it that were transplanted recently and are growing well, grins, and gives a thumbs-up before swimming on.

here is buffeted by strong winds. Connecting the Blue Lagoon and Enadala beaches, and snaking over the mass of gently sloping hills of the island's interior, is a well-trodden **track**. It takes about 30 minutes to walk from one beach to the other by using this track or following the coastline at low tide. But what could possibly draw anyone away from the Blue Lagoon's bright water? Cake could. **Lo's Tea Shop** – a blue shack on the edge of the water – sells banana cake and chocolate cake with sugary sauce for $2.50 a slice. Eat inside astride benches or, better still, outside with your toes in the sand. Both Lo's and **Grandma's Shell Market**, a few doors down, sell seashells by the seashore (along with sarongs and jewellery). Opening hours are Fiji time.

Diving is provided by **Westside Watersports** (☎666 1462; www.fiji-dive.com) at Nanuya Island Resort.

Sleeping & Eating

TOP CHOICE Nanuya Island Resort BOUTIQUE HOTEL $$
(☎666 7633; www.nanuyafiji.com; d incl breakfast $275-415; @) A short walk, even in flippers, from the azure waters of the Blue Lagoon, this swish and understated resort is the kind of place you picture when you dream of indulgence, beachside cocktails and exquisite vistas. The *bure* are Fiji-nouveau; the roofs may be thatched but the interiors are chic and elegant. All are fan-cooled and have their own bathroom with solar-heated hot water. Wedding packages are available and, as this place oozes romance, it's a favourite spot for couples (no children under seven), although the *bure* can accommodate families of up to four. It's worth noting that older guests may find the path to the hillside villas too steep and, if you are serious about staying here, you will need to book several months in advance. The beachside restaurant is very atmospheric and the à la carte fare (mains $25 to $35) deliciously inventive.

Gold Coast Inn HOMESTAY $
(☎665 1580; dm/d incl meals $82/185) Offering the only budget accommodation on this side of the island, the private timber *bure* here have a double and single bed as well as their own bathrooms. This is a smallish affair – there are only six bungalows and a small dormitory – but it's run by a family with a big heart.

NACULA

Nacula, a hilly volcanic island, is the third largest in the Yasawas. Blanketed with rugged hills and soft peaks, its interior is laced with well-trodden paths leading to villages and small coves. It is possible to follow a well-defined trail inland through mangroves from the resorts on the southern point to those at Long Beach. Keep an eye out for **mudskippers**, an amphibious fish that has uniquely evolved to be able to breathe out of water. They live in the tidal streams among the mangroves.

There are four villages on Nacula island, including **Nacula**, home of Ratu Epeli Vuetibau, the high chief of Nacula Tikina. The *tikina* (group of villages) includes the islands of Nacula, Tavewa, Nanuya Levu, Nanuya Lailai and Matacawalevu, and is home to about 3500 people. Catching a Sunday **church service** in one of the villages is a real treat; most resorts will arrange free transport for their guests.

Beach devotees will be ecstatic to know that Nacula also has some of the finest **beaches**, **swimming** and **snorkelling** in Fiji, particularly at **Long Beach**, and if you need some practice **hiking** on land, a decent two- to three-hour return hike above Nabua Lodge will take you to 360-degree views across the islands.

Diving is provided by **Vertical Blue Diving** (verticalbluediving@gmail.com) at Blue Lagoon Beach Resort.

Sleeping & Eating

SOUTH COAST

Safe Landing Resort HOSTEL $
(☎948 2180; www.safelandingfiji.com; sites per person incl meals $50, dm/d incl meals $70/180; @) Several small *bure* dot the waterfront here, overlooking the resort's trademark sandy cove: a pretty little beach framed between two rocky outcrops. Across a swath of green lawn, the restaurant looks out along the bay shared with Nabua. Australian-owned and managed, it's one of the few places to welcome BYO campers, with flat and shady sites under coconut palms. An airy dorm was under construction when we visited.

Nabua Lodge HOSTEL $
(☎665 0803; nabualodgefiji@connect.com.fj; dm incl meals $75, d with/without bathroom incl meals $180/150; @) Located just west of Safe Landing, on a nicely landscaped plot of grass with strategically placed hammocks. Local couple Sai and Vani Ratu are continuously upgrad-

ing on a small but significant scale: a wide new deck overlooks the water, and as we visited the engineers were putting the final touches to going solar, allowing for 24-hour power. Accommodation is simple, in small *bure*. The beach in front of Nabua Lodge is quite tidal and only a narrow strip of sand between rocky promontories is left exposed at high tide.

The two budget resorts are separated by a few hundred metres of waterfront, and sandwiched between them is **Travellers Tea House** – it's *the* place to go for afternoon tea. In a wonky kiosk with wobbly tables and seats, a serene and smiling local husband-and-wife team serve tea and fresh-baked cakes – banana, pineapple, choc and sometimes a combo of all the above – between 3pm and 5pm. It's a must, and all for the princely sum of $5.

LONG BEACH

Imagine a long swath of powdery sand easing into a glassy, cerulean sea and you will have some idea of what to expect at one of the best beaches in the Yasawas. And, unlike other beaches, it's possible to swim here at low tide without trudging over an exposed coral shelf to do so.

[TOP CHOICE] **Blue Lagoon Beach Resort** RESORT **$$** (✆603 0223; www.bluelagoonbeachresort.com.fj; dm/d $45/$179, villa $329-879; ❄) Blue Lagoon ticks all the right boxes. It's small enough to be low-key and relaxed, but big enough (about 70 guests when full) to have a bit of a buzz. It caters for all budgets in a compatible way; *bure* are stylish and the 16-bed air-con dorm is as clean as a whistle and great value. There's an interesting menu (daily meal plans $79 per person) served in a groovy sand-floored restaurant-bar with bean bags, lounges and hammocks over the water.

Oarsman's Bay Lodge RESORT **$** (✆672 2921; www.oarsmansbay.com; site per tent/dm/d/f $48/34/178/358; ❄@) Sharing the same prime slice of sandy real estate as Blue Lagoon Beach Resort, Oarsman's has seen its fair share of ups and downs over the last few years. It was in a down phase when we visited, and the out-of-date website bore no resemblance to reality – you might want to check it out before committing to a stay of any length.

Nanuya Levu (Turtle Island)

Nanuya Levu is a privately owned island (2 sq km) with protected sandy beaches and rugged volcanic cliffs. The 1980 film *The Blue Lagoon*, starring Brooke Shields, was partly filmed here, as was the original 1949 version starring Jean Simmons. It is off limits to all but resort guests.

One of the world's finest and most famous resorts, **Turtle Island Resort** (✆672 2921; www.turtlefiji.com; d from US$2700) lures the celebrities, romantics and wealthy from around the world to its 14 two-room exclusive beachfront *bure*. The resort is owned by American Richard Evanson, who, after making his fortune in cable TV, bought the island in 1972 for his personal hideaway. Rates include all food, drinks and most activities, including horse riding, scuba diving and big-game fishing. Recent developments here include a hydroponic and organic vegetable garden to supply the kitchen and green initiatives to protect local fauna. Transfers are by Turtle Airways seaplane charter, a 30-minute flight from Nadi.

Sawa-i-Lau

Sawa-i-Lau is the odd limestone island amid a string of high volcanic islands. The underwater limestone is thought to have formed a few hundred metres below the surface and then uplifted over time. Shafts of daylight enter a great dome-shaped cave – 15m tall above the water surface – where you can swim in a natural pool. With a guide, a torch and a bit of courage, you can also swim through an underwater passage into an adjoining chamber. The walls have carvings, paintings and inscriptions of unknown meaning. Similar inscriptions also occur on Vanua Levu in the hills near Vuinadi, Natewa Bay and near Dakuniba on the Tunuloa (Cakaudrove) Peninsula.

Most Yasawa budget resorts offer trips to the caves for around $45 per person.

Yasawa

Yasawa, the northernmost island in the group, has six small villages and a fabulous, five-star resort.

Set on a gorgeous beach, the 18 air-conditioned *bure* at **Yasawa Island Resort** (672 2266; www.yasawa.com; d from US$925;) are spacious, with separate living and bedroom areas, outdoor showers and their own private beach hut. Rates include lobster omelettes for breakfast, à la carte meals and most activities. Recommended activities include 4WD safaris and picnics to secluded beaches. Family weeks are offered twice a year, otherwise it's adults – and mostly couples – only.

Ovalau & the Lomaiviti Group

POP 12.064

Why Go?

Lomaiviti literally means 'Middle Fiji' and although the group is just off Viti Levu's east coast, it really does feel like the middle of nowhere. It is therefore hard to believe that it was in Levuka, the capital of the main island Ovalau, that the first Europeans settled and eventually made this the country's first capital. Today it's laid-back and the political machinations long departed, but with the right wind you may yet catch a whiff of the town's wild and immoral colonial days.

South of Ovalau, the tiny coral islands of Leleuvia and Caqalai have sandy beaches, good snorkelling and simple budget resorts. To the north is Koro with its fantastic diving, family-oriented Naigani and the luxury resort of Wakaya island. Hawksbill turtles visit to lay their eggs, and a pod of humpback whales passes the east coast of Ovalau on their annual migration between May and September.

Best Places to Stay

- » Caqalai Island Resort (p147)
- » Leleuvia Island Resort (p148)
- » Levuka Homestay (p143)
- » Royal Hotel (p143)
- » Silana Ecolodge (p147)

Best Sights

- » Levuka (p141)
- » Snake Island (p148)
- » Lovoni village (p145)
- » Niubasaga (p147)
- » Nadelaiovalu Peak (p140)

When to Go

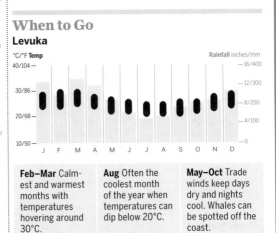

Levuka

Feb–Mar Calmest and warmest months with temperatures hovering around 30°C.

Aug Often the coolest month of the year when temperatures can dip below 20°C.

May–Oct Trade winds keep days dry and nights cool. Whales can be spotted off the coast.

🏃 Activities
DIVING & SNORKELLING

The Lomaiviti waters offer some wonderful, little-visited dive sites where you can encounter manta rays, hammerheads, turtles, white-tip reef sharks and lion fish, but at the time of writing few resorts offered diving. **Blue Ridge**, off Wakaya Island, is famous for its bright-blue ribbon eels. There is stunning soft coral at **Snake Island**, just off Caqalai, in the Moturiki Channel, and excellent hard coral at **Waitovu Passage**. The **Pipeline**, two minutes by boat from town at Levuka Passage, is for experienced divers only. Here the fishy waste from the Pafco tuna plant attracts gi-

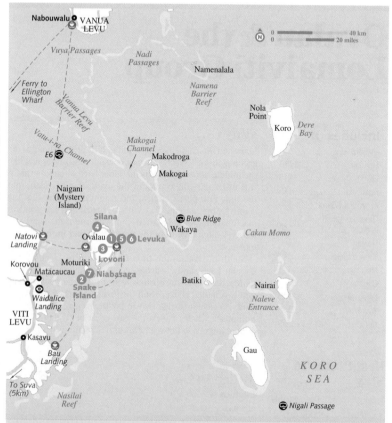

Ovalau & the Lomaiviti Group Highlights

❶ Enjoying the rickety colonial architecture of colourful **Levuka** (p141) and easily imagining its rowdy outpost atmosphere of times past

❷ Spotting Napoleon wrasses, banded sea snakes, phenomenally big schools of fish and psychedelic gardens of soft corals while snorkelling **Snake Island** (p148)

❸ Hiking through river jungles to the proud and remote village of Lovoni with **Epi's Midland Tour** (p141)

❹ Experiencing Fijian village life while staying with Seru and his welcoming family at **Silana Ecolodge** (p147)

❺ Walking down a noticeable slope on creaking floors to your bathroom at the **Royal Hotel** (p143), oldest hotel in the South Pacific

❻ Spotting whales from the terrace of **Levuka Homestay** (p143), cocktail in hand

❼ Getting spiritual with a melodious church service at **Niubasaga village** (p147) on remote Motoriki

ant groupers, eagle rays and bull sharks. The famous **E6** in the Vatu-i-Ra Channel is a huge pinnacle with soft corals and plenty of big pelagics. **Nigali Passage** off Gau island is a narrow channel in the reef that has a concentrations of pelagics such as gray reef sharks and barracuda. E6 and Nigali Passage can usually only be accessed on a liveaboard (see p35).

Wakaya Club, Naigani Island Resort and Caqalai Island Resort all offer diving.

Snorkelling off the outer islands is fantastic, especially around Snake Island. Napoleon wrasses, banded sea snakes and flourishing corals are highlights.

CYCLING

Levuka and its surrounding area is compact and it is easy to get around by bike – especially if you're heading south, as the road is quite flat. Head north and the road starts to get very hilly around Cawaci. If you're reasonably fit, it will take you about a day to cycle around the island. No one was officially renting out bikes at the time of research, but ask around and you're sure to find someone who will rent or lend you one.

YACHTING

Levuka is a port of entry into Fiji for yachties and there are a few good spots to put down anchor in the Lomaiviti Group. You can anchor in Levuka harbour to explore Ovalau, and good desert-island spots to park include Leleuvia island and Dere Bay on Koro island. You will find resort facilities at both of these spots. Try VHF Marine channel 16 to reach the appropriate authorities if entering the country at Levuka, but if no one answers, anchor near Queen's Wharf and make your way ashore. Formalities are usually simpler here than in Suva. There is a customs house by the main wharf, and ship supplies and repairs are available here. Call ahead if arriving outside normal working hours.

❶ Getting There & Around

From Suva **Northern Air** (☑347 5005; www. northernair.com.fj) flies to Ovalau ($80 one way, 12 minutes, Monday to Saturday) at 8am and returns to Suva at 8.40am. Book online or at the airport when there are departing or incoming flights. The airstrip is about 40 minutes' drive from Levuka. Minibuses to the airstrip ($10 per person) will pick you up from your hotel on request. A taxi costs about $40.

Patterson Brothers Shipping (☑344 0125; Beach St, Levuka; ☉8.30am-4.30pm Mon-Fri, to noon Sat) has a bus–ferry–bus service from Levuka to Suva via Natovi Landing ($35, four to six

hours, gather at 4.30am for 5am departure daily from Levuka; from Suva arrive at the far lot of Suva's bus terminal at 1pm for a 1.30pm departure). You can also opt to stay on the boat from Natovi to Nabouwalu (on Vanua Levu) and then continue by bus to Labasa ($65). **Venu Shipping** (☑339 5000; Rona St, Walu Bay, Suva) has direct services from Levuka to Walu Bay in Suva a couple of times a week, but the timetable can be erratic. **Goundar Shipping's** (☑330 1035) *Lomaiviti Princess* makes occasional stops in Levuka during busy periods on its Savusavu–Taveuni–Koro–Suva–Kandavu route.

The resorts on the islands near Ovalau (all except Koro) offer private transfers in their own boats to either Natovi, Bau or Waidalice Landings on Viti Levu and to Levuka. See each island's section for details.

OVALAU

Ovalau is the largest island in the Lomaiviti Group. The island itself is not as pretty as the little brothers and sisters scattered around it, but the capital, Levuka, is captivating and is the only place in the Lomaiviti Group with decent banks, shops and services.

The Bureta Airstrip and Buresala Landing (for ferries) are on the western side of Ovalau, while Levuka is on the eastern coast. A gravel road winds around the perimeter of the island and another follows the Bureta River inland to Lovoni village.

☞ Tours

Serai at **Ovalau Watersports** (☑960 9136) is the mover and shaker of Lomaiviti's small tourism world, and many guesthouses, resorts and tours use her as their booking agent. The office is officially at Levuka Holiday Cottage out near Gun Rock, but she can often be found at the back of the unnamed shop on the corner of Henning St and Beach St. Just go in and ask for Serai. She is the person to seek out for round-the-island 4WD tours as well as arranging all of the tours listed here.

Ovalau Tourist Information Centre offers a historical **walking tour** (per person $10; 2hr) around Levuka.

Silana Village Tour VILLAGE TOUR
(per person $35) Requires a minimum group of six with a few days' notice and includes a *meke* (dance performance that enacts stories and legends), a *lovo* (feast cooked in a pit oven) and a chance to make your own handicrafts from coconut and pandanus

Ovalau & Moturiki

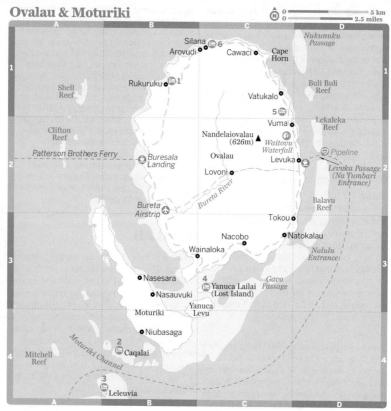

Ovalau & Moturiki

leaves. The guide, Seru, will also take you around Silana any time for $15 (including lunch).

Peak Hike With Samu   HIKING

Hike to 625m **Nadelaiovalu Peak**, the highest on the island with Samu, a young local. After an hour and a half of steep ascent through dense jungle you'll be rewarded with views over Levuka, the reefs and outer islands.

Tea & Talanoa Tours   CULTURAL

(per person $15) Led by Fijian grandmother Bubu Kara or long-term expat resident Duncan Chrichton (Mr Duncan). *Talanoa* means 'to chat'. Bubu makes delicious scones and Mr Duncan has a fabulous garden and some funky pets. Book in advance.

Levuka

POP 3750

There's no denying Levuka's visual appeal. It's one of the few places in the South Pacific that has retained its colonial buildings: along the main street, timber shop-fronts straight out of a Hollywood western are sandwiched between blue sea and fertile green mountains. The effect is quite beguiling – you can almost taste the wild frontier days of this former whaling outpost.

It is an extremely friendly place and you will be warmly welcomed by the mixture of indigenous Fijians, Indo-Fijians, Chinese Fijians, part-European Fijians and sometimes-eccentric expats who inhabit this sleepy town. Nearly everyone is welcoming to visitors, and if you stay for a few days, you'll meet half the town. There are a few good restaurants and cafes here, as well as a classically colonial bar, and the food, while perhaps not memorable, is tasty.

Levukans have been trying to protect the town's heritage by applying for Unesco World Heritage status, though they have so far been unsuccessful.

⊙ Sights

Levuka is small enough that you can see the sights in a single day of walking. Start your walking tour at Nasova, about 10 minutes' stroll south of the Pafco cannery. The Deed of Cession, handing over Fiji to Britain, was signed here in 1874. Cession Site, a memorial commemorating the event, is a pair of anchors and a scattering of plaque-bearing stones.

Across the road are faded Nasova House, once the governor's residence, and the thatched Provincial Bure. Prince Charles made his headquarters in the Provincial Bure when he represented Her Majesty's government during the transition to independence in 1970. It later served as a venue for Lomaiviti council meetings. A large, new meeting venue has been built next door, constructed in time for a 2006 Great Council of Chiefs meeting that never got off the ground because of the 2006 coup. According to our guide, it has yet to be used.

The Pafco tuna cannery at the southern end of Levuka employs almost 1000 townspeople and gives the whole town its distinctive odour. It was occupied by Lovoni villagers during the 2000 coup as part of a dispute about unloading cargo.

Head north along Beach St where the streetscape dates from the late 19th and early 20th centuries. Just in front of the post office is the site of the original Pigeon Post, marked by a nondescript drinking fountain in the centre of the road. From the timber loft that stood here, pigeons provided the first postal link between Levuka and Suva. The birds flew the distance in less than 30 minutes, and were considerably faster and more reliable than Post Fiji.

A few doors away stands the 1868 former Morris Hedstrom (MH) trading store, the original MH store in Fiji. Behind its restored facade are the Levuka Community Centre, a library and a branch of the Fiji Museum (admission $2; ⊙8am-1pm & 2-4.30pm Mon-Fri, 9am-1pm Sat), which holds a small exhibition detailing the history of Levuka, including some wonderful old photos of the town from colonial days.

Sacred Heart Church (Beach St) dates from 1858. The clock strikes twice each hour, with a minute in between. Locals say the first strike is an alarm to warn people who are operating on 'Fiji time'. The light on the spire guides ships through Levuka Passage. From the church, head west along Totoga Lane to explore the backstreets.

The Marist Convent School (1882) was a girls school opened by Catholic missionaries and run by Australian and French nuns. It is now a lively coed primary school. It was built largely out of coral stone in an attempt to protect it from the hurricanes that have claimed so many buildings in town, and it remains an impressive monument against the mountain backdrop.

The little weatherboard building on the corner of Garner Jones Rd and Totoga Lane

OVALAU & THE LOMAIVITI GROUP LEVUKA

DON'T MISS

EPI'S MIDLAND TOUR

Visit Lovoni village in the crater of an extinct volcano deep in the heart of Ovalau (although it resembles a flat valley floor surrounded by hills rather than anything else). Epi, who runs the tour (full day per person $80), is a Lovoni married to an Englishwoman and will take you through forest and past streams, pointing out all kinds of plants, bush food and local medicine along the way. The scenery is beautiful and Epi will regale you with the history and legends of the island and the Lovoni people. Once you've reached the village and presented your sevusevu (gift) to the village chief – assuming the chief is around – you can take a dip in the river. A delicious lunch in one of the village homes is laid on. The price includes transfers and lunch but requires a minimum of two people and the cost per person goes down with each additional person. Contact Serai at Ovalau Watersports (p139) to arrange a tour.

OVALAU & THE LOMAIVITI GROUP LEVUKA

Levuka

was Levuka's original **police station** (1874), and across Totoga Creek in Nasau Park you'll find Fiji's first private club – the 1904 colonial-style timber Ovalau Club. It's well worth stopping in for a beer, if it's open. Next door to the Ovalau Club is the **former town hall** (1898), built in typical British colonial style in honour of Queen Victoria's silver jubilee.

Alongside the former town hall you'll find the stone shell of the South Pacific's first **Masonic lodge**. Lodge Polynesia (1875) was once Levuka's only Romanesque building, but it was burnt to a husk in the 2000 coup by God-fearing villagers. Local Methodists had long alleged that Masons were in league with the devil and that tunnels led from beneath the lodge to Nasova House, the Royal

Hotel and through the centre of the world to Masonic headquarters in Scotland. This turned out not to be the case.

Return across the creek and follow Garner Jones Rd west to the **Levuka Public School** (1879). This was Fiji's first formal school and many of Fiji's prominent citizens were educated here, including Percy Morris and Maynard Hedstrom. Walk back down to Garner Jones Rd, turn left into Church St and pass Nasau Park. There are many old colonial homes on the hillsides, and the romantically named **199 Steps of Mission Hill** are worth climbing for the fantastic view – although if you count them, you might find there are closer to 185 steps. The very simple, coral-and-stone, Gothic-style **Navoka Methodist Church** (1864), near the foot of the steps, is one of the oldest churches in Fiji.

Head down Chapel St then left along Langham St. The **Royal Hotel** (1860s) is Fiji's oldest hotel, rebuilt in 1903. It is the lone survivor of the once-numerous pubs of that era. Originally it had an open verandah with lace balustrading, but this was built in to increase the size of the rooms. Check out the fantastic old snooker room, and play a game of hunt-the-Royal-Hotel-staff.

Back on Beach St, continue north to **Niukaube Hill**, on a point near the water. This was once the site of Ratu Cakobau's Supreme Court and Parliament House. This is also where the first indentured Indian labourers landed in Fiji, after being forced to anchor offshore for several weeks in an attempt to control an outbreak of cholera. The site now has a memorial to locals who fought and died in WWI and WWII.

North of here is the Anglican **Church of the Holy Redeemer** (1904), with its colourful stained-glass and altar of *yaka* and *dakua* wood. Tidy little **Levuka village**, once the home of Tui (Chief) Cakobau, is about 200m further north. In the **cemetery** next to the village's **Methodist Church** is the grave of former American consul John Brown Williams. It was his claim for financial compensation that led Cakobau to hand over Fiji to Britain (see p199 for more on this significant event in Fiji's history).

With the chief's permission you can climb one of two local sites known as **Gun Rock** for a great view over Levuka. In 1849 Commodore Charles Wilkes, of the US exploring expedition, pounded this peak with canon fire from his ship in an attempt to impress the chief of Levuka. Commodore James Graham Goodenough repeated the 'entertainment' in 1874. You can still find cannonball scars on the rock. (The other Gun Rock is much smaller, and named for the canon mounted upon it in the 1850s.) Gun Rock is a good place to spot **whales**, which swim past between May and September.

Walk, cycle or take a taxi 5km north to Cawaci, where you'll find the **Bishops' Tomb** (1922), a beautiful, fading, Gothic-style construction on a grassy point overlooking the ocean, where Fiji's first two Roman Catholic bishops are entombed. Our taxi driver told us that ghosts had been 'spotted' up here by locals and it's not hard to see how this place, with its Latin inscriptions, spooky acoustics, and a swaying cross on one of the graves in the foreground, could play upon the imagination. From here you can see the limestone-and-coral **St John's College** (1894), originally where the sons of Fijian chiefs were educated in English. These days girls are educated here too. The boys' and girls' dormitories are separated by a bridge that no student is allowed to cross after 6pm.

🛏 Sleeping

TOP CHOICE **Levuka Homestay**　　　B&B $
(☏344 0777; www.levukahomestay.com; Church St; s/d incl breakfast $126/148, extra person $42) Far and away the most chic choice in Levuka – a multilevel house with four large, comfortable, light-filled rooms with terraces, each one on its own level. The laid-back owners live on the highest level, where guests come to eat a spectacular breakfast or share a drink with them on their enormous deck overlooking the harbour (spot whales while imbibing from May to October). There is a high chair and a cot here for little ones.

TOP CHOICE **Royal Hotel**　　　HOTEL $
(☏344 0024; www.royallevuka.com; s/d $29/43, cottages from $85; ✳@☀) The Royal is the oldest hotel in the South Pacific, dating back to the 1860s (though it was rebuilt in the early 1900s after a fire) and it's got the character to back it up. This proud timber building is thick with colonial atmosphere, from the creaking wooden floorboards to the hallways plastered with black-and-white photographs of Levuka in times past. Upstairs each room is different and full of quirky old furniture, with iron bedsteads and sloping floors. The semi-enclosed private verandahs come complete with old-fashioned white cane chairs and wooden shutters. There are also some

LEVUKA'S WILD WEST HISTORY

In the 19th century the town of Levuka was a bolt-hole where embittered sailors jumped ship, escaped convicts hid out, polygamous drunks took strings of island brides and disputes were settled with the musket.

As early as 1806 European sandalwood traders stopped at Levuka in search of supplies. However, foreigners did not begin to settle here until the 1830s, when it became a popular whaling centre. The newcomers built schooners and traded for bêche-de-mer (sea cucumber), turtle shells and coconut oil. Some settled down with several Fijian women at a time, explaining to the local people that this was the custom where they came from.

The Lovoni people, warriors of the caldera in the centre of Ovalau, saw the settlers as interlopers and repeatedly burned down their timber town. The Europeans lived under the protection of the chief of Levuka, who was murdered by raiding Lovoni in 1846.

Levuka grew, and by the 1850s it had a reputation for drunkenness, violence and immorality. It attracted beachcombers and freebooters, con men and middlemen, dreamers and crooks. In the 1870s a flood of planters and other settlers came to Fiji, and the booming town reached a population of about 3000 Europeans, with 52 hotels for them to drink in. The cotton boom was brief and its aftermath bitter. A short-lived Ku Klux Klan was formed in Levuka with the (quickly frustrated) aim of installing a white supremacist government.

In 1825 the coastal villagers ended their alliance with the chief of Verata (a village on Viti Levu's Rewa Delta) and gave allegiance to Ratu Seru Cakobau, the powerful chief of Bau (an island off the southeast coast of Viti Levu). Cakobau attempted, unsuccessfully, to form a national government in 1871. In 1874 Great Britain acted on an earlier offer by Cakobau and Fiji was ceded to the Crown (for more information on this period see p200). Fiji thus became a British colony and Levuka was proclaimed its capital. The government was officially moved to Suva in 1882, and by the end of the 19th century trade was also shifting to Suva. With copra markets plummeting in the 1930s, Levuka declined further.

While the northern end of town was swept away in the hurricanes of 1888 and 1905, many of the boom-time buildings remain.

modern cottages in the grounds, which are more comfortable but don't quite match the charm of the main building. The biggest surprise is the small but lovely pool right next to a gym full of rusting workout equipment.

Levuka Holiday Cottage   SELF-CATERING $
(☎344 0166; cottage@owlfiji.com; d $80) About a 15-minute walk north of town ($3 by taxi), this is the only self-catering option close to town. There's a well-equipped kitchen and hot water, and it's right in the middle of a pretty, tropical garden under Gun Rock cliff.

New Mavida Lodge   HOTEL $
(☎344 0477; Beach St; incl breakfast dm $25, d $80-125) The New Mavida is an imposing (by Levuka standards) cream building sitting behind a white picket fence. Pass through the plain lobby to find comfortable rooms with hot-water bathrooms, TV and balconies, and a six-bed dorm.

Ovalau Holiday Resort   RESORT $
(Map p140; ☎344 0329; ohrfiji@connect.com.fj; camping per person $10, dm/s/d $12/15/28, self-contained bungalow s/d $45/77, extra person $25; ☒)

Three kilometres north of town, this resort consists of a cluster of ageing *bure* on a gentle slope across from the beach. There is a swimming pool here and the larger *bure* have kitchens.

Mary's Holiday Lodge   HOSTEL $
(☎344 0013; Beach St; dm/s/d with shared bathroom incl breakfast $20/30/50) Mary's rooms are pretty basic and tired, as are the shared, cold-water bathrooms. It's friendly enough though and very central.

✗ Eating

Whale's Tale   WESTERN $
(☎344 0235; Beach St; breakfast $6, sandwiches $8, mains $12; ⊘breakfast, lunch & dinner Mon-Sat) Ask a local to recommend a place to eat and they'll probably send you here. This is a perennial favourite serving 'the best fish and chips in Fiji' as one local resident told us. There are excellent burgers and sandwiches, an astoundingly good-value set-dinner menu ($17) and pretty good carafes of wine ($14). It's a cute little place with big windows for watching the world go by and a little bam-

boo thatched kitchen area at the back. Don't expect to get your food in a hurry though.

Kim's Paak Kum Loong
CHINESE $

(☎344 0059; Beach St; mains $8; ⊙lunch & dinner) This is the best place to get Chinese food in Levuka. There are two menus here – one has standard Chinese dishes, the other a mixture of Fijian-style fish and meat dishes and a selection of Thai curries. This place is usually busy and there's a good street-side balcony for voyeurs. Sunday night is buffet night.

Koro Makawa Restaurant
PIZZA $

(☎344 0429; Beach St; pizzas from $9; ⊙breakfast, lunch & dinner) You can get curries, fish and chips, and other European meals here, but locals recommend it because of the pizza, which is, apparently, very hit and miss – 'either one of the best pizzas you've ever tasted or a total disaster' was one comment. If you're willing to take the risk, go for one of the many fishy toppings – the tuna is the most fitting since the cannery's right on the doorstep.

🍷 Drinking & Entertainment

There are a number of pool halls where locals like to pot balls to pop music.

Ovalau Club
BAR $

(Nasau Park; ⊙4-9.30pm Mon-Thu, 2pm-midnight Fri, 10am-midnight Sat, 10am-9.30pm Sun) This is the main place in town to go for a drink. Fiji's first gentlemen's club, it's extremely atmospheric and the white timber colonial-style building is a sight in its own right. It's no longer a colonial club in any respect, but local residents (mostly expats) get together for a drink at 6pm every Tuesday and tourists are always welcome to join them. There's a snooker table, and at the weekend things can get pretty lively and local bands often play.

❶ Information

There are Westpac and BSP Bank ATMs right next to each other on Beach St.

Levuka Hospital (☎344 0221; Beach St; ⊙outpatient treatment 8am-1pm & 2-4pm Mon-Fri, to noon Sat, emergencies only after hours) A good, new hospital at the northern end of town.

Ovalau Tourist Information Centre (☎330 0356; Levuka Community Centre, Morris Hedstrom Bldg; ⊙8am-1pm & 2-4.30pm Mon-Fri, to 1pm Sat) Has an information board detailing Ovalau's accommodation and food options and also organises Levuka town tours.

Police station (☎344 0222; Totoga Lane)
Post office (Beach St) Near Queen's Wharf at the southern end of town; there's a cardphone outside.

Lovoni

Lovoni village is surrounded by thick, green rainforest in the centre of a flat-bottomed valley that is actually an extinct volcano crater. It is the island's beating heart and the centre of indigenous culture. There's no accommodation for travellers here, but guided tours are available from Levuka (see p139). Wear sturdy shoes and be prepared to face down some serious mud if it rains (which it does often, and suddenly). Your guide should provide a *sevusevu* for the chief (if the chief's around) and point out the **chiefs' burial site** opposite the church and the **Korolevu hill fortification** high on the crater rim, where villagers took refuge in times of war.

The Lovoni villagers are extremely proud of their heritage and our guide described them as the strongest and bravest people in all of Fiji. The fact that Chief Cakobau was only able to defeat them with trickery is held up as proof of this. On 7 July each year the enslavement of the Lovoni people is remembered. People of all religions gather in one church and the history is read out.

There is a Levuka–Lovoni truck that leaves Levuka at 7am and 11am Monday to Saturday and returns at about 3pm.

Rukuruku

Rukuruku village is a 17km drive north of Levuka, up a rough road with fantastic ocean vistas along the way. It's best to arrange a day out there with Bobo (of Bobo's Farm) to avoid trespassing on village property. Schoolchildren might sing you a song and

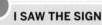

❶ I SAW THE SIGN

There is little signage and roads can be in very bad shape around the remote villages of Ovalau. If you decide to bike the island or independently travel by carrier truck, call Bobo's Farm or Silana Ecolodge in advance if you plan to stop or eat there or you may end up getting lost, going hungry or both. Carry snacks and water.

old people will share a bowl of kava. Tours are free to houseguests at Bobo's Farm.

Bobo's Farm (☑362 3873; www.bobosfarm. com; s/d $53/74) is a clean, tranquil, solar-powered, two-room timber cottage 15 minutes from Rukuruku and surrounded by thick rainforest on a massive farm. There's a shared living room and tiny kitchen, so you can self-cater if you wish, but the organic, homemade meals here are excellent (breakfast $8, lunch $10, dinner $14). You can also sit on the large main deck of Bobo and Karin's house, which often sets the stage for some kava drinking sessions with people from the local village.

You can walk to a black-sand beach (about 15 minutes), the local waterfall or natural waterslides and there's a freshwater stream for bathing or prawn catching. Bobo will gladly escort you to all of these and the village. He can also arrange island-hopping, snorkelling, fishing trips and a hike that can meet up with Epi's Midland Tour (p141). Book ahead through Ovalau Watersports in Levuka, which can also help organise transportation to the farm.

Arovudi & Silana

These small, delightful twin villages have their own little patch of pebbly beach. Poles were just going up to supply the area with electricity when we passed. The Method-ist village church (1918) is made of coral

cooked in a *lovo*. A *tabua* (whale's tooth) hangs by the side of the altar; it was presented to the village by the first missionaries to come here. There is one place to stay, run by the enterprising Seru, who also organises regular tours from Levuka.

OTHER LOMAIVITI ISLANDS

Lomaiviti's smaller islands are simply breathtaking. If you've been craving empty white-sand beaches and world-class snorkelling, look no further.

Naigani

Naigani (Mystery Island) is a mountainous island about 10km offshore from Ovalau. The island has white-sand beaches, lagoons, a fringing coral reef, the remains of a pre-colonial hillside fortification and 'cannibal caves'.

A former copra plantation and a friendly, unpretentious, family resort, Naigani Island Resort (☑603 0613, 995 7301; www.naiganiresort. com; studios/villas $170/200; ☏☒✈) is popular with antipodean time-sharers. The villas have clean, white, airy interiors and are strung out along palm-lined paths in an arrangement that's reminiscent of a retirement village. There's a pretty beach, and good

---

WARRIORS IN CHAINS: FIJI'S ONLY SLAVES

The saddest exhibit in the Fiji Museum at Levuka is the photograph of a 'dwarf' priest and two Lovoni warriors who were sold by Tui Cakobau to the Barnum & Bailey circus in the USA. In 1870 and 1871 Cakobau fought battle after battle with the ferocious Lovoni highlanders, who regularly sacked the settlement of Levuka and did not accept Cakobau's claim to be king of all Fiji. After repeated failed attempts to penetrate their hill, Cakobau sent a Methodist missionary to subdue the people. The Lovoni put their trust in a 'dwarf' (actually just a short bloke) priest who had the ability to foresee the future. The priest was the first to notice the approaching missionary and, seeing a brightness emanating from him, believed he came in peace. The missionary read from the Bible in Bauan, referring to the Lovoni villagers as the lost sheep of Fiji. He then invited them to a reconciliation feast with Cakobau.

On 29 June 1871 the Lovoni people came down from the safety of their village to Levuka and, in good faith, put aside their weapons. However, as they started their meal, Cakobau's warriors caught them off guard, quickly surrounding and capturing them.

Cakobau humiliated his captives horribly, then sold them as slaves for £3 a head. His takings helped him form his government. Families were separated as the villagers were dispersed as far as Kavala (in the Kadavu Group), Yavusania (near Nadi on Viti Levu), Lovoni-Ono (in the Lau Group) and Wailevu (on Vanua Levu). The Lovoni were the only Fijians ever to suffer this fate. When the British administration took over Fiji it freed the Lovoni slaves, and the blackbirding of other Pacific Islanders (see p199) began instead.

SILANA ECOLODGE

Off in a pretty beachside corner about a minute's walk from Silana Village, there are a few choices at this tranquil **homestay** (Map p140; ☑344 0166; silana@owlfiji.com; sites/ dm/bure from $15/25/55), all set in a big, lush family compound. There's one light-filled, two-room *bure* that sleeps four, with a rudimentary shared bathroom, and is located right in the centre of the bustle; another *bure* is bigger and more private with its own hot-water bathroom. The dorm has six beds in a dark house with a basic bathroom. Owner and father of five Seru will take you out on any number of activities from island-hopping to hiking during the day and meals ($25 for three meals plus snacks) are taken with the family – everyone in this family is a real character so expect plenty of laughs in between bites of *dalo*. At night, villagers come by to sing and play guitar around the kava bowl. It's a wonderful way to experience Fijian village life. The carrier from Levuka takes about 40 minutes and costs $3.

snorkelling about 50m out from the shore. The best snorkelling, though, is the next bay over at Picnic Beach. You can walk over at low tide (take a sturdy pair of shoes), take a kayak or get the resort boat to drop you off and pick you up a couple of hours later.

The food here is OK (mostly bland, European-style food) and there's a *lovo* every Saturday night. There's a small pool with a kids' slide, a baby pool and several inflatables. There's also a kids club in the holidays. Babysitting costs $10 an hour and wi-fi costs $15 an hour.

Return boat transfers to/from Suva, via Natovi Landing, or to/from Taviya village, near Rukuruku on Ovalau, are $100/50 per adult/child. Transfer to Ovalau takes around 30 minutes, or more if the weather is poor.

Yanuca Lailai

Yanuca Lailai (Lost Island) is the nearest to Ovalau of the small islands. Much of the shoreline is rocky but there is a patch of golden sand, good snorkelling from the shore, and a small mountain at the island's centre, which you can clamber up for fantastic views out to sea and of Ovalau.

Lost Island Resort (Map p140; sites/dm/ bure per person incl meals $30/30/60) has two rudimentary thatched *bure* with dirt floors next to owner Naca's simple wood house on a tiny, isolated strip of perfect white sand – the dorm is in the owner's house. Naca can take you trolling for $25 per hour, line fishing for $10 or snorkelling out on the reef. Book through Ovalau Watersports in Levuka. Transfers from the airstrip or Levuka are $35 one way. Transfers from Waidalice on Viti Levu (southeast of Korovou) cost $75.

Moturiki

The lush, hilly island of Moturiki is just southwest of Ovalau and home to 10 villages. Although it has no accommodation for travellers, both Leleuvia and Caqalai resorts will take guests to the village of **Niubasaga** for a typical Sunday church service, with beautiful singing and plenty of welcoming smiles. Be prepared: one of your party will have to get up and introduce the group to the congregation.

Caqalai

Teeny little Caqalai island (pronounced 'Thangalai') lies just south of Moturiki. It only takes 15 minutes to walk around the island perimeter's beautiful **golden-sand beaches**, which are fringed with palms, electric-blue water and spectacular reefs.

TOP CHOICE **Caqalai Island Resort** (☑343 0366; www.fijianholiday.com; sites/dm/bure per person incl meals $50/65/75) is a Shangri-La of peace, love and white sand. This gem of a backpackers is run by Moturiki's Methodist Church, but don't let that scare you – you'll find more kava here than kumbaya, although you'll have to bring your own alcohol if you prefer that to the muddy stuff. Accommodation is in big, basic thatched or wooden *bure,* scattered between the palm trees and hibiscus. Cold-water showers are in a shared block and toilets are in brightly painted stalls that are strategically placed near all the *bure*. Locals come over from Moturiki or Leleuvia in the evenings and there's usually some singing and dancing followed by the odd kava drinking session – it's very real and very local with no hype, just good

WHAT LIES BENEATH

Don't tempt the spirits of Gavo Passage. If you head out to the islands south of Ovalau, your boat will likely travel through a break in the reef. Many indigenous Fijians believe that beneath the waters of Gavo Passage lies a sunken village inhabited by ancestral spirits. Stories of fishermen hooking newly woven mats are whispered around Levuka. When passing over the *tabu* (sacred) site, Fijians remove their hats and sunglasses and talk in hushed tones. They believe the spirits will avenge any act of disrespect. Stay on the safe side, take off your baseball cap and give your sunnies a rest. Even if there are no spirits to annoy, irreverent behaviour might put the wind up your boatman.

fun. Snorkelling right off the beach is fantastic, but for some of the best snorkelling in Fiji walk out about 10 minutes to **Snake Island** (named after the many black-and-white-banded sea snakes here) at low tide and swim around the reef. Take some reef shoes though (and something to secure them while you're swimming), as the walkway can be hard on the feet. Underwater is a veritable wonderland of soft and hard corals and a mind-boggling array of fish including massive Napoleon wrasses. Watch for currents, though, and make sure you get in and out at the designated spot (marked with a buoy) so you don't damage the environment. There's a dive centre with a hodgepodge of ageing equipment and a local divemaster can be found on demand. Also on offer are village trips to Moturiki ($10), boat trips to tiny Honeymoon Island ($15) and day trips to Leleuvia ($10).

If you're coming from Levuka, you can book transport and accommodation from Ovalau Watersports or call for a pick-up. One-way transfers cost $30 per person. Transfers from Caqalai to Bureta airstrip on Ovalau cost $50 for one person, or $25 per person for two or more. From Suva, catch a bus heading down the Kings Road from the main bus terminal and get off at Waidalice Landing, which is next to Waidalice Bridge. You need to call ahead for a boat from Caqalai to pick you up here ($30 per person).

Leleuvia

Just south of Caqalai sits beautiful Leleuvia, another stunning palm-fringed coral island (slightly larger than Caqalai) wrapped in white powdery beaches with outstanding views out to sea.

TOP CHOICE **Leleuvia Island Resort**(Map p140; ☑973 0339; dovi@leleuvia.com; dm incl meals $50, bure $110; ☑) is less backpack-ery than nearby Caqalai: it's a better choice for couples looking for more comfort and a fantastic choice for families thanks to the sandy bottom and shallow swimming at the island's point. Thatched *bure* here are basic but classy with views of the sea and trade winds pouring through for natural ventilation. Wooden *bure* are actually duplexes so aren't the best for privacy, although they are simple, clean and comfortable; there are also a few family units with extra space and the small dorms have spotless, solid bunks. A large, open, sand-floored bar and restaurant area serves cold beer and tasty meals (three meals per day $32 per person; the Saturday *lovo* is a favourite) and at the resort's 'entrance' is a gorgeous wide stretch of beach with sun loungers and kayaks. The grand, shared thatched bathroom area oddly is the most striking architectural feature of the resort. The staff put on all kinds of entertainment (such as kava drinking and beach bonfires). While the snorkelling is not on a par with Caqalai, it is still excellent and you can hire equipment. Village trips, diving and fishing excursions are also possible.

Boat transfers to/from Waidalice or Bau Landing are $25 each way (call in advance for a pick-up; Waidalice is about a 1½-hour bus ride from Suva). Transfers to/from Levuka (one hour) also cost $30 each way. Call in advance for a pick-up or you can book via Ovalau Watersports.

Wakaya

About 20km east of Ovalau, Wakaya is a privately owned island visible from Levuka. It has forests, cliffs, beautiful white-sand beaches, and archaeological sites, including a **stone fish trap**. In some areas you'll find feral horses, pigs and deer roaming freely; in others there are millionaires' houses.

Wakaya Club (☑344 8128; www.wakaya.com; all-inclusive bure US$1900-7600; ❋☎) is one of Fiji's most beautiful and exclusive resorts.

If you've got several thousand dollars to spare, you can enjoy this utterly sublime isle with the likes of Bill Gates, Pierce Brosnan and Crown Prince Felipe of Spain. You'll be flown there via Cesna aircraft, served chilled Tattinger champagne on arrival and pampered to the absolute maximum.

Koro

Many villages are nestled in the lush tropical forests of Koro, northwest of Ovalau. Roads over the mountainous interior provide plenty of thrills and wonderful views. A portion of the island is freehold, so plenty of foreigners have bought up land to build their second homes.

At Dere Bay a wharf allows you to walk out to good swimming and snorkelling; inland is a waterfall and natural pool. The co-run resorts listed here are surrounded by residential developments and have been aimed at people visiting or building real estate on the island, although they are gearing up to be more tourist friendly.

Dere Bay Resort (☎331 1075; korobeach@connect.com.fj; d bure per person incl meals $200; ✆) has well-designed, intimate *bure* with soaring ceilings, 360-degree outlooks and spacious verandahs right on the beach. There's also a fantastic deck, a pier and a bar next door. Children under 12 pay half price. A few home rentals are also available from the website from $1500 a week.

Koro Beach Resort (☎331 1075; www.korobeach.com; d bure per person incl meals $180; ✆) has simple thatched, solar-powered *bure* with terraces and attached bathrooms lining a white sandy beach. For children under 12 the cost is $50 per person and meals are taken at the on-site restaurant.

Northern Air (www.northernair.com.fj) flies Koro–Suva on Sundays (one way $125), and **Pacific Island** (☎672 5644; www.pacificislandair.com) seaplanes will fly you in from Nadi. Ferries run by **Consort Shipping** (☎330 2877) and **Goundar Shipping** (☎330 1035) leave Suva twice weekly, stopping at Koro on their way to Savusavu and Taveuni. Enquire about transport when you book your accommodation. Pick-up from the ferry/airport is $20/30.

Vanua Levu & Taveuni

Includes »

Best Places to Stay

» Moody's Namena (p162)

» Maqai Resort (p179)

» Dolphin Bay Divers Retreat (p173)

» Taveuni Palms (p174)

» Naveria Heights Lodge (p156)

Best Dive Sites

» Namena Marine Park (p155)

» Great White Wall (p167)

» Nasonisoni Passage (p155)

» Rainbow Reef (p167)

» Dreamhouse (p155)

Why Go?

Vanua Levu (Big Island) and Taveuni look like a surrealist rendition of a mountainous, waterfall-lush rainforest lined with cerulean coasts. Vanua Levu's main settlement La-basa is a dusty patchwork of sugar cane and copra planta-tions but other than that, nature reigns. Most visitors stay around colonial-feeling Savusavu, where sailboats float in the shelter of slightly offshore islands, or in one of Taveuni's botanical-garden-like villages. Everyone, from the locals to the numerous expats, smile and act as if they've just awoken from a long sunny nap – and they probably have.

All around the islands you'll find traditional villages and calm, relaxing resorts. The Rainbow Reef and Namena Ma-rine Reserve have some of the best dive sites in the South Pacific and non-water babies can head into the rugged interior for hiking, rafting, plunging into waterfalls and birdwatching.

When To Go
Savusavu

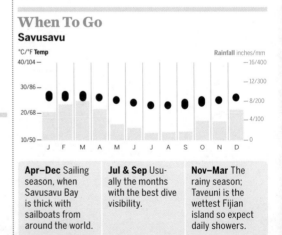

Apr–Dec Sailing season, when Savusavu Bay is thick with sailboats from around the world.

Jul & Sep Usu-ally the months with the best dive visibility.

Nov–Mar The rainy season; Taveuni is the wettest Fijian island so expect daily showers.

VANUA LEVU

POP 130,000

The few who make it to Fiji's second-biggest island smile smugly – they know they're onto one of the tropic's best-kept secrets. It's another world over here from the bustle of Viti Levu. Many roads on the east and west sides are rutted dirt and Labasa, the island's largest 'city', is a one-road strip of shops. Still, the island's few settlements are hard-working places filled with folks farming sugar cane and copra. Outside the small pockets of relative hustle are remote villages, mountain passes streaming with waterfalls, endless swaths of forest and an ever-changing coastline forgotten by the world. Take it slow, keep a smile on your face and enjoy exploring rural Fiji on its grandest scale.

ℹ️ Getting There & Away

AIR

Flying is the best way to get to Vanua Levu and Pacific Sun has regular flights from Labasa to Nadi ($225) and Suva ($240), and perhaps in the future, Taveuni (check the website). In Savusavu the office of **Pacific Sun** (☑885 2214) is in the Copra Shed and in Labasa, **Pacific Sun** (☑881 1454; Northern Travel Service office, Nasekula Rd) is off the main drag.

The Labasa airport is about 11km southwest of Labasa. There's a bus that passes the airport about every hour, but it doesn't link up with flights and you'll have to go out to the main road to flag it down. A taxi from Labasa costs $16.

Savusavu airstrip is 3km south of town, but only charter airlines were using it at the time of writing. Labasa is the main airport for Vanua Levu.

BOAT

TO TAVEUNI A bus leaves Savusavu every morning at 7am, arriving at the pier at Natuva at around 11am where a small boat leaves for Lovinivonu,

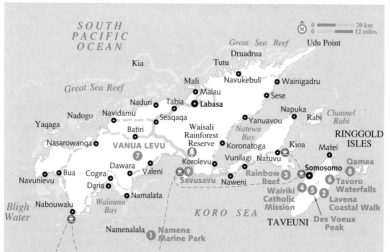

Vanua Levu & Taveuni Highlights

① Making bubbles around the pristine **Namena Marine Park** (p155)

② Exploring the lush beauty of the **Lavena Coastal Walk** (p178)

③ Diving the soft-coral wonderland of the **Rainbow Reef** (p167)

④ Feeling the Lord's power via booming song at **Wairiki Catholic Mission** (p171)

⑤ Finding the rare, delicate red-and-white *tagimaucia* flower high on the slopes of **Des Voeux Peak** (p172)

⑥ Swimming in all three glorious pools of the **Tavoro Waterfalls** (p177)

⑦ Bumping aimlessly along the rutted dirt tracks of **Vanua Levu** (p152)

⑧ Lounging on white sands, snorkelling and surfing at **Qamea** (p178)

⑨ Having a waterside sunset cocktail with yachties in **Savusavu** p160)

Vanua Levu

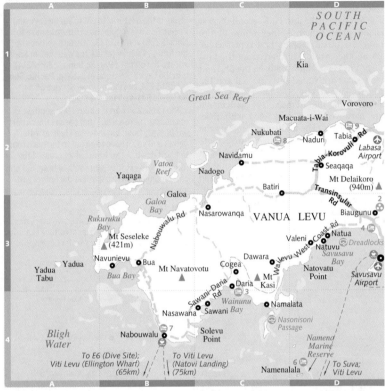

Vanua Levu

◎ Sights
1 Naag Mandir Temple..........................E2
2 Nukubolu...D3

🛏 Sleeping
3 Blue Parrot Bures...............................C4
4 Emaho Sekawa Luxury Retreat.........D3
5 La Dolce Vita Holiday Villas E3
6 Moody's Namena.................................D4
7 Nabouwalu Government
Guesthouse.......................................B4
8 Nukubati Island Resort C2
9 Palmlea Lodge D2
10 Rabi Island Council
Guesthouse.......................................G2
11 Salt Lake Lodge E3

Taveuni, arriving at around 1pm. In the reverse direction, boats leave Lovinivonu at 9am and connect to the bus at Natuva at 11am. On Tuesday, Thursday, Friday and Sunday this service ($20) is run by Grace Shipping – buy tickets at Mum's Country Kitchen. On other days you'll have to hop on the bus without a reservation, but the boat (the *Sunny*) is cheaper and slightly faster – on these days the bus costs $5 and the boat is $10.

The *Lomaiviti Princess* run by Goundar Shipping also crosses between Taveuni and Savusavu a few days a week as part of its Suva route.

TO SUVA Bligh Water Shipping (🖉885 3192), **Consort Shipping** (🖉885 0279) and **Goundar Shipping** (🖉883 3085) offer boat services to and from Vanua Levu via Koro, Taveuni and/or Ovalau. The best by far is the *Lomaiviti Princess* operated by Goundar; the office is located in Kong's shop on Main St.

CHARTERS & CRUISES

For those looking to charter their own boat, **SeaHawk Yacht Charters** (🖉885 0787; www.seahawkfiji.com) rents out a beautiful 16m yacht

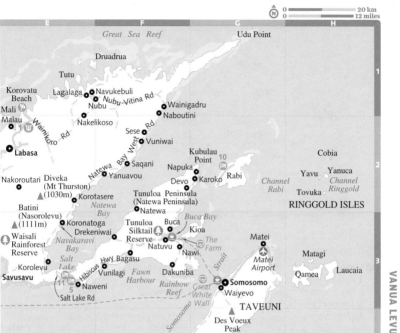

with captain and a cook/crew from US$150 per person per day. You can go practically anywhere in Fiji and the crew can help you arrange activities such as diving.

Getting Around

Vanua Levu's remote, tropical roads are crying out to be explored by 4WD. Hire cars are available in Labasa and Savusavu. Given the bumpy terrain, though, the available vehicles won't always be in top condition. There are unsealed roads around most of the island's perimeter. The road from Labasa to Savusavu is sealed but showing plenty of wear and you'll have to do a fair amount of pothole dodging. The first 20km of the Hibiscus Hwy from Savusavu along the scenic coast is similarly paved. Unfortunately, the rest of the highway is much rougher. Avoid driving at night as there are lots of wandering animals and there is often fog in the mountains. Petrol stations are scarce and usually closed on Sundays, so plan to fill up in Labasa, Savusavu or Seaqaqa. It's also a good idea to take some food with you on the road.

Just remember, you cannot wander on foot through the countryside without permission from the landowners.

It's also possible to navigate the island by bus but timetables can be erratic and it takes far longer.

Savusavu & Around

If you have ever dreamed of a sweetly scented South Pacific port nestled against a sweeping bay, backed by sloping green hills and filled with hibiscus flowers, chances are your image looks a lot like Savusavu (population 4970). It's a timeless little town where everyone smiles and says 'bula', and there are several good restaurants, bars and well-stocked stores. The stunning looks and ease of living continue to seduce folks to stay longer than planned and many foreigners have snapped up land in the hills and surrounding coast. As such, there's an uncommonly large but very laidback ex-pat community.

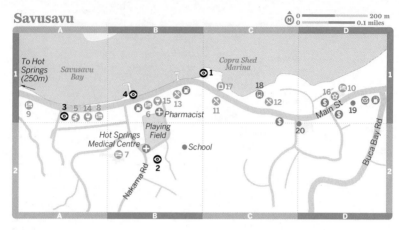

Savusavu

Savusavu is also the sole port of entry on Vanua Levu for yachts, and one of the most popular places in Fiji for visiting yachties to put down anchor. There are two excellent marinas here and Savusavu Bay fills up with vessels during the high season. A new marina complex (see www.marinavillagefiji.

com) is planned on the waterfront east of town. If it's ever completed, it will include an international marina, luxury villas and apartments, bars and cafes.

East of Savusavu the Hibiscus Hwy stretches for 70 miles up the coast. It's a lazy drive through avenues of palm trees, past blue bays and old plantations.

◎ Sights & Activities

Hot Springs   HOT SPRINGS

Those vents of steam you see along the water's edge are evidence of Savusavu's volcanic activity that simmers below the town's surface. There are hot springs behind the playing field and near the wharf. The shallow streams are literally boiling and locals come to cook food in them. You'll scald yourself if you touch them.

Diving & Snorkelling

Far and away the best diving around Vanua Levu, perhaps in all of Fiji, is about a two-hour boat ride from Savusavu at Namena Marine Park, (park fee is an additional $30 per person, valid for one year) a protected reserve of corals so vibrant and marine life so plentiful that it's become the poster child for Fiji's underwater world.

The best sites closer in are just outside Savusavu Bay (about a 20-minute boat ride) and include Dreamhouse, where you'll search for hammerheads in the blue before seeing great schools of barracuda, jacks and tuna at a coral outcrop; Dungeons and Dragons, which is a towering maze of dive-throughs; and Nasonisoni Passage, an incredible drift dive where you'll be sucked along by a strong current. The interior of Savusavu Bay itself has unfortunately been plagued by crown of thorns recently and the corals of the once-famous sites will take several years to grow back – the only two bay sites that were worth diving on at the time of writing were Mystery Reef and Alice in Wonderland.

KoroSun Dive   DIVING

(☎885 2452, 934 1033; www.korosundive.com; Hibiscus Hwy) Ideally located near the best dives outside of Savusavu Bay (at Koro Sun Resort), Colin and Janine run an attentive and professional centre that caters just as well to beginners as it does to advanced divers. Two-tank dives/PADI Open Water Courses, including all gear, cost $190/750. There are special rates for multiday diving and they also offer day trips to the Somosomo Strait or the Namena Marine Park. They'll pick you up and drop you off free of charge from anywhere around Savusavu.

Aboard A Dream   DIVING

(☎828 3030; www.aboardadream.com; charters from AU$400 per person) A live-aboard is the best way to dive the Namena Marine Reserve and fortunately this highly recommended outfit can take you there, as well as to other little-known sites, on three- to seven-day charters. The 15m ship takes a maximum of six passengers and your charming hosts have spent nearly a decade diving Fijian waters. It also offers nondive charters to Kiao Island.

L'Aventure Diving   DIVING

(☎885 0188; laventurefiji@connect.com.fj) This is a top-notch centre but since it doesn't provide pick-up, there's no point paying for the extra transport unless you're staying at the Jean-Michel Cousteau Fiji Islands Resort or want to dive Nasonisoni Passage (this is the only centre that often goes there). Two-tank dives/

BÊCHE-DE-MER

European traders flocked to Fiji in the early 19th century to hunt the lucrative bêche-de-mer (sea cucumber). It fetched huge profits in Asia, where it's still considered a delicacy and aphrodisiac. Savusavu was a major trading post.

You are likely to see some of these phallic, sluglike creatures while snorkelling or diving. They feed on organic matter in the sand and serve an important role as cleaners in the lagoon ecosystem. There are various types: some are smooth and sticky, some prickly, some black and some multicoloured. After being cut open and cleaned, they are boiled to remove the salt, then sun-dried or smoked. Many find the taste revolting but they are highly nutritious, being 50% to 60% protein.

Bêche-de-mer numbers have been depleted in Asian waters but they are still prevalent in the South Pacific. They make for a lucrative commodity, both for local use and for export, and traders are delivering dive equipment to remote areas and promising high rewards. Villagers of the Bua region are renowned for harvesting the creature. Usually untrained and unaware of the risks, they are encouraged by the traders to dive in deep waters, risking their lives by using old and/or not well-maintained scuba equipment. Many end up with the bends and a stint in the Fiji Recompression Chamber; several have died.

PADI Open Water Courses cost $280/860 with gear included.

Dive Namale
DIVING

(☎885 0435; www.namalefiji.com; Namale Resort & Spa, Hibiscus Hwy) Again only worth it if you're staying at the Namale Resort. Two-tank dives/PADI Open Water Courses, including all gear, are $220/850.

Rock n' Downunder Divers
DIVING

(☎885 3447, 932 8363; Waitui Marina) Not a bad choice if you're on a budget, but its equipment isn't tops and dives are usually to close-by sites inside Savusavu Bay. Two-tank dives/PADI Open Water Courses, including all gear, are $190/600.

J Hunter Pearls
SNORKELLING

(☎885 0821; www.pearlsfiji.com) Learn all about how black pearls are farmed before being boated out to the farm (now a floating structure since the grafting house was destroyed in a cyclone). If you want to snorkel the oyster lines, bring your own gear and jump in; otherwise you can check everything out from the glass-bottom of the boat. Tours depart at 9am weekdays ($25, 1½ hours). Afterwards you can head to the shop to buy pearls and shell jewellery.

Other Activities

Rock n' Downunder Divers — RENTALS
Kayaks for rent are $40 per day. You can also rent mountain bikes ($35 per day) and catamarans, and it can arrange a number of activities including village visits ($60 per person), beach cruises ($70), sunset cruises ($40) and boat charters ($60 per hour).

Naveria Heights Lodge
ADVENTURE TOUR

All sorts of adventures are available to guests as well as nonguests; see p156 for details.

SeaHawk Yacht Charters
CRUISES

(☎885 0787; www.seahawkfiji.com) Offers cruises around Savusavu Bay, including full-day picnic cruises ($85), half-day sail-and-snorkel trips ($55), sunset cruises ($50) and overnight cruises ($720 per couple).

Trip n Tour
ISLAND TOURS

(☎885 3154; tripntour@connect.com.fj; Copra Shed Marina) A range of tours around Vanua Levu are available including one to a copra plantation, full-day Labasa tours and fishing trips.

Marinas

Use VHF Marine channel 16 for assistance in locating moorings on arrival. The marinas can arrange for the relevant officials to visit your boat to process your arrival into Fiji.

Copra Shed Marina
MARINA

(☎885 0457; coprashed@connect.com.fj) Starting life as a copra mill back in the late 1800s, this marina is now a sort of service centre for yachties and visitors. You can arrange anything from car hire to day trips here – and when you're done, you can munch on a burger or enjoy a beer while looking out over the bay. If you've fallen in love with the place, you can even browse for properties at the estate agent. There are hot showers available for yachties ($4) and there's also a laundry service ($10 a load). Moorings in the pretty harbour between Savusavu and Nawi islet cost $10/260 per day/month in high season, and $8/210 in low season.

Waitui Marina
MARINA

(☎885 0536; waituimarina@connect.com.fj) The rougher-looking marina option a short walk from Copra Shed is the only outfit with helix moorings (very well maintained). It also offers showers ($3), laundry ($8 a load) and a club in a beautiful, restored boat shed. Moorings cost $10/225 per day/month in high season.

Savusavu Marina
MARINA

(☎885 3543; info@marinavillagefiji.com) This has been in the planning stages for a few years now but if it ever does get built, it will have space for 79 yachts, a clubhouse, laundry facilities, showers and lock-up facilities, just outside town, to the east.

🛏 Sleeping

Savusavu caters to long-term (often returning) visitors, so many of the sleeping options along the scenic south coast are self-catering single-home holiday rentals; some are luxurious while others are budget affairs. Resorts are out of town, either on Lesiaceva Point to the southwest, Savusavu Rd to the northwest or along the Hibiscus Hwy to the east; you can soak up South Sea sailor charm by staying in town. Buses service all locations regularly (see p161).

IN TOWN

TOP CHOICE **Naveria Heights Lodge** — B&B $$
(☎885 0348; www.naveriaheightsfiji.com; r incl breakfast $210; 🖳) This B&B is owned by some of the most fun people in the area: Sharon and Scott can lead yoga classes or take you

river tubing, mountain biking, hiking...the list goes on. If you just want to chill, they're good at that too and keep the fridge stocked with cold beer. No matter what you end up doing, you'll be awestruck by the view (overlooking the bay) straight from the B&B's two elegant, polished-wood rooms. Meals are prepared to order; Sharon is a nutritionist and can tailor a menu for you. The steep, 15-minute nature trail up the hill to reach the lodge is gorgeous, but you can also call for a pick-up.

Hidden Paradise Guest House   GUESTHOUSE $
(☑885 0106; s/d $30/60, with air-con $40/70; ❄) This is the best place to meet other budget travellers. It's a no-frills deal, with a shared bathroom and cold-water showers, but the rooms are spotless and the smiling owner Elenoa is often found playing a lively game of cards with her friends in the courtyard. A cooked breakfast is included in the price and you can watch life pass by from the Sea View Café at the front of the guesthouse.

Hot Springs Hotel   HOTEL $
(☑885 0195; www.savusavufiji.com; Nakama Rd; r with fan/air-con incl breakfast $55/125; ❄🛜🏊) The main thing going for this hotel is the view. Every room has a little balcony with fantastic, picture-postcard views over Savusavu Bay. The rooms are clean and spacious, but have a whiff of identikit motel about them (it *did* used to be a Travelodge). Lower-lever rooms are fan-cooled while the upper ones, with slightly better views, have air-con. The hotel also has a bar, a cafe and a pool with a view.

Copra Shed
Marina Apartments   APARTMENT $$
(☑885 0457; coprashed@connect.com.fj; Copra Shed Marina; apt $95-165; ❄🛜) The marina has two luxury units with good views in the most convenient location in town. They are a bit overpriced (especially the smaller unit, which doesn't have an en suite bathroom), but worth it if you plan to spend a lot of time in the Yacht Club.

Waterfront Apartment   APARTMENT $$
(☑885 0307; Waterfront Complex; r $165; 🌀❄) This is a compact waterfront studio apartment, with a TV and DVD player, queen-size bed, decent bathrooms and large windows on two sides. There's plenty of light and great views over the water.

Savusavu Budget Lodge   GUESTHOUSE $
(☑885 3127; r with fan/air-con $40/60; ❄) It's not as cute as Hidden Paradise, but the In-

dian owner here is very friendly and there are more amenities. Rooms are small and brightly painted, with private hot water bathrooms, and there's an upstairs lounge and a balcony overlooking the street and the water. Breakfast is included.

Savusavu Sunset Lodge   GUESTHOUSE $
(☑885 2171; r with fan/air-con $40/60; ❄) Set back from the road in a grassy garden, this place has simple rooms with hot-water bathrooms and not much else. Plump for a sea-facing room upstairs if you can.

LESIACEVA ROAD & SAVUSAVU ROAD

[TOP CHOICE] Fiji Beach Shack   HOLIDAY RENTAL $$$
(☑885 1002; www.fijibeachshacks.com; houses per day/week from $350/2380; 🛜🏊) These are seriously glam: the two-level 'House of Bamboo' has two bedrooms and a fabulous bathroom complete with a sunken bath and sea views from two large windows. There's a great DVD library and a good selection of children's board games (the house isn't suitable for very young children though). The 'Pod House' is an extremely private one-bedroom overlooking the bay. Both have a plunge pool, a deck and a day bed. You can snorkel out to gorgeous Split Rock from the beachfront across the road.

Hans' Place   HOLIDAY RENTAL $
(☑885 0621; www.fiji-holiday.com; Lesiaceva Rd; Yasiyasi studio per week $450, Yaka cottage per week $550) Sitting up on Lesiaceva Point among vibrant green lawns, a skip and a jump away from the ocean, are two excellent-value, cosy, self-contained cottages with comfortable decks. Yasiyasi is a studio built using native hardwoods. Yaka is a one-bedroom cottage, with the bed partitioned off from the living room. Both sleep two people. Each has a kitchenette with a gas stove and a fridge, a TV and a DVD player. They are fan-cooled and have hot showers. Bikes are available for hire at $10 a day.

Jean-Michel Cousteau Fiji
Islands Resort   RESORT $$$
(☑885 0188; www.fijiresort.com; d bure from $1000; @🏊♿) This outstanding, luxury ecoresort was started by the son of Jacques Cousteau. As you'd expect, it attracts divers but it also has one of the best kids clubs we've ever seen – with a children's pool, a trampoline and loving staff who cuddle babies and braid little girls' hair. The *bure* are massive and feature handmade furnishings, large decks and private garden areas. Great

gourmet meals are included in the price. The thin white beach is a bit rocky but OK and there's a pier to dive off into deeper water. All activities, except diving, are included in the rate. A taxi ride from town costs $9.

Emaho Sekawa
Luxury Retreat HOLIDAY RENTAL **$$$**
(☏851 0154, 993 2841; www.emahofiji.com; d incl 3 meals AU$895; ☎☒) If you're looking for your own private slice of rainforest, tawny beach and decadence with your own staff, gourmet chef and dive master, this retreat hits the dream mark. Accommodation is Balinese Crusoe-chic with heart-stopping sunset views and you get a golf cart to tool around the 2-hectare grounds. It's a five-minute walk to a 2km-long private beach where kayaks await. A three-night minimum stay applies.

Daku Resort
RESORT **$$**
(☏885 0046; www.dakuresort.com; Lesiaceva Rd; bure/villas from $195/320; @☒) A resort-cum-self-improvement centre, Daku attracts guests from around the world to participate in a surprisingly diverse array of courses from gospel singing to watercolour painting, meditation and yoga. If you'd rather sit back and relax than expend your creative juices, Daku still has plenty to offer. There's neat accommodation (in *bure* with sea-green-and-white tin roofs), a sweeping sea view, a pleasant pool and a good restaurant and bar. The beach across the road is pebble rather than sand, but at high tide you can swim out and find top-notch fish viewing. A taxi from town will cost about $4.

Tropic Splendor
Beachfront Cottage HOLIDAY RENTAL **$$$**
(☏851 0152; www.tropic-splendor-fiji.com; Savusavu Rd; cottages per day/week $360/2160;

@☒) This is a good option for a couple seeking something with privacy but still within reach of town. It's a charming, one-bedroom, beachfront cottage with a large deck and small pool overlooking the ocean. There's a full kitchen and lounge with a selection of DVDs and books, and a funky, outdoor, bamboo shower.

Bayside
Backpacker Cottage HOLIDAY RENTAL **$**
(☏885 3154; tripntour@connect.com.fj; Lesiaceva Rd; s/d $40/50) This sweet little cottage is in the grounds of travel agent Eddie Bower's home, sleeps two and has a decent kitchen with a gas stove, and TV and DVD player. There's a beach across the road but it's not fantastic; bring a snorkel, though, as underwater it's a different story. You can borrow mountain bikes to cycle the 3km to town and there's a minimum two-night stay.

HIBISCUS HIGHWAY
Dolphin Bay Divers Retreat and Almost Paradise are southeast of Buca Bay. Accessible only by boat, they are most easily reached from Taveuni; see p173 for details.

Namale Resort
RESORT **$$$**
(☏885 0435; www.namalefiji.com; Hibiscus Hwy; bure US$1170-2200; ☎☒) Namale is a hugely exclusive and pricey resort right by the water, 9km from Savusavu. Accommodation ranges from tropically delicious *bure*, hidden among the rainforest and reached by wooden walkways, to a jaw-droppingly luxurious grand villa complete with a mini movie theatre and private stretch of beach. You won't be able to drop by to sneak a peak though, because they shun the attentions of day trippers or drop-by visitors. The price

---

JEAN-MICHEL COUSTEAU

One of the world's greatest advocates for the preservation of oceans, Jean-Michel Cousteau is often overshadowed by his legendary, late father Jacques-Yves, but he was an indispensable player in his father's endeavours as well as the creator of his own. He has produced over 80 films and received Emmy, Peabody, 7 d'Or and Cable Ace Awards. Via his Ocean Futures Society he continues to produce programs for schoolchildren and TV as well as content for print media ranging from newspaper columns to books.

Despite the likeness in interests between father and son, the Costeaus didn't always get along, particularly after Jean-Michel's mother Simone passed away in 1990 and his father remarried. In 1995 Jean-Michel started the Cousteau Fiji Island Resort, a name that angered his father enough to launch a lawsuit. He dropped charges when the younger Cousteau added 'Jean-Michel' to the name. After this time the two became estranged until shortly before Jacques-Yves' death in 1997.

Jean-Michel still visits his namesake resort regularly.

THE TUI TAI

A trip with **Tui Tai Adventure Cruises** (☑885 3032; www.tuitai.com) combines the comfort, relaxation, fantastic food and luxury of an intimate, upscale resort with an ever-changing South Pacific backdrop. If you're put off the idea of cruising by visions of a cheesy behemoth, never fear: the *Tui Tai*, an elegant, motorised sailboat, is sexy as hell, and the small number of guests keeps the mood friendly and relaxed. You can lounge about in stylish, curved rattan chairs or day beds and spot dolphins from the deck; relax in the on-board spa; and eat delicious meals by lantern light or under the stars on a nearby beach. And then there are the activities – including snorkelling, kayaking, biking, diving, fishing and meeting local villagers. Setting off from Savusavu, a typical itinerary includes Taveuni, Kioa and Rabi islands, and provides the only way of reaching the Ringgold Isles (a beautiful, mostly uninhabited group of islands northeast of Vanua Levu), although your itinerary may vary according to the weather. All accommodation is in cabins with private bathroom and air-con. A five-night cruise costs from US$3851/2567 per person single/double, including all meals and activities except diving. Tui Tai also funds several community projects, has regular 'humanitarian' tours and uses ecofriendly practices.

includes all meals and activities except diving. Dive Namale operates here.

Salt Lake Lodge
LODGE $

(☑828 3005; www.saltlakelodgefiji.com; per week US$1000; ⌘⌘) This remote lodge was temporarily closed at the time of research but it gets fabulous reviews from our readers. The two bungalows are built with local tropical timber and sit on stilts at the edge of a lake with a beach bar, a lounge and an eating area between them and an outdoor kitchen. There's a strong eco ethos: all toilets are compost, rainwater is used for bathing and cooking, and there's solar power.

La Dolce Vita Holiday Villas
RESORT $$$

(☑828 0824; ladolcevitafiji.com; Hibiscus Hwy; d villas $400) Remote La Dolce has gorgeous, round, wooden *bure* with vaulted ceilings, great decking, large, modern bathrooms, lush manicured grounds and fabulous sea views. Rates include all meals. There is a bar and dining room, and even a pizza oven complete with thatched roof. Golfers are kept happy with a six-hole course, and if that doesn't float your boat there's boules, horse riding, jet skiing, bushwalking, snorkelling and trips with a 'dolphin caller' to see (and sometimes swim with) spinner dolphins. A taxi from Savusavu costs about $35. The power is on only from 5.30pm to 11pm.

Koro Sun Resort
RESORT $$$

(☑885 0262; www.korosunresort.com; Hibiscus Hwy; bure $400-1200; ❋⌘⌘⌘) The homey and welcoming Koro Sun has a handful of lavish two-story *bure* over a clear, blue lagoon; some bigger family-style units look out over a shady lily pond and a string of rather dated units sits on the hillside. Food is included in the price, as are numerous activities – there's a pool, tennis courts, a nine-hole golf course, kayaks, bikes and snorkelling gear. If you fancy being slathered with papaya, there's a 'rainforest spa'. The little ones can amuse themselves with sandcastle building, waterslide competitions and trips to nearby Bat Island (less ominous than it sounds) courtesy of an excellent kids club. Diving is available through KoroSun Dive. The resort is 13km east of Savusavu, and costs about $15 by taxi.

Olivia's Homestay
HOMESTAY $

(☑885 3099; silina@connect.com.fj; Nagigi; cabin per person $30) Guests at Olivia's live the village life at Nagigi and get educated in the Fijian way of doing everything from cookery to massage. No activity costs more than a few dollars, and both Olivia and the villagers are extremely welcoming. The no-frills homestay is a single cabin with four simple bedrooms and a cold-water shower. Children are adored. Buses from Savusavu to Nagigi ($2, 40 minutes) leave about every two hours.

SigaSiga Plantation
HOLIDAY RENTAL $$

(☑885 0413; www.theultimateparadise.com; Hibiscus Hwy; d bure $95-125, 2-bedroom villa $250) Situated on 119 acres just back from the best beach in the area (1.6km of white sand), these better-than-basic oceanfront self-catering cottages are 11km from Savusavu. The Thai and American owners make delicious Thai curries or you can order Indian Fijian specialities if you don't feel like cooking. It's a $13 taxi ride from town and the bus passes by as well.

Lomalagi Resort RESORT $$$
(☑851 0585; www.lomalagi.com; Salt Lake Rd; d incl meals US$210-499; ❄) This is the only resort at Natewa Bay, and what a spectacular setting it enjoys. Timber promenades wind their way through avenues of impossibly tall palm trees to a collection of *bure* built on a sunny hillside, all with unbeatable views. The beach is grey coral but the snorkelling is great and there's a 1km white-sand beach about 3km up the coast. A major reason to stay here is the spinner dolphins that frequent the bay, providing one of the best opportunities in Fiji to swim with the creatures. The villas have uninspired decor but are large, with decks.

Yau Kolo CAMPING $
(☑885 3089; yaukolo@yahoo.com; Hibiscus Hwy; sites per person $12, s/d onsite tent $20/30, dm $20) Camp in a veritable botanical garden complete with rushing jungle stream with a natural swimming pool about 13km from Savusavu. There are also a few basic dorm beds as well as cold showers, compost toilets and permanent tents complete with mattresses and bedding. There's a cafe serving cheap, good meals (there are no self-catering facilities). Breakfast is included.

✖ Eating

Surf and Turf INTERNATIONAL $$$
(Copra Shed Marina; mains $25-40; ☺lunch & dinner) This is the poshest restaurant in Savusavu town, with a lovely outside space overlooking the water. There are great wines available by the bottle or the glass, and tasty pasta, steaks, lobster and crayfish dishes and daily specials. Lunch is a lighter affair with burgers and sandwiches on offer. Surf and turf (lobster tail and fillet mignon) is $40 at dinner.

Captain's Table INTERNATIONAL $$
(Copra Shed Marina; pizza from $15, lunch/dinner $8/16; ☺breakfast, lunch & dinner) Dine overlooking the bay (from the Copra Shed Marina) on a creative assortment of international and Indian fare, like chicken stuffed with spinach, steaks and seafood. If you're feeling more casual, try Captain's Café on the street side that serves pizzas, pancakes, quesadillas and sandwiches from $9.

Decked Out Café INTERNATIONAL $$
(meals around $15; ☺lunch & dinner) Across the street from the Copra Shed Marina, this no-frills, semi-outdoor pad has become one of the more popular yachty hangouts. It serves pizzas (from $23), salads ($7), fish and chips

($9) and much more. Happy-hour (5pm to 7pm) beers are $3 and there's live music (6pm to 11pm) Thursday through Saturday. Wi-fi is free with a tab of $10 or more.

Sea View Café INDIAN/CHINESE $
(☑885 0106; Hidden Paradise Guest House; meals $8-10; ☺breakfast daily, lunch & dinner Mon-Sat) In front of Hidden Paradise, this place serves surprisingly excellent curries and Chinese specialities just above the roadside where you can watch village life go by.

Mum's Country Kitchen INDIAN $
(☑927 1372; breakfast $2-3, meals $6; ☺breakfast, lunch & dinner) One step up from a hole-in-the-wall, this place is popular with local Indo-Fijians for its curries – it's always packed.

Savusavu has a few grocery stores, including a well-stocked Morris Hedstrom Supermarket. The market has fruit and veggies as well as lots and lots of *yanqona* root, which is used to make the narcotic drink.

⚱ Drinking

Savusavu Yacht Club BAR
(Copra Shed Marina; ☺10am-10pm Sun-Thu, to midnight Fri & Sat) Tourists are considered temporary members of this friendly little drinking hole. There are tables out by the waterside, plenty of cold beer and some mingling yachties and ex-pats.

Waitui Marina BAR
(☺10am-10pm Mon-Sat) Sit on the balcony upstairs to enjoy classic South Pacific views of the yacht-speckled, palm-lined bay. The bar is well stocked and all foreigners on holiday are considered temporary members. Expect locals playing guitars and heavy drinking as the night wears on.

Planters' Club BAR
(☺10am-10pm Mon-Sat, to 8pm Sun) This was traditionally a place for planters to come and drink when they brought in the copra, and some of their descendants can still be found clustered around the bar today. It's a whiff of colonialism and teeming with expats. Happy hour is from 5.30pm to 6.30pm. Once a month the club holds a Sunday-lunch *lovo*. You're allowed two visits as a nonmember.

Savusavu Wines & Spirits LIQUOR STORE
(☺8am-6pm Mon-Fri, to 1pm Sat) It's amazing what you can find in this little bottle shop: a great wine and international spirits selection as well as imported gourmet coffees,

cheeses, cereals and more. There are a couple of tables outside if you wish to sit down and imbibe – and many do.

White Stork BAR
(☉10am-11pm) The rowdiest place in town, popular with locals, where everyone is blind drunk by around 11pm and fights are common.

⭐ Entertainment

Uros CLUB
(admission $5; ☉8pm-midnight) Meaning 'sexy' in Fijian, the only viable clubbing option in town is where anyone and everyone goes to bump and grind to local and international music. It's a smallish room up a dark flight of stairs and great fun.

🔒 Shopping

Next door to the Copra Shed is a handicrafts stall where a local man sells his wooden carvings. At the back of the market is Town Council Handicrafts, devoted to local, woven and wooden handicrafts.

ℹ️ Information

Being an official point of entry for yachts, there are customs, immigration, health and quarantine services available. ANZ, Colonial National and Westpac banks all have branches in the main street.

Customs (☑885 0727; ☉8am-1pm & 2-5pm Mon-Fri) Located west of the marinas on the main street.

Hospital (☑885 0444) The hospital is 1.5km east of town on the road to Labasa. Call the hospital if an ambulance is required.

Hot Springs Medical Centre (☑885 0721) Brand new and the best place to go.

Police (☑885 0222) The police station is 600m past the Buca Bay Rd turn-off.

Post office At the eastern end of town near Buca Bay Rd.

ℹ️ Getting There & Around

Bus

The Savusavu bus station is in the centre of town, near the market. Buses travelling the scenic, sealed (yet bumpy) highway from Savusavu over the mountains to Labasa ($8, three hours, four times daily) depart from 7.30am to 3.30pm. Some buses take the longer route from Savusavu along Natewa Bay, and these depart at 9am ($15, six hours).

Buses from Savusavu to Napuca ($7, 4½ hours), at the tip of the Tunuloa Peninsula, depart at 10.30am, 1pm and 2.30pm daily. The

afternoon bus stays there overnight and returns at 7am. A 4pm bus only goes as far as Naweni ($3). There is no bus from Savusavu to Nabouwalu; you have to catch a morning bus to Labasa and change buses there.

From Monday to Saturday there are five bus services from Savusavu to Lesiaceva Point ($1, 15 minutes) between 6am and 5pm. For confirmation of bus timetables in the south, ring **Vishnu Holdings** (☑885 0276).

Car

Cars can be booked through Trip n Tour (see p156); prices start at $110 for a two-door 4WD. A Yamaha scooter costs $45.

Taxi

Taxis are easy to find in Savusavu and the main taxi stand is right next to the bus station. Flagfall is $1.70 and 100m is $0.10.

North & East of Savusavu

Nestled in the mountains north of Savusavu, **Waisali Rainforest Reserve** (☑828 0267; Savusavu Rd; adult/child $8/2; ☉8am-5pm Mon-Sat) isn't particularly exciting, but there's a pleasant enough 30-minute walk through dense greenery down to a waterfall (but watch out for its death-trap-slippery rocks). You can enter the park 20km north of Savusavu, directly off the road to Labasa. Bus drivers should know where to drop you off (ask before you board), as should most carrier and taxi drivers. If you are driving, it's at km/culvert 14.4, which is also a good viewpoint.

DREKENIWAI TO DAKUNIBA

About 20km east of Savusavu, the Hibiscus Hwy veers right (south). The turn-off to the left (north) follows the western side of Natewa Bay, an alternative 4WD route to Labasa. About 35km further along the highway from this intersection is the turn-off into the village of **Drekeniwai**, where former prime minister Sitiveni Rabuka was born.

If you follow the Hibiscus Hwy to Buca Bay, the highway turns left (north), becoming more potholed as it heads through the **Tunuloa Silktail Reserve**, the habitat of the rare silktail bird. Found only on this peninsula and on Taveuni, the silktail has sadly made it onto the world's endangered-species list, with logging being its major threat. The average bird is about 8cm high and is black with a white patch on its tail.

If you turn right (south) at Buca Bay, you'll head through Natuvu village and then up over the mountain to the next village, **Dakuniba**.

NUKUBOLU

Deep in the mountains north of Savusavu, reachable by 4WD, lies the ruins of Nukubolu, an ancient Fijian village whose old stone foundations, terraces and thermal pools are in surprisingly good condition. The setting is lovely: a volcanic crater with steaming hot springs in the background. Nukubolu has myriad uses for the local villagers, who dry kava roots on corrugated-iron sheets laid over the pools and use the hot springs as a healing aid. The ruins are on the property of the village of Biaugunu, so take a *sevusevu* (gift) for the chief and ask permission before wandering around. The turn-off is about 20km northwest of Savusavu; continue about 8km inland and over a couple of river crossings. You can also rent a carrier from town to take you there; combine it with a trip to Waisali Rainforest Reserve.

The road is one big pothole and the going is slow, but you'll be rewarded with dazzling views over the forest and out to sea. In a beautiful forest setting, just outside Dakuniba, petroglyphs are inscribed on large boulders. They are thought to be of ceremonial or mystical significance. Be sure to bring a *sevusevu* (gift) for the village chief and read up about village etiquette before you arrive (see p221). The people of Dakuniba are very friendly and may offer to take you to a nearby beach to swim, fish or snorkel. The famous Rainbow Reef is offshore from Dakuniba, but is more easily accessible from the island of Taveuni.

Offshore Islands

NAMENALALA

The volcanic island of Namenalala rests on the Namena Barrier Reef, now one of the most spectacular protected marine reserves in the country, 25km off the southeastern coast of Vanua Levu and about 40km from Savusavu. Namenalala has the best diving and snorkelling in the region: sights include the shallow isolated offshore Chimneys, covered with soft and hard corals as well as plenty of nudibranchs, and Grand Canyon, a drop off at least a mile deep along Save-A-Tack Passage where there are great drift diving opportunities and plenty of marine life. The island also has lovely beaches and is a natural sailors' refuge. There's just one small, upmarket resort.

TOP CHOICE Moody's Namena (☎881 3764; www.moodysnamenafiji.com; all-inclusive packages for 5 nights incl transfers from Savusavu per person sharing from $1875; ☺closed April; ☎) is an outrageously located dive and snorkel ecoretreat that has six bamboo-and-timber *bure* on a forested ridge. Diving here is the best of the best and costs $300 for six tanks (divers must be certified). Other activities, which include windsurfing, fishing, snorkelling, reef excursions, barbecues, volleyball, and use of canoes and paddle boards, are included in the rate. The island has a nature reserve for birdwatching and trekking, and is home to seabirds, red-footed boobies and a giant-clam farm. From November to February hawksbill and green turtles lay their eggs on Namenalala beaches. There is a five-night minimum stay; no children under 16 years are allowed.

KIOA
POP 600

The island of Kioa (25 sq km) is inhabited by Polynesians originally from the tiny, coral-reef island of Vaitupu in Tuvalu. Because of weak soil and overcrowding on their home island, they decided that the best idea would be to buy another, more fertile island and start a relocation program. The people of Vaitupu had earned some money during WWII working for American soldiers who had occupied their islands, and in 1947 they purchased Kioa for the grand sum of $15,000. It was with some trepidation, however: those living on Kioa today speak wryly of their initial fears about how they would deal with the climate and whether they would be eaten by Fijian cannibals.

The residents of Kioa were finally granted Fijian citizenship in 2005. They are very warm and traditional people. Women make woven handicrafts that are sold to tourists on Taveuni and Vanua Levu, and fishing is done from small, traditional *drua* (double-hulled canoes). The people of Kioa have a speciality called *toddy,* which is a tradition that they imported from Tuvalu. It's a sweet syrup taken from coconut sap and can be made into a thick, spreadable syrup or fermented into a pungent alcoholic drink.

There is no accommodation or facilities for tourists; however, Tui Tai Adventure Cruises and Blue Lagoon Cruises do make stops here. Alternatively, the Taveuni ferry might be able to drop you off on its way past. For snorkellers and divers, the **Farm**, off the most easterly point of the island, has fantastic corals.

RABI
POP 4500

Rabi (66 sq km), east of the northern tip of the Tunuloa Peninsula, has four villages populated by Micronesians originally from Banaba, in Kiribati. At the turn of the 20th century the islanders of Banaba were first tricked and then pressed into selling the phosphate mining rights of Banaba for a small annual payment, and their tiny island was slowly ruined by the subsequent mining and influx of settlers. WWII brought further tragedy when the Japanese invaded Banaba and massacred many villagers. Following the war, Rabi was purchased for the Banabans by the British Government – with money from the islanders' own Provident Fund, set up by the British Government in 1931 for phosphate royalties – and 2000 survivors were resettled here. However, as they were dropped in the middle of the cyclone season with only army tents and two months' rations, and had never been so cold (Banaba is on the equator), many of the original settlers died.

If you're interested in visiting Rabi, you must first ask permission from the **island council** (☑881 2913). If you're extended an invitation, catch a bus from Savusavu to Karoko where small boats wait for passengers to Rabi ($70 one way).

Rabi Island Council Guesthouse (☑881 2913; dm $50; ☺Mon, Wed & Fri) has beds in basic, four-bed rooms. You'll eat with the villagers.

Labasa
POP 24,100

Labasa (pronounced 'Lambasa'), Vanua Levu's biggest settlement, is a bustling and dusty sugar and timber town that doesn't hold much allure for your average tourist. Sitting about 5km inland on the sweltering banks of the Labasa River and reclaimed mangrove swamps, the star attractions are a large sugar mill on the outskirts of town and a 'sugar-railway' that ka-chunks bushels of cane through Labasa centre. Labasa's population is predominantly Indo-Fijian, many of whom are descendants of girmitiyas (indentured labourers brought from India to work on the plantations; see p201 for more on girmitiyas). The town's main street is swarming with people. Bollywood music blasts out of stores selling trinkets, bangles and saris, while store owners and shop assistants stand chatting in the doorways.

Out of town are nearly undeveloped coastal areas that are rumoured to get great surf and have awesome diving.

⊙ Sights & Activities

Wasavula Ceremonial Site   HISTORIC SITE

This site is located just south of town, on Vunimoli Rd. At the entrance to the site there

---

MONOLITHIC GODS

Although the Wasavula Ceremonial Site is shrouded in mystery, it is thought to be related to similar sites of the *naga* (snake) cult found in Viti Levu's Sigatoka Valley. In the old religion those who betrayed ceremonial secrets would face insanity and death from the ancestral spirits and gods, so what is known about such places is mostly based on hearsay and vague memories.

Before the arrival of Christianity, ceremonial sites were venues for communicating with ancestral gods. Rituals performed at the sites provided a spiritual link between the people and the earth, time, crops and fertility. It is believed that this was where chiefs and priests were installed, where male initiation rites took place and where a *bokola* (the dead body of an enemy) was offered to the gods.

Stone monoliths at the sites were seen as actual gods or as the shrines of gods. These stones were often used for refuge; if someone who had committed a crime made it to the monolith before being caught, their life would be spared.

While the rituals of long ago are no longer practised at Wasavula Ceremonial Site, the ancestral gods haven't been evicted so easily. It is still revered as a sacred place by the village people and is now where they bury their dead. Some people continue to see the monolith as supernatural; it is said that in photos of villagers with the monolith, the villagers have often vanished from the developed pictures.

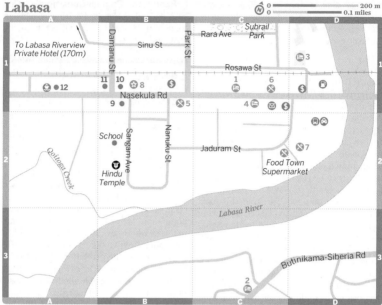

Labasa

is a sacred monolith that villagers believe grew from the ground. Behind the standing stone is the village cemetery. Beyond is the area that was used during cannibalistic ceremonies, and has a flat *vatu ni bokola* (head-chopping stone), another rock where the severed head was placed and a bowl-like stone in which the brain was placed for the chief. Unless you are given a guided tour you could probably walk right past most of these stones without noticing.

🛏 Sleeping

Grand Eastern Hotel   HOTEL $
(✆881 1022; grest@connect.com.fj; Rosawa St; r $100-130; ❋🛜🏊) This is the plushest and most convenient hotel in Labasa, located just off the main road for a whiff of calm. There's an airy, somewhat colonial atmosphere and the staff are helpful and wonderful. Standard rooms have porches facing the river, but it's worth paying the extra for the deluxe rooms that open out onto the courtyard swimming pool. All room interiors are plain and slightly careworn, however. There's also a decent restaurant and bar.

Friendly North Inn   HOTEL $
(✆881 1555; fni@connect.com.fj; Butinikama-Siberia Rd; r $70-90; ❋) For peace and quiet, head to the Friendly North Inn, which is a better deal that the Grand Eastern if you

don't mind the 20-minute walk to town. There are several surprisingly classy duplex villas set in a mellow, flower-studded garden; less-expensive pink 'apartments' share a common kitchen and lounge area between two or three rooms. The hotel has a large, open bar and restaurant, but meals need to be ordered in advance. A taxi into town will cost $5.

Labasa Riverview
Private Hotel   GUESTHOUSE $
(☏881 1367; Nadawa St; r with/without air-con $70/55; ❄) This is an unassuming house with ageing but cute rooms with cold-water bathrooms. A lounge area with a pool table overlooks a calm, murky river and the vibe is sweet. It's $3 for a taxi to town.

Hotel Takia   HOTEL $
(☏881 1655; hoteltakia@connect.com.fj; Nasekula Rd; r $85-150; ❄) Rooms here are large and clean, there's a restaurant that dishes out hefty servings of Chinese and Indian food for around $15, and a bar – though the drinkers can get rowdy. There's also a nightclub here, and sound carries.

Centerpoint Hotel   HOTEL $
(☏881 1057; cenhotel@connect.com.fj; Nasekula Rd; r $60-80; ❄) Bang in the centre of town, this place has large, if gloomy, rooms with bathrooms. It's basic but friendly and the cheapest place in the town centre.

✖ Eating

Labasa is full to the brim with basic cafes serving cheap plates of Indian and Chinese food. Note: most restaurants, although open for dinner, close by 7pm. There's also a cavernous market next to the bus station and a few well-stocked supermarkets.

Oriental Bar & Restaurant   CHINESE $
(Jaduram St; meals $8; ☉lunch & dinner Mon-Sat, dinner Sun; ☻) Look for the bright-orange door and pink balcony overlooking the bus station. Although you wouldn't guess it from the outside, this is one of Labasa's most upmarket and atmospheric restaurants, with a well-stocked bar and a wide choice of tasty Chinese dishes, including plenty of veggies and a few Fijian options.

Gopal's   VEGETARIAN $
(Nasekula Rd; thali $10; ☉breakfast, lunch & dinner; ☻) Specialises in vegetarian Indian food, and has fantastic thalis. There's also a sweets counter with a nice selection of sinful Indian treats.

Kwon Tung   CHINESE, INDIAN $
(Nasekula Rd; dishes from $5.50; ☉breakfast, lunch & dinner) Stomach-satisfying portions of Chinese and Indian food make this one of the most popular places in town.

♟ Drinking & Entertainment

There's not much going on in town. You might try the bar at the Grand Eastern Hotel for a poolside drink. A night out at the Labasa Club or the Farmers Club is *not* a good idea as it can get pretty rough.

Elite Cinema   CINEMA
(☏881 1260; Nasekula Rd; adult/child $3/1) Shows older films, the majority of which are in Hindi.

Bounty Night Club   CLUB
(☉8pm-1am Wed-Sat) Brave the caged bar – the owners assure us it's safe, but not only is the bar in a cage, the disco mirror ball is in a cage of its own!

ℹ Information

ANZ, Colonial National and Westpac banks all have branches in the main street and have 24-hour ATMs.

Hospital (☏881 1444; Butinikama-Siberia Rd) The hospital is southeast of the river.

Police (☏881 1222; Nadawa St)

Post office (Nasekula Rd) There are several cardphones outside.

ℹ Getting There & Around

There are regular buses that chug along the scenic mountain route between Labasa and Savusavu ($8, three hours, five times Monday to Saturday, four on Sunday) departing between 7am and 4.15pm. There is also a 9am bus that takes the long route ($15, six hours) to Savusavu around the northeast, following the even more scenic Natewa Bay. Buses to Nabouwalu depart three times per day Monday to Saturday ($10, six hours).

The majority of shops, businesses and hotels in Labasa are within walking distance of the centre. If you are going further afield, there is no shortage of taxis. You'll find the majority of them at the main stand near the bus station.

Northpole Rentals (☏881 8008; rentals@ northpole.com.fj) has an office at the hotel of the same name on the main drag. You can rent 4WD Suzuki Jimmys from $100 per day and it offers free airport pick-up and drop-off.

Around Labasa

The area around Labasa is a great place to explore by 4WD. There are a few points of interest; however, it's definitely the adventure of finding them rather than the sights themselves that make it worthwhile. For all of these sights, you'll need to turn left onto Wainikoro Rd, just past the sugar mill and across from a secondary school. This is the main road out of town to the east.

◉ Sights & Activities

Naag Mandir Temple   TEMPLE

Sacred **Cobra Rock** (so called because the 3m-high rock looks like an oversized cobra), housed inside the vibrant Naag Mandir Temple, is the area's most interesting attraction. The rock is constantly covered with bright, flower-and-tinsel garlands, and offerings of fruit, fire and *lolo* (coconut cream) are placed at its base. This is because, the locals told us, many people believe that the rock can cure the sick and the infertile. We were also told that the rock has magically grown bigger over the years and that the roof has had to be raised four times since the 1950s to accommodate it! Remove your shoes outside the beautifully tiled temple. A few buses pass the temple, including those to Natewa Bay ($1.20). A taxi costs about $17. If you're driving, the temple is 10km from the turning for Wainikoro Rd. The temple is heaving on Sunday mornings.

Korovatu Beach   BEACH

(admission per car $5) From Naag Mandir Temple, down through dense coconut trees and past the lounging cows lies Korovatu Beach, which is the closest stretch of beach to Labasa and makes an OK side trip if you're in the area for a few days.

⌂ Sleeping

⚑ Tribe Wanted   VILLAGE STAY $$

(☎992 0428; www.tribewanted.com) Tribe Wanted is a 'unique community tourism project' founded by two young English entrepreneurs who, in 2006, signed a three-year lease on Vorovoro island, offshore from Vanua Levu. The idea was to create a virtual tribe of members who could then pay to visit the island and, working with the local community, participate in the building of an ecovillage and a real-life tribe on Vorovoro. It worked and guests loved it, but the lease ran out and in late 2011 the project was closed. It is scheduled to open under new management in 2012.

⚑ Palmlea Lodge   BURE $$

(☎828 2220; www.palmleafarms.com; Tabia-Naduri Rd; bure from $259; ✱✸) This remote-feeling ecoresort is only 14km out of town off a dirt road and overlooks the Great Sea Reef. Simple bamboo thatched *bure* with verandahs sit on a gentle green slope a short walk to the resort's jetty – from here you can kayak to a private white-sand beach or just jump in for fantastic snorkelling. Fruit and veg is grown on an on-site organic farm and every effort is made to manage the resort in an ecofriendly fashion. Other activities including hiking, diving, fishing and crabbing with a local guide. Buses run past the resort five times a day making it easy to get to Savusavu.

⚑ Nukubati Island Resort   RESORT $$$

(☎881 3901; www.nukubati.com; d bure incl meals & activities from US$710) If you're looking for seclusion, this place should do the trick. *Bure* face a white-sand beach but are a little old-fashioned for the price. The prices include gourmet meals, all drinks (including alcohol) and most activities, including tennis, sailing, windsurfing and fishing. Game fishing, diving and massages cost extra. There is a maximum of 14 guests and only adults are allowed, unless you book the whole island, in which case children are accepted. A minimum five-night stay is required. Guided surf trips to the Great Sea Reef are possible from November to March.

Nabouwalu & Around

Nabouwalu is a small settlement on the island's southwestern point. Early in the 19th century European traders flocked to nearby **Bua Bay** to exploit *yasi dina* (sandalwood), which grew in the hills. Today, the ferry landing is about the only draw for travellers. Nabouwalu has administrative offices, a post office, a small market and a store. Offshore to the northwest, the island of **Yadua Tabu** is home to the last sizeable population of the rare and spectacular crested iguana. It became Fiji's first wildlife reserve in 1980.

Boats that arrive here are met by buses heading for Labasa, but if you want to stay in Nabouwalu, there is a basic, clean **government guesthouse** (☎883 6027; r per person $25). It's often booked out with government workers so be sure to call ahead to the district officer. There is a kitchen but no food; bring along some of your own supplies as there are no eateries nearby.

Nabouwalu can only be reached by bus from Labasa, not from Savusavu. The ferry bus is much quicker than the local bus.

The road from Nabouwalu around the southern coast to Savusavu (127km) is barely passable by 4WD or carrier.

Wainunu Bay

Hardly any travellers make it over to Wainunu Bay. The road here is poor and the land has escaped commercial logging, so the surrounding landscape – a patchwork of forest and waterfalls – remains untouched for the most part. Wainunu River, the third-largest river in Fiji, flows into Wainunu Bay. Today it's mostly populated with Fijian subsistence farmers who make money selling timber and kava.

Blue Parrot Bures (blueparrotbures@yahoo. com; dm/d $75/195) is actually an island at the point where two rivers meet to form a creek. Two traditional thatched *bure* have bamboo walls, bathrooms, cold-water showers and their own jetty onto the river. There are also four beds in the dorm-style loft in the main building. Rates include all meals and nonmotorised tours. Book via email, but be aware that emails are only answered about every two weeks. Children are accepted only if you book the entire resort.

Wainunu is three hours by very, very bad road from Savusavu, and about an hour from Nabouwalu. (It's actually closer to Viti Levu than Savusavu.) Contact Trip n Tour in Savusavu (p156), which can usually help with packages to the lodge.

TAVEUNI

POP 12,000

It's easy to see why Taveuni is called the Garden Island. Hot, steamy and often wet, this luscious strip of land is a carpet of green palms and tropical wildflowers, and its dense, prehistoric rainforest is a magnet for colourful bird life. Much of Taveuni's coastline is rugged, set against some of Fiji's highest peaks. Des Voeux Peak reaches up 1195m and the cloud-shrouded Mt Uluigalau, at 1241m, is the country's second-highest summit. A massive swath of the island's eastern side is a protected national park and here you can get sweaty on hillside hikes, cool off under waterfalls, enjoy a coastal walk along an impossibly beautiful beach trail or glide through clear waters on a traditional *bilibili* (bamboo raft). Dotted

around the island's perimeter are black-sand beaches, evidence of the island's volcanic past. If it's sheer indulgence you're after, the nearby islands of Laucala, Matagi and Qamea have stunning white beaches and luxury resorts.

It's not just on dry land that Taveuni makes an impression, though. The island's beauty descends below the water's surface, attracting divers from across the globe – all of them eager to explore the dazzling corals and diverse marine life of the world-famous Somosomo Strait.

🏃 Activities

DIVING & SNORKELLING

Taveuni has achieved mythical status among divers, who come to the Somosomo Strait to see incredible coral, a profusion of fish and the occasional shark, turtle or even pilot whale from September to November. The most famous of the vibrant soft-coral sites is **Rainbow Reef**, which fringes the southwest corner of Vanua Levu but is most easily accessed from Taveuni. Highlights include the luminescent **Great White Wall**, a vertical drop-off covered in white corals so that it almost looks like its blanketed in wavering, glimmery snow. The **Purple Wall**, covered in purple soft corals, gorgonia fans and sea whips, gets even more psychedelic, and **Annie's Brommies** is a fantastic outcrop teaming with fish. The island is especially hot and humid in January and February and the water clarity is reduced due to

VANUA LEVU & TAVEUNI TAVEUNI

ORIENTING YOURSELF ON TAVEUNI

The majority of visitors fly into Matei airport at the island's northernmost point, where most of the island's hotels, restaurants and dive shops are based. Head southeast from Matei and you'll eventually hit Bouma National Heritage Park, where the road stops at Lavena. Head southwest from Matei and you reach the towns of Somosomo, Naqara and Waiyevo, where there's some budget accommodation, shops and services but not much of interest to tourists. If you arrive by boat it will be at one of the two wharves in the Waiyevo area. Further south there are a few resorts near the village of Vuna. The road then goes only as far as the blowhole on South Cape, making much of the southeast coast almost inaccessible.

Taveuni

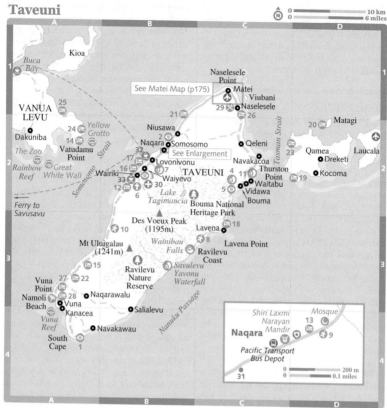

plankton blooms and northerly winds from the equator.

There is plenty for snorkellers, too. **Vuna Reef**, off southern Taveuni, boasts dazzling coral and improbable creatures. The three small islands immediately offshore from Naselesele Point in Matei also have good snorkelling (the third is known as the local 'Honeymoon Island'). You can also snorkel happily at Prince Charles or Beverly Beaches.

There are a number of dive operations on Taveuni, and the upmarket resorts on the off-shore islands of Matagi and Qamea have diving for their guests. All of the following companies organise dives in the Somosomo Strait.

Taveuni Ocean Sports DIVING
(☑888 1111; www.taveunioceansports.com) Based at Nakia Resort and Dive, this well-equipped, professional place gets top reviews from guests around the island. Each dive starts with a short lesson on local marine biology

and the centre is dedicated to protecting the environment. With group maximums at four people per dive you'll want to reserve in advance.

Taveuni Dive DIVING
(☑828 1063; www.taveunidive.com) This long-running team operates two recommended centres – one at Paradise Taveuni and the other at the upscale housing development of Taveuni Estates – so it can easily pick up from anywhere on the island. A two-tank dive/PADI Open Water Course costs $270/660 including equipment.

Dolphin Bay Divers DIVING
(☑992 4001, 828 3001; www.dolphinbaydivers.com) Located at Dolphin Bay Divers Retreat (on Vanua Levu but more easily accessed from Taveuni), this outfit offers two-tank dives/PADI Open Water Courses for $195/650 in-cluding equipment. The gear is in excellent condition.

Taveuni

◉ Sights

◈ Activities, Courses & Tours

◉ Sleeping

◈ Eating

ℹ Information

ℹ Transport

Garden Island Dive Centre   DIVING

(☏345 0324; www.gardenislandresort.com) Another professional place with a good reputation, this one is at the Garden Island Resort. A two-tank dive/PADI Open Water Course will cost $260/720.

Jewel Bubble Divers   DIVING

(☏888 2080; www.jeweldiversfiji.com; Matei) Check the gear here before going out, but the price beats anywhere on the island plus it's super friendly and locally owned. Two-tank dives cost from $180, and PADI Open Water Courses $590, including equipment.

HIKING

Taveuni's wild interior is perfect for exploring on foot. Bouma National Heritage Park is the place to head for hiking; you can amble beachside on the Lavena Coastal Walk, tramp up hills to the Tavoro Waterfalls or trek the guided Vidawa Rainforest Trail. If that's not hard-core enough you can slog it up to Des Voeux Peak or around Lake Tagimaucia.

WILDLIFE WATCHING

Taveuni is one of Fiji's best areas for birdwatching. Over 100 species of bird can be found here. Try Des Voeux Peak at dawn for a chance to see the rare orange dove (the male is bright orange with a green head, while the female is mostly green) and the silktail. Avid birdwatchers also recommend the Vidawa Rainforest Trail. On the Matei side of the village, follow a 4WD track for 3.5km up the mountain. Here you might see parrots and fantails, particularly in August and September when they're nesting. The deep-red feathers of the kula parrot were once an important trade item with the Tongans. The forested Lavena coast is also a good spot to see orange or flame doves, Fiji goshawk, wattled honeyeater, and grey and white heron. Vatuwiri Farm Resort at Vuna Point in the south is a great place for viewing fruit bats. Down south you can also see and hear magpies, introduced to control insects in the copra plantations.

DRUA

For assisting him in a war against the people of Rewa, Ratu Cakobau presented King George of Tonga with a *drua* (traditional catamaran). Named Ra Marama, the *drua* was built in Taveuni in the 1850s. It took seven years to complete, was over 30m long and could carry 150 people. Hewn from giant trees, it could outsail the European ships of the era.

Building *drua* could involve entire communities; some boats could carry up to 300 people. Their construction often involved ceremonial human sacrifices, and the completed vessel was launched over the bodies of slaves, which were used as rollers under the hulls. The last large *drua* was built in 1913 and is on display at the Fiji Museum in Suva. If you visit the island of Kioa, north of Taveuni, you can still see fishermen out in small, one-person *drua*.

OTHER ACTIVITIES

Tango Fishing Adventures   FISHING
(☎332 4303, 888 0680; makaira@connect.com. fj) Book through Makaira by the Sea in Matei. These folks will take you fishing for big game aboard the *Tango* with Captain John Llanes Jr, who has over 30 years' experience on the water. The boat has GPS, VHF and seven rod holders. A half-/full day costs $600/1000.

Taveuni Adventures   TOURS
(☎888 1700; www.taveuni.com.au; 1st fl, Garden State Price Point Bldg) Based in Naqara, this place can organise a range of activities including birdwatching excursions, hiking trips to Des Voeux Peak or Lake Tagimaucia, village tours and sunset cruises. It also acts as a booking agent for several accommodation options on the island.

Peckham Pearl Farm Tours   PEARL FARM
(☎888 2789) Snorkel the island's only saltwater black-pearl farm, in the Naselesele lagoon. Tours leave at 10am Monday to Friday from Audrey's Beach in Matei (opposite Audrey's Island Coffee & Pastries) and last for 1½ hours ($25/12 per adult/child). You can then browse the wares (pearls $24 and up).

Taveuni Estates   GOLF
(☎888 0441) Visitors are welcome to this nine-hole golf course ($40 green fee), plus the four tennis courts ($15) and a swimming pool.

Getting There & Away

AIR

At Matei airport, **Pacific Sun** (☎672 0888) has two flights a day to/from Nadi ($300 one way, 1½ hours) and Suva ($260 one way, 45 minutes), but be aware that routes are often heavily booked and are cancelled at the hint of bad weather. Leave yourself a grace period between Taveuni and your international flight in case you get stuck a day or two. At the time of research there were no direct flights between Vanua Levu and Taveuni.

BOAT

The Wairiki Wharf, for large vessels such as the MV *Suliven* and *Lomaviti Princess*, is about 1km south of Waiyevo. Smaller boats depart from the Korean Wharf, about 2km north. **Goundar Shipping** (☎in Savusavu 330 1035), **Consort Shipping** (☎in Suva 330 2877) and **Bligh Water Shipping** (☎888 0261, in Suva 331 8247) have regular Suva–Savusavu–Taveuni ferries with competitive rates – a ticket between Taveuni and Savusavu should cost around $35. Goundar is by far the most comfortable and reliable service. Bus–boat trips run to Savusavu and Labasa ($20 to $25; see p170). The boat departs from the Korean Wharf at 9am. The booking office is in Naqara.

For more information about these ferries see p236.

Getting Around

The one main road in Taveuni follows the coast, stretching from Lavena in the east, up north and around to Navakawau in the south. It is sealed from Matei to Wairiki, and there's also a sealed (though slightly potholed) section through Taveuni Estates. There are also a couple of inland 4WD tracks. Getting around Taveuni involves a bit of planning – the main disadvantage being the sporadic bus service. To get around cheaply and quickly you need to combine buses with walking, or take taxis – the driver will probably act as a tour guide too!

TO/FROM THE AIRPORT

From Matei airport expect to pay about $30 to Waiyevo, and $90 to Vuna (about one hour) in a taxi. Most upmarket resorts provide transfers for guests.

BUS

Pacific Transport (☎888 0278) has a depot in Naqara, opposite the Taveuni Central Indian School. From Monday to Saturday buses run from Wairiki to Bouma at 8.30am, 11.30am and 4.20pm. The last bus continues to Lavena where the first bus of each morning starts out at 5.45am. On Tuesday and Thursday all buses go as far as Lavena. On Sunday there is one bus at 3.30pm from Wairiki to Lavena, and one from Lavena to Wairiki at 6.45am.

Going south from Naqara, buses run to Navakawau at 9am, 11.30am and 4.45pm Monday to Saturday, returning at 5.30am and 8.15am. On Sunday a bus departs Navakawau at 6.45am and returns from Naqara at 4pm. From Matei, buses run to Wairiki at 11.30am Monday to Saturday and also at 7am and 3pm Monday to Friday during school terms.

The bus schedule is very lax: buses may show up early or an hour late. Be sure to double-check the time of the return bus when you board, just to make sure there is one.

CAR

At the time of research there were no official car-rental agencies on Taveuni, although locals are often willing to hire out their cars for around $125 per day. This of course means that there is no rental agreement and you will not be insured.

TAXI

It's easy to find taxis in the Matei, Waiyevo and Naqara areas, though on Sunday you might have to call one in advance. Hiring a taxi for a negotiated fee and touring most of the island's highlights in a day will work out cheaper than hiring a car. You should be able to get one from around $120 for the day, depending on how far you want to go. For destinations such as Lavena you can go one way by bus and have a taxi pick you up at the end at a designated time (but arrange this before you go).

Waiyevo, Somosomo & Around

This isn't the most beautiful part of Taveuni, but it is a good place to get things done and holds most of the island's facilities. It's also politically important – Somosomo is the largest village on Taveuni and headquarters for the Tui Cakau (high chief of Taveuni). The **Great Council of Chiefs' meeting hall** (*bure bose*) was built here in 1986 for the gathering of chiefs from all over Fiji. Just south of Somosomo is Naqara, Taveuni's metropolis – if you take metropolis to mean a few supermarkets, a budget hotel and the island's only bank. Head another 2km down the coast and you'll hit Waiyevo, which is Taveuni's administrative centre and home to the hospital, police station, more ferry links and a resort. About 2km further south of Waiyevo is Wairiki village, which has a general store and a beautiful old hilltop Catholic mission.

◉ Sights

International Dateline LANDMARK

The International Dateline twists its way round Fiji, but the 180-degree meridian actually cuts straight through Taveuni, about a 10-minute walk south of Waiyevo. Along the side of the road to Wairiki, a small, red survey beacon marks the spot. If you take the road uphill from Waiyevo (towards the hospital) and cross the field on the right, you'll find a big, wooden Taveuni map that's split in two to mark the two sides of the dateline. If you're easily amused you'll enjoy jumping from one day to another.

Waitavala Water Slide WATERFALL

If you've always wanted to launch yourself down a series of mini waterfalls, then here's your chance. You can slide down on your bum or attempt to do it standing up, surfer style, like the local kids. Either way, you'll end up (perhaps a little battered) in a small pool at the bottom. It could be a good idea to watch a local go down before you attempt it yourself – there are usually a few kids around to show you how. Be warned, though: local kids say never to attempt to begin your slide from the very top of the falls – it's too dangerous even for them. Also, if there's too much water the slides become

WORTH A TRIP

WAIRIKI CATHOLIC MISSION

This faded beauty has bags of colonial charm, and the setting is equally beguiling – standing on a slope peering over the Somosomo Strait. Its interior has an impressive beam ceiling and beautiful stained glass, reputedly from France. In the presbytery there's a painting of a legendary battle in which a Catholic missionary helped Taveuni's warriors defeat their Tongan attackers. It's worth attending Mass at 7am, 9am or 11am on Sunday when the congregation lets rip with some impressive vocals. There are no pews here, though: the congregation sits on woven mats on the floor. And you'll have to take off your shoes.

The mission is about 20 minutes' walk south along the coast from Waiyevo. You can't miss it on the hill to the left. A dirt track behind leads up to a huge white cross. The views from here are superb.

too hazardous and even the locals won't go down.

The slide is a 20-minute walk from Waiyevo. With the Garden Island Resort on your left, head north and take the first right at the bus stop. Take another right at the branch in the road, pass a shed and then go left down a hill. You'll see a 'waterfall' sign. The river is on the Waitavala estate, which is private land, so if you pass anyone on your way there, ask if you can visit.

Lake Tagimaucia
LAKE

Lake Tagimaucia is in an old volcanic crater in the mountains above Somosomo. Masses of vegetation float on the lake, which is situated 823m above sea level, and the national flower, the rare *tagimaucia* (an epiphytic plant), grows on the lake's shores. This red-and-white flower blooms only at high altitude from late September to late December.

It is a difficult trek around the lake as it is overgrown and often very muddy; you'll need a stick (to find firm ground) and a guide. Ask around in Naqara or arrange a guide through your accommodation as it's easy to get lost on your way up. Taveuni Adventures also organises day trips. The track starts from Naqara. Take lunch and allow eight hours for the round trip.

Des Voeux Peak
MOUNTAIN

At 1195m, Des Voeux Peak is the island's second-highest mountain. On a clear day the views from the peak are fantastic: it's possible to see Lake Tagimaucia and perhaps even the Lau Group. Allow three to four hours to walk the 6km, and at least two to return. It's a steep, arduous climb in the heat, so it's best to start out early. Try to make it up there by dawn if you are a keen birdwatcher. To get here, take the inland track just before you reach Wairiki Catholic Mission (coming from Waiyevo). Alternatively, arrange for a lift up and then walk back at your leisure.

🛏 Sleeping & Eating

🍃 Nakia Resort and Dive
BURE **$$**

(☑888 1111; www.nakiafiji.com; bure US$220; 🛜) Four simple, dark yet comfortable *bure* sit on a cheerful, grassy hillside looking out to sea at this raved-about ecoresort. These guys use alternative energy wherever possible, are into composting and recycling, and have a large organic garden where they get fresh fruit and veg for their restaurant. This is a place to flex your grin and make friends with the other inevitably happy guests. The

dive shop is excellent and takes the same eco-bent.

Aroha Resort
BURE **$$**

(☑888 1882; www.arohataveuni.com; bure from $216; 🛜🏊🍴) Simple but elegant varnished-wood rooms with louvred windows look out over a black-sand beach. Two rooms can be adjoined for families and each unit has its own airy kitchen and open-to-sky bathroom. There's a small infinity pool, a barbecue, bikes and kayaks, all for free use by guests. It's a short walk to Wairiki and its shops and restaurants. In all, it's excellent value.

Garden Island Resort
HOTEL **$$$**

(☑888 0286; www.gardenislandresort.com; r $350-500; ❄🛜🏊) A plain block-like exterior opens to a surprisingly chic nest streamlined with white tile and hip black furniture. Rooms are luxe, the pool beckons you with stylish lounging chairs and the snorkelling off the rocky beach is great, but what we like the most is the magnificent tree dripping with sleeping bats at the water's edge. Get the best deals with online packages.

First Light Inn
GUESTHOUSE **$**

(☑888 0339; firstlight@connect.com.fj; Waiyevo; r with fan/air-con $56/66; ❄) Convenient for the ferries, this is a relaxed and friendly place with a spotless self-catering kitchen for guests and satellite TV. Try to ring before you turn up as it might not always be staffed.

Chottu's Motel
GUESTHOUSE **$**

(☑888 0233; Naqara; budget s/d/tr $40/50/60, deluxe s/d $58.75/70.50) Chottu's has two types of room: budget, which are basic and share cold-water bathrooms; and deluxe, which are still pretty bare bones but have small TVs, private facilities and kitchenettes.

Wathi-po-ee Restaurant
FIJIAN **$**

(Waiyevo; meals around $7; ⊙breakfast, lunch & dinner Mon-Fri, breakfast & lunch Sat & Sun) A basic place that serves big plates of chow mein, curries and Fijian dishes as well as eggs, bacon and toast for breakfast.

❶ Information

Colonial National Bank (☑888 0433; Naqara; ⊙9.30am-4pm Mon, from 9am Tue-Fri) The only bank on the island will exchange currency and travellers cheques and has an ATM.

Hospital (☑888 0444; Waiyevo)

Police (☑888 0222; Waiyevo) The main police station is at the government compound behind

THE LEGEND OF THE TAGIMAUCIA

Fiji's emblem flower, the *tagimaucia* (*Medinilla waterhousei*), only grows above 600m in the mountains of Taveuni and in a small area of Vanua Levu. The unusual and very rare flower has white petals with a layer of leaf-like crimson red petals underneath and hangs off a vine. It blooms from October to December and its legend is a Fijian favourite.

There once lived a young girl with a wild spirit and a tendency to be disobedient. One fateful day her mother lost her patience with the girl and beat her with a bundle of coconut leaves, saying she never wanted to see her face again. The distraught girl ran away until she was deep in the forest. She came upon a large vine-covered *ivi* (Polynesian chestnut) tree and decided to climb it. The higher she climbed, the more entangled she became in the vine and, unable to break free, she began to weep. As giant tears rolled down her face they turned to blood and, where they fell onto the vine, they became beautiful white-and-red *tagimaucia* flowers. Calmed by the sight of the flowers, the girl managed to escape the forest and, upon returning home, was relieved to find an equally calm mother.

the Garden Island Resort in Waiyevo. There is also a police station in Naqara.

Post office (☑888 0027; Waiyevo; ☺8am-1pm & 2-4pm Mon-Fri) Among the shops beneath the First Light Inn.

Southern Taveuni

The southern part of the island isn't well serviced by public transport but it's a beautiful place to visit. Check out the **blowhole** on the dramatic, windswept South Cape. As the water jumps up through the volcanic rock it creates rainbows in the air. Southern Taveuni is also home to Vuna Reef, which is perfect for snorkellers and novice divers. The main villages on southern Taveuni are Naqarawalu in the hills and, on the southern coast near Vuna Reef, Kanacea, Vuna and Navakawau.

🛏 Sleeping

Dolphin Bay Divers Retreat   BURE $
(☑828 3001, 926 0145; www.dolphinbaydivers.com; Vanaira Bay, Vanua Levu; tent sites per person $15, d safari tents/bure $55/115; @) Just a bay over from Sau Bay on Vanua Levu (but most easily accessed from Taveuni), this is a friendly place with simple *bure,* space for camping and some permanent safari tents. It's very popular with divers, who make up most of the guests, but there's also good snorkelling from the beach. The food here is good, plentiful and eaten family style. You can also help yourself to snacks throughout the day. Transfers from Matei cost $60 one way. Meal plans are $75 per day with snacks. Important: this is a very remote location and you'll have to organise transfers in advance. Transfers from Vanua Levu are discouraged and

cost $180 from Buca Bay (where there's no Vodafone connection so you won't be able to call). Dives cost $195/650 for a two-tank dive/PADI Open Water Course.

Paradise Taveuni   RESORT $$$
(☑888 0125; www.paradiseinfiji.com; d incl all meals & transfers $650-700; ❉🛜🏊) Set on a former plantation, this oceanfront place has stunning sunset views and plenty of strategically placed hammocks and sun loungers from which to enjoy them. The *bure* and *vale* (rooms) are luxury all the way with large decks, locally handmade day beds, separate living and sleeping quarters, and huge bathrooms, some with the added bonus of outdoor jacuzzis and rock showers. The place is seamlessly run with smiling efficiency. There's diving through Taveuni Dive and incredible snorkelling right off the shore on the house reef, although there's not much of a beach. Activities include fishing, guided walks and wild-boar hunting, plus there's a spa overlooking the water.

Sau Bay Fiji Retreat   BURE $$$
(☑828 3000; www.saubay.com; Vanua Levu; bure $355-525; @) This place is in a sheltered bay on Vanua Levu, but is accessible only by boat and this is more easily done from Taveuni. There are two wooden bungalows and a luxury safari tent here with en suite bathrooms. There's no beach, but there are some sun loungers on a grassy lawn overlooking the water. There's hiking, good snorkelling at the house reef and you can hire kayaks and paddle in the mangroves up a small river. Diving can be arranged at nearby Dolphin Bay Divers. A full meal plan is $95 per person.

VANUA LEVU & TAVEUNI SOUTHERN TAVEUNI

FEEL THE POWER

All of Taveuni's electricity is supplied by generator. Upmarket resorts have 24-hour power; however, some budget and midrange places only run their generators in the evening, usually between 6pm and 10pm. Keep a torch handy.

Vatuwiri Farm Resort
BURE $$$

(⏱888 0316; vatuwirifiji.com; d cottages incl meals $500) This one is different: a huge estate, one of the last in the South Pacific still in the hands of the founding family, offering the rare opportunity to stay on a working farm in Fiji. The Tartes produce copra, beef, cocoa and vanilla. Accommodation is in two small cottages down by the water's edge and companionable dinners are taken in the main house with the Tartes, a fascinating family who are happy to talk about their family's and Fijian history. There's plenty to do on the farm such as birdwatching, horse riding, swimming or just enjoying the peace and quiet.

Remote Resort
RESORT $$$

(⏱9201 334; www.theremoteresort.com; Villas from $1600; ✴🖾🖾🖾🖾) Private villas on the doorstep of the Rainbow Reef (it's only a 10-minute boat ride to the White Wall) make this luxury diving heaven. There's a spa, any or as little activity you could hope for on a beach like this, all meals are included and the views are beyond the imagination.

Vuna Lagoon Lodge
GUESTHOUSE $

(⏱822 1963; dm/s/d $25/35/75) Stay in a simple, blue, wooden house a few steps from a black volcanic rock beach. Run by a local family, there's a self-catering kitchen and laundry facilities. It's also just a couple of minutes from the Fijian village of Vuna, so it's a great place to hang out and make friends with the locals. Good, home-cooked meals are available for between $7 and $12. It's best to call ahead.

Dolphin Bay Divers Taveuni
Guest House
GUESTHOUSE $

(⏱8880531;www.dolphinbaydivers.com;dm/d$25/55) This is a big, spotless house with two double bedrooms with shared bathroom. It is generally used by guests of Dolphin Bay Divers before or after their stay at the resort. You'll share the house with a friendly Indo-Fijian family who cook delicious Indian food and are happy to act as tour guides around the island.

Matei

A residential area on Taveuni's northern point, Matei is the main 'tourist hub,' if you can call it that, with a scarcely visible string of guesthouses, hotels and rental properties strewn along a long stretch of road crowned by stately palm trees and skirted by beach. The airport is tiny and, if you're travelling light, you can step off the plane and wander down the street five minutes later. Only a couple of beaches are suitable for swimming and sunbathing, but this is a good place to base yourself for diving and activities. It's a very warm place and it's easy to fall into conversation with locals and expats in the street.

🛏 Sleeping

Tuvununu
HOSTEL $

(⏱625 0582; tuvununu@gmail.com; dm/s/d $30/60/80; 🛜) Backpacker bliss with a long stretch of hammocked, waterfront deck, guitar-playing locals and a magically refilling kava bowl. Rooms are clean and comfy but a bit loud and nothing special. What you come here for is the convivial ambiance, the huge home-cooked meals around a big table and the majestic view over offshore islands (grab a kayak to get a little closer). Wi-fi is free. The backpackers is about a 10-minute walk from Matei through forest and a scenic village, and many folks stay here as a jumping-off point for Maqai Beach on Qamea.

TOP CHOICE Bibi's Hideaway
BURE $

(⏱888 0443; bure $32-118) A rambling, quiet 5-acre hillside plot hides a selection of adorable, colourful *bure* in varying sizes among the fruit and palm trees. Pick a pineapple for breakfast and papayas for lunch – if you don't your charming host Pauline will probably bring you fruit anyway. There are self-catering facilities here and plenty of room for exploring. The small blue house on the roadside at the bottom of the property will make Indian food on demand for $10 a plate if you don't feel like cooking. The resort was started by its affable Fijian owners on the suggestion of the author of the first Lonely Planet guide to Fiji.

TOP CHOICE Taveuni Palms
VILLAS $$$

(⏱888 0032; www.taveunipalmsfiji.com; d villas all inclusive except alcohol US$1400-2000; ✴🖾🖾🖾) Breathtakingly beautiful, completely tasteful and private, Taveuni Palms boasts three villas, each on its own beach and equipped with its own a swimming pool and staff, including

Matei

To Honeymoon Island (100m)

Naselesele Point

Beverly Beach

Prince Charles Beach

Matei Airport

Audrey's Beach

Matei

To Naqara (10km)

Viubani

To Naselesele (200m)

Matei

VANUA LEVU & TAVEUNI MATEI

a personal chef and one babysitter per child if you bring the kids. The cook will prepare a five-course meal for you every night, but the villas have kitchens anyway. One villa has an attached sleepout for kids and another has its own spa, but all are fitted with incredible entertainment centres with big TVs, DVD players and stereos. Activities include kayaking, snorkelling and cooking lessons. All the fruit and veggies are organically grown on the sprawling, manicured property.

Coconut Grove Beachfront Cottages
BURE $$

(☏888 0328; www.coconutgrovefiji.com; bure $300-390; ☎) A stone path studded with fish mosaics leads down to three calm, tasteful and bright cottages and a gorgeous slice of golden sandy beach. Two of the *bure* have rock showers with sea views and plenty of attention has

been spent to ensure that everything you'll need in your bungalow will be just where you need it. The restaurant here is one of the best on the island and the American owner, Ronna, likes to let her staff run things for a more Fijian feel – although she stays firmly on the sidelines to make sure every detail is attended to. This place doesn't accept children under 12.

Makaira by the Sea
BURE $$

(☏888 0680; fijibeachfrontatmakaira.com; bure $170-248; ☎) Makaira has two *bure:* one has a living room and panoramic views from both the deck and the bath; the other is smaller, with an outdoor 'jungle shower'. They both come equipped with kitchenettes but there's also a small cafe where breakfast and dinner can be provided. The family that runs Makaira also owns Tango Fishing Adventures across the road and it also offers a 'fishing kayak' rental for $125 per day.

Todra Ni Siga
BURE **$$**

(☏941 3985; bure incl breakfast US$160-175; ☎) Two private and self-contained cottages sit on the edge of a slope that meanders down to a small beach. Both are modern and comfortable but the smaller one has the better setting, with a fantastic view of the sea; the bigger cottage has a better bathroom, however, with an ocean view from the open-to-sky shower. There's an on-site craft shop selling handmade clothes and cards, and the owner May's house is in the centre of the property – she is super helpful and often has yummy Fijian treats on offer for her guests to try.

Tovu Tovu Resort
BURE **$**

(☏888 0560; www.tovutovu.com; bure from $95; ☎) This is a friendly place with a selection of ageing wooden *bure* with wooden verandahs, kitchenettes, hot-water bathrooms and fans. It is built on a subdivided copra estate, and owned by the Petersen family, which once ran the plantation. The best thing is the vibe – it's very welcoming and they'll go out of their way to make sure you're comfortable. The resort is a 20-minute walk southeast of Matei airport, past the Bhula Bhai & Sons Supermarket. Even if you don't stay here you should stop by for the restaurant.

Taveuni Island Resort
RESORT **$$$**

(☏888 0441; www.taveuniislandresort.com; bure from US$500, honeymoon villa US$1800; ☎❄) A luxury jaw-dropper reminiscent of a sort of late-1960s minimalist chic, Taveuni Island Resort has 12 *bure* with polished wood walls, white tiled floors, wicker furniture, outdoor rock showers and complete privacy, all balanced on a hilltop. If you've serious cash to splash, there's a private villa complete with plunge pool and your own private team of staff. Meals are a gourmet's delight, are included in the price and can be taken by the pool or in your *bure*. No children under 15 are allowed.

Beverly Campground
CAMPGROUND **$**

(☏888 0381; sites per person/permanent tent/dm $17/20/40) One of those magical spots where everybody makes friends easily and camping isn't a chore, this small site is set on a white-sand beach, beneath fantastic, huge poison-fish trees. The camp has very basic facilities including flush toilets, showers and a sheltered area for cooking and dining. The owner sometimes brings around fresh fruit and vegetables in the morning. He can also provide equipment for snorkelling, fishing and kayaking.

Taveuni Rental Properties
HOLIDAY RENTAL **$$**

(☏888 0522; www.fiji-rental-accommodations.com; houses US$210-300) Longtime Taveuni resident Bob Godess rents out three family-friendly beachfront holiday homes; all have full kitchen, polished wood floors, great outside deck areas, plenty of lush garden as well as beach access. Rates include a housekeeper.

Karin's Garden
GUESTHOUSE **$$**

(☏888 0511; www.karinsgardenfiji.com; cottage US$175) A wooden, two-bedroom cottage (one double and one twin) in the grounds of the owner's house, it has views out towards the reef and beach (which you can access from the property), a kitchen, a sitting room and a verandah. The rooms are big and cosy, the owners affable and they'll cook delicious meals for guests with enough notice.

Little Dolphin
GUESTHOUSE **$**

(☏888 0130; www.littledolphintaveuni.com; d cottage $100) This tiny, two-storey, top-heavy cottage has a breezy bedroom and a verandah overlooking the ocean. Downstairs is a kitchen and hot-water bathroom.

✖ Eating

There are several good choices in Matei. If you're here on a Wednesday, try the *lovo* (feast cooked in a pit oven) or buffet (complete with entertainment) at Naselesele village; your accommodation will be able to arrange this for you. Profits go to the local school.

Really good rotis ($1.50) can be bought at Matei airport.

Restaurant Tramonto
WESTERN **$$**

(☏888 2224; pizza from $25, meals $20-25; ☺lunch & dinner) If you're in the market for a pizza the size of a small child, then Tramonto won't disappoint – they're huge and mightily topped. You can consume said pizza in a nice raised building overlooking the water. If cheesiness turns you cold then there are a couple of other well-prepared dishes available daily, including fish 'n' chips and lamb shanks. On Sunday there's a buffet dinner and on Wednesday a barbecue; reservations are required.

Coconut Grove Restaurant
INTERNATIONAL **$$**

(☏888 0328; lunch $7-22, dinner $14-35; ☺breakfast, lunch & dinner) Take off your shoes and enjoy the sea views from the deck of this guesthouse's lovely restaurant. The menu includes wonderfully fresh vegetarian dishes, homemade pasta, soups, salads and fish. You can just turn up for breakfast or lunch, but you'll have to let them know you're coming for dinner. They pin up the night's choices on the restaurant door during the day, and you have to write your name down before 4pm. There are usually only three or four choices, always including one fish and one meat.

TOP CHOICE Audrey's Island Coffee and Pastries
CAFE $

(coffee & cake $10; ⊙10am-6pm) You can sit on the deck of US-born Audrey's house and enjoy fabulous cakes (moist chocolate cake and white-chocolate coconut slabs are just a couple of the possibilities – it depends on what she's been baking) and coffee while looking down the sweeping coast road and out to sea. If you're lucky, she may break out the Kahlúa and offer you a shot or three. She'll even let you have the recipe.

Vunibokoi Restaurant
FIJIAN $$

(dinner mains $18; ⊙breakfast, lunch & dinner) Tovu Tovu Resort's restaurant has large windows overlooking the island of Viubani. At lunch there are burgers and sandwiches, and there a few choices (usually changing daily) on the dinner board in the evenings, including delights such as crab curry, stir-fried prawns and *rourou* (boiled taro leaves in coconut cream) soup. Food is tasty and very good value and, on Friday, there's a popular 'buffet and music night' ($20).

Bhula Bhai & Sons Supermarket
GROCERY $

(☏888 0462; ⊙7.30am-6pm Mon-Sat, 8am-11am & 3-5pm Sun) Sells a range of groceries (including disposable nappies, but not beer), phonecards, stationery and film, and accepts Visa and MasterCard (10% commission, $90 limit). It has a public phone and a petrol pump (petrol is not served on Sundays).

Eastern Taveuni

The local landowners of beautiful eastern Taveuni have rejected logging in favour of ecotourism, under the banner of the Bouma Environmental Tourism Project. Scenes for the 1991 movie *Return to the Blue Lagoon* were filmed at Bouma National Heritage Park's Tavoro Waterfalls and at Lavena Beach.

BOUMA NATIONAL HERITAGE PARK
This **national park** (www.bnho.org) protects over 80% of Taveuni's total area, covering about 150 sq km of rainforest and coastal forest.

Sights & Activities

Tavoro Waterfalls
WATERFALL

There are three waterfalls here, each with natural swimming pools.

The first waterfall is about 24m high and has a change area, picnic tables and barbecue plates and is only 10 minutes' gentle stroll along a flat, cultivated path from the **visitors centre** (☏888 0390; falls admission $15; ⊙9am-4pm). Don't be fooled, however: getting to the other falls isn't so easy – it's a good 30-minute climb up and down hills to the second one. Luckily there are a few lookout points where you can stop and rest along the way. What's more, as you approach the waterfall you'll have to make like a frog and jump from boulder to boulder to cross a river; there's a rope you can use to balance but be careful as the rocks are very slippery. It's not quite as big as the first but is more secluded and beautiful. Getting to the third fall involves a hike along a less-maintained, often muddy, path through the forest for another 20 minutes, and if it's been raining it can be difficult to access. Smaller than the other two (about 10m high), it has a great swimming pool and rocks for jumping off (check for obstructions first!). If you bring your snorkelling gear you'll be able to see the hundreds of prawns in the water.

Vidawa Rainforest Trail
WALKING

If you are a keen walker, try this full-day, guided trek led by shamans. Beginning at Vidawa village, it passes through the historic fortified village sites of Navuga and follows trails into the rainforest where you'll see lots of birdlife. The trek then takes you to the Tavoro Waterfalls. You can only do this walk with a guide and need to book in advance. The trip runs Monday to Saturday and can take a maximum of eight people ($50). It includes guides, lunch, afternoon tea and park admission fee. Book through the Tavoro Waterfalls visitors centre.

If you are in the mood for a marathon, it is possible to catch the early morning bus to Bouma (45 minutes from Matei, 1½ hours from Naqara), make a flying visit to all three waterfalls and catch the early afternoon bus at about 1.40pm on to Lavena. In a rush, you can also do the coastal walk before dark and either stay overnight at Lavena or be picked up by a prearranged taxi. But this is Fiji – you'll be the only one rushing. For transport information see p170.

DON'T MISS

LAVENA COASTAL WALK

The 5km Lavena Coastal Walk follows the forest edge along stunning white-sand Lavena beach (known as Blue Lagoon Beach to the locals ever since the movie was filmed here, our guide told us), then a volcanic black-sand beach, past peaceful villages, before climbing up through a landscape straight out of *Jurassic Park* to a gushing waterfall. There's some good snorkelling and kayaking here and Lavena Point is fine for swimming.

The path is well maintained and clearly marked. About halfway along the trek, watch for the *vatuni'epa*, bizarre rock pedestals formed by the erosion of the coral base along the coast, which, according to our guide, the locals refer to as mushrooms because of their shape. Past these, the path seems to disappear at Naba settlement: follow the path onto the beach, then follow the shore past the *bure* and cross the stream to where the path reappears. Further ahead is a suspension bridge and eventually the trail takes you up the ancient valley of Wainibau Creek.

To reach the falls at the end of the trail you have to clamber over rocks and swim a short distance through two deep pools. Two cascades fall at different angles into a deep pool with sheer walls. The hardy can climb up the rocks to the left-hand side and jump into the deep pool. If you're visiting in the rainy season, the rocks near the falls can be slippery, if not flooded; it can be difficult and dangerous to reach the falls at this time. Ask at Lavena Lodge for current conditions. At any time of year (even if it hasn't been raining), violent flash floods can occur and readers have advised staying to the left of the pool, where you can make an easier getaway.

The walk is managed through Lavena Lodge. Entrance is $15. You can also take a guided sea-kayak journey and coastal walk for $50 (including lunch) or arrange to take a boat one way and walk back ($200 for the whole boat). Usually you can order a meal for when you return to the lodge ($10), but it's a good idea to bring along some food and definitely bring water.

Lavena village is about 15 minutes' drive past Bouma and 35 minutes from Matei. However, by local bus it takes about one hour from Matei or just under two from Waiyevo. Expect to pay about $75 for a taxi to/from Matei.

Waitabu Marine Park
MARINE PARK

This area has decent snorkelling and a gorgeous white-sand beach. It is only possible to visit the park with a guide. The village of Waitabu has set up a half-day tour that includes a local guide, guided snorkelling, a *bilibili* ride, and afternoon tea and singing in the village ($40 per person). There's also a Backpackers' Tour with guided snorkelling ($30 per person). You can't just turn up though and will have to book in advance, as trips will depend on the tides that day. Bookings are taken on ☑888 0451 or 820 1999. You can also arrange to stay the night at the new **campground** (per person with own tent $12, incl hire tent $17). There are toilets and showers and you can order a meal for $10. A return trip in a taxi should cost about $70.

🛏 Sleeping & Eating

Lavena Lodge
GUESTHOUSE $

(☑888 0116; tw per person incl Lavena Coastal Walk $30) Run by friendly, informative staff, the lodge has basic, clean rooms and a shared kitchen and bathroom. Electricity is supplied in the evening. There's a bench underneath a tree on the gorgeous beach from which to watch the sun go down, and when everything is quiet in the late afternoon it seems like a perfect slice of paradise. Meals are available ($7 breakfast, $10 lunch or dinner). There's a tiny shop in the village, but if you're planning to cook, bring your own supplies.

Offshore Islands

Qamea, Matagi and Laucala are a group of islands just east of Thurston Point, across the Tasman Strait from northeastern Taveuni. All three of the islands have lovely, white-sand beaches.

QAMEA

The closest of the three islands to Taveuni is Qamea (34 sq km), only 2.5km east of Thurston Point. Its coastline is riddled with deep bays and lined with white-sand beaches; the interior is fertile, green and rich in bird life. The island is also notable for the *lairo* (annual migration of land crabs). For a few days from late November to early December, at the start of their breeding season, masses of crabs move from the mudflats towards the sea.

Sleeping

TOP CHOICE Maqai Resort BACKPACKERS $

(☑990 7900; www.maqai.com; sites per person $20, dm/bure from $35/60; @) A private white-sand beach, excellent snorkelling just over the reef, a fickle but sometimes epic surfing wave and nightly entertainment from music around the kava bowl to fire shows – and believe it or not, this is a backpackers. Accommodation is in sturdy, clean safari tents and meals are taken in a Crusoe-like common area with sand floors, couches and a pool table. There's a boat to take you out to the breaks and snorkelling, village visits and hiking. If you have a few days don't miss the chance to stay on the backpacker's other outpost on Nunuku Island in simple thatched bures on the beach ($120 including transport). Three (huge) meals per day cost $50 and return transfers to Tuvununu on Taveuni are $50 per person. The best deals, however, are through packages from Bamboo Backpackers in Nadi that include boat transport, food, activities and lodging from Viti Levu (six-night trips from $495).

Qamea Resort & Spa RESORT $$$

(☑888 0220; www.qamea.com; bure US$690-950; ✳✉) The magnificently thatched *bure* lie on a long stretch of beautiful white-sand beach. The huge air-conditioned *bure* are decorated with Fijian art, and some have plunge pools, spa baths or rock showers. Rates include meals and transfers to and from Taveuni; children under 16 are not accepted unless you book the entire resort! There is excellent snorkelling just offshore as well as windsurfing, sailing, outrigger canoeing, nature walks, village visits and fishing trips. There's a dive shop where two-tank dives/ PADI Open Water Courses cost $260/950, including gear.

MATAGI

Tiny, horseshoe-shaped Matagi (1 sq km), formed by a submerged volcanic crater, is 10km off Taveuni's coast and just north of Qamea. Its steep rainforest sides rise to 130m. The bay faces north to open sea and there is a fringing reef on the southwest side of the island.

The *bure* at **Matangi Island Resort** (☑888 0260; www.matangiisland.com; bure incl all meals & nonmotorised activities US$730-1250; ☎✉) are huge, vaulted-ceilinged affairs with massive beds, plenty of windows to let in the light and separate seating areas. Each *bure* is surrounded by a neat tropical garden. It's romance run amok in the 'treehouse', perched 5m up in the tree canopy

---

THE CURSE OF THE AMERICAN IGUANA

It's thought that the first *iguana iguana* (technically called the common or green iguana but known as the American iguana in Fiji) arrived in Fiji with a foreign national on Qamea in 2000, who set it free. Twelve years later the species has spread to Laucala, Matagi, Taveuni and Vanua Levu, and it's widely believed it was brought to Viti Levu in 2010. This incredibly destructive animal can grow up to 2m in length, weighs up to 15kg and has no natural predators in Fiji. Besides regularly scaring the bejeezus out of the islanders, the iguanas eat *dalo,* kava and other staples, and risk spreading disease to the country's three native and endangered iguana species (two of which are endemic).

In general iguanas stay away from people, but when threatened they can become vicious. People have been bitten by the lizards and in these cases the risk of salmonella infection is very high. There are also concerns that iguanas could infect the crops they frequent.

Some islanders have started eating the iguanas, which are a tasty food source (apparently 'just like chicken') in the Americas. The local government, however, has warned people not to eat them since the salmonella they carry may cause food poisoning. In the meantime fines have been set for the possession of the animals or their eggs (up to $50,000) and resorts that keep them as pets can be fined up to $250,000; moving American iguanas from one island to another can get you 15 years in prison. But even though the media regularly highlights the concerns and there has been a government effort to contain the animals, by early 2012 little had been done in terms of eradication.

with wraparound decks, views to the beach, outdoor jacuzzis, lanterns aplenty and day beds. The pretty restaurant, where all meals are taken, looks over Qamea and out to the ocean.

Matangi boasts 30 dive spots within 10 to 30 minutes of the island; a two-tank dive is $225 (including gear) at the resort's dive shop. The resort is not suitable for children under the age of 12.

LAUCALA

Just 500m east across the strait from Qamea, 30-sq-km Laucala was once owned by the estate of the late US millionaire Malcolm Forbes. The resort was purchased by Red Bull billionaire Dietrich Mateschitz in 2003, who has turned it into his own resort, Laucala Island (www.laucala.com; villas from US$3800), complete with an 18-hole championship-standard golf course and private international airport.

Kadavu, Lau & Moala Groups

POP 20,850

Best Places to Stay

» Oneta Resort (p187)

» Mai Dive Astrolabe Reef Resort (p187)

» Matava (p185)

» Papageno Eco-Resort (p185)

» Koro Makawa (p187)

Best Dive Sites

» Naiqoro Passage (p186)

» Manta Reef (p183)

» Eagle Rock (p186)

» Yellow Wall (p183)

» Broken Stone (p186)

» Pacific Voyager (p183)

Why Go

This is where you wish you were right now. Remote and authentic yet easily accessed from Viti Levu and home to comfortable, ecofriendly resorts, Kadavu blends Fiji's best assets. As your plane lands on a tiny airstrip surrounded by luminescent sea, volcanic peaks and intense forest, you'll feel like an adventurer. Your flight will be followed by a long, and sometimes bumpy, boat ride to your resort past prehistoric-looking coves chirping with rare birds and fringed by the world's fourth-largest barrier reef.

Meanwhile, the Lau and Moala Groups are for those who have the time and endurance to seek out even more pristine paradises. Think turquoise waters, hardly touched jungle and traditional villages worthy of a BBC documentary. Yet of the group's 30 inhabited islands there are only two humble guesthouses and it takes lots of planning just to figure out how to get there and back.

When to Go

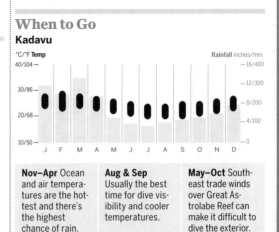

Kadavu

Nov–Apr Ocean and air temperatures are the hottest and there's the highest chance of rain.

Aug & Sep Usually the best time for dive visibility and cooler temperatures.

May–Oct Southeast trade winds over Great Astrolabe Reef can make it difficult to dive the exterior.

Kadavu, Lau & Moala Groups Highlights

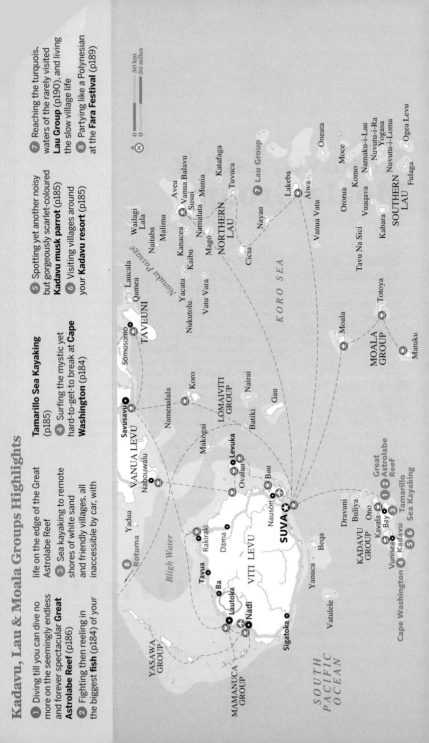

1 Diving till you can dive no more on the seemingly endless and forever spectacular **Great Astrolabe Reef** (p186)

2 Fighting then reeling in the biggest **fish** (p184) of your life on the edge of the Great Astrolabe Reef

3 Sea kayaking to remote shores of white sand and friendly villages, all inaccessible by car, with **Tamarillo Sea Kayaking** (p185)

4 Surfing the mystic yet hard-to-get-to break at **Cape Washington** (p184)

5 Spotting yet another noisy but gorgeously scarlet-coloured **Kadavu musk parrot** (p185)

6 Visiting villages around your **Kadavu resort** (p185)

7 Reaching the turquoise waters of the rarely visited **Lau Group** (p190), and living the slow village life

8 Partying like a Polynesian at the **Fara Festival** (p189)

KADAVU GROUP

Sitting sleepily 100km south of Viti Levu, the ruggedly beautiful Kadavu Group (pronounced 'Kandavu') offers a slice of wild and untamed Fiji. There is one small town here and next to no roads.

Snaking its way around the islands, the Great Astrolabe Reef is justifiably renowned in diving circles. People come from all over the world to sample its underwater delights. Handsome stretches of long, sandy beach and sheltered coves ring the islands' perimeters. In the interior you'll find all manner of bird life, including the colourful Kadavu musk parrot, thriving in an impossibly green rainforest that's ripe for scrambling up hillsides, splashing about under waterfalls and kayaking through mangroves.

The group is made up of several islands including Kadavu (the country's fourth-largest island), Ono, Galoa and Yaukuve Levu. Kadavu is irregular in shape and is almost split into three by deep bays along its length. At its southern tip sits its highest peak, the impressive 838m-high Nabukelevu (Mt Washington).

Most visitors will stay on Kadavu, where you'll find the bulk of the accommodation and the group's only town, petite Vunisea.

🏃 Activities

The Kadavu Group's rich landscape and underwater seascapes make it a perfect destination for nature lovers, divers, hikers and birdwatchers.

Hiking

Kadavu's hilly rainforest interior is sprinkled with waterfalls and hiking trails. There are good treks into the interior from several of the resorts. Resort staff will act as guides for the tougher treks. For shorter journeys you can set off on your own, but be sure to ask locals beforehand if a track is safe and about the proper etiquette for visiting a village.

Diving & Snorkelling

Buliya island, just north of Ono, is a great manta snorkelling site, where you're pretty much guaranteed an amazing encounter with the rays, and Matava Resort takes people diving at a site off Kadavu accurately called **Manta Reef**, where divers have a good chance of seeing massive manta rays cruising alongside the reef. Novice divers should head to **Yellow Wall**, with abundant yellow soft corals among a series of arches, and the **Pacific Voyager**, a 61m wrecked

---

TRANSPORT ISSUES

The ferry trip to Kadavu from Suva can be rough but the *Lomaiviti Princess*, run by Goundar Shipping, is relatively comfortable and it can be more reliable than flying. Flights tend to get cancelled for the slightest reasons and travellers can find themselves stuck in paradise a few days longer than they anticipated. If you end up stranded at the airport, compassionate Matana Beach Resort Dive Kadavu, the closest resort to the airport, offers special 'cancelled flight' rates (prices are negotiable) or you may find local villagers who will put you up for a night or two.

The small boats used by budget resorts for transfers to/from the airstrip sometimes don't have covers, life jackets or radios. The Group often falls prey to rough weather and the southeast coast in particular is often assaulted by wind and rain. You may get lucky, but expect a rough ride.

---

tanker on the more protected western side of the island. The following operators have excellent equipment and instructors.

Mai Dive   DIVING
(☑603 0842) Located at Mai Dive Astrolabe Reef Resort, this extremely professional place is the best-located dive centre for the Great Astrolabe Reef. Groups are small, the boat is clean, fast and sheltered and the equipment is excellent. A two-tank dive/PADI Open Water Course including equipment costs $218/710.

Mad Fish Dive Centre   DIVING
(☑333 6222) At the Matava Resort, this gem of a centre offers dives all over the reef system, including fantastic manta ray, cave and shark dives. It has a fleet of big comfortable dive boats. Two-tank dives/PADI Open Water Courses cost $245/850. It strongly supports reef conservation and environmentally friendly diving practices.

Papageno Eco-Resort   DIVING
(☑603 0466) Knowledgeable instructors will take you to the best sites, taking into account weather conditions. It's also within easy reach of the tanker wreck *Pacific Voyager*. A two-tank dive/PADI Open Water Course costs $220/800 including equipment. It uses

Kadavu Group

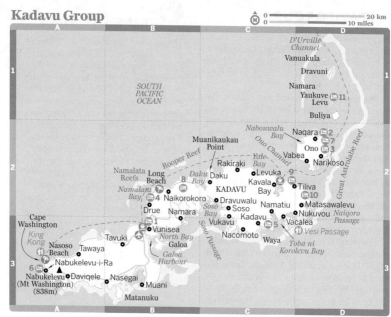

Kadavu Group

Activities, Courses & Tours

Sleeping

fixed moorings for its dives and encourages tourists to help protect the reefs.

Dive Kadavu   DIVING
(☎368 3502; www.divekadavu.com) A favourite haunt is Namalata Reefs, which is about 5km off the west coast of the island and more sheltered from the prevailing winds than the Great Astrolabe Reef. Expect to pay $190/700 for a two-tank dive/PADI Open Water Course including equipment.

Viti Water Sports   DIVING
(☎331 7281) Based at Waisalima Beach Resort, this is a small, personable operation with instructors who come by when there are clients. It charges $215/800 for a two-tank dive/ PADI Open Water Course, with equipment.

Fishing

Australia's *Modern Fishing* magazine has stated that the area around the Great Astrolabe Reef 'may well be the hottest poppering and jigging locations on the planet.' Dogtail tuna, giant trevally and red bass are regulars on the line and many of Kadavu's resorts (Ono's Oneta Resort and Kadavu's Matava Resort in particular) will take you out beyond the reef for some serious fishing action. You may be able to take some of your catch home for dinner too.

Surfing

The best surfing in Kadavu is found around **Cape Washington**, at the southernmost end of Kadavu. It gets plenty of swell activity year-round, including the excellent King Kong Lefts, off Nagigia island. **Vesi Pas-**

sage, near Matava Resort, also has powerful surf, but the waves often get blown out.

Keen surfers should head for Nagigia Island Resort at Cape Washington, which has daily boats heading out to the surf as well as several private breaks suitable for beginners.

Sea Kayaking

Organised kayaking trips take place from May to September and all of the resorts have two-person ocean kayaks free or for hire.

Tamarillo Sea Kayaking — SEA KAYAKING
(☑761 6140; www.tamarillo.co.nz/fiji) These recommended, interesting and well-organised jaunts run five to seven days and cost from $2400 per person. All tours include meals and accommodation (at the centre's own homestay, Matava Resort or Waisalima Resort) as well as a village stay. It also offers day and overnight trips. There's a two-person minimum.

Birdwatching

The lush rainforests, especially on Kadavu's eastern side, are home to a wide variety of bird life, including the indigenous Kadavu honeyeater, Kadavu fantail, velvet fruit dove and the colourful Kadavu musk parrot. Most of the resorts will be able to arrange a guide, but you'll see many species fluttering around the resorts as well.

Yachting

While there are no facilities aimed directly at yachties, Kadavu has several sheltered bays that are suitable for putting down anchor, including Daku Bay near Papageno Eco-Resort, Toba ni Korolevu Bay near Kadavu village, and Nabouwalu Bay on Ono island. Yachties are usually welcome to have a meal or a drink, get laundry done or arrange a dive course at a nearby resort.

Fiji Safari — YACHTING
(☑921 1403; www.fijisafari.net) Offers yacht charters around Kadavu on a 36ft Jeaneau. Yacht charters can also be arranged through Matava Resort.

🛏 Sleeping

Take into account the time and cost of transfers when choosing your accommodation. In Kadavu most of the places to stay are a fair way from the airport, and the only way to get there is by boat. Most places have a three-night minimum and offer package rates from their websites that are more economical than per night rates.

KADAVU

🗒 **Papageno Eco-Resort** — RESORT $$
(☑603 0466; www.papagenoresortfiji.com; s/d incl meals & transfers from $355/540; 🛜 🎏) Low-key Papageno is the stuff of island fantasies. Large, dark-wood *bure,* with decks looking out to sea, are spread sparingly (to ensure plenty of privacy) around manicured tropical gardens. Towards the back of the resort are four connected 'garden rooms', which share a single verandah, are surrounded by greenery and overlook a small stream. All rooms are decked out with local artwork and have bigger-than-average bathrooms. The welcoming central lodge has a small bar, some comfy chairs and an excellent selection of books. The resort prides itself on its ecocredentials, using solar and micro-hydro energy to complement its generator, composting organic waste on site, and investing heavily in environmental and local community development projects. The food is excellent and plentiful, and breakfasts alone – gargantuan feasts including eggs from the resort's own hens, homemade pastries, pancakes, sausage, fresh fruit, juices, porridge and an array of cereals – could set you up for the day. Kava ceremonies, sea kayaking and hiking are all free. Snorkelling, fishing and surfing are extra. There are family rooms here and a babysitting service is available.

🗒 TOP CHOICE **Matava Resort** — RESORT $$
(☑333 6222; www.matava.com; d per person incl meals & transfers from $305; 🎏) Fun is the best word to describe this social, active and impeccably run place. Anything you want to do on Kadavu, from diving to sportfishing, birding or hiking, the enthusiastic team here can set you up and you'll have plenty of new friends to enjoy your outing with. Meanwhile stay in spacious and clean hard-wood *bure* with heaps of windows to maximise the views (there are both garden and hillside options) and good solid beds. The resort runs on solar power, has a large organic garden and employs strict recycling policies. Fantastic meals, using vegetables and herbs from the organic garden, are eaten communally in the big restaurant-bar *bure,* which is beautifully lit by lanterns in the evening. The resort doesn't have a sunbather-friendly strip of beach, but there are suitable spots a short kayak away and there is plenty of space to lounge on ample decks or in the grassy grounds. A reef links

DON'T MISS

THE GREAT ASTROLABE REEF

The famous Great Astrolabe Reef, which is a major pull for most visitors to Kadavu and is the fourth-largest barrier reef in the world, hugs the eastern side of the Group. It is bisected by the **Naiqoro Passage**, home to brilliantly coloured soft and hard corals, a fantastic assortment of tunnels, caverns and canyons, and a variety of marine life, including plenty of reef sharks and graceful manta rays. Particularly recommended dive sites are **Eagle Rock**, a group of rock pinnacles with abundant hard corals and masses of fishlife including pelagics; and **Broken Stone**, which is a beautiful underwater landscape with a maze of swim-throughs, caverns and tunnels. The weather often dictates which sites are suitable to dive, and visibility can range from 15m to 70m. Most of the resorts will also take snorkellers out to the reef.

Matava to Waya, a picturesque offshore island, which makes for a great snorkelling or kayaking trip – or it's a short walk to a village and its magnificent waterfall where local kids try to impress with their high-diving skills.

Matana Beach Resort
Dive Kadavu
RESORT $$

(☏368 3502; www.divekadavu.com; per person incl meals & transfers s/d/tr/q $290/225/198/180; ☏🖳) This resort has *bure* with nearly all the walls covered in louvres so you can open them up for plenty of ventilation. They all have comfortable beds, verandahs, hot water and tidy bathrooms, but the brighter choices are the smaller units at the southern end. Diving is the main reason folks come here (this sheltered side of the island has less-fickle conditions than the Great Astrolabe Reef), but there are myriad other activities available from massage to village tours and bird nerds will happily spot most endemic species at the resort itself. Sheltered from the prevailing southeasterly winds, it boasts an excellent beach where the snorkelling and swimming is wonderful, regardless of the tide. There's also a social, oceanfront bar that hosts regular *lovo* (feast cooked in a pit oven), barbecue and curry nights.

Waisalima Beach Resort
BURE $$

(☏331 7281; www.waisalima.com; bure per couple per night incl meals & transfers from $345) Adorable, large thatched *bure* grace a remote stretch of white sand lined by coconut palms. All units have a single and double bed, prop-style windows and mosquito nets. The newest *bure* have flashier tiled bathrooms but all have hot water. Plenty of hammocks are strung up beachside, there are views of Ono island and if you tire of being surrounded by quiet you can go sit in the common area with its beautiful mosaic tiled floor and funky tunes on the sound system. Dine on superb meals including fresh baked goods while the trade winds keep you cool and the sand is breezed out from between your toes. The bar is stocked and stress is a dirty word. There's also a dive shop, Viti Water Sports, here.

Tiliva Resort
RESORT $$

(☏333 7127; www.tilivaresortfiji.com; s/d incl meals & transfers $300/500; ☏) This place was temporarily closed when we passed, but its location on a twist of coast just around the corner from Tiliva village is beautiful. It's one of the few Fijian-owned resorts on Kadavu and has just six *bure*, so you can expect lots of individual attention. Plenty of activities that revolve around the village are on offer as well as diving and it gets great traveller reviews.

Naninya Island Resort
RESORT $$

(☏603 0454; www.fijisurf.com; per person incl meals & transfers from $170 per night) Apparently hit or miss, when this place is good, the remote and staggeringly photogenic location near Cape Washington makes it unforgettable. Unfortunately we've heard complaints from travellers about lack of food and poor service. It's a surfers' resort and has a choice of five breaks that produce rideable waves year-round, with bigger swells during mid-year. For those who are not surfboard savvy there's fabulous snorkelling in the lagoon, village visits, windsurfing, kite surfing and plenty of great walks, including one to Cape Washington lighthouse for a swim in the Nasoso Beach caves.

Biana Accommodation
GUESTHOUSE $

(☏333 6010; s/d $45/65) Staying in Vunisea really defeats the purpose of coming to Kadavu but if you get stuck here, this place is about 2km north of the airport, near the wharf. It has basic rooms with mosquito nets. Rates include breakfast; lunch or dinner is $8.

ONO

TOP CHOICE **Oneta Resort** RESORT $$

(☑603 0778; www.onetafiji.com; dm/d per person incl meals & transfers $280/467; ☎) The architecturally lovely thatched *bure* with hard-wood floors, woven walls and louvred, netted windows are among this region's most luxurious and are definitely the most classy. Mattresses have been imported from Italy and beds are draped with gauzy white mosquito nets and topped with Southeast Asian embroidered linens. All units from the private honeymoon suite to the stylish six-bed dorm complex have giant open-to-sky bamboo showers. All this wonderfulness sits in an artfully landscaped garden complete with fruit trees and organic veggies, and there's a lush white-sand beach out front. Meals are made with the Italian owner's family's olive oil and organic produce and the homemade gelato is worthy of a Roman gelateria. This place is mostly meant to be a fishing lodge but diving (with nearby Mai Dive) and so many other activities are on offer, anyone would be happy here. At night watch movies on a full-sized movie screen and hang out with charming Piero and his Fijian girlfriend Vuli.

TOP CHOICE **Mai Dive Astrolabe Reef Resort** RESORT $$

(☑603 0842; www.maidive.com; sites per person incl meals $75, s/d incl meals $180/270; ☎) Pretty tongue-and-groove-built bungalows line the beach at this very tidy, streamlined resort (just a few minutes' boat ride from the fantabulous Great Astrolabe Reef) run by an Australian-Fijian family. All *bure* have polished timber floors and wooden verandahs and are right by the water; they are simple but stylish and have an incredibly happy feel to them. Some units have showers that are open to the elements so you can wash under the stars. Underfoot you'll find either white sand or Japanese grass, and frangipani trees perfume the air with tropical bliss. The dive centre here has become one of the island's most respected. There's plenty to do for nondivers, but honestly you'd be better off elsewhere; serious divers, however, should make this their first choice. There's a one-week minimum stay.

Koro Makawa HOLIDAY RENTAL $$$

(☑603 0782; www.koromakawa.com.fj; d per night all inclusive $1035; ☎☀) This lavish two-bedroom pad with a wraparound deck, a plunge pool and private sea views is so surreally out of place in its remote location, if you blink you may think you've been transported to Malibu. If you're not content with enjoying the good life on your private white-sand beach, your private staff can arrange secluded beach picnics and nature walks or nanny service, among other things. You can snorkel with manta rays five minutes away or go diving with Spenser, the friendly American owner. It's particularly popular with newlyweds for its supreme privacy. All nonmotorised activities are included.

YAUKUVE LEVU

This beautiful, reef-fringed volcanic island may one day be the site of a luxury resort – if it doesn't hit any more snags.

Yaukuve Island Resort RESORT $$$

(☑327 0011; www.yaukuve.com) This glamorous place has been being built for years but, despite the claims on its website, still wasn't open in early 2012. When it is finished this will be the most luxurious resort in the area with massive *bure* with their own living rooms, plasma TVs, sunken baths and rain showers. Plus there's a gym, a spa, a screening room and a couple of restaurants.

✖ Eating

The airport has a kiosk selling snacks, drinks and rotis. There are small grocery stores in Vunisea and Kavala Bay, and a regular weekday market in Vunisea. Most of the resorts are very remote, so even if all your meals are provided it may be an idea to take along snacks.

THE BATTLE OF THE SHARK & OCTOPUS GODS

Dakuwaqa, the Shark God, once cruised the Fiji islands challenging other reef guardians. On hearing rumours of a rival monster in Kadavu waters, he sped down to the island to prove his superior strength. Adopting his usual battle strategy he charged at the giant octopus with his mouth wide open and sharp teeth prepared. The octopus, however, anchored itself to the coral reef and swiftly clasped the shark in a death lock. In return for mercy the octopus demanded that the people of Kadavu be forever protected from shark attack. In Kadavu the people now fish without fear and regard the shark as their protector. Most won't eat shark or octopus out of respect for their gods.

ⓘ Information

Many resorts offer wi-fi but service is very slow. Some resorts, especially the more upmarket ones, accept credit cards, but check before you fly out. You can't change foreign currency in Vunisea and there's no ATM, so bring however much money you'll need.

The **Vunisea post and telephone office** (☺8am-3pm Mon-Fri) is on top of the hill, a short walk from the airstrip. It also sells some groceries, clothes and stationery. Kavala Bay, at the northeastern end of the island, also has a post office.

Emergency & Medical Services

Hospital (☎333 6008) Opened in 1996 with the help of Australian aid, Vunisea's hospital only has limited services. For more serious ailments you're better off heading back to Viti Levu. Divers suffering from the bends can be transferred to the Fiji Recompression Chamber Facility (see p104) in Suva by Medivac helicopter service.

Police (☎333 6007)

ⓘ Getting There & Away

Air

Pacific Sun (☎672 0888; www.airpacific.com) has daily flights to Kadavu from Suva ($185 one way, 40 minutes) and Nadi ($220 one way, 50 minutes). It is advisable to check timetables and confirm flights the day before departure as they are often late or cancelled.

Transfers to Yaukuve Levu take 45 minutes from Nadi by private seaplane or helicopter, which can be organised through your resort.

Ideally, have your accommodation and transfers booked in advance, otherwise you could be stranded in Vunisea.

Boat

Goundar Shipping (☎330 1035) runs the clean and reliable MV *Lomaiviti Princess*, which departs Suva late Wednesday night and arrives at Vunisea four to five hours later ($50 one way); it departs Kadavu Thursday afternoon and arrives in Suva that night connecting onwards to Vanua Levu and Taveuni. **Venu Shipping** (☎in Suva 339 5000, 330 7349; Rona St, Walu Bay, Suva) operates the much less reliable MV *Sinu-i-Wasa* to Suva from $55 per person one way on Tuesday nights.

ⓘ Getting Around

Kadavu's few roads are restricted to the Vunisea area, except for one rough, unsealed road to Nabukelevu-i-Ra around the southern end of Kadavu. Small boats are the island group's principal mode of transport. Each resort has its own boat and will pick up guests from Vunisea airstrip. Make sure you make arrangements in advance. Boat trips are expensive due to fuel

costs. In rough weather it can be a wet and bone-crunching trip to the more remote resorts.

To get to Ono island you'll have to fly to Vunisea on Kadavu, where you'll be picked up by your resort. Transfers take anything from one to two hours.

LAU & MOALA GROUPS

Fiji's final frontier, the Lau islands are strewn across the southwest corner of Fiji's vast archipelago like green champagne bubbles on the blue Pacific. Few visit here, but those who do report countless bays, deserted, reef-rimmed atolls and sparsely populated islands with hilly interiors. For the hardened and patiently adventurous, Lau and Moala offer the opportunity to create your own trail and go where few outsiders have been.

Vanua Balavu and Lakeba in the Lau Group are the only two of the 30 or so inhabited islands that see a slow dribble of visitors. Both have basic amenities, weekly flights and a simple guesthouse.

Although much closer to the mainland, the Moala Group is even further removed from the reaches of tourists and has no facilities whatsoever.

🏃 Activities & Tours

The biggest draw is the isolation of the islands: a chance to interact with local communities and experience a way of life seldom seen by outsiders. **Hiking** is the most accessible activity and easily arranged, and as long as you follow polite etiquette (see p221).

Lau Group is still relatively unexplored in terms of **diving**. The Fijian Government protects the waters, and commercial fishing is prohibited in the area. In the absence of diving companies, **snorkelling** is the next best way to experience the sizeable reefs and their marine life. Guesthouses should be able to arrange for local boats to run you out to the reefs.

Sailing around the Lau Group requires a cruising permit, which is now relatively easy to obtain and is issued at any official port of entry (you cannot legally enter Fiji via the Lau Group) and yachts are charged an anchorage fee of $10 per day. These poor islands need the funds so if the anchorage fee isn't asked for offer it anyway.

ⓘ Information

There is little infrastructure for locals, let alone for travellers, but you'll find a couple of general stores in Lomaloma and on Lakeba. Currently

ROTUMA

Far flung and isolated, the 43-sq-km volcanic island of Rotuma drifts in the Pacific 460km northwest of Viti Levu. The vast distance between its tiny frame and the mainland is what has allowed the Rotumans to develop such an inimitable culture.

Ethnically and linguistically distinct from Fiji, the Rotuman culture resembles that of Tonga and the Polynesian islands to the east. Strong emphasis on communal sharing and *kainaga* (kinship), combined with a slow pace of life, mean that visitors encounter a close-knit people with an elastic sense of time. And that is how the Rotumans prefer it to remain.

In 1985, wary of Western influence, 85% of Rotumans voted against opening the island up to tourism and while it's perfectly feasible to visit, genuine travellers here are few. Most who do so have been invited or are returning residents visiting 'home'.

There are more than twice as many Rotumans living abroad than there are left on Rotuma. Most have left to find work and opportunities in Fiji, New Zealand and Australia, and this mass exodus means that young people can seem relatively scarce on this beautiful island outpost.

Hiking, Archaeology & Beaches

Rotuma's volcanic curves offer excellent hiking and there are spectacular views from **Solroroa Bluff** and **Mt Suelhof** (256m), Rotuma's highest peak. Between Losa and Solroroa Bluff is **Mamfiri**, a volcanic vent that drops around 25m.

Twenty stone tombs were recorded at **Sisilo Hill** in 1824 and this archaeological site is also known as the Graveyard of Kings. If you're lucky you may spot some endemic wildlife including the Rotuman gecko and the red-and-black Rotuman honeyeater.

Rotuma also has some of the loveliest beaches in Fiji. The best are at **Oinafa**, **Losa** and **Vai'oa**, west of Solroroa Bluff. There are also some fine surfing areas around the island.

Fara Festival

An annual festival known as Fara begins on 1 December, leading into six weeks of dancing, parties and revelry. The emphasis is on hospitality and celebrating friends, family, visitors, life and love. At this time the population increases by around one-third; it's the best time to be on the island.

Where to Stay

The easiest way to stay on Rotuma is to organise a homestay. If you're lucky enough to be invited to the island, discuss with your Rotuman contact how best to compensate the family during your stay. You can also contact the Fiji Visitor Bureau in either Nadi or Suva to get the contact details for the Rotuman Island Council, which is the group you should contact if you want to visit. You can also simply ask the visitor's bureau for their advice.

Another option would be to post a message on www.rotuma.net. This online forum is used by Rotumans to keep in contact across the globe and somebody there may be willing to offer a homestay.

Mojito's Barfly (☎889 1144; Motusa) has simple rooms with shared facilities but they are generally reserved for government workers. Travellers also stay at **Jasmine's Accommodation** (Motusa) from time to time in simple rooms. Phone the **District Office** (☎889 1011) to arrange in advance.

Getting There

Pacific Sun (www.airpacific.com) flies to Nadi ($632) and continues onto Suva ($805) on Wednesdays; the trip takes 1½ hours.

Western Shipping (☎331 4467; Narain's Wharf, Walu Bay, Suva) operates the *Cagi Mai Ba* to Rotuma (deck/seat/cabin $118/165/180) the first Saturday of every month. The journey takes 36 hours and the conditions on board are very basic.

Yachts occasionally visit the island and to anchor they must obtain permission from the Ahau government station in Maka Bay, on the northern side of the island. Rotuma is a designated port of entry; see p234 for details.

ℹ **KNOW BEFORE YOU GO**

» The Lau and Moala islands are Fiji's wild frontier. There are no hotels, bars, restaurants, dive shops, banks or tourist shops. Only two islands, Vanua Balavu and Lakeba, have guesthouses. Neither accepts credit cards.

» Meals will be mostly whatever the locals can catch or grow. Expect fresh seafood of various kinds and local fruits and (often starchy) vegetables.

» Book flights well in advance and confirm your reservation. Flights are infrequent, sometimes rescheduled and generally full. If it rains and the grass on the landing strip is dangerously slippery, the plane will return to Suva.

» Boats can run weeks behind their published timetables and if they do, the local shops will run out of goods. BYO snacks.

there is only spotty Vodafone mobile coverage on Vanua Balavu. There is the **Lomaloma post office** (☑889 5000) on Vanua Balavu, and the **Tubou post office** (☑882 3001) on Lakeba. Tubou also has a **police station** (☑882 3043) and **hospital** (☑882 3153).

ℹ **Getting There & Away**

Pacific Sun (☑347 8077; www.airpacific.com) flies between Suva and Vanua Balavu on Wednesdays ($225 one way, one hour) and to Lakeba on Thursdays ($225 one way, 1½ hours). There's also a flight on Tuesday from Suva to Cica ($265).

Bligh Water Shipping (☑331 8247; www. blighwatershipping.com.fj) has slow monthly trips from Suva to Vanua Balavu and Cicia. One-way fares, including meals, are $135.

Lau Shipping's MV *Lau Trader* runs between Suva and Northern Lau, Upper Southern Lau, Lower Southern Lau, while Seaview Shipping's MV *Sandy* travels from Suva to Upper Southern Lau and Lower Southern Lau (see p236).

At the time of writing the more reliable **Goundar Shipping** (☑330 1035) was planning to start servicing Vanuabalavu and Lakeba via Cicia once a month as well.

Lau Group

The 57 isles of Lau are subdivided into northern and southern Lau and it is said that on the southernmost island of Ono-i-Lau you can see Tonga on a clear day. This proximity to its Pacific neighbour has had a profound influence on the group's cultural development. The southeast trade winds made it easy for Tongan warlords to reach Fiji and with them came Tongan language, food, decoration and architecture. The winds that blew them so favourably over were less inclined to blow them back and Lau islanders still bear the names and physical traits of their Tongan ancestors.

VANUA BALAVU

Vanua Balavu, 355km east of Nadi, about halfway to Tonga, is Northern Lau's largest island, and has a grass airstrip.

Arguably the most scenic of Lau's islands, it averages about 2km wide and resides with eight other smaller islands inside a barrier reef. The islands curl their way around the surrounding water, creating sheltered bays and corridors of calm sea. The interior of Vanua Balavu is scattered with rugged hills and pristine, sandy beaches ring the group's perimeter. The celebrated **Bay of Islands**, also known as Qilaqila, sits in the northwest pocket and is a spectacular site for snorkelling, kayaking and swimming. It's also a lovely place for yachties to draw anchor and a known hurricane shelter. Within the rugged limestone hills is **Vale Ni Bose** (literally the Meeting House of the Gods), a gaping cave with limestone walls and a pool of crystalline water.

Vanua Balavu's largest village is Lomaloma on the southeast coast. In the mid-19th century Tonga conquered the island, and the village of Sawana was built next to Lomaloma. Fifth-generation Tongan descendants still live in Sawana, and the houses with rounded ends show the influence of Tongan architecture.

At one time ships trading in the Pacific regularly visited Lomaloma and it had the first port in Fiji. In its heyday Lomaloma had many hotels and shops, as well as Fiji's first botanical gardens, though little remains of its past grandeur.

One week after the full moon in November, the people of Vanua Balavu witness the annual rising of the balolo (tiny green and brown sea worms). At sunrise the Susui villagers collect worms by the thousands. The fishy-tasting baked worms are considered a delicacy.

🛏 **Sleeping**

Moana's Guesthouse   GUESTHOUSE $

(☑822 1148, 820 1125; www.moanasguesthouses. com; r per person incl meals $95, children under 12yr $50; @) This hospitable place covers all the basics with beach *bure* and guesthouse options. The three simple *bure* are a 1km walk from Sawana village and mere metres from a tidal beach. The *bure* are simple, thatched affairs with mosquito nets, solar power, private bathrooms and mats laid over concrete floors. Moana's can arrange boat, snorkelling and fishing trips and collects travellers from the airstrip for $60 return. There is internet but it's slow and not always working.

OTHER NORTHERN LAU ISLANDS

Mago island made headlines in 2005 when Hollywood actor Mel Gibson bought the former copra estate for nearly US$15 million from a Japanese hotel chain, making it one of the largest privately owned islands in the world. The Yavusa Vuaniivi clan, who claimed their ancestors were cheated by 19th-century British settlers who allegedly gave the islanders 2000 coconut plants in return for Mago, challenged the sale's validity.

Kaibu is another privately owned island in the northern Lau Group, 55km west of Vanua Balavu. It has a grass airstrip, shares a fringing reef with the larger island of Yacata and is home to the now defunct, but previously exclusive, Kaimbu Island Resort. It has been in a state of renovation and sale for several years and conflicting rumours of its imminent operation or demise abound.

Cicia is a 34-sq-km dot in the Pacific southwest of Vanua Balavu that's covered in coconut palms.

LAKEBA

Lakeba, being the hereditary seat of the Tui Nayau (Chief of Lau), is the most important island in southern Lau. It is a roughly circular volcanic island, approximately 9km in diameter, with a small peninsula at its southern end. Its 54-sq-km area is home to about 2000 people. In days of yore the islanders lived in an interior hilltop fort, far from marauding neighbours. Today they live in the eight coastal villages that are connected by a road that circles the island. To the east is a wide **lagoon** enclosed by a barrier reef.

Lakeba was historically a meeting place for Fijians and Tongans; it was also the place where Christian missionaries first entered Fiji via Tonga and Tahiti. Two missionaries, Cross and Cargill, developed a system for written Fijian here and produced the first book in that language. Lake-

ba was frequently visited by Europeans before the trading settlement was established at Levuka in the Lomaiviti Group.

The **provincial office** (☑882 3164) for the Lau Group is in **Tubou** at the southern end of Lakeba. There is also a guesthouse, a post office, a police station and a hospital here, and some of the nearby **beaches** are good for snorkelling and swimming. For transport you can utilise the carriers and buses that circle the island.

The island has caves worth visiting, especially **Oso Nabukete**, which translates as 'too narrow for pregnant women'. Adorned with huge pillars of limestone stalactites and inhabited by bats, it's an awesome example of nature's might.

🛏 Sleeping

Jeke Qica's Guesthouse GUESTHOUSE $
(☑882 3188; r per person incl meals $65) In Tubou, this small guesthouse offers two rooms with private bathrooms inside 'Jack's house'. Meals are simple but filling and Jack can provide interesting commentary on the area's culture and history. If you have a hard time reaching Jeke by phone call the provincial office on ☑882 3164.

OTHER SOUTHERN LAU ISLANDS

There are 16 other southern Lau islands, mostly within a radius of 100km southeast of Lakeba. Vatoa and Ono-i-Lau are more isolated and much further south.

The islanders of southern Lau are well known for their crafts: Moce, Vatoa, Ono-i-Lau and Namuka-i-Lau produce *masi* (bark

---

FATAL ATTRACTION

There's a freshwater lake near the village of Mavana, on the northeast corner of Vanua Balavu, where the people of Mavana gather annually for a fun ceremony authorised by their traditional priest. Naked except for a leaf skirt, they jump around in the lake to stir up the muddy waters. This provokes the large fish known as *yawa* (a type of mullet usually only found in the sea) to spring into the air. It's believed that the male fish are attracted to the female villagers and thus easily trapped in the nets. Legend has it that the fish were dropped into the lake by a Tongan princess while flying over the island on her way to visit her lover on Taveuni.

cloth) and the artisans of Fulaga are excellent woodcarvers. You may be able to purchase crafts from villages on the islands or from handicrafts shops in Suva.

Moala Group

The three islands of this group – Moala, Totoya and Matuku – are geographically removed from Lau, but administered as part of the Eastern Division. The islands are the eroded tops of previously submerged volcanic cones that have lifted more than 3km to the sea surface. Totoya's horseshoe shape is the result of a sunken volcano crater forming a land-locked lagoon. Matuku has rich volcanic soil, steep wooded peaks and a submerged crater on its western side. However, this beautiful island is generally inaccessible to visitors. Each of the islands has villages.

MOALA

Moala (65 sq km) is the largest and most northerly of the group and is about 160km from Suva. The highest peak reaches 460m and has two small crater lakes. It has extremely fertile soil and supports nine villages that produce copra and bananas.

Moala has no tourist infrastructure and although you don't need to be formally invited as such, your only option for accommodation is with a local family and you'll need to organise this before you arrive.

Understand
Fiji

population per sq km

FIJI   AUSTRALIA   USA

≈ 3 people

Fiji Today

Coup-coup Land

Since the 2006 military coup, Commodore Frank Bainimarama has strengthened his power base and attempted to legitimise his position as Fiji's rightful prime minister in a series of complex political manoeuvrings. In 2009 when the Court of Appeal declared Bainimarama's interim government illegal, Commodore Bainimarama and his entire government immediately stepped down so that President Iloilo was free to appoint 'a distinguished person' as caretaker prime minister.

President Iloilo then surprised everyone – well, perhaps not Bainimarama – when he then promptly dismissed the Court of Appeal, suspended the constitution and declared a new legal order with himself as Fiji's new head of state. His first order of business: to reinstate Bainimarama as interim prime minister, who in turn reinstated his cabinet. The shuffle effectively restored Commodore Frank Bainimarama to power while removing the previous barriers restricting his governance.

Fiji is an archipelago of 332 islands and a further 500 smaller islets covering a total area of more than 1.3 million sq km, with a land area of 18,300 sq km.

A Little Less Conversation

In early 2012 the Public Emergency Regulations (PER), which had been put in place during the 2009 political turmoil, were lifted. These regulations restricted people's freedom of speech, freedom of assembly and freedom of the media. Despite the abolishment of the PER, new public order decrees continue to oppress political opposition and Bainimarama continues to be labelled as a dictator by international press and his detractors. For his part, Bainimarama insists he's only doing what's necessary to stamp out the corruption and systemic racism that characterised previous governments. He's said it before (in 2010) and he'll undoubtedly say it again, he's 'committed to free and fair elections'. It's just the date that's proving tricky to pin down. Recently 2014 has been earmarked as the year Fiji returns to democracy.

Sport

Fijians are fanatical about sports and their fondness for rugby union, the most popular game in the country, crosses many of the racial and cultural divides so evident elsewhere in Fijian society. The Fijian rugby sevens team is one of the most successful sevens teams in the world and a considerable source of national pride. The 'Flying Fijians' have won two Sevens World Cup titles, a number of Hong Kong Sevens titles and the 2005/06 IRB Sevens World Series.

Press

From April 2009 until late 2011 the government's infamous PER laws led to censorship across all major newsrooms, while during the 1987 coup the *Fiji Times* famously published a newspaper with large blank spaces to highlight censored articles.

if Fiji were 100 people

57 would be Fijian
38 would be Indo-Fijian

4 would be other (European,
Pacific Islander or Chinese)

belief systems
(% of population)

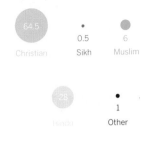

64.5 Christian

0.5 Sikh

6 Muslim

28 Hindu

1 Other

Local Views

While this may sound all doom and gloom, Fijians themselves have a deep well of optimism, and it is their unfailing friendliness and unrestrained warmth that has so endeared them to travellers the world over. Fijians are typically both politically savvy and carefree enough to take such shenanigans in their stride. Many enjoy nothing more than a good debate on the subtle ramifications of the latest government proposal and, now that the PER has been lifted, don't be surprised if newspaper editorials aren't once again choked with letters pouring scorn on surreptitious politicians. The locals are also just as likely to blame irresponsible scaremongering by overseas interests (particularly the New Zealand and Australian governments) as primary reasons for the downturn in their economy as they are their own country's political instability.

» Life expectancy: 71.6 years

» Population below poverty line: 25.5%

» Inflation rate: 8.6%

» Coups since 1987: 4

» Most popular sports: rugby, football, cricket

What Lies Beneath

The 2006 coup underpins one of Fiji's most contentious issues – who qualifies to be a 'Fijian' and enjoy the rights that go with it? In the late 1870s Britain brought indentured Indian labourers to work the sugarcane fields. More than 130 years on Indo-Fijians are still not entitled to the civil liberties that are the right of indigenous Fijians. Today the tension between the ethnic Fijian landowners and the entrepreneurial Indo-Fijians is one of the key problems facing Fiji. Fearful of an Indian-led government, many Fijian landowners have refused to renew Indo-Fijian sugar-cane farmers' land leases. Farmers and their families have suddenly found themselves homeless, and have drifted into a cycle of poverty in squatters' camps around the main centres. Meanwhile, a declining sugar yield and the EU's decision to cut sugar subsidies is dealing a double blow of woe to Fiji's beleaguered main industry.

'Fiji Time'

Fijians are noteworthy for their elastic sense of time; for some travellers the transition between the fast-food, quick-fix West and the chilled-out, take-it-as-it-comes islands can be frustrating. This languid pace is called 'Fiji time' and it refers as much to a philosophy of *kerekere* (a concept that time and property is communal) as to anything that can be read off a clock.

Fiji on Film

Fiji's cobalt-blue waters have provided cinematic eye candy for:

Cast Away (2000)
Starring Tom Hanks

The Blue Lagoon (1979)
Starring Brooke Shields

Contact (1997)
Starring Jodie Foster

History

The Fijian islands are strewn across the Pacific's southwest corner like a rash of green spots on the skin of a blue giant, and it is the vastness of that mighty ocean that has defined, shaped, hindered and helped the country become the nation it is today. Up until relatively recently the ocean represented a formable barrier for human expansion and it wasn't until 3500 years ago – a mere blink of an eye in historical terms – that Fiji first felt a human footfall.

Since then its location at the 'crossroads of the Pacific' has had a profound influence on the cultural development of the archipelago. The southeast trade winds blew in Tongan warlords and with them came Polynesian customs to temper Melanesian traditions. It was also the Tongans who gave the islands their name. The story goes that when Captain James Cook asked the Tongans what the islands to their west were called, he heard them reply 'Feegee', the Tongan pronunciation of Viti. Therefore the country we now know as 'Fiji' owes its name to an Englishman's mishearing of a Tongan's mispronunciation.

Early Arrivals

According to oral folklore, the indigenous Fijians of today are descendants of the chief Lutunasobasoba who, along with his companions, reached Vuda (near Lautoka on Viti Levu) in their canoe *Kaunitoni*. Though this story hasn't been independently substantiated, the Fijian government officially promotes it, and many tribes today claim to be descended from Fiji's first chief.

In academic circles debate continues as to exactly when and how Fiji was colonised, but most agree that Fiji was settled by a wave or waves of Polynesians and Melanesians from Papua New Guinea who had descended from earlier Austronesian migrations from Southeast Asia. Archaeological findings suggest Fiji's original inhabitants were Polynesians, who arrived about 1220 BC and stayed for only a short time before myste-

TIMELINE	1220 BC	500 BC	AD 1000
	The Austronesian people arrive, choosing to settle only along the coast and to live off fishing, just as they did in Tonga before gradually moving to Samoa.	Melanesians from elsewhere in the Pacific arrive and begin permanent settlement, which includes moving inland and establishing farms and other more sustainable ways of life.	Tongan and Samoan warriors begin a series of incursions into Vitian territory, forcing Fijians to create fortified sites and adopt a warlike lifestyle.

TABUA

Tabua (carefully polished and shaped whales' teeth) were believed to be shrines for the ancestor spirits. They were, and still are, highly valued items and essential to diplomacy. The acceptance of a *tabua,* which is a powerful *sevusevu* (a gift presented as a token of esteem or atonement), binds a chief to the gift-giver. Traditionally, a chief's body was accompanied to the grave by a *tabua.*

Originally *tabua* were rare, obtained only from washed-up sperm whales or through trade with Tonga. However, European traders introduced thousands of whale teeth and replicas made of whalebone, elephant tusk and walrus tusk. These negotiation tools became concentrated in the hands of a few dominant chiefdoms, increasing their power.

riously disappearing from the archaeological record. It is theorised that a thousand years later new arrivals from Melanesia assimilated, displaced or killed the descendants of the first Polynesian colonists and it was the blending of these two cultures that gave rise to the indigenous Fijian culture of today.

Around 500 BC a shift from a coastal, fishing lifestyle towards agriculture occurred, along with an expansion of population – probably due to further immigration from other parts of Melanesia – that led to an increase in intertribal feuding. Cannibalism became a ritual for humiliating defeated foes. New architecture developed around this martial culture, with villages moving to ring moat-fortified sites during times of war. Around AD 1000 Tongan incursions began, continuing until the arrival of Europeans.

While there were extended periods of peace, Fiji was undergoing intense social upheaval at the time of the first European settlement in the early 19th century, and these regular tribal skirmishes led Europeans to believe that it was in a constant state of war.

When Cultures Collide

By the early 19th century Europeans were in regular contact with indigenous Fijians: some were washed ashore in shipwrecks, some came to plunder natural resources and some to spread the word of God. With them came new technologies, religions, languages and, eventually, an entire new workforce. All have left an indelible mark on Fiji.

Early European Encounters

Europeans sailed the Pacific during the 17th and 18th centuries, ostensibly to find *terra australis incognita,* the great 'unknown southern land' later called Australia. Some of them bumped into Fiji on the way.

The first traders to reach Fiji were Tongan who came to trade colourful kula (a type of parrot) feathers, *masi* (printed bark cloth) and weapons with the eastern Fiji islands.

1643	1774	1789
Dutchman Abel Tasman's ship is almost wrecked off the northern islands; he manages to chart the eastern portion of Vanua Levu so that others can avoid it.	After landing at Australia, Captain Cook visits – although he limits his contact, due to the islands' reputation as the Cannibal Isles.	Captain William Bligh and 18 others make rough navigation charts while drifting between the Vitian islands after being cast adrift near Tonga following the *Bounty* mutiny.

POPPERFOTO / GETTYIMAGES ©

» Captain James Cook

The first European to sail the area was a Dutchman, Abel Tasman, who sailed past in 1643 on his way back from Van Diemen's Land. His descriptions of treacherous reefs kept mariners away for the next 130 years. English navigator James Cook stopped over on Vatoa in the southern Lau Group in 1774 and his countryman, Captain Bligh, passed between Vanua Levu and Viti Levu after he was thrown off the *Bounty* in 1789. The channel is known as Bligh Water in memory of the mutinied captain.

By the early 19th century European whalers and traders of sandalwood and bêche-de-mer began to visit as better maps of the surrounding reefs were developed. Fragrant sandalwood was highly valued in Europe and Southeast Asia. Tongans initially controlled the trade, obtaining sandalwood from the chiefs on Vanua Levu and then selling it to the Europeans, but when a shipwrecked survivor of the *Argo*, Oliver Slater, discovered the location of the supply, news quickly spread of its whereabouts. In 1805 Europeans began to trade directly with Fijians, bartering metal tools, tobacco, cloth, muskets and gunpowder. By 1813 the sandalwood supply was exhausted, but firearms and the resulting increase in violent tribal warfare were lasting consequences.

The other commodity that brought trade to the area, bêche-de-mer, was an Asian delicacy. The intensive harvesting and drying required to process the seafood required hundreds of workers at each bêche-de-mer station. Chiefs who sent their villagers to work boosted their own wealth and power, with an estimated 5000 muskets traded during this period. Bêche-de-mer was a short-lived trade, lasting only from 1830 to 1850.

In ancient times a war club was a warrior's most treasured possession and came in many forms. Some were bulbous, ideal for braining your opponent, while others were designed to be thrown or jabbed. Clubs that had killed many acquired their own *mana* (prestige) and were both feared and revered.

CHIEF CAKOBAU: KING OF FIJI

By 1829 the chiefdom of Bau, in eastern Viti Levu where European trade was most intense, had accumulated great power. Chief Seru Epenisa Cakobau was at the height of his influence by the 1850s and asserted himself as the king of Fiji *(Tui Viti)*, although this claim wasn't accepted by all chiefs and many regarded him as, at best, first among equals. Despite having no real claim over most of Fiji, this did not deter him from offering to sell the islands to Britain.

By 1862 Cakobau needed some serious allies, both militarily and financially, and he again proposed to Britain's consul that he would cede the islands to Queen Victoria in return for the payment of his debts. The consul declined, doubting Cakobau's claims on the kingdom, but the rumours caused a large influx of settlers to Levuka, who bickered among themselves. Disputes also erupted with Fijians over land ownership and the town became a lawless and greedy outpost, on the verge of anarchy and racial war.

And what of Cakobau's huge debt? This was not cleared until 1868 when the Australian Polynesia Company agreed to pay it in exchange for land.

1804	1822	1830	1840
After trading with Tongans, Europeans discover sandalwood on Vanua Levu and begin a direct trade, which utterly depletes the supply by 1813; some chiefs become briefly wealthy.	Fiji's first modern town, Levuka, is established by European settlers. Its population consists mostly of traders, missionaries, shipwrights, opportunists and drifters.	The first London Missionary Society pastors arrive from Tahiti and begin to devise a written language, which they will teach in schools and use to record early-contact culture.	The first US navy visit, commanded by Captain Charles Wilkes, occurs; an incident at Malolo island results in the deaths of two sailors and over 70 Fijians.

A New God

In the 1830s London Missionary Society (LMS) pastors and Wesleyan Methodist missionaries arrived in southern Lau to find converts and preach against cannibalism.

Conversion of chiefs became the most successful strategy, with the powerful Cakobau adopting Christianity in 1854. Acceptance of Christianity was further made palatable by its similarity with existing beliefs of *tabu* (sacred prohibitions) and *mana* (spiritual power). Early adoption, however, usually meant that Christianity was tempered with traditional spirituality rather than supplanting it outright. Villagers attended church but also continued to worship ancestral gods through such practices as the kava ceremony, and codes of conduct.

Commercial Settlers

A whaling settlement was established at Levuka, on Ovalau, in the 1830s, and became a major port in the South Pacific for traders and warships. In 1840 Charles Wilkes led a US expedition that produced the first reasonably complete chart of the Fijian islands. He also negotiated a port-regulation treaty under which Cakobau and his subchiefs were paid for the protection of foreign ships and the supply of provisions.

However, this seemingly mutually beneficial relationship was fraught with tension. Relations began to deteriorate in 1841 when Levuka was razed by fires, which the settlers suspected Cakobau of instigating. Later, during the 1849 US Independence Day celebrations, the Nukulau island home of US consul John Brown Williams was also destroyed by fire, and locals helped themselves to his possessions. Williams held Cakobau (as nominal king of Fiji) responsible for the actions of his people and sent him a substantial damages bill, which was a significant source of Cakobau's debts.

Blackbirding

When the American Civil War created a worldwide cotton shortage, Fiji enjoyed a cotton boom that indirectly stimulated blackbirding, a trade in labourers. Europeans brought other Pacific Islanders, particularly from the Solomon Islands and New Hebrides (now Vanuatu), to labour on the Fijian cotton (and copra and sugar) plantations.

Initially, people were coaxed, bribed and tricked into agreeing to work for three years in return for minimal wages, food and clothing. Later, however, chiefs were bribed and men and women traded for ammunition.

On completion of the three-year contract, regulations required that labourers be given passage back to their villages, but more often than not they were dropped at the first island the captain saw fit outside of Fijian territorial waters.

For a clear, concise and readable overview of Fijian and regional history, dip into *Worlds Apart: A History of the Pacific Islands* by IC Campbell.

Samples of Lapita pottery found at the Sigatoka Sand Dunes, which is now open to the public, suggests this was one of the earliest settlements in Viti.

HISTORY WHEN CULTURES COLLIDE

1867

After several conversions in coastal areas, Methodist minister Reverend Thomas Baker heads into the Western Highlands, but villagers disagree with him about his god and the pastor is killed and eaten.

1874

After much debate and negotiation, Cakobau and 12 other chiefs cede Fiji to Queen Victoria and Britain on 10 October in a ceremony at Levuka.

CHRIS HELLIER / ALAMY ©

» Engraving of Chief Ratu Seru Cakobau, 1855

By the 1860s and '70s the practice had developed into an organised system of kidnapping. Stories of the atrocities and abuses inflicted by recruiters resulted in pressure on Britain to stop the trade, and in 1872 the Imperial Kidnapping Act was passed; but it was little more than a gesture, as Britain had no power to enforce it.

The Colonial Period

Missionaries developed written Fijian language – called Bauan – from the dialect spoken in the powerful chiefdom of Bau during the 1830s.

The end of the American Civil War in 1865 brought a slump in the world cotton market, which severely affected the Fijian economy. In the following years new arrivals brought diseases to Fiji, such as measles, which had dramatic effects on the Fijian population.

By 1873 Britain was interested in annexing Fiji, citing the need to abolish blackbirding as justification. In reality, they were also interested in protecting Commonwealth commercial interests and bailing out an economy that was drastically overspent. Taking advantage of this interest, Cakobau, who had acquired new debt, again approached the British consul to cede the islands to Queen Victoria. Besides financial stability, Cakobau believed cession to British rule would also bring Christianity and civilisation to the islands. Fiji was pronounced a British crown colony on 10 October 1874, at Levuka.

THE REVEREND BAKER'S LAST SUPPER

Thomas Baker, a Wesleyan Methodist missionary, was killed on 21 July 1867 by the Vatusila people of Nabutautau village deep in the isolated Nausori Highlands. A few years earlier Baker had been given the task of converting the people of the interior to Christianity. Baker's predecessors had been able to convert many groups peacefully and he was advised to keep to these areas. But whether due to impatience, martyrdom, foolhardiness or the urge for success, he ignored the advice and with it crucial cultural know-how.

The highlanders associated conversion to Christianity with subservience to the chiefdom of Bau. As they were opposed to any kind of extended authority, knocking off the reverend may well have been a political manoeuvre. However, a second and more widely believed theory maintains that it was Baker's own behaviour that brought about his nasty end. Apparently, the local chief had borrowed Baker's comb to festoon his voluptuous hairdo. Insensitive or forgetful of the fact that the chief's head was considered sacred, Baker grabbed the comb from the chief's hair. Villagers were furious at the missionary for committing this sacrilege and killed and ate him and seven of his followers in disgust.

In 2003, believing they had suffered a curse of bad luck as a result of their ancestors' culinary habits, the people of Nabutautau held a tribal ceremony to apologise to the descendants of the missionary. Around 600 people attended, including Thomas Baker's great-great-grandson and Prime Minister Lasenia Qarase.

1875	1879	1882	1916
Without the benefit of the immunity that Europeans had built up to the disease, a third of the population is killed by a savage measles outbreak, creating further tensions in the colony.	Following the outlawing of blackbirding, Britain introduces the first group of girmitiyas (Indian indentured labourers) to work in the labour-intensive sugar-cane fields of the main island.	As Levuka's difficult geography impedes further expansion, the government is forced to relocate; Suva officially becomes the capital, although the town has barely a dozen buildings.	The importation of indentured Indian labourers ends after agitation within India and the visit to Fiji by Anglican clergyman Rev Charles Freer Andrews.

From Girmitiyas to Indo-Fijians

To maintain good relations with its subjects, the colonial government combated exploitation of indigenous Fijians by prohibiting their employment as plantation labourers. However, plantation crops such as cotton, copra and sugar cane, while extremely profitable, demanded large pools of cheap labour. If the colony were to avoid blackbirding then a new labour source had to be found.

In 1878 negotiations were entered into with the Indian colonial government for indentured labourers to come to Fiji on five-year contracts. After this term the labourers (known as girmitiyas) would be free to return home. Indian indentured labourers soon began arriving in Fiji, at a rate of about 2000 per year.

The girmitiyas were a diverse group from all over India, with 80% Hindu, 14% Muslim and the remainder mostly Sikhs and Christians. Overcrowded accommodation gave little privacy, different castes and religions were forced to mix, and social and religious structures crumbled. Despite the hardship, most girmitiyas decided to stay in Fiji once they had served their contract and many brought their families from India to join them.

By the early 1900s India's colonial government was being pressured by antislavery groups in Britain to abolish the indenture system. In 1916 recruitment stopped and indenture ended officially in January 1919. By this time 60,537 indentured labourers were in Fiji.

Fiji's first coup took place 108 years to the day after the arrival of the *Leonidas* carrying the first group of Indian indentured labourers.

Independence & the New Political Landscape

The 1960s saw a movement towards Fijian self-government and, after 96 years of colonial administration, Fiji became independent on 10 October 1970. In the rush towards independence, important problems such as land ownership and leases and how to protect the interests of a racially divided country were not resolved. Despite an economic boom in the immediate post-independence years, by the early 1980s the price of sugar had fallen and the country's dependence on it resulted in massive foreign debt.

Economic woes exacerbated ethnic tensions. In Fiji most shops and transport services were (and still are) run by Indo-Fijian families. Stereotypes developed portraying Indo-Fijians as money obsessed, despite the fact that most belonged to poorer working classes and Indo-Fijians – unlike indigenous Fijians – could never secure land tenure on their farming leases.

Fiji's first government (the Fijian Alliance Party) became associated with economic failure, and greater unity among workers led to the formation of the Fiji Labour Party (FLP). In April 1987 an FLP government was elected in coalition with the National Federation Party (NFP). Despite having an indigenous Fijian prime minister, Timoci Bavadra, and a cabinet comprising an indigenous Fijian majority, the new government

Contact with the firearms and diseases of Europeans had a marked impact on Fiji's ethnic population, which has only recently returned to its 18th-century level.

HISTORY INDEPENDENCE & THE NEW POLITICAL LANDSCAPE

1951	1958	1963	1970
Fiji Airways, called Air Pacific since 1971, is founded by Australian aviator Harold Gatty, offering one of the first services to another new capital, Canberra, Australia.	Fiji's favourite statesman, Ratu Sir Lal Sukana, dies. Born a chief of the Bau Royal House, he is best remembered for his tireless work creating the Native Land Trust Board.	Indigenous Fijian men and women are given the vote, and the 38-member Legislative Council is divided almost equally into indigenous Fijian, Indo-Fijian and European groups.	After 96 years of colonial rule Fiji becomes independent (on 10 October), adopting a British model of parliament with two houses, including a 'House of Lords' made up of Fijian chiefs.

was labelled 'Indian dominated' because the majority of its MPs were Indo-Fijian.

The Early Coups

With the FLP labelled 'Indian dominated', racial tensions got out of hand. The extremist Taukei movement played on Fijian fears of losing their land rights and of Indo-Fijian political and economic domination. On 14 May 1987, one month after the elections, Lieutenant Colonel Sitiveni Rabuka took over from the elected government in a bloodless coup, and formed a civil interim government supported by the Great Council of Chiefs.

In September 1987 Rabuka again intervened with military force. The 1970 constitution was invalidated, Fiji was declared a republic and Rabuka proclaimed himself head of state. The following month Fiji was dismissed from the Commonwealth of Nations.

The coups returned power to an elite minority, with Indo-Fijians effectively removed from the political process. Conflicts resurfaced: between chiefs from eastern and western Fiji, between high chiefs and village chiefs, between urban and rural dwellers, and within the church and trade-union movement. Economically the coups were disastrous, with the two main industries, tourism and sugar, severely affected. Development aid was suspended, and from 1987 to 1992 about 50,000 people, mostly Indo-Fijians, emigrated.

For daily news, views and sports check out *Fiji Village* (www. fijivillage.com), a Fijian-based media source that remains surprisingly honest.

Rewriting the Constitution

In 1995 a Constitutional Review Commission (CRC) presented its findings. It called for a return to a multiethnic democracy and, while concluding that the position of president should be reserved for an indigenous Fijian, proposed no restriction on ethnicity for the prime minister.

FIJI IN ARMS

Fiji had only a minor involvement in WWI, as colonial authorities prevented many Fijians from enlisting. Nevertheless, about 700 of Fiji's European residents and about 100 Fijians served in Europe.

The conflict in the Pacific during WWII was much closer to home. Fiji itself was used as an Allied training base from an airstrip at Nadi that today has become the international airport. Around 8000 Fijians were recruited into the Fiji Military Force (FMF) and from 1942 to 1943 fought against the Japanese in the Solomon Islands.

Today Fiji, considering its size, has fairly large armed forces, and has been a surprisingly major contributor to UN peacekeeping missions in various parts of the world; in 2004 Fiji was the first country to volunteer troops to protect UN officials in Iraq.

1977	1979	1987	1990
The National Federation Party wins an election but fails to put together a government, so election results are overturned by the governor-general. The following election is a landslide for the Alliance Party.	A remake of *The Blue Lagoon*, in the Yasawas, catapults Brooke Shields to teenage stardom and puts Fiji on the top of the romantic-holiday-makers' list.	Two military coups take place in quick succession under the leadership of Lieutenant Colonel Sitiveni Rabuka; Fiji is expelled from the Commonwealth and becomes a republic.	A new constitution is created, which asserts ethnic Fijians' role in the political system, marginalises Indo-Fijians and reserves two seats for the army in the cabinet.

WHERE ARE THE CHIEFS?

One of Fiji's most powerful institutions was the Great Council of Chiefs, which was founded by British colonisers in 1876. The Council consists of 55 members, who are mostly hereditary chiefs, charged with safeguarding the political system. It gained even greater power after the military coups of the 1980s and introduction of the 1990 constitution.

When Commodore Frank Bainimarama seized power the Council refused to recognise him, insisting that Lasenia Qarase be present at meetings. Bainimarama suspended, although didn't abolish, the Council in 2007.

The government acted on most of the CRC's recommendations and a new constitution was declared in 1997.

In the same year Rabuka apologised to Queen Elizabeth for the 1987 military coups and presented her with a *tabua* as a gesture of atonement; in the following month Fiji was readmitted to the Commonwealth.

The 2000 Coup

In the May 1999 elections voters rejected Rabuka's SVT. The FLP won the majority of seats and its leader, Mahendra Chaudhry, fleetingly became Fiji's first Indo-Fijian prime minister.

Many indigenous Fijians feared for their traditional land rights and began protesting. Many refused to renew expiring 99-year land leases to Indo-Fijian farmers. On 19 May 2000 armed men entered the parliamentary compound in Suva and took 30 hostages, including Prime Minister Chaudhry. Failed businessman George Speight quickly became the face of the coup, demanding the resignation of Chaudhry and President Ratu Sir Kamisese Mara. He also wanted the 1997 multiethnic constitution rescinded.

Support for Speight was widespread and Indo-Fijians suffered such harassment that many fled the country. With lawlessness increasing and Chaudhry removed from power, the head of Fiji's military, Commodore Josaia Voreqe 'Frank' Bainimarama, instituted martial law. After long negotiations between Speight's rebels and Bainimarama's military, the 1997 constitution was revoked.

In March 2001 the appeal court decided to uphold the 1997 constitution and ordered that Fiji be taken to the polls to restore democracy. Lasenia Qarase, heading the Fijian People's Party (SLD), won 32 of the 71 parliamentary seats in the 2001 elections. Claiming that a multiparty cabinet would be unworkable, Qarase defied the constitution by including no FLP members in his 18-strong cabinet.

In 2006 the discovery of an ancient Fijian village possibly dating back as far as the 13th century brought excitement to the village of Kuku in Nausori. Locals have been rebuilding the site in the hopes of creating a tourist attraction.

1997	1998	2000	2001
Under increasing pressure, Rabuka unveils a new constitution, which calls for a return to multiethnic democracy; this leads to democratic elections and a Bill of Rights that outlaws racial discrimination.	Mahendra Chaudhry becomes the first Indo-Fijian prime minister, promising change, which unnerves many indigenous Fijians and leads to protests in the capital and around the country.	Failed businessman George Speight heads a 19 May coup; 30 hostages are held in parliament for eight weeks as Speight demands the resignation of Mahendra Chaudhry and the president. Speight is later jailed.	In a tough election campaign, interim Prime Minister Lasenia Qarase defeats Mahendra Chaudhry; George Speight (using the name Ilikimi Naitini) is also briefly elected before being prevented from taking his seat.

CANNIBAL

Fiji's most notorious cannibal was Ratu (Chief) Udreudre, the holder of the *Guinness Book of Records* title for the most people eaten: 872.

The 2006 Coup

While Speight's coup was quick, there was much that was unresolved. The Qarase government's draft Promotion of Reconciliation, Tolerance and Unity (PRTU) Bill divided the country during 2004 and 2005. Though the aim was to heal the wounds of the past, opponents saw the amnesty provisions for those involved in the coup as untenable. One of the opponents of the bill, Commodore Frank Bainimarama, presented a list of demands including dropping the PRTU and other controversial bills. He gave a deadline of 4 December 2006 to Qarase, and began military exercises around Suva to support his intention.

Qarase met several of the demands, agreeing to put three contentious bills on ice, but it wasn't enough. On 5 December President Ratu Josefa Iloilo dissolved parliament on Bainimarama's order and Qarase was put under house arrest. Several key groups did not approve of Bainimarama's coup, including the Methodist Church and the Great Council of Chiefs who refused to meet without Qarase and continued to recognise President Iloilo, who Bainimarama had ousted by declaring a state of emergency.

In January 2007 Iloilo was sworn back in as president, though many speculate that he is now purely a figurehead with little influence. In 2009 he annulled the constitution and disbanded the Court of Appeal after it ruled the 2006 coup illegal. The following day he reappointed Bainimarama as interim prime minister.

In 2009 Fiji was suspended from participation in the Pacific Islands Forum and dismissed (again) from the Commonwealth of Nations for failing to return to democracy.

2006	2007	2009	2009
Commodore Frank Bainimarama begins military manoeuvres in Suva that eventually depose the government of Lasenia Qarase; he then declares himself acting president of Fiji.	Bainimarama restores Ratu Josefa Iloilo to the presidency, who in turn appoints Bainimarama prime minister.	The Fijian constitutional crisis sees President Iloilo abrogate the constitution and remove all constitutional office holders including judges. He then reappoints Bainimarama as prime minister under his 'new order'.	Fiji is suspended from both the Pacific Islands Forum and the Commonwealth for failing to hold democratic elections.

The Environment

The Land & Ocean

Fiji has long been defined by the ocean that surrounds it and the vast stretches of the South Pacific have both protected and isolated the locals for much of their history. In Fiji's vast territorial waters, spinning on the periphery around the hub of Viti Levu, are 332 other islands, of which 110 are permanently inhabited.

The Fijian archipelago was formed by a series of complex geographical events, although its principal architect has been the volcanic activity that first started in the region 150 million years ago. Other geological processes led to the formation of coral and limestone islands, and vast colonies of tiny individual animals (coral polyps) have formed coral reefs in the surrounding waters. Fiji's reefs take three different forms: fringing, barrier and atoll.

The country's territorial limits cover an enormous 1.3 million sq km, but only about 18,300 sq km of this – less than 1.5% – is dry land.

Volcanic Islands

Although there are no active volcanoes in Fiji today, it was ancient volcanic activity that gave Fiji its backbone and laid down the building blocks for the creation of further islands.

Fiji's volcanic islands generally have a series of conical hills rising to a central summit. Pinnacles indicate the sites of old volcanoes, with crystallised lava flows reaching the coast as ridges, forming cliffs or bluffs. Between these ridges are green valleys and generally the only flat land to be found on these islands is that found in the valleys' river basins.

Although Viti Levu and Kadavu were both created this way, Fiji's volcanic legacy is best appreciated on Vanua Levu, where locals in Savusavu still use the hot springs to cook in.

Limestone Islands

Limestone islands are characteristically rocky land masses that have risen from the sea. Volcanic materials thrust up through the limestone, and the islands are often made up of cliffs, undercut by the sea and topped with shrubs and trees. Other characteristics include a central depression surrounded by fertile, undulating hills. Vanua Balavu in the Lau Group is a limestone island.

The most notable consequence of global warming in Fiji has been coral bleaching. When physiologically stressed by raised water temperatures, coral loses the symbiotic algae that provide its colour and nutrition. In 2001 and 2002 Fiji's reefs experienced huge amounts of bleaching, affecting 65% of reefs and killing 15%.

Coral Islands

If you're looking for somewhere to swim or snorkel, head to one of Fiji's coral islands. Small and low, they are generally found in areas protected by barrier reefs, with surface levels at the height at which waves and winds can deposit sand and coral fragments. Their coasts have bright, white-sand beaches, and mangroves are found in the lagoon shallows. Examples of coral islands are Beachcomber and Treasure Islands in the Mamanucas, and Leleuvia and Caqalai in the Lomaivitis.

VITI LEVU'S GEOLOGY

Viti Levu, the main island, is 10,390 sq km and includes Fiji's highest point, Tomanivi (1323m; also called Mt Victoria), near the northern end of a range of mountains that separates the island's east and west. This mountain range also acts as a weather barrier; Suva, the country's capital, is located on the island's wetter side, while both Nadi and Lautoka are on the drier, western side of the island.

Scientists maintain that Viti Levu owes its existence to plate tectonics. Volcanoes formed when the Pacific plate was pushed under the Australian plate. Fiji's oral tradition sees things differently. According to legend, the snake-god, Degei, created Viti Levu as a home for the two humans (and their progeny) who hatched from eggs he had found in an abandoned hawk's nest. Degei now sleeps in Viti Levi's Nakauvadra Range and it is the opening and closing of his eyes that prompt day and night.

Fringing Reefs

Narrow fringing reefs link to the shore of an island, stretching seaward, and are exposed during low tide. Often the bigger fringing reefs have higher sections at the open-sea edge and drainage channels on the inside, which remain water-filled and navigable by small boats. Where rivers and streams break the reefs, fresh water prevents coral growth. The Coral Coast on southern Viti Levu is an extensive fringing reef.

Suva's beautiful (but under-resourced) public gardens, opened in 1913, are named after botanist John Bates Thurston, who introduced many ornamental plants to Fiji.

Barrier Reefs

Barrier reefs are large strips of continuous reef, broken only by occasional channels. Fiji's Great Sea Reef extends about 500km from the coast of southwestern Viti Levu to the northernmost point of Vanua Levu. A section of this, lying between 15km and 30km off the coast of Vanua Levu, is unbroken for more than 150km. The Great Astrolabe Reef circling Kadavu is a barrier reef, as are the smaller reefs encircling Beqa.

Atolls

Atolls are small rings of coral reef with land and vegetation on top, just above sea level and enclosing a lagoon. Despite their idyllic representation in tales of the South Pacific, most have inhospitable environments. The porous soil derived from dead coral, sand and driftwood retains little water and is often subject to drought. The vegetation is made up of hardy pandanus, coconut palms, shrubs and coarse grasses. Of Fiji's few atolls the best-known is Wailagi Lala in the Lau Group.

Top Birding Spots

» Bouma National Park

» Colo-i-Suva Forest Park

» Tunuloa Silktail Reserve

» Des Voeux Peak

Wildlife

Like many isolated oceanic islands, Fiji's native wildlife includes a few gems but is otherwise relatively sparse. Many of the plants and animals are related to those of Indonesia and Malaysia, and are thought to have drifted in on the winds and tides.

Native Animals

The only native terrestrial mammals in Fiji are six species of bat, of which you'll almost certainly see *beka* (large fruit bats or flying foxes) flying out at sunset to feed, or roosting during the day in colonies in tall trees. Two species of insectivorous bats are cave dwellers and are seldom seen.

Over 130 species of birds live or pass through Fiji, making birdlife the main wildlife attraction; birdwatching is best during the dry season. There are 27 endemics including beautiful members of the pigeon (orange doves) and parrot (including the widespread collared lory) families.

Fiji's 27 species of reptiles are mostly lizards. The endemic crested iguana, identified in 1979, is found on the Yasawas and on Yadua Taba off the west coast of Vanua Levu. Its ancestors are thought to have floated to Fiji on vegetation from South America. There are also two terrestrial snakes – a small, nonpoisonous Pacific boa and the Fiji burrowing snake.

Introduced Animals

Besides the bats, all other land-dwelling mammals have been introduced from elsewhere. More than 3500 years ago the first settlers introduced poultry, Polynesian rats, dogs and pigs to Fiji. In the 19th century Europeans brought additional domestic animals and, inadvertently but inevitably, brought brown and black rats and house mice.

The common Indian mongoose was introduced in 1883 to control rats in sugar-cane plantations. Unfortunately, the mongoose mostly chose to eat Fiji's native snakes, frogs, birds and eggs, while the rats continued to prosper.

Undaunted by the consequences of these early introductions, authorities imported the cane toad in 1936 to control insects in the cane plantations. It too has now become a pest, preying upon native ground frogs in coastal and lowland regions, as well as competing with them for food.

In 2000 a small number of common iguana (known locally as the American iguana) were smuggled into Fiji and released on Qamea Island. They have since spread to several other islands, including Taveuni, and environmentalists predict far-reaching consequences on the ecosystem.

Marine Life

Fiji's richest animal life is underwater. There are hundreds of species of hard and soft coral, sea fans and sponges, often intensely colourful and fantastically shaped.

As coral needs sunlight and oxygen to survive, it's restricted to depths of less than 50m. Corals on a reef break are generally of the densely packed varieties, such as brain coral (which looks like a human brain), which are able to resist the force of the surf. Fragile corals such as staghorn grow in lagoons where the water is quieter.

Fiji's tropical fish are exquisite. Among the many you're likely to see are yellow-and-black butterflyfish; coral-chomping, blue-green parrotfish; wraithlike needlefish; and tiny, territorial, black-and-white clownfish guarding their anemone homes. Fat-fingered blue starfish and delicate feathered starfish are common. Some marine creatures, such as fire corals, scorpionfish and lionfish, are highly venomous; if in doubt, don't touch! And watch where you put your bare feet.

Of the four sea snakes found in Fiji most are rarely seen, except for the *dadakulaci* (banded sea krait), which occasionally enters freshwater inlets to mate and lay its eggs on land. Although the *dadakulaci* are placid and can't open their jaws wide enough to bite humans, their venom is highly poisonous so it is worth being careful around them.

Five turtle species are found in Fijian waters: the hawksbill, loggerhead, green (named after the colour of its fat), Pacific Ridley and leatherback.

Plants

Most of Fiji is lush with fragrant flowers and giant, leafy plants and trees; 1596 plant species have been identified, of which about 60% are endemic. Many are used for food, medicine, implements and building materials.

Rainforest Plants

Forest giants include valuable timbers such as *dakua* (Fijian kauri), a hard, durable timber with a beautiful grain used for furniture making. Of the many different fern species in Fiji, a number are edible and known as *ota*.

You'll see *noni* (evergreen) products – cordials and soaps – for sale throughout Fiji. *Noni* produce a warty, foul-smelling, bitter-tasting fruit,

THE ENVIRONMENT WILDLIFE

Can't tell a batfish from a butterflyfish? *Tropical Reef Life – a Getting to Know You & Identification Guide,* by Michael Aw, gives an informally detailed overview of underwater life, plus photographic tips.

RESPECT & PROTECT

Many of Fiji's endangered animals and plants are protected by the Convention on International Trade in Endangered Species (CITES). Others are protected by national legislation. If you buy a souvenir made from a protected or endangered species and don't get a permit, you're breaking the law and chances are that customs will confiscate it at your overseas destination. In particular, remember the following:

» *Tabua* are *tabu* (sacred) – whale's teeth are protected.

» Turtle shell looks best on live turtles.

» Leave seashells on the seashore; protected species include giant clams, helmet shells, trochus and tritons.

» Tread lightly. Stepping on live coral is like stepping on a live budgie: you'll kill it.

» Many plants, including most orchids, are protected.

Trash & Carry

Your litter will become someone else's problem, especially on small islands; where possible, recycle or remove your own.

Don't Rush to Flush

Fresh water is precious everywhere, especially on small islands; take short showers and drink boiled or rainwater rather than buy another plastic bottle.

which, despite its unattractive properties, is gaining credibility worldwide for its ability to help relieve complaints including arthritis, chronic fatigue, high blood pressure, rheumatism and digestive disorders.

The *tagimaucia,* with its white petals and bright red branches, is Fiji's national flower. It only grows at high altitudes on the island of Taveuni and on one mountain on Vanua Levu.

Coastal & River Plants

Mangroves are the most distinctive plant communities along the coasts of Fiji. They provide important protection against erosion for seashores, and are breeding grounds for prawns and crabs.

Casuarina, also known as ironwood or *nokonoko,* grows on sandy beaches and atolls. As its name suggests, the timber is heavy and strong and was used to make war clubs and parts of canoes.

An icon of the tropics, the coconut palm continues to support human settlement. Coconuts provide food and drink, shells are used for making cups and charcoal, leaves are used for baskets and mats, and oil is used for cooking and lighting, and as body and hair lotion.

Other common coastal plants include the beach morning glory, with its dawn-blooming purple flowers, the beach hibiscus, with its large, yellow flowers, and the night-flowering *vutu* tree.

National Parks & Reserves

Fiji has several protected conservation areas, though lack of resources means that conservation is difficult. The Bouma National Heritage Park and Ravilevu Nature Reserve now protect over 40% of Taveuni and contain some well-maintained walking tracks. Koroyanitu National Heritage Park, near Lautoka in the highlands of Viti Levu, is also well established.

Other significant sites include the Sigatoka Sand Dunes on Viti Levu's Coral Coast, Colo-i-Suva Park and Garrick Reserve near Suva, and Tunuloa Silktail Reserve near Navua on Vanua Levu. For permits to go to Yadua Taba (home to the crested iguana), Garrick Reserve and several other sites of ecological and historical importance you will need to contact the National Trust for Fiji in Suva.

Fijian Culture

It's true – loincloths, grass skirts, cannibalism, old beliefs and traditional sports have given way to *sulu* and Western clothing, Christianity and rugby. But Fijian culture is alive and well. Traditional core values of respect, communal living, sex-defined roles and hereditary titles still underpin indigenous Fijian culture, and traditional arts such as woodcarving and weaving are as vibrant as ever. Gardening and fishing continue to put food on Fijian tables (or should that be pandanus mats?).

This chapter explores the indigenous Fijian culture and the 57% of the population it represents. The following chapter, Indo-Fijian Culture (p217), looks at the rich tapestry of customs the Indian indentured labourers brought to these islands.

Indigenous Fijians

In most places you go in Fiji you'll be met with a cheery '*bula*' (cheers! hello! welcome!; literally 'life') and a toothy grin. Fijians welcome *kaivalagi* (foreigners; literally 'people from far away') warmly, openly and at times positively enthusiastically. Consequently, Fijians have earned themselves a reputation as some of the friendliest people on earth; it's a reputation that is well deserved.

Face-to-face confrontation is rare and frowned upon in Fiji. Village life is subject to complex rules of etiquette and land (*vanua*) is owned collectively by the community and cherished. Consequently, it is seldom sold.

Unlike other Melanesian societies where chiefs are appointed on merit, in Fiji a chief's position is hereditary (though the title may past to a kinsman and not necessarily the chief's own son or daughter). This is common in nearby Polynesian societies and illustrates how Fiji, as the crossroads of the Pacific, has been influenced by those around it, most notably the Tongans and Rotumans.

At the moment only a person of indigenous Fijian decent has the lawful right to be called 'Fijian'. Indo-Fijians who have lived in Fiji for several generations are referred to as 'Indian' and all other Fiji nationals are similarly referred to by the nationality of their ancestors.

Arts

Traditional arts and crafts such as woodcarving and weaving, along with dancing and music, remain an integral part of life in many villages and a major tourist attraction. These traditions have inspired much of the small but thriving Fijian contemporary arts scene, of which Suva is the epicentre.

The University of the South Pacific's Oceania Centre for Arts & Culture in Suva provides working space for artists, musicians and dancers. The Fiji Arts Club has an annual exhibition, usually in August or September, in Suva. Suva is also the literary hub for Fiji, hosting occasional readings by members of the Pacific Writing Forum, and performances of work by Fijian playwrights and poets.

Pottery

Pottery is thought to have initially been brought to Fiji by the Lapita people over 3000 years ago, and some modern potters still use traditional techniques. The pots are beaten into shape with wooden paddles of various shapes and sizes, while the form is held from within using a pebble anvil. Coil and slab-building techniques are also used. Once dried, pots are fired outdoors in an open blaze on coconut husks, and are often sealed with resin varnish taken from the *dakua* tree.

Woodcarving

Traditional woodcarving skills are largely kept alive by the tourist trade, providing a ready market for war clubs, spears and cannibal forks. *Tanoa* (drinking bowls) and *bilo* (kava cups of coconut shell) remain part of everyday life. *Tanoa* shaped like turtles are thought to have derived from turtle-shaped *ibuburau,* vessels used in indigenous Vitian *yaqona* rites.

Bark Cloth

Masi (also known as *malo* or *tapa*) is bark cloth with rust-coloured and black printed designs. In Vitian culture *masi* was invested with status and associated with celebrations and rituals. It was worn as a loincloth by men during initiation rituals and renaming ceremonies, and as an adornment in dance, festivity and war. *Masi* was also an important exchange item, used in bonding ceremonies between related tribes. Chiefs were swathed in a huge puffball of *masi,* later given to members of the other tribe.

While men wore the *masi,* production has traditionally been by women. Made from the inner white bark of the paper mulberry bush that has been soaked in water and scraped clean, it's then beaten and felted for hours into sheets of a fine, even texture. Intricate designs are added by hand or stencil and often carry symbolic meaning. Rust-coloured paints are traditionally made from an infusion of candlenut and mangrove bark; pinker browns are made from red clays; and black from the soot of burnt *dakua* resin and charred candlenuts.

It is difficult to see *masi* being made, though you'll see the end product used for postcards, wall hangings and other decorative items. Textile designers have begun incorporating traditional *masi* motifs in their fabrics.

See Traditional Potters at Work

» Nakabuta

» Nasilai

» Fiji Museum (Tuesdays and Thursdays)

Mat & Basket Weaving

Most indigenous Fijian homes use woven *voivoi* (pandanus leaf) to make baskets, floor coverings and fine sleeping mats. Traditionally, girls living in villages learned to weave and many still do. Pandanus leaves are cut and laid outdoors to cure, stripped of the spiny edges, and boiled and dried. The traditional method of blackening leaves for contrasting patterns is to bury them in mud for days before reboiling. The dried leaves are made flexible by scraping with shells and then split into strips of about 1cm to 2cm and woven. Mat borders are now often decorated with brightly coloured wools instead of the more traditional parrot feathers.

Fiji's Treasured Culture (www.museum.vic.gov.au/fiji) is an online exhibition of fabulous artefacts held in Museum Victoria (in Melbourne, Australia) and Suva's Fiji Museum.

Music & Dance

Fiji has an active music scene influenced by reggae, hip hop and rock. Popular older acts include Seru Serevi, Lia Osborne and Daniel Rae Costello, and bands such as Delai Sea and Voqa ni Delai Dokidoki. Black Rose is one of Fiji's most successful rock bands. For most Fijian musicians, such as rappers D Kamali who moved to Auckland or Hawaiian-based performer Fiji, success means moving overseas.

Meke

Most visitors first encounter Fijian dance when they're welcomed at resorts and hotels with *meke,* a performance that enacts ancient lore. Traditionally, *meke* were accompanied by a chanting chorus or by 'spiritually possessed seers'. Rhythm was supplied by clapping, the thumping and

MELODIOUS MEASURES

Replaced by guitars and keyboards, traditional indigenous instruments are a rare find in Fiji these days. Yet once upon a time, nose flutes were all the rage. Made from a single piece of bamboo, some 70cm long, the flute would be intricately carved and played by your typical laid-back Fijian, reclining on a pandanus mat and resting his or her head on a bamboo pillow. Whether it was the music or the pose, flutes were believed to have the power to attract the opposite sex and were a favourite for serenading.

Other traditional instruments had more practical purposes, such as shell trumpets and whistles, which were used for communication. Portable war drums were used as warnings and for communicating tactics on the battlefield. One instrument you are still likely to see (and hear) is the *lali*, a large slit drum made of resonant timbers. Audible over large distances, its deep call continues to beckon people to the chief's *bure* or to church.

stamping of bamboo clacking sticks and the beating of slit drums. The whole community participated in *meke*. In times of war, men performed the *cibi* (death dance), and women the *dele* or *wate,* a dance in which they sexually humiliated enemy corpses and captives. Dancing often took place by moonlight or torchlight, with the performers in costume, their bodies oiled, faces painted and combs and flowers decorating their hair.

Vilavilairevo (Fire-Walking)

Although famous throughout Fiji and performed in many of the Coral Coast resorts, *vilvilairevo* (fire-walking) was originally performed only by the Sawau tribe of Beqa, an island off Viti Levu's southern coast. Traditionally, strict taboos dictated the men's behaviour leading up to the ceremony and it was believed adherence to these protected them from burns. See the boxed text, p89, for further details.

Architecture

Since colonial times some communities have grown to sizeable towns and small cities. Today these urban centres are more heavily influenced by modern building practices than rural villages, which still retain some aspects of traditional architecture.

Traditional

Fijian villagers once resided in traditional thatched dwellings known as *bure*. In the past these homes were dark and smoky inside, with no windows, usually only one low door and hearth pits for cooking. The packed-earth floor was covered with grass or fern leaves and then finely woven pandanus-leaf or coarse coconut-leaf mats. Sleeping compartments were at one end, behind a bark-cloth curtain, with wooden headrests.

Traditional *bure* are usually rectangular in plan, with timber poles and a hipped or gabled roof structure lashed together with coconut-fibre string. Thatch, woven coconut leaves or split bamboo is used as wall cladding, and roofs are thatched with grass or coconut leaves. Most villages still have some traditional-style *bure* but, as village life adapts and changes and natural materials become scarcer, most Fijians find it easier and cheaper to use concrete blocks, corrugated iron and even flattened oil drums.

Colonial

Historic Levuka was once the capital of Fiji and has been nominated for World Heritage listing. A number of its buildings date from its heyday of the late 19th century, particularly the main street, which is surprisingly intact.

The village of Navala, nestled in the Viti Levu highlands, is an exemplar of traditional Fijian architecture. It's the only village remaining where every home is a *bure*.

ays of the old religion, every village had a *bure kalou* (ancient temple), which was
d as a meeting house. These buildings had a high-pitched roof and usually stood
on terraced foundations. The *bete* (priest), who was an intermediary between the villagers
and spirits, lived in the temple and performed various rituals, including feasting on slain
enemies and burying important people. A strip of white *masi* (bark cloth) was usually hung
from the ceiling, to serve as a connection to the spirits. The construction of such a temple
reputedly required that a strong man be buried alive in each of the corner-post holes.

The British influence on Suva is reflected in its many grand colonial buildings, including Government House, Suva City Library and the
Grand Pacific Hotel (see the boxed text, p95).

Sport

Almost a religion among indigenous Fijians, rugby union is the one sport
that has continually put Fiji on the world stage since the first match between Fijian and British soldiers in 1884. Fijians are prized internationally as players, often having contracts in Europe, NZ or Australia that
prevent them from playing for Fiji. Still, Fiji has won the most Pacific
Tri-Nations titles and is a tough draw for any international side.

The rugby season is from April to September and every village in Viti
Levu seems to have its own rugby field. Even if you're not a footy fan, it's
worth going to a local Friday afternoon or Saturday morning match just
to watch the excited crowd.

Soccer (football), a favourite in the Indo-Fijian community, is also on
the up and up with indigenous Fijians.

Netball has the same popularity among Fiji's women as rugby does
with men. The Fijian team is consistently in the top 10 in the world and
you'll see local games on weekends throughout the islands.

Church

Since the 1830s Christianity has been developing in Fiji and remains an
important part of cultural and political life. Indigenous Fijians maintain
their traditional culture, but practices such as cannibalism and ancestor
worship were erased by Christian values long ago.

Today 53% of Fijians are Christian, the majority of whom (about 34%)
are Methodist, and the church remains a powerful force in internal affairs. There's a Catholic minority of around 7%, and evangelical Christian
churches are becoming increasingly popular.

Religion and politics have often gone hand in hand in Fiji and church
approval is often sought as a way of legitimising power structures, particularly after coups. However, there are now calls for a greater separation
between church and state, and the current differences between Commodore Frank Bainimarama and the powerful Methodist church may assist
implementation of this profound change.

Sunday is a day to worship and rest and a time spent with family. Most
businesses close for the day and streets are deserted. If you find yourself
at loose ends, consider attending a Sunday service. It is a real treat; Fijians love to sing and choir groups don't hold back. Many resorts now
incorporate church services into their cultural tours.

Fiji is more urban-
ised that many
might imagine
and two-thirds of
the population
now live in urban
centres – prin-
cipally Suva, the
capital, and Viti
Levu towns.

Celebrate Fiji

Fijians are a famously hospitable people, with personalities as sunny as the islands they live on, and few visitors escape without being befriended by at least some of the hotel staff. For those who dig a little deeper, a land rich with traditional etiquette and a fascinating history awaits. Blend this with the colourful Indo-Fijian culture, the influence of neighbouring South Pacific nations and a Christian inheritance courtesy of Western missionaries and it's easy to see why Fiji has such a rich cultural cocktail.

Young girl in Nadi, Viti Levu

Meeting the Locals

Village life today is a far cry from the days of cannibalism and ritualised warfare, and it's ironic that the islands that were once feared by early sailors are now revered by today's travellers. To meet some of these friendly locals, ditch the poolside lounger and head to any of the places below.

Hindu Temples

1 For a gaudy slice of India in Melanesia, visit one of the country's many Hindu temples. Nadi's Sri Siva Subramaniya Swami Temple (p46) is a particularly fine example of traditional Dravidian architecture.

Sunday Church

2 Throughout Fiji, Sunday church services are filled with beautiful songs and skilfully harmonised vocals. Our favourite? The hymns sung by the congregation at Taveuni's Wairiki Catholic Mission (p171).

Rugby

3 Rugby is an integral part of the *vaka i taukei* (Fijian way of life) and every village has a team. To enjoy a game, bring a loud, barracking voice and join the scrum of supporters on the sidelines of a village rugby field.

Suva Nightlife

4 Spending a night on the dance floors of Suva (p102) is not only fun but it may force you to re-evaluate your thoughts about Fijian youth and Fiji's cultural landscape.

The Market

5 Most markets are simple, open-air affairs where villagers gather to sell produce, swap stories and share jokes. Suva's Municipal Market (p95) is one of the biggest in the South Pacific and the perfect place to buy a *sevusevu* (p222) or sample local delicacies such as *bila* (fermented cassava).

Clockwise from top
1 Sri Siva Subramaniya Swami Temple (p46), Nadi
2 Locals outside church following Sunday service, Nadi
3 Rugby match, Viti Levu

Festivals & Arts

Meke & Lovo

1 Many resorts have weekly *meke* nights (p210) which include meals cooked in a *lovo* (pit oven) and traditional song-and-dance performances.

Indo-Fijian Fire-Walking

2 To witness the incredible commitment exhibited by Hindi devotees as they pierce their bodies with metal skewers and walk over hot embers, attend Suva's South Indian fire-walking festival (p97).

Hibiscus Festival

3 Fiji's largest festival (p97) draws crowds that converge on Suva's Albert Park to partake of the stalls, carnival rides and free entertainment.

Fiji Museum

4 Fiji's traditional arts are best appreciated at the Fiji Museum (p93), with its treasure-trove of war clubs, cannibal utensils and chiefly ornaments.

Right
1 Locals celebrating, Rotuma 2 Fire-walker (p89), Suva

Indo-Fijian Culture

Clement Paligaru
An Australian of Indo-Fijian descent, Clement is a radio and television journalist specialising in Asia Pacific affairs. He has worked for the Australian Broadcasting Corporation for almost 20 years.

Masala is a heady, aromatic concoction of Indian curry spices that can seduce, enthral and mystify the senses. Step away from Fiji's laid-back resorts, languid beaches and villages and you get a sense that a lot of the country has been touched by some magical masala-wand. Indo-Fijian presence is almost everywhere, bringing colour, flavour and heat to most aspects of Fiji life. This is the legacy of Indo-Fijians living here for over a century, transforming Fiji's social, political and culinary traditions.

Indo-Fijians have their own distinct Hindi dialect. It is an amalgam of regional dialects once spoken by indentured labourers from India.

A Sweet & Spicy Route

Many of the ways of the Indo-Fijians were forged in the sugar-cane belts of Viti Levu and Vanua Levu. They remain so etched that at times travelling through these parts offers a more Indian than indigenous Fijian experience. Fijian villages may punctuate the main roads, but Indian presence is robust.

Most of the large cane farms, which flank the main roads, are leased and managed by Indo-Fijians. Quite a few have remained in the same families since Indo-Fijians were first allowed to stay in Fiji. This is where generations have laboured, thrived and built foundations for life elsewhere.

Today some are facing forced evictions as their leases of the native land expire. Their children are increasingly opting for work in towns. But it will be a while before the farms and their ways of life disappear.

The Indo-Fijian men you see tilling the fields and loading cane work, as their ancestors did, from dawn till dusk. The harsh sun still beats down at midday. But the whips of colonial overseers disappeared a long time ago. For lunch they may share a curry prepared by their wives and daughters. In the evening they will relax over a few bowls of kava and probably banter with their Fijian mates in each other's languages. It is in these fields and smaller towns where camaraderie has defied the tensions that exist between the two main ethnic groups.

Arranged marriages remain a serious option for many young Indo-Fijians seeking a life partner. A high proportion of Indo-Fijians who have migrated overseas still consider returning home to find a bride or bridegroom.

The vegetable gardens near the colourfully painted Indo-Fijian homes provide produce for the families and market stalls. Almost a century ago selling surplus vegetables was one of the earliest ventures of enterprising indentured labourers freed of their contracts. Visit a market in any of Fiji's main centres and you'll find a delicious array of the many weird and wonderful gourds, fruits and vegetables from home and market gardens.

THE MILAAP PROJECT & MORE

There is now a growing volume of works in print, film and online reflecting the Indo-Fijian experience. Dr Satish Rai is among the more prolific producers. In his films he has documented the growing interest in ancestral history among Indo-Fijians as well as recorded testimonials and commentaries about Fiji's recent political and social history. His films include *Milaap: Discover Your Indian Roots* (2001), *Once Were Farmers* (2004) and *In Exile at Home: A Fiji Indian Story* (2008). Other writers and raconteurs have posted stories on internet sites such as www.girmitunited.org, which is also a comprehensive guide to publications and films about Indo-Fijians.

Nearby there will always be piles of colourful spices, indispensible for Indian cuisine.

You won't need to go too far to find a restaurant, a tiny cafe or even a mall to taste delicious home-style curries made from pumpkin, jackfruit and other vegetables in season. Fiji's curries are truly like no other, so try not to skip this experience. It's a must for non-vegetarians to try inimitable Fiji specialities such as goat, river clam *(na kai)* and duck curries. So infused is Fiji with this cuisine that in many indigenous Fijian homes curry has become a regular staple as well.

In roadside stalls near villages you will also find enterprising indigenous Fijians tapping into Indian cravings for piquancy. The piles of quartered mangoes you might find them selling will be dried and pickled in a mouthwatering and heady concoction of hot Indian spices. Try picking up a jar of these Fiji-style pickles at a supermarket or in a duty free shop before you head home.

Fiji has a fledgling Indo-Fijian film scene which has a small but supportive local and overseas fan base. Notable feature releases include Adhura Sapna (Director: Vimal Reddy), Tum Jo Mille (Param Sivan) and Ghar Pardes (Vimal Reddy). The stories tap into history, culture and cross-cultural themes.

A Sprinkling of Holiness

Among the more colourful reminders that Indian communities thrive in Fiji are the myriad temples, mosques and family shrines. Most Indo-Fijians are Hindus, Muslims and Sikhs who still practise the ancient rituals of their ancestors.

If you haven't been to the Indian subcontinent but want a snapshot of some of these Eastern religions, you can always start in Fiji.

The architecture and rituals in the Hindu temples, Muslim mosques and Sikh gurdwaras will impress and mystify. But delve deeper and you'll see that the devotees have also built them to reflect Indian regional differences and sects within the religions.

A must-see is the near-fluoro South Indian–style Sri Siva Subramaniya Swami Hindu temple in Fiji. Another North Indian–style temple near Labasa boasts a large rock, which devotees believe has been growing in the form of a snake, which is sacred to Hindus. Meanwhile, the major Sikh temples across Fiji follow Indian tradition and regularly offer free meals to all visitors and devotees.

While the large shrines are hard to miss, keep an eye out for red flags atop bamboo poles next to Hindu family homes. They mark tiny personal shrines often decorated with statues, marigold garlands and offerings.

The early indentured-labourer experience and postcoup reflections have inspired countless pages of Indo-Fijian poetry and fiction by authors such as Satendra Nandan, Raymond Pillai, Subramani, Sudesh Mishra, Mohit Prasad and Kavita Nandan.

This devotion among the faithful doesn't just demonstrate strong adherence to India's main religions. It also shows how determined the early Indian migrants were to restore order and dignity to their lives after the horrors of indenture. Rape and violence were common on the plantations. Religion helped purge the indignities. It helped communities organise themselves politically along Hindu/Muslim lines. But this also led to conflict within the Indo-Fijian community, sometimes compromising their dreams of a stable, secure future in the Pacific.

Religious organisations also set up the very first schools for the children of indenture, allowing them to pursue dreams beyond the cane fields. In many places you will see signage for these Hindu, Muslim and Sikh schools. They still churn out some of the nations brightest. Many have gone on to become Fiji's leading scholars, businesspeople, politicians and bureaucrats.

Little India Everywhere

In many of the world's major cities, enclaves with names like Chinatown, Little India and Latin Quarter contain bustling microcosms of migrant life. In Fiji, most of the main centres feel like Little Indias. Many shops and businesses are run by Indo-Fijians.

Take a bus into town and you will pass billboards enticing you to shopping meccas like New Delhi Fashions and promising great deals from the Tappoos, Khans and Motibhais. Towns like Ba, Lautoka, Labasa and Levuka are still caught in a time warp with old-style shopfronts and aisles cluttered with Indian homewares, fashions and pantry essentials.

Some of these businesses were set up early last century during the final years of indenture. On completion of their labour contracts a small number of Indian farmers became shopkeepers. But the explosion of Indian commerce really happened when Indians from the state of Gujarat set up shop, tapping into the needs of the rural folk. Today they still own many of the shops lining the streets of Fiji as well as the upmarket malls in cities like Suva.

It can be fun to venture into some of the smaller shops. But if you've been to India and enjoyed bargaining with shopkeepers, don't expect the same thrill in Fiji. These folk drive a hard bargain, which has at times worked against them. During coups, nationalist leaders have harnessed anti-Indian sentiment by conjuring caricatures of stingy, acquisitive Indians to take over the country.

Where Paths Cross – a Cultural Interchange

Bus stands in smaller towns offer a snapshot of the changing Indo-Fijian ways. These busy interchanges are where the rural and urban communities cross paths and where you can catch a glimpse of life and ways on farms and far-flung settlements. Years ago Indo-Fijian women, especially from rural areas, would be seen in elaborate saris juggling shopping bags and kids in the heat. Today, you'll be lucky to spot any.

On the street, most now opt for Western-style dress. But look closer and you'll notice that some still retain quintessentially Indian practices. Many married Hindu women still stain the parting in their hair with bright red vermillion. Gold jewellery is de rigueur, but more restrained than in the past. During and after the coups, these and other public displays of wealth attracted much vilification. But private functions like weddings still feel like Indian movie sets with glitter, silk attire, music and dance in abundance.

One decidedly Indian fixture at the bus stands is the deceptively humble sweet cart. These roofed glass cabinets on wheels carry an array of

Even though they are far away from the heartland of Vedic astrology in India, many Indo-Fijians regularly consult with pundits (priests) for readings and predictions about the future.

To visualise the lives of Fiji's early Indo-Fijian settlers, visit the Fiji Museum's Indo-Fijian gallery in Suva. It reconstructs the history of Indo-Fijian indentured labourers, and their customs and traditions, with the help of family heirlooms, artefacts and personal belongings.

THE BOLLYWOOD BEAUTY BY SHALINI AKHIL

Kesh is a feminist, loves pubs, swears a lot and was born and raised in Australia. Her Indo-Fijian cousin Rupa is the exact opposite. She diligently cooks curries, wears saris and is heading for an arranged marriage. When Rupa comes to live with Kesh in Melbourne, their worlds collide. Wicked humour and disarming honesty spice up this tale of culture clash, identity struggle and the Indo-Fijian way.

Read Shalini Akhil's blog at www.iwriter.blogspot.com.

The Indo-Fijian social and cultural experience is very similar to the experience of descendants of Indian indentured labourers in the West Indies, Surinam and Mauritius. Shared traditions include food, spoken dialects and religious rituals.

The word *girmit* is used to describe the indenture system. It entered the Indo-Fijian lexicon when the *girmitiyas* (early labourers) mispronounced the word agreement.

dangerously sweet and calorie-laden delights, laced with cardamom, milk and sweet syrup. As in India, no spicy meal or snack here is complete without one of these indulgences afterwards. If you have a sweet tooth, you could be in trouble. During the year, most Indo-Fijians get their fix from these carts or sweet shops around town. It's really only during big religious festivals that the sweets are made en masse at home.

The bus depots, streets and markets are also places of spontaneous, friendly exchange between Indo-Fijians and indigenous Fijians. Yes, political and race tensions have spilt over into these public spaces occasionally. But stick around long enough and you'll see this is also neutral territory where cultural exchange is possible. The Indian and Fijian having a chat are probably quipping in each other's languages. The traditional Fijian taro an Indo-Fijian is buying from a vendor might end up curried. The indigenous Fijian lining up at the nearby cinema might be about to watch the latest Bollywood hit.

For two cultures that are quite distinct, Indians and Fijians have co-existed remarkably well over the years. They live side by side, work together, go to the same schools, and enjoy each other's company in sport and entertainment. There's still a fair way to go as far as intermarriages are concerned. Much of this has to do with different educational, cultural and social priorities. But this is slowly changing, just as things have evolved in the past.

Over a century ago the early Indian migrants to Fiji lost little time dispensing with many social and cultural rigidities of India. Today they regard themselves among the most laid-back and sociable of the Indian diaspora in the world. Ask any Indo-Fijian just what makes them different from the folk in India – reticence will soon give way to a robust conversation bursting with anecdotes and pride about just how Fijian they have become.

Village Life

Fijian villagers live in land-owning *mataqali* (extended family groups) under a hereditary chief, who allocates land to each family for farming. Village life is more conservative than its urban counterpart. Fiercely independent thinking is not encouraged and being too different or too ambitious is seen as a threat. Concepts such as *kerekere* and *sevusevu* are still strong, especially in remote areas. *Kerekere* is unconditional giving based on the concept that time and property is communal. *Sevusevu* is the presentation of a gift such as kava for, say, permission to visit a village, or more powerfully, a *tabua* (whale's tooth) as a token of reconciliation or wedding gift.

In a Fijian village you will see few, if any, fences between homes and children run from one home to the next at will and without thought. This communal sense of living forms the cornerstone of village life and most Fijians would find it downright unneighbourly to erect a fence or wall between their homes.

As warm and as friendly as Fijians are, it is important to remember that villages are private places and it is considered rude to just turn up and wander around. If you do need to visit a village uninvited, ask to see the headmen at once and be sure to bring a *sevusevu*.

For a look at the indigenous Fijian diaspora, search out *No 2* (2006), a New Zealand film about a Fijian family living in Auckland and the resulting breakdown of their traditional family structure.

Village Etiquette

If you have been invited to someone's village, you're in for a treat. Fijians are famously hospitable and although villages are governed by complex codes of behaviour, Fijians are likely to shrug off any social faux pas with a joke. The best way to gauge what is appropriate is to simply ask your hosts, but the following tips will stand you in good stead.

» Bring a *sevusevu*.

» Never wander around unaccompanied: beaches, reefs and gardens are all someone's private realm.

» Dress modestly: sleeves and *sulu* (skirt or wrapped cloth, worn to below the knees) or sarongs are fine for both men and women. You will rarely see adult Fijians swimming and when they do they cover up with a T-shirt and *sulu*. Wear slip-on shoes: they're easier to take off when entering houses.

» Take off your hat and sunglasses, and carry bags in your hands, not over your shoulder; it's considered rude to do otherwise.

» It is rare to see public displays of affection between men and women so curtail your passions in public to avoid embarrassing or offending locals.

» Check with your host if you can take photos and wait until after the *sevusevu* to start snapping.

» Stoop when entering a *bure* (thatched dwelling) and quietly sit cross-legged on the mat. It is polite to keep your head at a lower level than your host's.

» Fijians regard the head as sacred – never ever touch a person's head.

» If you're staying overnight, and had planned to camp but are offered a bed, accept it; it may embarrass your hosts if they think their *bure* is not good enough.

Fiji's most common garden plant is the hibiscus. Its large, beautiful flowers only last a day but are in plentiful supply. You'll find them everywhere – tucked behind ears, decorating tables and adorning pillows. Don't be afraid to tuck one behind your own ear – you know you want to.

SEVUSEVU

When visiting a village it's customary to bring a gift of *yaqona* (kava) with you. *Yaqona* is sold at most markets and you should buy a minimum of half a kilo in *waka* (root) form rather than the inferior pounded variety. This is for your *sevusevu* ceremony during which guests request permission to visit the village from the *turaga-ni-koro* (hereditary chief) and, in effect, the ancestral gods. The chief will welcome you in a small ritual (involving the drinking of the gifted *yaqona*) that will likely develop into a *talanoa* (gossip session) around the *tanoa* (*yaqona* bowl). There are certain protocols to be followed at a *yaqona* ceremony and although there are many regional variations, most require you to observe the following rules.

» Sit cross-legged, facing the chief and the *tanoa* (large wooden bowl).

» Women usually sit behind the men.

» Never walk across the circle of participants, turn your back to or point your feet at the *tanoa*, or step over the cord – if there is one – that leads from the *tanoa* to a white cowrie shell, which represents a link with the spirits.

» When you are presented with the *bilo* (a coconut shell cup) of *yaqona*, clap once with cupped hands before taking and drinking from it. Although concessions are frequently made for tourists, it is polite to drink the cup's entire contents in a single draft before handing it back to the bearer.

The custom throughout Fiji is to finish drinking *yaqona* before dining. Be warned – this can result in some very late meals, a long recounting of your life story and a singalong to a guitar.

» If you'll be bathing in the river or at a shared tap, wear a *sulu* while you wash.

» The custom of *kerekere* means that people may ask you for things. If you don't want to give an item away, just say that you can't do without it; but be sensitive to people's lack of material goods, and take minimum gear on village visits.

» Travel with thank-you gifts of tea, tinned meat or sugar, or contribute some cash to cover costs.

» Sunday is for church and family so avoid visiting then unless invited.

Legend has it that the plant that kava is made from sprung from the grave of a Tongan princess who died of a broken heart.

Daily Life

Fijian's are early risers and if you spend a night in a village expect to hear the first clatter of pots and pans and hushed tones of conversation at around 5.30am. As a recipient of Fijian hospitality, you may well be given the best, and in some cases only, bed in the house (many people still sleep on woven pandanus mats on the floor).

The *balabala* (tree ferns) of Fiji are similar to those in Australia and New Zealand; once used on the gable ends of *bure* (traditional thatched dwellings), the trunks are now commonly seen carved into garden warriors – the Fijian counterpart of the Western gnome.

Most homes are no longer built in the traditional thatched *bure* style but are simple, rectangular, pitched-roof houses made from industrialised materials requiring less maintenance. Rural homes are unlikely to have electricity or plumbing and people wash and get water from a communal tap fixed above a concrete square. Cooking is done over small kerosene stoves. Toilets may be of the long-drop variety, usually in a row of tin sheds tucked away behind the houses.

The women tend to most of the domestic duties – washing, cooking, cleaning and looking after the children. Their days are full but often interspersed with loud peals of laughter and chatter.

Men spend their days farming, fishing and performing communal obligations. Evenings are often spent sitting in the chief's (or one of the other elder's) house talking and drinking *yaqona*.

Survival Guide

Directory A–Z

Accommodation

Five-star hotels, B&Bs, hostels, motels, resorts, tree-houses, bungalows on the beach, campgrounds and village homestays – there's no shortage of accommodation options in Fiji. See the 'Which Island?' chapter, p25, for booking tips and a run-down on all these options.

Activities

Fiji has plenty to offer the adventurous and active. See p30 for details on what the region has to offer.

Business Hours

Fijians are not known for their punctuality, often observing 'Fiji time'. A few internet cafes and shops are open for limited hours on Sunday, but the general rule is to assume everything will be closed. Many places in Fiji close for lunch from 1pm to 2pm.

Banks 9.30am to 4pm Monday to Thursday and 9.30am to 3pm Friday

Government offices 8am to 4.30pm Monday to Thursday and 8am to 4pm Friday

Post offices 8am to 4pm Monday to Friday and 8am to 11.30am Saturday

Restaurants lunch 11am to 2pm, dinner 6pm to 9pm or 10pm

Shops 9am to 5pm Monday to Friday and 9am to 1pm Saturday

Customs Regulations

Visitors can leave Fiji without paying VAT on the following:

» $400 per person of duty-assessed goods

» 2L of liqueur or spirits, or 4L of wine or beer

» 500 cigarettes or 500g of cigars or tobacco, or all three under a total of 500g

» personal effects

Further points worth noting:

» Pottery shards, turtle shells, coral, trochus shells and giant clamshells cannot be taken out of the country without a permit.

» You can bring as much currency as you like into the country, but you will need to declare any amount over $10,000 and you can't take out more than you brought in.

» Importation of vegetable matter, seeds, animals, meat or dairy produce is prohibited without a licence from the Ministry of Agriculture & Fisheries.

» If you're taking a domestic pet into Fiji you need to write to the **Director of Animal Health and Production** (☎331 5322; fax 330 5043; GPO Box 15829, Suva) and send them your animal's details including an up-to-date vet report. The department will send you a licence or approval to take your pet into Fiji.

Discount Cards

STA Travel and other student-travel agencies give discounts on international airfares to full-time students who have an International Student Identity Card (ISIC). Application forms are available at these travel agencies. Student discounts are occasionally given for entry fees, restaurants and accommodation in Fiji. You can also use the student health service at the University of the South Pacific (USP) in Suva.

Electricity

240V/50Hz

Embassies & Consulates

Generally speaking, your country's embassy won't be much help if the trouble you're in is remotely your own fault. Remember, you are bound by the laws of the country you are in.

The following countries have diplomatic representation in Fiji (a complete list can be found at www.fiji.gov. fj). All embassies are in Suva.

Australia (Map p90; ☑338 2211; www.fiji.highcommis sion.gov.au; 37 Princes Rd, Tamavua)

China (Map p90; ☑330 0251; http://fj.china-embassy.org/ eng/; 183 Queen Elizabeth Dr)

European Union (Map p92; ☑331 3633; 4th fl, Fiji Development Bank Centre, Victoria Pde)

Federated States of Micronesia (Map p92; ☑330 4566; 37 Loftus St)

France (Map p92; ☑331 0526; www.ambafrance-fj.org; 7th fl, Dominion House, Thomson St)

Japan (Map p92; ☑330 4633; www.fjemb-japan.go.jp; 2nd fl, Dominion House, Thomson St)

Korea (Map p92; ☑330 0977; 8th fl, Vanua House, Victoria Pde)

Nauru (Map p92; ☑331 3566; 7th fl, Ratu Sukuna House, Macarthur St)

Netherlands (Map p92; ☑330 1499; 1st fl, Crompton Solicitors Suite, 10 Victoria Arcade)

New Zealand (Map p92; ☑331 1422; 10th fl, Reserve Bank Bldg, Pratt St)

Tuvalu (Map p92; ☑330 1355; 16 Gorrie St)

UK (Map p92; ☑322 9100; www.britishhighcommission. gov.uk/fiji; Victoria House, 47 Gladstone Rd)

USA (Map p90; ☑331 4466; http://suva.usembassy.gov; 158 Princes Rd, Tamavua)

Food

Fiji's food reflects the country's position as the multicultural hub of the Pacific, with its blend of indigenous Fijian, Polynesian, Indian, Chinese and Western tastes.

Staples & Specialities

Starchy carbohydrates play a big part in Pacific diets. Traditional Fijian foods include *tavioka* (cassava) and *dalo* (taro) roots, boiled or baked fish, and seafood in *lolo* (coconut cream). Meat is usually fried and accompanied with *dalo* and *rourou* (boiled *dalo* leaves in *lolo*), though you'll often find the colossally popular corned beef substituting for the real thing. *Kokoda* is a popular dish made of raw fish marinated in *lolo* and lime juice, with a spicy kick.

Indo-Fijian dishes are usually spicy, and a typical meal comprises meat (but never beef or pork), fish or veggie curry with rice, dhal (lentil soup) and roti (a type of Indian flat bread). Chinese food is generally a Western-style takeaway affair with stir-fries, fried rice, chop suey, chow mein and noodle soups.

Celebrations

Lovo are traditional indigenous Fijian banquets where food is prepared in an underground oven. A hole is dug in the ground and stones are put inside and heated by an open fire. The food – whole chickens, legs of pork, fragrant stuffed *palusami* (meat or corned beef, onions and *lolo*) or *dalo* – is wrapped in banana leaves and slowly half baked and half steamed on top of the hot stones. Delicious! Traditionally, *lovo* is served for family get-togethers as well as for more formal occasions such as church festivals and funerals.

Self-Catering

» Every large town in Fiji has a fresh fruit-and-vegetable market and at least one supermarket where you can buy basic groceries.

» Most villages have a small shop but, as villagers grow their own fresh produce, stock is often limited to tinned fish, corned beef and packets of instant noodles.

» If your accommodation has cooking facilities, it will generally sell (very) basic supplies; but you'll be better off stocking up in town.

Vegetarians & Vegans

Being vegetarian in Fiji is pretty easy, especially if you're partial to Indian food. Many Indo-Fijians are strict vegetarians, so most Indo-Fijian restaurants have lots of veggie options, and there are Govinda's or Hare Krishna vegetarian restaurants in most sizeable towns. Most resorts and tourist restaurants have at least one token veggie meal on the menu.

Gay & Lesbian Travellers

In 1997 Fiji became the second country in the world to protect against discrimination based on sexual orientation in its constitution. But in Fiji constitutions come and go and since the last one was abolished in 2009 (a new one is due to be released in 2013) the Crimes Act of 2010 takes precedent. Under this act adult, consensual and non-commercial male and female homosexual conduct is legal; however, discrimination based on sexual orientation or gender identity is not banned. Same-sex marriages and civil unions are not recognised in Fijian family law, which means visiting gay couples are unable to marry while on vacation.

Given the popularity of Christianity and the church's 'homosexuality is morally reprehensible' stance, the local gay scene is fairly closeted. Nonetheless there is some indication of changing attitudes in the community; a large number of openly gay men work in the hospitality industry and some nightclubs in Lautoka, Nadi and Suva are gay-tolerant.

As public displays of affection in general are considered offensive, as a gay or lesbian couple the risks of receiving unwanted attention for outwardly homosexual behaviour is high. But gay couples who are relatively private are extremely unlikely to have any trouble in Fiji. Gay singles should exercise some caution; don't give anyone an excuse to even think you are paying for sex, and be very careful not to give the impression you are after young Fijian men.

The website www.global gayz.com/oceania/fiji tracks gay developments in Fiji.

Health

There is no malaria or rabies in Fiji. Health facilities are good; however, this is a small country with a limited budget so 'good' does not necessarily equate with the facilities of a well-developed country.

The overall risk of illness for a normally healthy person is low; the most common problems are diarrhoeal upsets, viral sore throats and ear and skin infections – all of which can mainly be treated with self-medication. For serious symptoms, eg sustained fever, chest or abdominal pains, it is best to go to the nearest clinic or doctor.

Dengue Fever

Dengue fever is a virus spread by the bite of a day-biting mosquito. It causes a feverish illness with headache and severe muscle pains similar to those experienced with a bad, prolonged attack of influenza. Another name for the disease is 'break-bone fever' and that's what it feels like. Danger signs include prolonged vomiting, blood in the vomit and a blotchy rash. There is no preventive vaccine and mosquito bites should be avoided whenever possible. Dengue fever requires medical care.

Recommended Vaccinations

The World Health Organization (WHO) recommends that all travellers be covered for diphtheria, tetanus, measles, mumps, rubella and polio, regardless of their destination. Since most vaccines don't produce immunity until at least two weeks after they're given, visit a physician at least six weeks before

departure. A recent influenza vaccination is always a good idea when travelling, as are vaccinations for hepatitis A, hepatitis B and typhoid fever.

If you have been in a country affected by yellow fever within six days of arriving in Fiji, you will need an International Certificate of Vaccination for yellow fever to be allowed entry into the country.

Availability of Health Care

Fiji has readily available doctors in private practice and standard hospital and laboratory facilities with consultants. Private dentists, opticians and pharmacists are also available. The further you get from main cities the more basic the services.

Private consultation and private hospital fees are approximately equivalent to Australian costs. Fees for government-provided services vary from modest to negligible but waiting times can be very long. Direct pay-

PRACTICALITIES

» The *Fiji Times* (www.fijitimes.com) and the *Fiji Sun* (www.fijisun.com.fj) are the country's principal newspapers; both are based in Suva.

» *Fiji Magic* (www.fijilive.com/fijimagic) is a free, monthly publication with details and prices of accommodation, restaurants, activities and tours.

» The government-sponsored Fiji Broadcasting Commission (www.radiofiji.com.fj) has radio stations in English (2Day FM – Suva 100.4 FM and Nadi 107.4 FM), Fijian (Radio Fiji 1 – 558 AM) and Fiji-Hindi (Radio Fiji 2 – 620 AM and 98 FM).

» Bula FM (Suva 100.2 FM and Nadi 102.4 FM) plays an eclectic mix of pop, rock, reggae, dance, folk, country and local music. Radio Fiji Gold (Suva 100.4 FM and Nadi 94.6 FM) appeals to an older generation.

» Fiji has three free-to-air TV stations: Fiji One (www.fijitv.info), Mai Television (www.tv.com.fj) and FBC TV (www.fbc.com.fj) and several pay-to-view subscription channels provided by Sky Fiji, Pacific Broadcasting Services Fiji and Sky Pacific.

» The video and DVD system used in Fiji is PAL.

» Fiji follows the metric system: kilometres, kilograms, litres and degrees in Celsius.

ment is required everywhere except where a specific arrangement is made, eg in the case of evacuation or where a prolonged hospital stay is necessary; you will need to contact your insurer.

Medications

Most commonly used medications are available. Private pharmacies are not allowed by law to dispense listed drugs without a prescription from a locally registered practitioner, but many will do so for travellers if shown the container or a prescription from home.

Water

The municipal water supply in Suva, Nadi and other large towns can usually be trusted, but elsewhere avoid untreated tap water, and after heavy rain it's worth boiling the water before you drink it.

Insurance

Having a travel-insurance policy to cover theft, loss and medical problems is a very good idea, but always check the small print.

» You may prefer a policy that pays doctors or hospitals direct, rather than you having to pay on the spot and claim later. If you have to claim later, make sure you keep all the documentation.

» It's a smart idea to email a copy of your insurance to yourself. That way, should everything be lost, you can access the information online (ditto for passports).

» Some policies specifically exclude so-called 'dangerous activities', which can include diving, motorcycling and even hiking. If you're planning to dive, it's best to purchase either comprehensive cover or pay extra for this activity.

» The Australian Department of Foreign Affairs and Trade warns travellers that some insurance companies will not pay claims that arise when travellers have disregarded the government's travel advice.

Worldwide travel insurance is available at www.lonelyplanet.com/travel_services. You can buy, extend and claim online anytime – even if you're already on the road.

Internet Access

» Internet cafes are fairly prolific in Suva, Lautoka and Nadi; competition means that you can jump online with broadband access for as little as $3 per hour.

» Budget resorts in Nadi also have internet access, some using prepay cards that deduct credits in 15-minute allotments (which works out at around $10 an hour).

» Outside of urban centres access is more limited, slower and pricier (up to $8 an hour in internet cafes), but thanks to the new VTSat, a satellite-based telecommunication network, even the remote islands like Rotuma now have internet access.

» If you're carrying your own laptop or iPad you can sign up for a prepay account with a service provider such as **Connect** (www.connect.com.fj), **Unwired Fiji** (www.unwired.com.fj) or **Vodafone** (www.vodafone.com.fj). The latter sells modem sticks for $79 and 1GB of data costs $15.

» Many midrange and top-end resorts have internet connections, so you simply need to plug in your computer.

Legal Matters

The only drug you are likely to come across when travelling in Fiji is marijuana – which is illegal. Don't seek it out or buy it, as the consequences if you are caught can be serious – it is not uncommon for drug users in Fiji to be imprisoned in the psychiatric hospital.

Most travellers manage to avoid any run-ins with the local authorities. If you are arrested, though, you have the right to contact your embassy or consulate, which will be allowed to provide you with legal representation but can do little else.

Maps

Map Shop (Map p92; ☎321 1395; Room 10, Department of Lands & Surveys, Southern Cross Rd, Suva; ☉8am-3.30pm Mon-Thu, to 3pm Fri) Beyond the maps found at the front of each telephone book, this shop in the Government Buildings stocks a good map of Suva and the surrounding areas, as well as big (1:50,000) and detailed topographic maps of each island or island group.

Fiji Hydrographic Office (Map p90; ☎336 1099; Toga Leva Naval Base, Queens Rd, Suva) Yachties after navigational charts of the Yasawa Group, the Kadavu Group, eastern Vanua Levu and the Lau Group can buy them here. The base is about a 20-minute drive west of the yacht club.

Carpenters Shipping (Map p90; ☎331 2244; 22 Edinburgh Dr) The rest of Fiji is covered by the British Admiralty Charts available here for $106 each. Ring before heading out.

At specialist book and map shops overseas you can usually purchase the latest Hema map of Fiji. Specialist marine charts are usually available at Fijian ports but are expensive.

Money

The local currency is the Fiji dollar ($); it's fairly stable relative to Australian and New Zealand dollars. All prices quoted in this book are in Fiji dollars unless otherwise specified. See p14 for exchange rates and costs.

The dollar is broken down into 100 cents. Bank notes come in denominations of

$100, $50, $20, $10 and $5. There are coins to the value of $2, $1, $0.50, $0.20, $0.10 and $0.05.

It's good to have a few options for accessing money – take a credit card, a debit card, some travellers cheques and a small amount of foreign currency. The best currencies to carry are Australian, New Zealand or US dollars, which can be exchanged at all banks.

Before you head out to remote parts of Fiji, check in the appropriate destination chapter to make sure you can access money, exchange currency or cash travellers cheques.

ATMs

ATMs are common in major urban areas and most accept the main international debit cards including Cirrus and Plus. The ANZ bank has an ATM at Nadi International Airport. Although they are increasingly commonplace, you won't find ATMs in remote areas, including the Yasawas, so plan ahead.

Credit Cards

Restaurants, shops, midrange to top-end hotels, car-rental agencies and tour and travel agents will usually accept all major credit cards. Visa, Amex and MasterCard are widely used. Some resorts charge an additional 5% for payment by credit card. Cash advances are available through credit cards at most banks in larger towns.

Tipping

Tipping is not expected or overtly encouraged in Fiji; however, if you feel that the service is worth it, tips are always appreciated.

Post

Post Fiji (www.postfiji.com.fj) is generally quick with its actual delivery, if a little slow at the counter, and has offices throughout the country.

DHL (Map p90; ☎337 2766; dhlinfo@fj.dhl.com; Grantham Rd, Suva) has representatives throughout the country, as well as its main office in Suva.

Public Holidays

Fijians celebrate a variety of holidays and festivals; for details of the latter, see p19.

Exact dates vary from year to year but are given a year in advance on the government's website, www.fiji.gov.fj. Look for the public holiday link in the quick links footer at the bottom of the homepage.

Annual public holidays include the following:

New Year's Day 1 January
Prophet Mohammed's Birthday February or March
Easter (Good Friday & Easter Monday) March/April
National Youth Day March
Queen's Birthday Mid-June
Fiji Day (Independence Day) Early October
Diwali Festival October/November
Christmas Day 25 December
Boxing Day 26 December

Safe Travel

Fiji is a very safe place for travellers and common sense is all you really need to ensure a safe and happy holiday. That said, Fiji isn't immune to crime and occasionally tourists are targeted. It is worth keeping the following in mind.

» When you're in Nadi or Suva do not walk around at night, even in a group. Locals catch cabs after dark and you should do the same.
» Sword sellers are not as common as they used to be, but if anyone becomes overly friendly, wants to know your life story and begins carving your name on a long piece of wood, just walk away, even if they pursue you claiming that you have to pay for the rubbishy item.
» Male travellers in particular are often approached and asked if they want marijuana and/or prostitutes.

Shopping

The main tourist centres of Nadi, the Coral Coast and Suva have lots of handicraft shops. Savusavu (on Vanua Levu) and Lautoka also have lots of handicraft shops, which are quieter and where the salespeople are less pushy. Also, you can often buy interesting handicrafts direct from villages, particularly woven goods and carvings.

» Popular souvenirs include traditional artefacts such as war clubs, spears and chieftain cannibal forks, as well as kava bowls of various sizes, woven pandanus mats, baskets from Kioa, sandalwood or coconut soap, and *masi* (bark cloth) sold in the form of wall hangings, covered books and postcards.

GOVERNMENT TRAVEL ADVICE

For the latest travel warnings and cautious advice, log onto the following websites:
Australian Department of Foreign Affairs & Trade (www.smartraveller.gov.au)
New Zealand Ministry of Foreign Affairs & Trade (www.safetravel.govt.nz)
UK Foreign & Commonwealth Office (www.fco.gov.uk/en/travel-and-living-abroad)
USA Department of State/Bureau of Consular Affairs (www.travel.state.gov)

» Stuffed, *masi*-patterned teddies called Bula Bears are Taveuni and Ovalau specialities and are quite cute.

» Pottery can be a good buy – if you can get it home in one piece.

» Don't buy any products derived from endangered species such as turtle, and avoid the temptation to buy seashells.

» Be cautious about buying wooden artefacts. A label reading 'treated wood' doesn't guarantee an absence of borers. Inspect items closely for holes or other marks, or you may end up paying more for quarantine in your own country than you did for the actual piece.

» Clothing shops in Suva and Nadi have *bula* shirts (a *masi*- or floral-design shirt) and fashion items by local designers. There are also vibrant saris and Indian jewellery on sale.

Bargaining

Indigenous Fijians generally do not like to bargain; however, it's customary in Indo-Fijian stores, especially in Nadi and Suva. Indo-Fijian shop owners and taxi drivers consider it bad luck to lose their first customer of the day, so you can expect an especially hard sales pitch in the morning.

Telephone

There are no area codes within Fiji. Outer islands are linked by cable and satellite to worldwide networks.

Country code	☎679
International access code	☎00
Operator assistance	☎010
International operator assistance	☎022

Mobile Phones

Vodafone (www.vodafone.com.fj) is the only mobile-phone company in Fiji. It operates a GSM digital service and has roaming agreements with Vodafone in Australia, New Zealand and the UK, as well as Optus in Australia. Ask for rates charged in Fiji for your mobile-phone calls before you leave home – you may end up paying international rates for local calls.

Mobile phones can be rented from Vodafone Rentals (Map p54; ☎672 6226; Nadi airport concourse) for $6 per day, but as you can buy a cheap phone in town for $20 including $40 free talk-time, there is little sense in renting one. SIM cards can be purchased for $9.95, including $10 free talk-time.

Mobile phone numbers in Fiji generally start with ☎9.

Phonecards

The easiest way to make local calls within Fiji is to buy a Transtel Tele Card, available in denominations from $3 to $50. Dial ☎101 and enter the code on the card by following the automated instructions (in English). Local calls cost $0.36 for the first 20 minutes (and then $0.18 per minute thereafter), national calls cost $0.34 per minute and mobile calls cost $0.63 per minute.

VOIP

Fintel (Map p92; ☎331 2933; 158 Victoria Pde) in downtown Suva is the only provider of international VOIP (voice over internet protocol) calls and these are a fraction of the cost of using traditional lines.

Time

Fiji is 12 hours ahead of GMT/UTC. When it's noon in Suva, corresponding times elsewhere are as follows:

CITY	TIME
Same Day	
Sydney	10am
Auckland	noon
Honolulu	2pm
Previous Day	
London	midnight
Los Angeles	4pm
New York	7pm

Add one hour to these times if the other country has daylight saving in place.

Tourist Information

The Fiji Visitors Bureau (FVB; www.fijime.com) in Nadi is the only tourist information body in Fiji. The website is excellent but the office deals mainly with promoting Fiji abroad and has little to offer walk-in travellers.

The South Pacific Tourism Organisation (Map p92; ☎330 4177; www.spto.org; 3rd fl, Dolphin Plaza, cnr Loftus St & Victoria Pde, Suva) promotes cooperation between the South Pacific island nations for the development of tourism in the region including Fiji.

Travellers with Disabilities

In Pacific countries people with disabilities are simply part of the community, looked after by family where necessary. In some cities there are schools for children with disabilities, but access facilities such as ramps, lifts, accessible toilets and Braille, are rare. Buses do not have wheelchair access and pavements have high kerbs.

Nevertheless, people will go out of their way to give you assistance when you need it. This includes scooping you up in their arms so that they can carry you on and off boats.

IT'S A SAILOR'S LIFE FOR ME

Fiji's islands are a popular destination and stopover for yachts cruising the Pacific. The best time to sail is in the 'winter', from early May to November, when the south-easterly trade winds are blowing. During the 'summer' months (November to April), winds change direction more often and the chance of finding yourself in a storm or cyclone is greater. Races and regattas are held throughout the year.

Obviously the Fijian reefs necessitate good charts and crews with sailing experience. Contact individual yacht clubs and marinas for further information, and pick up a copy of the *Yacht Help Booklet, Fiji,* available from the FVB. Other popular references include *Landfalls of Paradise – The Guide to Pacific Islands,* by Earl R Hinz, or Michael Calder's *Yachtsman's Fiji.* You can also visit www.noon site.com/Countries/Fiji, an excellent resource that details port facilities and has a library of online trip accounts.

For the rundown on sailing to Fiji from elsewhere see p234, and for customs formalities see p237.

MARINA	LOCATION	DESIGNATED PORT OF ENTRY
Royal Suva Yacht Club	Suva, Viti Levu	Yes
Vuda Point Marina	Vuda Point, Viti Levu	Yes (via Lautoka)
Denarau Marina	Port Denarau, Viti Levu	No
Musket Cove	Malololailai, Mamanucas	No
Copra Shed Marina	Savusavu, Vanua Levu	Yes
Waitui Marina	Savusavu, Vanua Levu	Yes
Anchorage in harbour	Levuka, Ovalau	Yes
Anchorage at Oinafa	Rotuma	Yes

Crewing on a Yacht

Crewing on a yacht across the blue of the Pacific can sound romantic, and often it is – remote beaches, pristine reefs and the soft slap of the ocean against the hull. It all sounds fab, but before you grab that bottle of rum and train a parrot to whistle sea shanties, scan through these tips.

» Long passages between landfalls, cooped up with strangers, can get mighty boring on a 15m-long piece of fibreglass. Spend as much time with the captain as possible before committing. This way you can both see how compatible you are likely to be with the rest of the crew.

» Expect to share a room. Yachts are semiprivate at best.

» Fresh water on a boat is a premium. It is unlikely that you will use it to wash with.

» Your attitude is supremely important. Once at sea you can't get off. Be willing to do all kinds of jobs and know a yacht is no place for lofty creature comforts.

» Discuss in detail the skipper's expectations of you and if you are expected to contribute to the kitty before you leave.

» Expect to take your turn at night watches.

» To find a crewing position be proactive: use the noticeboards at marinas, knock on doors and learn where the boats will be at different times of the year. It is no use looking in Fiji if all the boats are still in Tonga.

» To enter the Pacific islands you need to prove onward transportation, which means the skipper must vouch for you. They are well within their rights to hold your passport or deny you shore leave.

» Try to gauge the experience of the skipper and the condition of the boat. Your life depends on it.

Most top-end hotels have at least one disabled-friendly room with wheelchair access, paths, walk-in showers and handrails, but this may be tucked away at the back of the resort. It's a good idea to check exactly what facilities it has to ensure it suits your needs. Resorts with multiple levels, lots of stairs and sandy paths can be problematic.

Even if the resort is disabled-friendly, consider how you plan to reach your destination. Mamanuca and Yasawa resorts are commonly accessed by catamarans, which are met by small dinghies that run guests to the beach. Those with mobility impairments would find arriving this way challenging. Instead opt for islands that can be reached by plane or, at the very least, have a wharf.

Organisations

The **Fiji Disabled People's Association** (Map p90; ☑ 330 1161; www.fdpa.org.fj; 3 Brown St, Toorak, Suva) may be able to offer pretrip planning advice.

Visas

Entering Fiji is very straightforward. To get a visa you'll need an onward ticket and a passport valid for at least three months longer than your intended stay. A free tourist visa for four months is granted on arrival to citizens of more than 100 countries, including most countries belonging to the British Commonwealth, North America, much of South America and Western Europe, India, Indonesia, Israel, Japan, Mexico, the Philippines, Russia, Samoa, Solomon Islands, South Korea, Tonga, Tuvalu, Vanuatu and many others. Check Fiji Visitors Bureau's website (www.fijime.com) for a full list.

Nationals from countries excluded from the list will have to apply for visas through a Fijian embassy prior to arrival.

Visitors cannot partake in political activity or study, and work permits are needed if you intend to live and work in Fiji for more than six months. Foreign journalists will require a work visa if they spend more than 14 days in Fiji.

Arriving by Boat

Those entering Fiji by boat are subject to the same visa requirements as those arriving by plane. See p234) and p237 for a full rundown on the other requirements for those entering Fiji by yacht.

Visa Extensions

Tourist visas can be extended for up to six months by applying through the **Immigration Department** (Map p92; ☑331 2622, fax 3301653; Government Bldgs, Suva). You'll need to show an onward ticket and proof of sufficient funds, and your passport must be valid for three months after your proposed departure.

Volunteering

Cocooning yourself in five-star resorts, dining at exclusive restaurants and sipping on poolside cocktails all help pump much-needed dollars into the cash-strapped economy, but these experiences bear little resemblance to the day-to-day life of most Fijians. If you are eager to spend your time as well as your money helping the locals, a vacation incorporating some volunteer work might be the way to go. Different organisations are on the lookout for different skill sets, so do your research well. If at all possible, make contact with the volunteers who went before you to see if they felt the work they participated in was rewarding. It is safe to assume that volunteering often takes place in fairly remote locations under fairly primitive conditions. If you are liable to faint at the sight of a gecko clinging to the roof of your thatched hut, it may not be for you.

Lonely Planet's **volunteering website** (www.lonelyplanet.com/volunteer/index.cfm) has excellent resources for those interested in making a contribution to Fiji or elsewhere.

The following organisations all have volunteering opportunities within Fiji.

Fiji Aid International (www.fijiaidinternational.com)

Mad Venturer (www.madventurer.com)

Peace Corps (www.peacecorps.gov)

Women Travellers

Fiji is a fairly male-dominated society, but it is unlikely that solo women travellers will experience any difficulties as a result. Be aware, however, that men in this environment may view the influence of Western women as a threat to their own position, and therefore might discourage their wives from talking with you.

If you're travelling alone, you may experience whistles and stares but you're unlikely to feel threatened. Nevertheless, some men will assume lone females are fair game and several female readers have complained of being harassed or ripped off, particularly in touristy areas.

On rare occasions lone women have been harassed and raped on mainland beaches and forest trails. We haven't heard of any incidents on the small outlying islands, but while on Viti Levu, exercise caution before visiting a secluded spot by yourself.

Generally speaking, though, female travellers will find Fijian men friendly and helpful, especially if you are travelling with a male partner.

Transport

GETTING THERE & AWAY

Centrally situated in the South Pacific, Fiji is one of the main airline hubs of the Pacific region (Hawaii is the other) and often features as an extended stopover on travellers' itineraries as they travel to or from Australia and New Zealand to the northern hemisphere.

Flights and tours can be booked online at www.lonelyplanet.com/bookings.

Entering the Country

» Ensure you have a valid passport and, if necessary, an appropriate visa before arriving in Fiji; see p231 for more details.

» Immigration procedures are straightforward: it's highly unlikely that travellers will experience difficulty.

» In general, visitors do not need to show immunisation cards on entry, although it's always wise to check with your local authorities before leaving in case this changes.

Air

Airports & Airlines

As we went to print, Air Pacific – Fiji's national carrier – was rebranding itself as Fiji Airways, and the airline information in this book may be subject to change.

Most visitors to Fiji arrive at Nadi International Airport (NAN), situated 9km north of central Nadi. Nausori Airport, about 23km northeast of Suva, is used for domestic flights by Pacific Sun and Air Pacific (Fiji Airways) and the odd flight to neighbouring South Pacific countries.

On arrival at Nadi International Airport a sea of smiling faces and guitar serenading will greet you. Most of these people represent local accommodation or the many travel agencies in the airport. The airport has an ANZ bank with currency exchange and ATM, an information desk, several travel agencies, airline offices and car-rental offices in the arrivals area, as well as a post office, a cafeteria, a restaurant, a duty-free shop, a newsagency and a luggage storage area. Luggage storage costs $3 to $6 per day with a surcharge for oversized items like surfboards.

Code-sharing arrangements mean that Qantas, United Airlines and Air New Zealand ticket holders are sometimes carried on Air Pacific (Fiji Airways) planes.

Air New Zealand (www.airnewzealand.co.nz) Flies to Nadi from Auckland once or twice daily.

Air Niugini (www.airniugini.com.pg) Flies between Nadi and Port Moresby via Honiara (Solomon Islands) three times a week.

Air Pacific (fiji airways; www.airpacific.com) Fiji's international carrier flies to Australia (Brisbane, Sydney and Melbourne), New Zealand (Auckland and Christchurch), (China) Hong Kong, the US (Hawaii and Los Angeles) and several Pacific nations – Kiribati (Tarawa), Solomon Islands (Honiara), Vanuatu (Port Vila), Tuvalu (Funafuti), Samoa (Apia) and Tonga (Nuku'alofa).

Air Vanuatu (www.airvanuatu.com) Connects Nadi and Port Vila twice a week.

Aircalin (www.aircalin.nc) Flies between Nadi and Noumea twice a week.

Jetstar Airways (www.jetstar.com) A low-cost airline that flies between Melbourne and Nadi via Sydney every other day.

Korean Air (www.koreanair.com) Has three flights a week between Seoul and Nadi.

Qantas Airways (www.qantas.com.au) Operates direct flights from Australia (Brisbane, Gold Coast, Sydney and Melbourne), New Zealand (Auckland) and the United States (Honolulu) to Nadi.

Solomon Airlines (www.flysolomons.com) It is possible to fly nonstop between Honiara and Nadi or via Port Vila (Vanuatu).

Virgin Australia (www.virginaustralia.com) Operates flights from Sydney, Brisbane and Melbourne to Fiji. It is possible to incorporate Fiji into a Virgin Australia Airpass.

Tickets

» High-season travel to Fiji is between April and October, as well as the peak Christmas and New Year period.

» Airfares peak between April and June, and in December and January.

» If you book well in advance it's possible to escape the seasonal price variations.

» Fiji is a popular destination for Australian and New Zealand families; school holidays in these countries are considered high periods in Fiji.

» For the exact dates of antipodean vacation periods search 'school term' at http://australia.gov.au (for Australia) and www.minedu.govt.nz (for New Zealand).

Asia

The only direct flights to Fiji are from Seoul (South Korea) with Korean Air or with Air Pacific (Fiji Airways) from Hong Kong. Most flights to/from Southeast Asia go via Australia or New Zealand.

Australia

Australia and Fiji are well connected. Qantas, Air Pacific (Fiji Airways), Virgin Australia and Jetstar all operate routes out of Australia and competition is cutthroat, making it possible to pick up bargain flights if you shop around and wait for specials. There are direct flights from Melbourne, Sydney, Gold Coast and Brisbane to Fiji. The flight time is about four hours from Sydney and 4½ hours from Melbourne.

If you're collecting air-miles on Qantas, read the fine print carefully, as code-sharing agreements mean that Air Pacific operates some Qantas flights.

New Zealand

Kiwis have three options: fly with Air Pacific (Fiji Airways) from either Auckland or Christchurch or fly with either Air New Zealand or Qantas out of Auckland.

Air New Zealand has at least one flight a day to Nadi. The flight time between Nadi and Auckland is three hours.

Pacific Countries

In the past it was possible to buy air passes for travel within the South Pacific. The terms and conditions varied from pass to pass, but the general idea was that you could work your way around several island nations provided that you met certain mileage requirements. It is worth keeping an eye out for such passes should they ever be reinstated as they offered good value to those wishing to explore the Pacific.

Currently the only flights between Fiji and its Pacific neighbours are Air Pacific (Fiji Airways) flights to Samoa, Tuvalu, Solomon Islands, Hawaii, Tonga, Vanuatu and Kiribati.

Pacific island nations' airlines that fly directly to Fiji are Air Vanuatu (from Port Vila, Vanuatu), Aircalin (from Noumea, New Caledonia), Solomon Airlines (from Honiara, Solomon islands) and Air Niugini (from Port Moresby, Papua New Guinea).

UK & Europe

Generally there is not much variation in airfares for departures from the main European cities, but sometimes deals can be had – particularly in London, the travel-discount capital of Europe.

Broadly speaking, when travelling from the UK or Europe you have two choices; to fly via either Honolulu or Los Angeles in the US where you can pick up a connecting Qantas or Air Pacific (Fiji Airways) flight, or via Hong Kong or Seoul in Asia and pick up a connecting Korea Air or Air Pacific flight. Another popular route is to buy a Qantas or Air Pacific (Fiji Airways) flight to either Australia or New Zealand with a stopover in Fiji.

US & Canada

Fiji is a possible stopover between the west coast of the US and Australia or New Zealand. Fares from the US vary greatly depending on the season and ticket restrictions. Air Pacific (Fiji Airways) flies direct from Fiji to Los Angeles and on to Vancouver thanks to a code-sharing agreement with Alaska Airlines. It also flies between Nadi and Hawaii, as does Qantas.

Fiji is about six/12 hours from Hawaii/west coast US.

Sea

Travelling to Fiji by sea is difficult unless you're on a cruise ship or a yacht.

Cargo Ship

Few of the shipping companies will take passengers on cargo ships and those that do will usually charge hefty rates. It is virtually impossible to

CLIMATE CHANGE & TRAVEL

Every form of transport that relies on carbon-based fuel generates CO_2, the main cause of human-induced climate change. Modern travel is dependent on aeroplanes, which might use less fuel per kilometre per person than most cars but travel much greater distances. The altitude at which aircraft emit gases (including CO_2) and particles also contributes to their climate change impact. Many websites offer 'carbon calculators' that allow people to estimate the carbon emissions generated by their journey and, for those who wish to do so, to offset the impact of the greenhouse gases emitted with contributions to portfolios of climate-friendly initiatives throughout the world. Lonely Planet offsets the carbon footprint of all staff and author travel.

leave Fiji by cargo ship unless passage has been prearranged. A useful American company is **Freighter World Cruises** (☎800-531-7774; www.freighterworld.com), which can organise travel on a freighter ship around the South Pacific. You could also try asking your local shipping agents, or go to the docks and personally approach the captains.

Cruise Ships

Surprisingly, the Fijian archipelago does not feature in many cruising itineraries and few cruise ships call here. Notable exceptions are the trips offered by **P&O Cruises** (www.pocruises.com.au) that call into Fiji as part of a larger South Pacific circuit. Most departures are out of Sydney or Brisbane (Australia), although there are also some less-frequent departures from Auckland, New Zealand. Trips typically take between 12 and 16 days and also call into islands belonging to Vanuatu, New Caledonia and Tonga as well as Norfolk Island and Bounty Island, depending on the trip you sign up for.

Yacht

Strict laws govern the entry of yachts into Fiji and skippers should immediately make for one of designated ports before exploring Fijian waters and understand the following:

» Yachts can only enter through the designated ports of Suva, Lautoka, Savusavu, Levuka and Rotuma (dock at Oinafa).

» Yachts have to be cleared by immigration and customs, and are prohibited from visiting *any* outer islands before doing so.

» You must email or fax a completed Advanced Notice of Arrival Form (C2C) to **FRCA** (Fiji Revenue & Customs Authority; ☎324 3000; www.frca.org.fj; yachtsreport@frca.org.fj) Suva (fax 330 2864); Lautoka (fax 666 7734); Savusavu (fax 885 0728); Levuka (fax 344 0425), a minimum of 48 hours prior to arriving. Failure

to do so attracts heavy fines. Forms can be downloaded from the website.

» In 2011 a port health quarantine fee ($172.50) and a biosecurity levy ($102) were introduced.

» Extra surcharges apply if you arrive outside of operational hours (8am to 1pm and 2pm to 4.30pm Monday to Thursday, 8.30am to 1pm and 2pm to 4pm Friday).

» To complete customs formalities when you arrive you will require a certificate of clearance from the previous port of call, a crew list and passports for everyone on board except children travelling on their parent's passport.

» If you wish to visit any place beside a port of entry, a cruising permit from the Ministry of Fijian Affairs is required. These are easily obtained and free of charge.

» On arrival contact Port Control on VHF channel 16 to be directed to the quarantine area and await the arrival of customs officials. Several forms including various declarations and crew lists will need to be completed at this time.

» Before departing you'll need to complete clearance formalities (within 24 hours), providing inbound clearance papers, your vessel's details and your next port of call.

The Coconut Milk Run is a popular route cruising from California to New Zealand via Hawaii, Tahiti, Rarotonga, Vava'u and Fiji. To make the most of the weather, most yachts depart California in February and reach Fiji in July or August.

Boats from New Zealand often time their departure to coincide with the Auckland-to-Fiji yacht race in June. By the end of October most yachts head south to Australia and New Zealand via New Caledonia to spend the summer there.

For further information about cruising Fijian waters, marinas and finding crewing positions, see p230.

GETTING AROUND

By using local buses, carriers (small trucks) and ferries you can get around Fiji's main islands relatively cheaply and easily. If you'd like more comfort or are short on time you can utilise air-conditioned express buses, rental vehicles, charter boats and small planes.

Air

Viti Levu's airports at Nadi and Nausori (near Suva) are the main domestic hubs. Other domestic airports include Savusavu and Labasa on Vanua Levu, Matei on Taveuni, Vunisea on Kadavu, Bureta on Ovalau in the Lomaiviti Group, and Malololailai and Mana in the Mamanucas. Many other small islands also have airstrips. There are flights to some outer islands where there is no accommodation for tourists and an invitation is needed to visit – in some cases it is illegal to turn up uninvited. Rotuma, Gau and Koro in the Lomaiviti Group, Moala and Vanua Balavu (in the Moala Group) and Lakeba in Lau have airstrips but receive few visitors, while other islands such as Vatulele (off Viti Levu), Yasawa and Wakaya (in the Lomaiviti Group) have their own airstrips that serve the upmarket resorts.

Airlines in Fiji

Since Air Fiji went belly up in 2009, virtually all domestic routes are serviced by **Pacific Sun** (☎672 0888, 330 4388; www.airpacific.com), which was formed when Fiji's international carrier, Air Pacific (Fiji Airways), bought Sun Air in 2006. Pacific Sun has six aircraft, four DH-6 Twin-Otters and two ATR 42-500, and operates scheduled services to 10 destinations within the Fijian islands. It sometimes transports passengers' luggage in a separate plane, and arriving before or after your possessions is a common occurrence. It is a smart policy to take a change of clothes and all your valuables in your carry-on luggage.

Some may find the light planes scary, especially if it's windy or turbulent, but the views of the islands, coral reefs and lagoons are fantastic. Most flights are turnaround flights that return to Suva after unloading and reloading passengers. As some flights only go once a week it is advisable to book well in advance to secure a seat.

Fares are sold in four categories. The cheapest are 'Bula Specials' followed by 'Bula Saver', 'Bula Flexi' and 'Bula Plus'. A one-way Nadi–Suva flight for a Special/Saver/Flexi/Plus fare costs $103/180/210/230; naturally, the cheap seats are the first to sell. The tables here list Bula Saver fares as the Bula Specials are hard to come by.

Pacific Sun flights departing Suva:

DESTINATION	PRICE ONE WAY
Cicia	$265
Kadavu	$185
Labasa	$240
Lakeba	$225
Nadi	$180
Savusavu	$265
Taveuni	$260
Vanua Balavu	$225

Pacific Sun flights departing Nadi:

DESTINATION	PRICE ONE WAY
Kadavu	$220
Labasa	$225
Rotuma	$632
Savusavu	$310
Suva	$180
Taveuni	$300

To help fill the vacuum created by the downsizing of Pacific Sun's fleet and the closure of Air Fiji, a small operator called **Northern Air** (☎3475 005; www.northernair.com.fj) has sprung up. It principally serves northern Fiji with scheduled flights from Suva to Levuka, Kadavu, Moala, Lababsa, Koro and Ovalau. It also supplies charter services.

Charter Services

Charter services are most commonly used by those wishing to maximise their time at island resorts.

Island Hoppers (☎675 0670; www.helicopters.com.fj) Offers transfers to most of the Mamanuca islands' resorts, as well as helicopter flights departing from Denarau island and Nadi airport.

Turtle Airways (☎672 1888; www.turtleairways.com) Has a fleet of seaplanes departing from New Town Beach or Denarau, near Nadi. As well as joy flights, it provides transfer services to the Mamanucas, Yasawas, the Fijian Resort (on the Queens Road), Pacific Harbour, Suva, Toberua Island Resort and other islands as required. Turtle Airways also charters a five-seater Cessna and a seven-seater de Havilland Canadian Beaver.

Pacific Island Air (☎672 5644; www.pacificislandair.com) Offers transfers to islands in the Mamanuca, Yasawa and Lau Groups.

Bicycle

Cycling not only allows you to see the countryside at your own pace but reduce your carbon footprint at the same time. It's a particularly good way to explore Viti Levu, Vanua Levu (the Hibiscus Hwy) and parts of Ovalau and Taveuni. With the exception of the Kings and Queens Roads, most roads, especially inland, are rough, hilly and unsealed, so mountain bikes are the best option.

The best time to go is the drier season (May to October); note that the eastern sides of the larger islands receive higher rainfall. If you intend to cycle around Fiji as a main form of transport, bring your own bike, helmet, waterproof gear, repair kit and all other equipment. It is difficult to get bike parts in Fiji. If you wish to take a bike on a domestic flight, make sure it is demountable. There is only one company (Stoney Creek Resort near Nadi) that rents bikes of a standard suitable for a multiday ride.

The biggest hazard for cyclists is the unpredictable traffic – drivers can be pretty manic and are not used to cyclists. Avoid riding in the evening when visibility is low. Travel light but carry plenty of water – it can be hot and dusty or humid. The cheapest place to store bikes is at backpacker hostels.

Boat

With the exception of the ferries listed here, often the only means of transport between neighbouring islands is by small local boats. These rarely have radio-phones or life jackets. If the weather looks ominous or the boat is overcrowded, consider postponing the trip or opting for a flight.

Ferry

Regular ferry services link Viti Levu to Vanua Levu, Taveuni, and Ovalau. The bigger boats have canteens where you can buy drinks, snacks and light meals. Ferry timetables are notorious for changing frequently, plus boats sometimes leave at odd hours with a lengthy waiting period at stopovers. The worst thing about the long trips is that the toilets can become disgusting (take your own toilet paper). There are irregular boats that take passengers from Suva to Lau, Rotuma and Kadavu.

NADI–MAMANUCA GROUP

Every day a small flotilla of high-speed catamarans departs Denarau Marina to the resorts on the Mamanuca islands. All boats have a free pick-up and drop-off service between the port and Nadi Hotels. Mana Island is the only island with a wharf; at all the other islands the arriving catamarans are meet by a swarm of resort dinghies that take turns to pull alongside the bigger catamaran and deposit or collect travellers. Luggage is colour-coded with tags but it's a good idea to check your bags have followed you into the dinghy. In calm weather the transfer of passengers from big boat to little boat goes smoothly but when there is motion in the ocean, things become interesting.

See p116 for details on the following companies.

Awesome Adventures Fiji (☎675 0499; www.awesomefiji. com) Calls into four Mamanuca islands on its daily run to the Yasawas.

Malolo Cat I & II (☎675 0205) Are both owned by Plantation and Musket Cove resorts and travel between Port Denarau and Malololailai.

South Sea Cruises (☎675 0500; www.ssc.com.fj) Operates two fast catamarans from Denarau Marina to most of the Mamanuca islands.

NADI–YASAWA GROUP

Awesome Adventures Fiji (☎675 0499; www.awesomefiji. com) Owned by the same company as South Sea Cruises, it operates the lurid-yellow *Yasawa Flyer*, a large catamaran that services all of the resorts on the Yasawa islands. It's a large boat with a comfortable interior including a snack shop and toilets, but you'll still feel the swell on choppy days. See the boxed text, p126, for more details.

SUVA–VANUA LEVU & TAVEUNI

The three ferry companies listed here connect Suva and Savusavu, often via Koro, Taveuni and/or Ovalau.

It takes around 12 hours to reach Savusavu. For those bound for Labasa, a bus often meets the boats at Savusavu and tickets can be bought in Suva that include the Labasa bus transfer. Sometimes the boats depart from Natovi Landing, a half-hour bus ride north of Suva.

Bligh Water Shipping (Map p90; ☎in Suva 331 8247; www. blighwatershipping.com.fj; 1-2 Matua St, Walu Bay) Has regular Suva–Savusavu–Taveuni departures aboard the MV *Suliven* in five classes. Even the cheapest class has comfortable seats but for a good night's sleep, splurge for the bunks in the sleeper class or those in the two- or three-bed cabins.

Consort Shipping (Map p92; ☎in Suva 330 2877; fax 330 3389; consortship@connect.com.fj; Ground fl, Dominion House Arcade, Thomson St, Suva) Also runs a Suva–Savusavu–Taveuni service.

Goundar Shipping (Map p154; ☎in Savusavu 330 1035; Kong's Shop, Main St, Savusavu) Began operations in 2011; its boat, the *Lomaiviti Princess*, was formerly the *Queen of Prince Rupert*, which was the main ferry between the Queen Charlotte Islands and mainland British Columbia in Canada. At the time of research timetables had yet to be finalised, but it is expected that the boat will bring a new level of comfort and much-needed professionalism to the Suva–Vanua Levu route.

LAUTOKA–VANUA LEVU

Bligh Water Shipping (Map p90; ☎in Suva 331 8247; www. blighwatershipping.com.fj; 1-2 Matua St, Walu Bay) Operates the MV *Westerland*, between Lautoka and Labasa (Malau) two or three times a week.

NATOVI (SUVA)–OVALAU (LEVUKA)

Suva ferries actually leave from Natovi Landing, which is just north of the city, and arrive at Buresala Landing on Ovalau, where a waiting bus transfers passengers to Levuka.

Patterson Brothers Shipping (Map p90; ☎331 5644; fax 330 1652; suite 1 & 2, Epworth Arcade, Nina St) Operates a daily service between Ovalau and the mainland.

Venu Shipping (☎339 5000; Rona St, Walu Bay, Suva) Runs an erratic service from Levuka to Walu Bay

See p139 for more information.

SUVA–KADAVU

Viti Levu is connected to Kadavu by only two companies. Both sail out of Suva. See p188 for details.

Goundar Shipping (☎in Savusavu 330 1035; Kong's Shop, Main St, Savusavu)

Venu Shipping (☎339 5000; Rona St, Walu Bay, Suva)

OUTER ISLANDS

There are very few services to the Lau, Moala and Rotuma groups. Those that run are slow, uncomfortable and erratic. Many islands only receive one ferry a month, making this an unreliable option for anyone on any kind of schedule. There are rumours that the new Goundar Shipping plans to service Vanuabalavu and Lakeba via Cicia once a month.

If you are planning on travelling to any of the remote outer islands contact Tomi Finau or Atelaite Cama at **Procure Fiji** (☎in Suva 331 8151; procurefiji@gmail.com; Shop 8, Port of Mua-i-Walu no 2, Walu Bay). They run the procurement office for the outer islands and know exactly what boats are going where, when and whether they take passengers. They can also hook up outer-island homestays.

Bligh Water Shipping (Map p90; ☎in Suva 331 8247;

www.blighwatershipping.com.fj; 1-2 Matua St, Walu Bay) Has once-a-month trips from Suva to Vanuabalavu and Cicia.

Lau Shipping (Office 12; Mua-i-walu Jetty 2, Walu Bay, Suva) Operates MV *Lau Trader* between Suva and Northern Lau, Upper Southern Lau and Lower Southern Lau.

Seaview Shipping (☑in Suva 330 9515; www.seaviewfiji.com) MV *Sandy* travels from Suva to Upper Southern Lau and Lower Southern Lau.

Western Shipping (☑in Suva 331 4467; Narain's Wharf, Walu Bay, Suva) Operates the *Cagi Mai Ba* to Rotuma. The journey takes 36 hours; phone for departure times and dates.

Yacht

Yachting is a great way to explore the Fiji archipelago but remember if you wish to visit any place except a port of entry, a cruising permit from the Ministry of Fijian Affairs is required. These are free of charge and usually issued on the spot. Port agents will often apply on your behalf for a small fee. A special permit (beyond the normal cruising permit) to travel to the Lau Group is no longer required.

For further information about cruising Fijian waters, marinas and finding crewing positions, see p230.

Bus

Fiji's larger islands have extensive and inexpensive bus networks. Local buses are cheap and regular and a great way to mix with the locals. While they can be fairly noisy and smoky, they are perfect for the tropics, with unglazed windows and pull-down tarpaulins when it rains. There are bus stops but you can hail buses along the road, especially in rural areas. Most drivers prefer to go downhill at the maximum speed their vehicle allows to make up for the excruciatingly slow speed they travel going uphill.

It's a lot like being on a roller coaster, only cheaper.

Air-conditioned express buses run on some major routes such as Nadi to Suva. Sunbeam Transport and Pacific Transport are the main carriers on Viti Levu; see p46 for more information. Pacific Transport also operates services on Taveuni (see p170). Coral Sun's Scania coaches only stop at the major resorts between Nadi airport and Suva. The buses are more comfortable than those of the other operators, are only a few dollars more expensive and are predominantly used by tourists.

Local companies operate buses on Vanua Levu but they can be slow and their timetables are often erratic.

Reservations are not necessary for local buses. If you are on a tight schedule or have an appointment, though, it's a good idea to buy your ticket in advance, especially for bus trips and tours over longer distances (eg Suva to Nadi). Pacific Transport and Sunbeam issue timetables, but for most of the local buses you should just ask around at the bus stations.

Car & Motorcycle

About 90% of Fiji's 5100km of roads are on Viti Levu and Vanua Levu, of which about one-fifth are sealed. Both of these islands are fun to explore by car, 4WD or motorcycle.

Driving Licence

If you hold a current driving licence from an English-speaking country you are entitled to drive in Fiji. Otherwise you will need an international driving permit, which should be obtained in your home country before travelling.

Fuel

Petrol stations are common and easy to find on Viti Levu and Vanua Levu. They are most prolific and competitive in the cities. Once you get

off the beaten track, however, they become fewer and further between. If you plan to do some driving by 4WD into Viti Levu's interior, you should take a full tank with you. If you do run out of fuel it might be available in village shops (but don't assume so).

Hire

Rental cars are relatively expensive in Fiji. Despite this, it is a good way to explore the larger islands, especially if you can split the cost with others.

Some rental agencies will not allow their cars to be driven on unpaved roads, which greatly limits your ability to explore the highlands. It is possible to take vehicles on roll-on, roll-off ferries to Vanua Levu or Taveuni but, again, some companies do not allow this. The ferry costs are pretty expensive and vehicles are available to rent on both of these islands anyway. If you do take a car on a ferry to Vanua Levu it's best if the car's a 4WD.

The shorter the hire period, the higher the rate. Delivery and collection are often included in the price. Rates for a week or more with an international company start at around $125 per day, excluding tax, but the same car can cost half as much again per day for just one or two days' hire. Some companies will hire at an hourly rate or per half-day, while some have a minimum hire of three days. It's usual to pay a deposit by credit card. If you don't have a credit card you'll need to leave a hefty cash bond.

A valid overseas or international driving licence is required. The minimum-age requirement is 21, or in some cases 25.

Generally, the larger, well-known companies have better cars and support but are more expensive. Consider what's appropriate for you, including how inconvenienced you might be if the car breaks down, what support services are provided, the likely distance to services, cost

THE FEEJEE EXPERIENCE

Feejee Experience (☑672 5950; www.feejeeexperience.com) offers coach transfers with or without accommodation for budget travellers. The transfer-only passes are valid for a year and you can hop on and off anywhere you like along a set route as long as you don't backtrack. The four-day Hula Loop ($449) starts at Nadi and incorporates stops at Mango Bay, Pacific Harbour and Volivoli Beach. Sandboarding down the Sigatoka Dunes, village visits, the mud pools at Sabeto and snorkelling at Volivoli (Rakiraki) are included, but accommodation and food isn't. The 11-day Big Kahuna ($799) also includes the Viti Levu circuit plus seven days travel through the Yasawa islands.

The accommodation-inclusive deals cost $279/449/799/854/1399 for 3/4/6/8/10-day packages.

These tours are popular with the 20-something crowd who do not want to use the public buses. Nightly activities are catered to this age group and are very social, fortified with alcohol and lots of fun. Feejee Experience has a stellar reputation and those who sign up for a tour rave about their experiences. Before you book, however, it is worth keeping in mind that a perfectly comfortable Sunbeam Bus will also take you around the island for $38.45.

of insurance, if value-added tax (VAT) is included and the excess or excess-waiver amount. Regardless of where you rent from, check brakes, water and tyre pressure and condition before heading off.

The easiest place to rent vehicles is on Viti Levu. Most rental agencies have offices at Nadi International Airport; the established companies also have offices in other towns and rental desks at larger hotels. Car-rental agencies on Vanua Levu and Taveuni have mostly 4WDs due to the islands' rough roads.

Some of the more reputable car-rental agencies on Viti Levu:

Avis Rent a Car (www.avis.com.fj) Nadi airport (☑672 2233); Nausori airport (☑337 8361); Port Denarau (☑672 2233); Suva (☑337 8361)

Budget Rent a Car (www.budget.com.fj) Labasa (☑881 1999); Lautoka (☑666 6166); Nadi airport (☑672 2636); Nausori airport (☑347 9299); Port Denarau (☑675 0888); Savusavu (☑881 1999);

Sigatoka (☑650 0986); Suva (☑331 5899)

Hertz (www.hertzfiji.net) Nadi airport (☑672 3466); Pacific Harbour (☑992 3923); Suva (☑338 0981)

Thrifty Car Rental (www.thrifty.com) Nadi airport (☑672 2935); Suva (☑331 4436)

Although not widely available, motorcycles and scooters are not a bad way to travel in Fiji. Similar traffic rules and rental conditions as mentioned previously for car rental apply to motorcycles and scooters.

INSURANCE

Third-party insurance is compulsory. Some car-rental companies include it in their daily rates while others add it at the end (count on $22 to $30 at least). Personal accident insurance is highly recommended if you are not already covered by travel insurance. Renters are liable for the first $500 damage. Common exclusions, or problems that won't be paid for

by the insurance company, include tyre damage, underbody and overhead damage, windscreen damage and theft of the vehicle.

Road Conditions

The perimeter of Viti Levu is easy to get to know by car. The Queens Road and most of the Kings Road are sealed, although the section between Korovou and Dama is still unsealed. It takes about 3½ hours to drive the 200km from Nadi International Airport to Suva (via the Queens Road), but this depends on how many lorries you get caught behind on the hills. Roads into Viti Levu's interior are unsealed and a 4WD is generally necessary.

There are unsealed roads around most of Vanua Levu's perimeter, but there's a sealed road from Labasa to Savusavu and the first 20km of the Hibiscus Hwy from Savusavu along the scenic coast is also paved. The remainder of the Hibiscus Hwy is quite rough.

Road Hazards

Some locals drive with a fairly heavy foot on the accelerator pedal and many ignore the whole idea of sticking to the left-hand side when navigating bends (particularly along the Coral Coast). Local drivers also tend to stop suddenly and to overtake on blind corners, so take care, especially on gravel roads. Buses also stop where and when they please. There are lots of potholes and sometimes the roads are too narrow for two vehicles to pass, so be aware of oncoming traffic.

Watch for sugar trains in the cane-cutting season because they have right of way. Dogs wandering onto the road can be a major hazard so observe the speed-hump-enforced 20km/h rule when driving through villages. Avoid driving at night as there are many pedestrians and wandering animals – especially along the southeast coast of Viti Levu, on Vanua Levu and on Taveuni.

Road Rules

Drive on the left-hand side of the road. The speed limit is 80km/h, which drops to 50km/h in villages. Many villages have speed humps to force drivers to slow down. Seatbelts are compulsory for front-seat passengers.

Hitching

Hitching is never entirely safe in any country and we don't recommend it. Travellers who decide to hitch should understand that they are taking a small but potentially serious risk.

Hitching in Fiji, however, is common. Locals do it all the time, especially with carriers. It is customary to pay the equivalent of the relevant bus fare to the driver. Hitchhikers will be safer if they travel in pairs and let someone know where they are planning to go. Crime is more prevalent around Suva, although there have been cases of hitchhikers being mugged around Nadi.

Local Transport

Many locals drive small trucks (known as carriers) with a tarpaulin-covered frame on the back. These often have passenger seating and some run trips between Nadi and Suva. You can pick one up in Nadi's main street; they leave when they are full and are quicker and only slightly more expensive than taking the bus.

Minivans are also an increasingly common sight on the road. Popular with locals, they're also quicker and more expensive than a bus but much cheaper than a taxi. Your ride won't necessarily be more comfortable, though – it's generally a sardine-type affair. Minivans plough up and down the Queens Road around Nadi.

Taxi

You will find taxis on Viti Levu, Vanua Levu, Taveuni and Ovalau. The bus stations in the main towns usually have taxi depots and there is often an oversupply of taxis, with drivers competing for business. There are some good cabs, but most are rickety old dinosaurs bound for or retrieved from the wrecker. Most taxi drivers are Indo-Fijians keen to discuss life and local issues. They invariably have relatives in Australia, New Zealand or Canada.

Unlike in Suva, the taxi drivers in Nadi, Lautoka and most rural areas don't use their meters. First ask locals what an acceptable rate for a particular trip is. Then, if there is no meter, confirm an approximate price with the driver before you agree to travel. Cabs can be shared for long trips. For touring around areas with limited public transport, such as Taveuni, forming a group and negotiating a taxi fee for a half or full day may be an option.

Always ask if the cab is a return taxi (returning to its base). If so, you can expect to pay $1 per person or less, as long as the taxi doesn't have to go out of its way. To make up for the low fare the driver will usually pick up extra passengers from bus stops. You can usually recognise a return taxi because most have the name of their home depot on the bumper bar.

WANT MORE?

For in-depth language information and handy phrases, check out Lonely Planet's Fijian Phrasebook. You'll find it at **shop .lonelyplanet.com**, or you can buy Lonely Planet's iPhone phrasebooks at the Apple App Store.

Language

The majority of the local people in Fiji you're likely to come in contact with speak English, and all signs and official forms are also in English. At the same time, English is not the mother tongue for almost all local people, – at home, indigenous Fijians speak Fijian and Indo-Fijians speak Fiji-Hindi (also known as Fijian Hindi or Fiji Hindustani).

FIJIAN

The many regional dialects found in Fiji today all descend from the language spoken by the original inhabitants. All the people in this vast area speak related languages belonging to the Austronesian family. There are some 300 regional varieties of Fijian, but there are two major groups: varieties spoken to the west of a line extending north–south, with a couple of kinks, across the centre of Viti Levu belong to the Western Fijian group, while all others are Eastern Fijian.

The dialect which is based on the eastern varieties of the Bau–Rewa area is understood by Fijians throughout the islands. This standard form of Fijian is popularly known as *vosa vakabau* (Bauan). It's used in conversation among Fijians from different areas, on the radio and in schools, and is the variety used in this chapter.

Pronunciation

Fijian pronunciation isn't particularly difficult for the English speaker, since most of the sounds found in Fijian have similar counterparts in English. Standard Fijian is written in the Roman alphabet, and it is phonetically consistent – each letter represents only one sound and vice versa.

Fijian's five vowels are pronounced as follows: a as in 'father', e as in 'bet', i as in 'machine', o as in 'more', and u as in 'flute'. Vowels have short and long variants. In this chapter a long sound is written as a double vowel, eg *aa*. Vowel length is important for distinguishing the meaning of words. For example, *mama* means 'a ring' and *maamaa* means 'light' (in weight).

Most consonants are pronounced as they are in English, with a few differences: b is pronounced with a preceding nasal sound, as 'mb'; c as the 'th' in 'this'; d with a preceding nasal sound, as 'nd'; g as the 'ng' in 'sing'; j as the 'ch' in 'charm' (without a puff of breath); k as in 'kick' (without a puff of breath); p as in 'pip' (without a puff of breath); q as the 'ng' in 'angry'; r is trilled; t as in 'tap' (without a puff of breath; often pronounced 'ch' before 'i'); and v is pronounced between a 'v' and a 'b'.

Occasionally on maps and in tourist publications you'll find a variation on the spelling system used in this guide – it's intended to be easier for English speakers to negotiate. In this alternative system, Yanuca is spelt 'Yanutha', Beqa 'Mbengga', and so on.

Basics

In Fijian, there are two ways of saying 'you', 'your' and 'yours'. When speaking to an adult stranger or someone who is your superior, you should use the longer 'polite' form. This form is easy to remember because it always ends in -*ni*. In all other situations, a shorter 'informal' address is used.

'Fijinglish'

Some English phrases are used in Fijian with slightly different meanings.

Fijian English	English
grog	kava
bluff	lie, deceive
chow	food, eat
set	OK, ready
step	cut school, wag
Good luck to ...!	It serves ... right!
Not even!	No way!

Hello.	Bula!
Hello. (reply)	Io, bula./Ia, bula. (more respectful)
Good morning.	Yadra.
Goodbye.	Moce. (if you don't expect to see them again)
See you later.	Au saa liu mada.
Where are you going?	O(ni) lai vei? (as the question 'How are you?')
Nowhere special, just wandering around.	Sega, gaade gaa. (as the reply to 'How are you')
Let's shake hands.	Daru lululu mada.
Yes./No.	Io./Sega.
Thank you (very much).	Vinaka (vakalevu).
Sorry.	(Ni) Vosota sara.
What's your name?	O cei na yacamu(ni)?
My name is ...	O yau o ...
Pleased to meet you.	Ia, (ni) bula.
Where are you from?	O iko/kemuni mai vei?
I'm from ...	O yau mai ...
How old are you?	O yabaki vica?
I'm ... years old.	Au yabaki ...
Are you married?	O(ni) vakawati?
How many children do you have?	Le vica na luvemu(ni)?
I don't have any children.	E sega na luvequ.
I have a daughter/ son.	E dua na luvequ yalewa/ tagane.
I don't speak Fijian/English.	Au sega ni kilaa na vosa vakaviti/vakavaalagi.
Do you speak English?	O(ni) kilaa na vosa vakavaalagi?
I understand.	Saa macala.
I don't understand.	E sega ni macala.
Can I take your photo?	Au tabaki iko mada?
I'll send you the photo.	Au na vaakauta yani na itaba.

Accommodation

Note that the term 'guesthouse' and its Fijian equivalent, *dua na bure ni vulagi,* often refer to establishments offering rooms for hire by the hour.

Where's a hotel?	I vei dua na otela?
Where's a cheap hotel?	I vei otela saurawarawa?
I'll stay for one day/ week.	Au na siga/maacawa dua.
I'm not sure how long I'm staying.	Sega ni macala na dede ni noqu tiko.
Where's the bathroom/ toilet?	I vei na valenisili/ valelailai?

Emergencies & Health

Help!	Oilei!
Go away!	Lako tani!
I'm lost.	Au saa sese.
Call the police!	Qiria na ovisa!
Call an ambulance!	Qiria na lori ni valenibula!
Call a doctor!	Qiria na vuniwai!

Where's the hospital?	I vei na valenibula?
I need a doctor.	Au via raici vuniwai.
I have a stomachache.	E mosi na ketequ.
I'm diabetic.	Au tauvi matenisuka.
I'm allergic to penicillin.	E dau lako vakacaa vei au na penisilini.

condoms	rapa, kodom
contraceptive	wai ni yalani
diarrhoea	coka
medicine	wainimate
nausea	lomalomacaa
sanitary napkin	qamuqamu

Shopping & Services

I'm looking for a/the ...	Au vaaqaraa ...
church	na valenilotu
market	na maakete
museum	na vale ni yau maaroroi
police	na ovisa
post office	na posi(tovesi)
public toilet	na valelailai
tourist office	na valenivolavola ni saravanua

What time does it open/close?	E dola/sogo ina vica?
I'm just looking.	Sarasara gaa.
How much is it?	E vica?
That's too expensive.	Au sega ni rawata.

bookshop	sitoa ni vola
clothing shop	sitoa ni sulu
laundry	valenisavasava
pharmacy	kemesi

Time & Dates

What time is it?	Saa vica na kaloko?
yesterday	nanoa
today	nikua
tonight	na bogi nikua
tomorrow	nimataka

Monday	Moniti
Tuesday	Tusiti
Wednesday	Vukelulu
Thursday	Lotulevu
Friday	Vakaraubuka
Saturday	Vakarauwai
Sunday	Sigatabu

Transport & Directions

Where's the ...?	I vei na ...?
airport	raaraa ni waqavuka
(main) bus station	basten
bus stop	ikelekele ni basi

When does the ... leave/arrive?	Vica na kaloko e lako/kele kina na ...?
boat	waqa
bus	basi
plane	waqavuka

I want to go to ...	Au via lako i ...
How do I get to ...?	I vei na sala i ...?
Is it far?	E yawa?
Can I walk there?	E rawa niu taubale kina?
Can you show me (on the map)?	Vakaraitaka mada (ena mape)?
Go straight ahead.	Vakadodonu.
Turn left.	Gole i na imawi.
Turn right.	Gole i na imatau.

Numbers – Fijian

1	dua
2	rua
3	tolu
4	vaa
5	lima
6	ono
7	vitu
8	walu
9	ciwa
10	tini
11	tinikadua
12	tinikarua
20	ruasagavulu
21	ruasagavulukadua
30	tolusagavulu
100	dua na drau
1000	dua na udolu

Compass points (north, south etc) are never used. Instead, you'll hear these expressions:

on the sea side of ...	mai ... i wai
on the land side of ...	mai ... i vanua
the far side of ...	mai ... i liu
this side of ...	mai ... i muri

FIJI-HINDI

Fiji-Hindi is the language of all Indo-Fijians. It has features of the many regional dialects of Hindi spoken by the Indian indentured labourers who were brought to Fiji from 1879 to 1916. Some people call Fiji-Hindi 'Bhojpuri', but this is the name of just one of the dialects that contributed to the language.

Many words from English are found in Fiji-Hindi (eg 'room', 'towel', 'book', 'reef'), but some have slightly different meanings. For example, 'book' in Fiji-Hindi includes magazines and pamphlets, and if you refer to a person of the opposite sex as a 'friend', it implies that he/she is your sexual partner.

Fiji-Hindi is used in all informal settings, such as in the family and among friends, but the standard Hindi of India is considered appropriate for formal contexts, eg in public speaking, radio broadcasting and writing. The Hindu majority write in standard Hindi using the Devanagari script. The Muslims use the Perso-Arabic script – when written this way, it's considered a separate language, Urdu (the language of Pakistan). Indo-Fijians have to learn standard Hindi or Urdu in school along with English; however, they all speak Fiji-Hindi informally.

Some people say that Fiji-Hindi is just a 'corrupted' version of standard Hindi. In fact, it is a legitimate dialect with its own grammatical rules and vocabulary unique to Fiji.

Pronunciation

Fiji-Hindi is normally written only in guides for foreigners, such as this, and transcribed using the English alphabet. In our pronunciation guides, the vowels are pronounced as follows: a as in 'about' or 'sofa', aa as the 'a' in 'father', e as in 'bet', i as in 'police', o as in 'obey', u as in 'rule', ai as in 'hail', aai as the 'ai' in 'aisle', au as the 'o' in 'own', and oi as in 'boil'.

The consonant sounds b, ch, f, g, h, j, k, l, m, n, p, s, sh, v, y, w and z are similar to those in English. The pronunciation of d, r and t in Fiji-Hindi differs from English – however, in this chapter we've used a simplified pronunciation guide and haven't made these distinctions. If you pronounce these sounds as the English 'd', 'r' and 't', you'll be understood.

Fiji-Hindi also has 'aspirated' consonants (pronounced with a puff of air). Aspiration is important in distinguishing meaning, and it's indicated with the letter 'h' after the consonant – eg pul/phul (bridge/flower), kaalaa/khaalaa (black/valley), taali/thaali (clapping/brass plate). Other aspirated consonants are bh (as in 'grab him', said quickly), chh (as in 'church hat', said quickly), dh (as in 'mad house'), gh (as in 'slug him'), jh (as in 'bridge house') and th (as in 'out house').

Basics

There are no exact equivalents for 'hello' and 'goodbye' in Fiji-Hindi. The most common greeting is kaise (How are you?). The usual reply is tik (fine). In parting, it's common to say fir milegaa (We'll meet again). More formal greetings are: namaste (for Hindus) or salaam alaykum (for Muslims) – the reply to the latter is alaykum as-salaam.

There are no equivalents for 'please' and 'thank you'. To make a polite request, people use the word thoraa (a little) and a special form of the verb ending in -naa, eg thoraa nimak denaa (Please pass the salt). For 'thanks', often just achhaa (good) is used. English 'please' and 'thank you' are also commonly used. The word dhanyavaad, meaning something like 'blessings be bestowed upon you', is used to thank someone who has done something special for you.

The polite form of the word 'you', ap, should be used with people you don't know well. The informal mode uses the word tum. Polite and informal modes of address are indicated in this chapter by the abbreviations 'pol' and 'inf', respectively.

Yes./No.	ha/nahi
Maybe.	saayit
I'm sorry. (used for something serious)	maaf karnaa
What's your name?	aapke naam kaa hai? (pol) tumaar naam kaa hai? (inf)
My name is ...	hamaar naam ...
Where are you from?	aap/tum kaha ke hai? (pol/inf)
I'm from ...	ham ... ke hai
Are you married?	shaadi ho gayaa?
How many children do you have?	kitnaa larkaa hai?
I don't have any children.	larkaa nahi hai
Two boys and three girls.	dui larkaa aur tin larki
Do you speak English?	aap/tum English boltaa? (pol/inf)
Does anyone here speak English?	koi English bole?
I don't understand.	ham nahi samajhtaa

Emergencies & Health

Help me!	hame madad karo!
Go away!	jaao!
Call the doctor/police.	doktaa ke/pulis ke bulaao
Where's the hospital?	aaspataal kaha hai?
I'm diabetic.	hame chini ke bimaari hai
I'm allergic to penicillin.	penesilin se ham bimaar ho jaai
I have a stomachache.	hamaar pet piraawe
I feel nauseous.	hame chhaant lage
condom	kondom/raba
contraceptive	pariwaar niyojan ke dawaai
medicine	dawaai
sanitary napkin	ped, nepkin
tampon	tampon

Time & Dates

English days of the week are generally used.

What time is it?	kitnaa baje?
It's ... o'clock.	... baje
When?	kab?
yesterday	kal
today	aaj
tonight	aaj raatke
tomorrow	bihaan

Numbers – Fiji-Hindi
English is used for numbers 20 to 99.

1	ek
2	dui
3	tin
4	chaar
5	paanch
6	chhe
7	saat
8	aath
9	nau
10	das
100	sau
1000	hazaar

Transport & Directions

When does the ... leave/arrive?	kitnaa baje ... chale/pahunche?
car	mottar
ship	jahaaj

Where's the ...?	... kaha hai?
airport	eyapot
(main) bus station	basten
church	chech
market	maaket
mosque	masjid
shop	dukaan
temple	mandir

I want to go to ...	ham ... jaae mangtaa
Please write down the address.	thoraa edres likh denaa
Is it near/far?	nagich/dur hai?
Can I go by foot?	paidar jaae saktaa?
Go straight ahead.	sidhaa jaao

By the ...	... ke paas
coconut tree	nariyal ke per
mango tree	aam ke per
breadfruit tree	belfut ke per
sugar-cane field	gannaa khet

GLOSSARY

This glossary is a list of Fijian (F), Fijian-Hindi/Hindi (FH) and other (O) terms you may come across in Fiji.

balabala (F) – tree fern with the unique property of not igniting over hot stones; good for fire-walking rituals

bêche-de-mer (O) – elongated, leathery sea cucumber, with a cluster of tentacles at the mouth; considered a delicacy in Asia – you may find it on your menu

beka (F) – flying fox or fruit bat

bete (F) – priests of the old Fijian religion

bilibili (F) – bamboo raft

bilo (F) – drinking vessel made from half a coconut shell

bokola (F) – the dead body of an enemy

bula (F) – cheers! hello! welcome! (literally, 'life')

bure (F) – traditional thatched dwelling or whatever your resort decides it to be

bure bose (F) – meeting house

bure kalou (F) – ancient temple

bure lailai (F) – little house (toilet)

cibi (F) – death dance

copra (O) – dried coconut kernel, used for making coconut oil

dadakulaci (F) – banded sea krait, Fiji's most common snake

dakua (F) – a tree of the kauri family

dele (F) – a dance where women sexually humiliate enemy corpses and captives; also called *wate*

drua (F) – double-hulled canoe; traditional catamaran

FVB – Fiji Visitors Bureau

girmitiya (FH) – indentured labourer; the word comes from *girmit*, the Indian labourers' pronunciation of agreement

ibe (F) – a mat

ibuburau (F) – drinking vessels used in *kava* rites

ivi (F) – Polynesian chestnut tree

kaivalagi (F) – literally, 'people from far away'; Europeans

kava (F) – Piper methysticum (Polynesian pepper shrub); more importantly the mildly narcotic, muddy and odd-tasting drink made from its aromatic roots; also called *yaqona*

kerekere (F) – custom of unconditional giving based on the concept that time and property is communal; also means please

koro (F) – village headed by a hereditary chief

kula – a type of parrot, Fiji's national bird

lau toka (F) – spear hit

lovo (F) – Fijian feast cooked in a pit oven

mana (F) – spiritual power

masi (F) – bark cloth with designs printed in black and rust; also known as *malo* or *tapa*

mataqali (F) – extended family or landowning group

meke (F) – a dance performance that enacts stories and legends

naga (F) – snake

NAUI (O) – National Association of Underwater Instructors

nokonoko (F) – Casuarina; also known as ironwood

noni (F) – an evergreen that produces a warty, foul-smelling, bitter-tasting fruit gaining credibility worldwide for its ability to help relieve complaints including arthritis, chronic fatigue, high blood pressure, rheumatism and digestive disorders

ota (F) – edible fern

PADI (O) – Professional Association of Diving Instructors

pandanus (O) – a plant common to the tropics whose sword-shaped leaves are used to make mats and baskets

pelagic (O) – large predatory fish, or whale

puja (O) – Hare Krishna prayer

rara (F) – ceremonial ground

ratu (F) – male chief

sevusevu (F) – presentation of a gift to a village chief and, consequently, the ancestral gods and spirits; the gift is often *kava (yaqona)*; however, *tabua* is the most powerful *sevusevu*; acceptance of the gift means the giver will be granted certain privileges or favours

sulu (F) – skirt or wrapped cloth worn to below the knees

tabu (F) – forbidden or sacred, implying a religious sanction

tabua (F) – the teeth of sperm whales, which carry a special ceremonial value for Fijians; they are still used as negotiating tokens to symbolise esteem or atonement

tagimaucia (F) – a flower with white petals and bright red branches; Fiji's national flower

talanoa (F) – to chat, to tell stories, to have a yarn

tanoa (F) – *kava* drinking bowl

tapa (F) – see *masi*

tikina (F) – a group of Fijian villages linked together

trade winds (O) – the near-constant (and annoying) winds that buffer most of the tropics

tui (F) – king or chief

turaga-ni-koro (F) – hereditary chief

vale (F) – a family house

vale ne bose lawa (F) – parliament house

vanua (F) – land, region, place

vatu ni bokola (F) – head-chopping stone used during cannibalistic rituals

vatuni'epa (F) – rock pedestals formed by the erosion of the coral base along the coast

vilavilairevo (F) – fire-walking (literally, 'jumping into the oven')

Viti (F) – the name indigenous Fijians used for Fiji before the arrival of Europeans (whose mispronunciation gave Fiji its current name)

waka (F) – bunch of *kava* roots

wate (F) – see *dele*

waqa tabus (F) – double-hulled canoe

yaka (F) – breadfruit tree

yaqona (F) – see *kava*

yavu (F) – base for housing

behind the scenes

SEND US YOUR FEEDBACK

We love to hear from travellers – your comments keep us on our toes and help make our books better. Our well-travelled team reads every word on what you loved or loathed about this book. Although we cannot reply individually to postal submissions, we always guarantee that your feedback goes straight to the appropriate authors, in time for the next edition. Each person who sends us information is thanked in the next edition – the most useful submissions are rewarded with a selection of digital PDF chapters.

Visit **lonelyplanet.com/contact** to submit your updates and suggestions or to ask for help. Our award-winning website also features inspirational travel stories, news and discussions.

Note: We may edit, reproduce and incorporate your comments in Lonely Planet products such as guidebooks, websites and digital products, so let us know if you don't want your comments reproduced or your name acknowledged. For a copy of our privacy policy visit lonelyplanet.com/privacy.

OUR READERS

Many thanks to the travellers who used the last edition and wrote to us with helpful hints, useful advice and interesting anecdotes:

Nicolas Benoit, Ilona Bicker, Isabelle Billaud, Richard Carrick, Bram Cassidy, Alan Clarkson, Chris Cottier, Regina Fellner, Philippe Gerbeaux, Max Goldsack, Patti Harris, Nick Henry, Thum Herbert, Arne Johannesen, Julie Lauzier, Jade Lynch, Charlotte Mcdonnell, Rusiate Naulivou, Peter Saunders, Lisa Smieja, William Su, David Waite

AUTHOR THANKS

Dean Starnes

I owe a large *vinaka vakalevu* (and probably a few Fiji Bitters) to my fellow authors Virginia Jealous and Celeste Brash and the team at Lonely Planet, especially Maryanne Netto, who tirelessly answered all my formatting queries. My warmest thanks go to my parents, Julie and Alan Starnes, and my expectant wife Debbie, all of whom supported me tirelessly through the write-up period and without whose help I wouldn't have met a single deadline.

Celeste Brash

Most thanks to my family for putting up with my absences. In Savusavu thanks to Sharon and Scott and to Colin and Janine. On Taveuni to Harry my intrepid taxi driver and to Ursula (Mila) and folks at Tuvununu. On Kadavu *vinaka* to Peiro and Vuli, drinks with Richard at Matava, diving with Richard at Mai Dive, and good help from Christian Bannard. For the Lomaivitis a wholehearted *vinaka* to Seru and Sala, my new Fijian family, to Serai and to the awesome boatman who caught me two fish.

Virginia Jealous

Vinaka vakalevu to Hugh, Cristelle and Tahi for my Suva home-away-from-home; Mafa for language skills and laughs; Sashi for my Lautoka home-away-from-home; Elenoa from SSC and the boat crews who, every day, treated me like a long-lost friend; Sushil from Rosie's; the GVI crew on Nacula; Bulou for the gift of bananas; Tui who shared an unexpected long 4WD trip with me (lucky we had the bananas).

ACKNOWLEDGMENTS

Climate map data adapted from Peel MC, Finlayson BL & McMahon TA (2007) 'Updated World Map of the Köppen-Geiger Climate Classification', *Hydrology and Earth System Sciences*, 11, 163344.

Cover photograph: Frangipani flower, Michael DeFreitas Pacific/Alamy. Many of the images in this guide are available for licensing from Lonely Planet Images: www.lonelyplanetimages.com.

THIS BOOK

This 9th edition of Lonely Planet's *Fiji* guidebook was researched and written by Dean Starnes, Celeste Brash and Virginia Jealous. Clement Paligaru continues his work on this title, updating his original content in the chapter on Indo-Fijian Culture. The previous edition was written by Dean Starnes, Nana Luckham and George Dunford, with Jean-Bernard Carillet contributing to the Diving chapter. The team on *Fiji* 7 consisted of Justine Vaisutis, Mark Dapin, Virginia Jealous and Claire Waddell. This guidebook was commissioned in Lonely Planet's Melbourne office, and produced by the following:

Commissioning Editor Maryanne Netto

Coordinating Editors Andrea Dobbin, Samantha Forge

Coordinating Cartographers Corey Hutchison, Alex Leung

Coordinating Layout Designer Jacqui Saunders

Managing Editors Barbara Delissen, Annelies Mertens

Senior Editor Susan Paterson

Managing Cartographer David Connolly

Managing Layout Designer Jane Hart

Assisting Editors Elin Berglund, Peter Cruttenden, Kate Kiely

Cover Research Naomi Parker

Internal Image Research Rebecca Skinner

Language Content Branislava Vladisavljevic

Thanks to Ryan Evans, Larissa Frost, William Gourlay, Trent Paton, Gerard Walker

NOTES

index

how to use this book

These symbols will help you find the listings you want:

- ⊙ Sights
- 🏄 Beaches
- 🏃 Activities
- 🛶 Courses
- 👉 Tours
- 🎉 Festivals & Events
- 🛏 Sleeping
- 🍴 Eating
- 🍷 Drinking
- ☆ Entertainment
- 🛍 Shopping
- ℹ Information/Transport

Look out for these icons:

- TOP CHOICE — Our author's recommendation
- FREE — No payment required
- 🍃 — A green or sustainable option

Our authors have nominated these places as demonstrating a strong commitment to sustainability – for example by supporting local communities and producers, operating in an environmentally friendly way, or supporting conservation projects.

These symbols give you the vital information for each listing:

- ♪ Telephone Numbers
- ☉ Opening Hours
- P Parking
- ⊝ Nonsmoking
- ✳ Air-Conditioning
- @ Internet Access
- 🛜 Wi-Fi Access
- 🏊 Swimming Pool
- 🥗 Vegetarian Selection
- 📖 English-Language Menu
- 👪 Family-Friendly
- 🐾 Pet-Friendly
- 🚌 Bus
- ⛴ Ferry
- Ⓜ Metro
- Ⓢ Subway
- 🚊 Tram
- 🚆 Train

Reviews are organised by author preference.

Map Legend

Sights
- 🏖 Beach
- 🛕 Buddhist
- 🏰 Castle
- ✝ Christian
- 🕉 Hindu
- ☪ Islamic
- ✡ Jewish
- ❶ Monument
- 🏛 Museum/Gallery
- 🏚 Ruin
- 🍇 Winery/Vineyard
- 🦁 Zoo
- ⊙ Other Sight

Activities, Courses & Tours
- 🤿 Diving/Snorkelling
- 🛶 Canoeing/Kayaking
- ⛷ Skiing
- 🏄 Surfing
- 🏊 Swimming/Pool
- 🚶 Walking
- 🏄 Windsurfing
- 🔵 Other Activity/Course/Tour

Sleeping
- 🛏 Sleeping
- ⛺ Camping

Eating
- 🍴 Eating

Drinking
- ☕ Drinking
- ☕ Cafe

Entertainment
- 🎭 Entertainment

Shopping
- 🛍 Shopping

Information
- 🏦 Bank
- 🏛 Embassy/Consulate
- ➕ Hospital/Medical
- @ Internet
- 👮 Police
- ✉ Post Office
- ☎ Telephone
- 🚻 Toilet
- ℹ Tourist Information
- • Other Information

Transport
- ✈ Airport
- ⊗ Border Crossing
- 🚍 Bus
- ⊕⊕ Cable Car/Funicular
- Cycling
- Ferry
- Ⓜ Metro
- Monorail
- P Parking
- ⛽ Petrol Station
- 🚕 Taxi
- Train/Railway
- Tram
- • Other Transport

Routes
- Tollway
- Freeway
- Primary
- Secondary
- Tertiary
- Lane
- Unsealed Road
- Plaza/Mall
- Steps
- Tunnel
- Pedestrian Overpass
- Walking Tour
- Walking Tour Detour
- Path

Geographic
- 🛖 Hut/Shelter
- 🚨 Lighthouse
- 👁 Lookout
- ▲ Mountain/Volcano
- 🌴 Oasis
- 🌳 Park
-)(Pass
- ⛱ Picnic Area
- 💧 Waterfall

Population
- ❂ Capital (National)
- ◉ Capital (State/Province)
- ● City/Large Town
- ○ Town/Village

Boundaries
- ——— International
- ----- State/Province
- – - Disputed
- – – Regional/Suburb
- ∿∿ Marine Park
- ⌐⌐ Cliff
- ▪▪▪ Wall

Hydrography
- River, Creek
- Intermittent River
- Swamp/Mangrove
- Reef
- Canal
- Water
- Dry/Salt/Intermittent Lake
- Glacier

Areas
- Beach/Desert
- + + + Cemetery (Christian)
- × × × Cemetery (Other)
- Park/Forest
- Sportsground
- Sight (Building)
- Top Sight (Building)

OUR STORY

A beat-up old car, a few dollars in the pocket and a sense of adventure. In 1972 that's all Tony and Maureen Wheeler needed for the trip of a lifetime – across Europe and Asia overland to Australia. It took several months, and at the end – broke but inspired – they sat at their kitchen table writing and stapling together their first travel guide, *Across Asia on the Cheap*. Within a week they'd sold 1500 copies. Lonely Planet was born.

Today, Lonely Planet has offices in Melbourne, London and Oakland, with more than 600 staff and writers. We share Tony's belief that 'a great guidebook should do three things: inform, educate and amuse'.

OUR WRITERS

Dean Starnes

Coordinating Author Dean was an impressionable six when he first travelled to Fiji. The week he spent bobbing above the Mamanuca reefs with a leaky mask and a pair of floaties ignited a passion that has drawn him back on many occasions. Dean was also the coordinating author on the 8th edition of this guide and has worked on Lonely Planet titles for such far-flung destinations as Papua New Guinea, Mongolia and East Africa. Dean now lives in Auckland where he alternates between writing for Lonely Planet, freelancing as a graphic designer and shirking responsibilities. His book, *Roam; the Art of Travel,* and his website, www.deanstarnes.com, feature photography and stories about his wayfaring ways.

Read more about Dean at:
lonelyplanet.com/members/dean_starnes

Celeste Brash

Ovalau & the Lomaiviti Group; Vanua Levu & Taveuni; Kadavu, Lau & Moala Groups Celeste first visited Fiji in 1987 and seriously considered running away from home so she could stay there. As an adult she moved to sort-of-nearby French Polynesia, where she lived for 15 years before recently moving back to the US. Her award-winning travel articles and stories have appeared in *Travelers' Tales, LA Times* and *Islands* magazine and numerous other publications. She's written around 30 Lonely Planet guides on destinations around the world but considers the South Pacific her speciality.

Read more about Celeste at:
lonelyplanet.com/members/celestebrash

Virginia Jealous

Nadi, Suva & Viti Levu; The Mamanuca & Yasawa Groups Virginia lived, worked and travelled widely in the Pacific from 2004 to 2006, and contributed to Lonely Planet's South Pacific guides and the 7th edition of *Fiji*. Since then she's been looking for a reason to go back, and was very happy to share a few kava sessions with old friends while shamelessly picking their brains about the current Fiji scene. She was also reassured to find that, despite the vagaries of politics and economics, Fiji welcomes travellers as warmly as ever.

Contributing Author

Clement Paligaru Clement wrote the Indo-Fijian Culture chapter. An Australian of Indo-Fijian descent, Clement is a radio and television journalist specialising in Asia-Pacific affairs. He has worked for the Australian Broadcasting Corporation for almost 20 years.

Published by Lonely Planet Publications Pty Ltd
ABN 36 005 607 983
9th edition – September 2012
ISBN 978 1 74179 697 1
© Lonely Planet 2012   Photographs © as indicated 2012
10 9 8 7 6 5 4 3 2
Printed in China